Thomas Clarke is Professor of International Management at the
University of Technology, Sydney. He is a member of the St
Partnership, an international business consultancy. He is Visiting
Professor at UAM Mexico, CEIBS Shanghai and FGV, Sao Paulo,
Brazil. Formerly he was Professor of Corporate Governance at
Leeds Business School, UK.

Stewart Clegg is Professor of Management at the University of
Technology, Sydney. He is acknowledged as a leading authority
throughout the world on the study of power in organizations. He
has been Visiting Professor at the University of Hong Kong Business
School and Hong Hong Baptist University as well as at a number
of leading Business Schools in the United States, New Zealand,
Europe and Latin America.

D1324932

WA 1189572 1

CHANGING PARADIGMS

*The Transformation of Management
Knowledge for the 21st Century*

THOMAS CLARKE
and
STEWART CLEGG

HarperCollinsBusiness
An Imprint of HarperCollinsPublishers

HarperCollinsBusiness
An imprint of HarperCollins*Publishers*
77–85 Fulham Palace Road,
Hammersmith, London W6 8JB

www.harpercollinsbusiness.com.

This paperback edition 2000
1 3 5 7 9 8 6 4 2

First published in Great Britain by
HarperCollins*Publishers* 1998

Copyright © 1998 Thomas Clarke and Stewart Clegg

The Authors assert the moral right to
be identified as the authors of this work

ISBN 0 00 638731 4

Set in Meridien

Printed and bound in Great Britain by
Caledonian International Book Manufacturing Ltd, Glasgow

All rights reserved. No part of this publication may be
reproduced, stored in a retrieval system, or transmitted,
in any form or by any means, electronic, mechanical,
photocopying, recording or otherwise, without the prior
permission of the publishers.

This book is sold subject to the condition that it shall not,
by way of trade or otherwise, be lent, re-sold, hired out or
otherwise circulated without the publisher's prior consent
in any form of binding or cover other than that in which it
is published and without a similar condition including this
condition being imposed on the subsequent purchaser.

1189572 1

Learning Resources
Centre

CONTENTS

Nothing is as powerful as an idea whose time has come.

VICTOR HUGO (1802–1885)

The mark of true intelligence is to be able to hold two entirely contradictory ideas in your mind at the same time, and still be able to function normally.

F. SCOTT FITZGERALD (1896–1940)

There are solutions to the major problems of our time; some of them even simple. But they require a radical shift in our perceptions, our thinking, our values ... we are now at the beginning of such a fundamental change of world view in science and society, a change of paradigms as radical as the Copernican revolution.

FRITJOF CAPRA, *The Web of Life*, 1996

The belief in new paradigms.

Millenarian optimism has provided a surfeit of such visions. The technology-based transformation of the US economy, Asia as the manufacturing workplace of the world economy. A flexible, competitive Britain. The virtual company. The global consumer. The service based economy. And so on.

Paradoxical as it may seem, new paradigms cause problems not when they are wrong but when they are manifestly right. Almost all on that list are correct, important and inevitable. But the more obviously accurate they are, the more immediate the impact foreseen for them by bull market sentiment. Long term trends, by definition, work in the long term. Yet – in Asia until the spring and in the US this summer – the markets have been treating the long term as if it were already here.

PETER MARTIN, *Financial Times*, 29 October 1997

Only the paranoid survive.

ANDY GROVE, Chief Executive, Intel

When anyone mentions new paradigms you must, in all circumstances, take cover immediately.

J. K. GALBRAITH, 17 June 1998, address to
Harvard University Club, London

PREFACE

This book was written in Leeds, Sydney, São Paulo, Mexico City, Hong Kong and Shanghai in circumstances that closely reflect the central themes of the volume. We were attempting to come to terms with rapidly changing management ideas, improving practice and a massive proliferation of management literature in the context of a series of major transformations in the international business environment. As we travelled to meet frequent international academic commitments, we occasionally collided at various points of the globe. Our meetings in cities, universities and airports were supplemented by constant communication by e-mail.

This is not the first book to be written essentially on the Internet, as countless different drafts of chapters, transformed into electronic impulses, oscillated backwards and forwards tens of thousands of miles between two authors on different sides of the world. We trust that the many other writers who adopt this mode of collaboration will have more luck with compatibility of software systems than we experienced.

This book on the future of management was conceived, paradoxically, in the cobbled streets, dimly lit pubs and medieval cloistered corridors of St Andrews University. We were both in the management department there (the Principal, Professor Struther-Arnot, used to enjoy astounding government mandarins with the observation, 'You must remember, I am the chief executive of a corporation that is 600 years old, and, therefore, I *must* take the long view').

On moving to Leeds Business School in 1992, Thomas Clarke became a member of the task force of the R S A Tomorrow's Company Inquiry into the sources of sustainable business success, and directed the national conference of the inquiry at the West Yorkshire Playhouse in 1994. Meanwhile, Stewart Clegg was heading for Australia, and had received an invitation to conduct research for the Karpin Task Force on Leadership and Management, established by the Australian government in 1993. This research into the formation of embryonic industries was conducted at the University of Western Sydney, with an international group of consultant researchers.

We rejoined forces in the Australian summer of 1994/95 and began work on this volume, which we hoped would synthesize the central shifts of management thought and practice in the late twentieth century and into the next millennium. We wanted to write about how changes in management thinking reflected and impelled the substantive changes that were taking place around us.

Many people have helped along this journey. In Sydney, Stewart Clegg would like to thank Geoff De Lacy and Peter Ivanoff of the Karpin Industry Task Force into Leadership and Management, who were invaluable mentors during the research process. Additionally he would like to thank Larry Dwyer, John Gary, Jane Marceau, Sharon Kemp and Eddie O'Mara, all of whom were co-researchers on the project.

Roger Alexander at the University of Western Sydney was a supportive and helpful Dean of the Faculty of Business and Technology at Macarthur. At the University of Technology, Sydney, Stewart would like to thank his graduate students and colleagues in the Collaboration Research Group, who were very understanding at the time when this volume was being completed. The members of the University of Hong Kong Business School provided opportunities to test the ideas in the book.

In Leeds, Thomas Clarke would like to thank the members of Leeds Business School, particularly Rex Clark, Allan Blake, Elaine Monkhouse, Richard Bostock and Jeff Gold and, for his superb sense of humour, David Band. John Shutt has been a source of strength and inspiration in recent years, and is an academic of prodigious energy.

At the China Europe International Business School in Shanghai, Thomas would like to thank the former executive president and dean, Joachim Frohn, who provided great academic leadership; the present executive president, Bill Fischer; also vice-president David Southworth, Du Qian, Kenneth Xu, Maggie Zhu, Karen Zhang and the many colleagues there who are building the finest business school in China. A special word of thanks goes to Du

Yuxing, a research associate of immense capability and a genius with Microsoft software.

Thomas Clarke would also like to thank Mark Goyder of the Centre for Tomorrow's Company, and Peter Smith of the Strategic Partnership Limited. Bob Tricker, editor of *Corporate Governance – An International Review*, has constantly proved to be a source of considerable enthusiasm and wisdom. Bob Garratt has offered consistent support in the long gestation of this volume. At DBM plc, Peter Trigg was always interested in the progress of the book, and will, we hope, be pleased with the result; Michele Cozzi, who has now departed for her vineyard in Australia, was wonderful, and Ruby Malik was very kind.

We would both like to thank our colleagues and research students at FGV in São Paulo, and especially Peter Spink and Roberto Venosa. We are indebted to the members of the European Group on Organization Studies (EGOS), and to the Asia-Pacific Researchers on Organization Studies (APROS) for their academic collaboration and support. Jean-François Chanlat of HEC Montreal inspired us both with his intellectual *joie de vivre*. Bianke Ralle has looked after us both over the years with great skill and affection. Finally our thanks to Lucinda McNeile of HarperCollins Business, who has patiently encouraged this project from its inception to its completion.

We are also deeply grateful to Lynne, Jonathan, William, Elizabeth and Jesus for putting up with our literary pursuits.

Thomas Clarke, Shanghai
Stewart Clegg, Sydney
March 1998

INTRODUCTION

REPLACING CERTAINTY

The business world is rapidly transforming, and management thinking is racing to keep pace. The result is a bewildering profusion of management theories, concepts and fashions that often replace each other before they can become widely established. Attempting to bring coherence to this fast-fusion of management ideas is potentially dangerous. Intellectual syntheses that apparently explain all quickly fragment in the face of suddenly emerging economic realities. However, we believe it is possible to discern emerging trends in the development of management paradigms, defining paradigms as means of understanding the world and the basis for informing action.

It is our central argument that the development of management ideas is essential for effectively interpreting and intervening in contemporary business. The increasing number and sophistication of paradigms make greater intellectual demands upon managers but need to be understood rather than ignored. This makes the job of being a manager today a great deal more complex and demanding than ever before, but also makes managing a more creative, and sometimes exciting activity.

Replacing the certainties of an ideology and value system that were formed with industrialization over the last century is not easy. These were based on classical management orthodoxies concerning business objectives, performance indicators, organization and control, and are now being displaced by a new, diverse and challenging set of ideas and values. This accelerating change in thinking is fuelled by the transformation of technology, markets, products and processes. Multiple technological breakthroughs, shortening product life-cycles, and rapidly changing markets are together

forcing the pace of paradigm shifts in management. Today management thinking must continually confront uncertainty, paradoxes,
trade-offs and contingencies, whilst achieving balance, direction
and motivation. The capacity for learning becomes the critical attribute, enabling managers to adapt quickly to the unknown, and to
anticipate changes in the business environment.

Illustrative of the speed of change, extreme uncertainty, but
immense opportunity of contemporary business is the recent
career of Microsoft Corporation. In 1999 Microsoft became the
US$500 billion corporation in the world, with a market capitaliz-
ation exceeding that of the largest corporations such as General
Electric and Shell which were established over generations of
industrial activity. Microsoft did not exist 25 years ago, and makes
software products for a technology, personal computers, that did
not exist 30 years ago. Microsoft achieved this huge market valuation at a time the software corporation had net fixed assets, at a
generous estimate, of just a few billion dollars.

The explanation for the difference between the vast market capitalization of Microsoft Corporation and its small fixed asset base
lies in the stock market assessment of the creativity, market position and consequent revenue flow of the company. Yet Microsoft,
facing legal and legislative challenges to its monopoly position,
direct technological challenges to the personal computer from the
network technology of major mainframe and software manufacturers and from unpredictably inventive micro-companies that
populate the software development industry, could earn the distinction of following the fastest rise in corporate history with the
quickest descent.

Intellectual Capital

Microsoft is exceptional but not unique: in 1999 a range of high
technology companies in computers, telecommunications, and
pharmaceuticals, have ascended into the leading positions in the
FT500 including Intel, Merck, Novartis, IBM, Roche, Glaxo,
WorldCom and Vodaphone. In a survey of US industry Margaret
Blair of the Brookings Institute discovered that intangibles (brands,
intellectual property, licences) now greatly exceed the value of
tangible assets (property, plant and equipment) in most industries.[1]
The knowledge-based information economy has arrived, in which

creativity, intelligence and ideas are the core capability for sustainable business success. Frequent paradigm shifts are essential for survival in this business context.

Constant innovation is necessary to sustain viability in many markets today. In the Japanese consumer electronics industry the model life of products is now just a few months; at the same time the total number of products on offer is increasing dramatically. What was happening before in the personal computer and consumer electronics industry, and other high technology businesses, is now happening in many other industries. Firms have to be faster, smarter, more market-sensitive, flexible and intelligent in order to succeed. Since the time of Adam Smith business has been about capitalizing on opportunities created by economic and technological change, but managers today are continually confronted with *discontinuous* change: the business environment has become less predictable, with more frequent unknowns that are less readily subject to rational interpretation.

The predictable pattern of traditional business change was a gradual but continuous curve of improvement. This allowed a patient, and often slow process of careful adjustment on the part of companies; penalties for those companies that did not change at all, caught up with them much later. Increasingly, incremental change in industry is displaced by discontinuous change: the graph goes off the chart; things suddenly become more unpredictable and less easily manageable. In this turbulent world standard answers and structured processes can no longer cope with the complexity of the new demands. New problems are confronted requiring new solutions that often involve fundamental transformation of business thinking and practice.[2]

When companies fail to make this leap into the unknown they often find themselves quickly supplanted by new entrepreneurs and companies who are not encumbered by the technology, organizational structures and assumptions of traditional players. This has happened in computer software, telecommunications, airlines, financial services and a host of other industries. As Hamel and Prahalad and many others have emphasized, the companies most likely to succeed in this challenge are those that can most effectively rethink their organization, business and industry in the most creative ways to respond to the new market environment.[3]

Global Connections

The environment in which businesses compete has moved to the world stage. The globalization of the world economy presents a new business environment in which competition is international in a growing number of industries, and only world-class standards will satisfy customers. Finance, markets, technology, consumption, culture and consciousness are all becoming global. This international integration of economic activity offers new opportunities for overseas investment and trade, and collaboration in production and marketing. However, the price of access to new international markets is greater competition in domestic markets. Globalization promises greater mobility of people and ideas, freedom of choice, and more rapid technological diffusion. But the arrival of new centres of global production and expertise make international co-ordination of the world economy more difficult to accomplish, and involves significant decentralization. Hence the paradox that conceptions of 'one world' have released a wave of multiculturalism, which international companies are struggling to come to terms with.

The economic implications of the new information and communication technologies are closely connected with globalizing forces. As *The Economist* recently commented, information and communication technologies have helped to globalize production, and in turn globalization speeds up the diffusion of technology. The combination of information technology and globalization are transforming concepts of time and space. As Negroponte suggests, the physical world is becoming digitalized with the creation of new products and markets, and the transformation of organizational activity.[4] The convergence of computing power and telecommunications reach is providing new technological and information resources with which to pursue business opportunities, but this is only achievable if the management and organization of enterprises are transformed to capture the potential of new technologies.

As stable markets and long production runs disappear and are replaced by niche markets and shortening product life-cycles, earlier methods of strategic planning based on rational modes of analysis become too rigid and are replaced by more creative strategic thinking which responds more sensitively to rapid shifts in demand. It is the collateral of human creativity which creates options for the future, together with the networks linking multiple partners on an international basis, enabling companies to tackle gaps in their innovation capability.

Sustaining Capability

The resource-based view of the firm is becoming the most influential theoretical paradigm in management strategy, with the definition of critical resources stretching across core competence, invisible assets, capabilities, organizational processes, firm attributes, information and knowledge, which enable companies effectively to implement strategies to improve performance. At the centre of this is the conception of collective entrepreneurship, which encourages the development of organizations and people, promotes trust and open confrontation of problems, with a high value placed on internal relationships and processes. Traditional command-and-control forms of organization that have predominated in twentieth-century industry are unable to respond quickly and creatively enough to meet the developing demands of consumers and emerging market opportunities: intelligent, networked forms of organization are needed. Hierarchical and centralized organizations of functional specialists delivering mass-produced goods give way to flatter, networked, more open and decentralized firms that allow mass customization of products for specific niche markets. The new paradigm of organization emphasizes vision, high achievement focus and managing paradox. Highly adaptive and hungry for learning, organizations are becoming equipped to face complexity, uncertainty and change.

The world-class organization transcends the customer-driven orientation of total quantity management: an openness to ideas and to the external environment in the learning organization means that it can excel by exceeding customers' expectations and benchmarking against the best in the class. The virtual organization is fluid: through training and development, people can provide state-of-the-art products and services within an egalitarian environment and with leading-edge technological support. Of course, any organization, regardless of size or type, can strive to become world class, and this achievement is not the sole property of existing leading corporations.

Changing Paradigms in Management Theory and Practice

CHANGING PARADIGMS

From	In	To
Classical/ neo-classical management orthodoxy	**Ideas and values**	Multiple changing management paradigms
Local/national international	**Market environment**	Glocalization/ globalization
Manual/analogue stand alone	**Processing and communication**	Electronic/digital network
Strategic planning rational strategy	**Orientation**	Strategic thinking/ innovation/core competence
Taylorism/Fordism	**Organization and control**	Intelligent/ networked virtuality
Shareholders/ financial performance indicators	**Measures**	Stakeholders/non-financial performance indicators
Profit/growth/ control	**Objectives**	Sustainable enterprise

If companies are to succeed in this more complex and demanding competitive environment it is clear that they need to build better relationships with everyone they do business with. Part of this effort involves improving relations with investors, but companies also have to improve the measurement and management of their relationships with customers, employees, suppliers, creditors and the wider community. This wider stakeholding conception of the corporation is often proposed as an ethical new basis for business enterprise. In fact, increasingly, the stakeholder approach reflects the practicalities of how to raise business performance. The importance of improving business relationships is the main lesson of supply chain management, total quality management, investor relations, employee relations and relationship marketing. The reciprocity and partnership which increasingly typifies contemporary business relationships is based partly on the more open communication now prevalent, which makes it difficult for companies to sustain the practice of upholding different messages and values for different audiences.

The most critical business relationship is between the company and the physical environment. Traditional corporate objectives of profit, growth and control are increasingly tempered by the politically enforced duty to respect the environment, and to engage only in business pursuits that are sustainable. Sustainability is the crucial test of whether a company is genuinely creating wealth or simply destroying it. To be sustainable, business activity should take no more from the physical environment than it is capable of restoring to it. Business needs to meet present demands without endangering the needs of future generations.

Developing Themes

In this book we explore the nature of new management paradigms. We examine the impact of the new drivers of business change. We investigate the parameters of the knowledge based organization, and how the next generation of managers will face the challenges of managing more complex business relationships and demanding performance indicators. We develop these themes in chapters concerned with paradigms, globalization, digitalization, strategy, organization, stakeholders and sustainability. In summary, the central paradigm shifts considered are presented in the table opposite. Some of these shifts have already occurred in large sectors of the economy; others are beginning to happen. We believe they are all important, and together will help to define the direction of business activity in the twenty-first century.

Chapter 1

PARADIGMS

The concept of paradigm is at once ancient and contemporary. Its name derives from the ancient Greek *paradeigma*. Classically, it meant model, framework, pattern or example, and this meaning has survived to the present day. Different concepts of management paradigms have been at the centre of critical debate in recent years, and the notion of changing paradigms captures the flux of organizational transformation resulting from the surging changes in the business environment.

It was a historian of science, Thomas Kuhn, who pioneered the idea of changing paradigms in *The Structure of Scientific Revolutions* (1970). For Kuhn, science was characterized by the dominance of succeeding paradigms as *models for thinking or*, as he put it, 'a constellation of concepts, values, perceptions and practices shared by a community which forms a particular vision of reality that is the way a community organizes itself'. A paradigm is a systematic set of ideas and values, methods and problem fields, as well as standard solutions, that explain the world and inform action. 'It's the way we see the world – not in terms of our visual sense of sight, but in terms of perceiving, understanding, interpreting.'[1]

The use of the term paradigm has proliferated greatly since Kuhn first popularized it. Within academic circles, and increasingly among practising managers, two distinct usages have crystallized. The first we might refer to as that of the paradigm police; the second as the paradigm warriors:

On the one hand it has come to mean a single approach in which theory, method, the interpretation of findings and the way research should develop are all laid out and agreed by a community of scholars ... On the other hand, there are members of another group who see things very differently

where paradigms are concerned. They do not see before them
a single unifying paradigm but many – or at least several
paradigms lying alongside each other in a relationship characterized by hostility and conflict . . . engaged in a struggle for
survival.[2]

While the idea of paradigms has been widely received in management, it has been so more as a contested than a settled domain.
Management paradigms are far more numerous than those of the
natural sciences that Kuhn studied. Kuhn expected the long
periods of normality to be marked by an absence of paradigmatic
questioning and strife. One paradigm would hold unquestioned
sway for some years.

In management, at any time, there are a number of competing
paradigms available. One popular view is that paradigms are a kind
of Platonist form: eternal in their mutations and variation. Different
paradigms (sometimes they are termed metaphors or frames of
reference) reveal different facets of our understanding of management.[3] Today, many MBA and executive management programmes use such a method of 'switching frames' as a learning
device: re-framing encourages the ability to see things, situations or
people in other ways, to put them in another perspective. Managers
operating in a particular era typically see the world through one
overarching paradigm, within which the separate frames, metaphors and perspectives that they use stand in some coherence to
each other, but differ radically from those in use in preceding and
succeeding eras. Using new frames or seeing through the assumptions of different forms means that the managerial and organizational world not only looks different; it becomes different
(sometimes presented as the social construction of reality).

BUSINESS PARADIGMS

'You manage within a paradigm. You lead between paradigms.'[4]
Paradigms allow us to see certain things in a certain way – but
they also make it difficult to see certain other things that do not
'belong' within the paradigm. We cling to our paradigms and see
only what they enable us to see, even when their assumptions
are not clearly or strongly stated. Indeed, the more implicit the
paradigm, in some ways the stronger it is, because we are less

aware of it. This aspect of paradigms is of particular significance for managers: a paradigm can be a set of unwritten regulations or practices that establishes or defines boundaries, and tells you how to behave inside the boundaries. Being locked into a paradigm can, at its worst, become a form of conceptual imprisonment. Most large business organizations have multiple paradigms, multiple rules, applying to multiple games. Different paradigms may help us to see better where to go, what questions to ask, what evidence to seek, what to deny, but every paradigm eventually encounters new problems which it cannot solve. Unsolvable problems provide the catalyst for triggering a paradigm revolution.[5]

Why Do Paradigms Change?

Kuhn set out to chart how changing realities of investigation were tied up with changing perceptions. In business the focus has been much more on the changing realities rather than changing perspectives. Kuhn (1970) stressed the political nature of paradigms, but did not really tell us why the adherents of subordinated paradigms suddenly triumphed when they did, other than to say that the anomalies were becoming an embarrassment for the powerful adherents of the existing paradigm.[6] Burrell and Morgan never really answer this question either because, for them, the paradigms never really change: there is simply a circulation of élites and their adherents in which the politics of careers play out.[7] As the existing dominant paradigm becomes overcrowded a few pioneers will build intellectual capital in other paradigms.

In management theory some theorists suggest that periods of flux are characteristic effects of 'long waves'. It was a Soviet economist called Kondratiev who first pioneered long-wave theory, but it has gained many adherents.[8] Long-wave theory proposes that the world economy displays a rhythmical pattern, as rapid expansion and stagnation alternate with a periodicity of around about fifty years. A single wave is estimated to have a fifty-year cycle through initial growth to decline. Some theorists emphasize, as did Kondratiev, that the seismic changes that long waves represent are the result of massive investments in, and the subsequent depreciation of, major aspects of infrastructure such as canals, railways and roads. Others follow Schumpeter and think that it is less the decline in infrastructure that is responsible and more the fact that clusters of innovation bunch together, creating new and discontinuous leading-edge sectors in the world economy, driving macro-economic growth.[9] Eventually further innovation restarts the whole cycle around further discontinuous innovation.

The world economy is presented at a crucial point of transition in the long-wave scenario. The post Second World War boom would be expected to have had an approximate fifty-year cycle, with a twenty-five-year upswing and a twenty-five-year downswing. Twenty-five years have elapsed since the world economy, centred on the developed OECD states, shifted into the OPEC-induced downturn of the early 1970s. According to the theory, the new upswing wave, and a shift to a new paradigm, should be beginning about now. The convergence of communications and computer technology, combined with rapid advances in other generic technologies, including bio-engineering, materials, energy and space technology, is helping to create an exploding cluster of discontinuous change.

Paradigm Shifts

In any system that is ecologically interdependent, if you change any paradigmatic part then you change the whole. When there is sufficient change and fluidity in a system then we can speak of a 'paradigm shift': that period when a shift occurs from one paradigm set to another, the transition from one wave to the next. When the rules change across the board, all changes. When we have such a paradigm shift we have a widespread shift in the rules, a shift to a new set of games. In these conditions uncertainty and ambiguity will apply. People will be unsure how to proceed. 'Discontinuities change the rules of competition – both existing and new competition. Don't try to deal with them by applying the old rules faster or better. Rather, start challenging assumptions in order to drive strategic process change. The first question to ask is which elements of environmental change signal an impending discontinuity?'[10] In these circumstances, the champions will be those who can read the new game, and master its rules, quickly and successfully. Literally, they will be those who can ride the next wave.

Change can be viewed as a curve where the slope, whether steep or gentle, is continuous and driven by economic trends, rates of growth, technological advance and competition.[11] Discontinuous change is a step shift in the rate of change that invalidates existing assumptions and begins to transform the rules of competition. Examples of discontinuous change include the breakdown of the communist bloc in Eastern Europe; the formation of the regional economic blocs of the European Union, NAFTA and ASEAN and the resulting deregulation between borders; the convergence of computers and telecommunications to create the information superhighway, and the further convergence with the information and entertainment industries to create multimedia. In this way paradigm shifts are triggered by significant political, economic or technological breakthroughs that create a whole new frame of reference.

Such discontinuities invalidate old paradigms, including those which may have been the basis of a firm's success, strategy and culture. Company characteristics that were key attributes suddenly become liabilities. There are three potential responses to discontinuity (Figure 1.1):

- Sustained effort within existing methods to carry the company up a steeper change curve
- Transforming the organization's methods with a step shift that will get ahead of the change curve
- Establishing new operating paradigms and organizational infrastructure.

An illustration of a company that pursued the third option is Direct Line, which responded to the deregulation of the financial services industry in the UK by establishing a telephone sales and service, capturing 10 per cent of the car insurance market in less than two years. Another dramatic illustration was the remarkable success Marc Andreessen had with the Netscape Navigator web browser, which he originally launched as Mosaic, a giveaway software that created a market; he went on to capture 80 per cent of this market. His aim was to have Netscape products running on 500 million machines by the year 2000 – potentially achievable if the paradigmatic domination of Microsoft did not prevent it. However, the meteoric rise of Netscape faltered when Microsoft began including a web browser in its standard package.

Paradigm *mismatches* occur when people retain the old paradigms after a breakthrough has triggered a paradigm shift. Many companies utilized new information technology simply to speed up

Figure 1.1: Patterns of Change

1. Change as a Continuous Curve

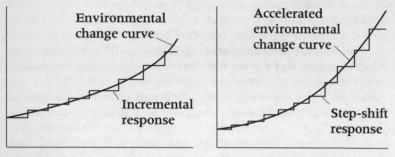

Environmental
change curve

Incremental
response

Accelerated
environmental
change curve

Step-shift
response

1a. Continuous environmental
change

1b. Continuous accelerated
environmental change

2. Change as a Discontinuous Curve

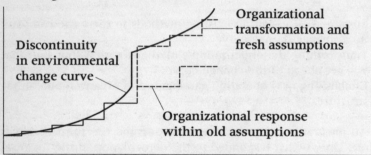

Organizational
transformation and
fresh assumptions

Discontinuity
in environmental
change curve

Organizational response
within old assumptions

3. Discontinuous Change as Exploited by Process Predators

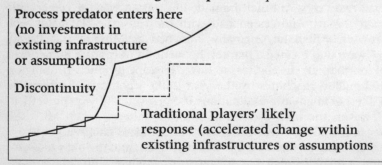

Process predator enters here
(no investment in
existing infrastructure
or assumptions

Discontinuity

Traditional players' likely
response (accelerated change within
existing infrastructures or assumptions

Source: Keen and Knapp, *Every Manager's Guide to Business Processes* (1996), p. 89

their existing manual processes, rather than taking the opportunity to rethink business processes in order to capitalize on what the new technology was capable of achieving. Technologically this can be as inept as driving an airplane as if it were a car: you may still reach your destination eventually, but there are easier ways to travel. Frequently paradigm mismatches are a drag on organizational efficiency, and can lead to complete breakdown. Moreover, failure to capture the potential of new paradigms and technology completely stifles the process of innovation.

Paradigm shifts are today more challenging because the pace of economic and technological change has accelerated beyond belief. The central processing unit (CPU) of computers used to execute instructions in a sequential manner, the basis of the von Neumann electronic digital computer. But by the late 1980s computer scientists had developed parallel computers, in which hundreds or thousands of CPUs operate in parallel and in co-operation with one another. This explosive increase in the power and speed of computers is a metaphor for what is occurring in many other fields of technology and commerce (partly as a result of the massive processing power that is now widely available). Suddenly, instead of being achieved sequentially and gradually, everything is being done rapidly and simultaneously. This means that, for people and for companies, continual multi-learning and life-long learning are essential if they are to keep up.

Constant innovation is necessary for survival. Figures 1.2 and 1.3 show that the model life of products in the Japanese consumer electronics industry had fallen to less than a year by the late 1980s, at the same time as the cumulative total number of products on offer had increased by more than five times in less than five years. Multiple technological breakthroughs, shortening product life-cycles, and rapidly changing markets are together forcing the pace of paradigm shifts. Breathless commentators on the latest series of paradigm shifts add to the excitement.

Desperately Seeking Newness

The sense of urgency about stimulating and developing the management knowledge necessary to deal with accelerating paradigm shifts has precipitated a rapidly growing profusion of management ideas, books and gurus. The desperate search for newness, to

Figure 1.2: Decline in Model Life in the Consumer Electronics Industry

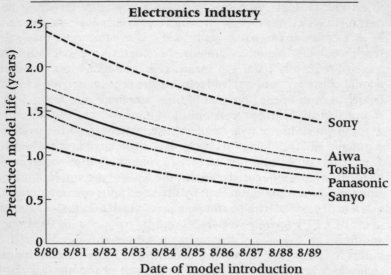

Date of model introduction

Source: DTI, Innovation Plans Handbook, London:
Innovation Advisory Board, 1993

become *excellent, leading-edge, high performing, innovative,* can be a distraction from the practical, and lead us to misunderstand the past and undervalue what is important in the present. In *Beyond the Hype: Rediscovering the Essence of Management,* Eccles and Nohria make an impassioned, and probably forlorn appeal for reason:

> The desperate search for quick solutions to eternal manage-
> ment challenges – combined with the opportunities this has
> created for managers, academics, consultants and journalists
> who proffer solutions to these problems – has resulted in an
> impressive proliferation of nostrums, techniques, and philo-
> sophies of management. Typically these 'new' ideas are pre-
> sented as universally applicable quick-fix solutions – along
> with the obligatory and explicit caution that their recommen-
> dations are *not* quick fixes and will require substantial man-
> agement understanding and commitment. As many managers
> will attest, the result has been a dazzling array of what are often
> perceived as management fads – fads that frequently become
> discredited soon after they have been widely propagated.[12]

Figure 1.3: Product Proliferation in the Consumer Electronics Industry

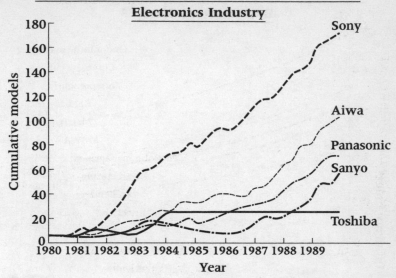

Source: DTI, Innovation Plans Handbook, London: Innovation Advisory Board, 1993

As the fortunes of Western companies began to decline in the 1970s, companies became more willing to experiment with new ideas according to Richard Pascale. In *Managing on the Edge* (1990) he takes the consumption rate and shelf life of management fads as an indicator of managerial panic. Pascale identifies several dozen such fads in the post-war period and suggests that, while there are valid aspects to most of these ideas, what is wrong is the piecemeal fashion in which they are implemented; he sees an impatient shift from one to another without any sense of the context in which they must be embedded (Figure 1.4). Pascale encountered a manufacturer from the mid-west, who lamented, 'In the past eighteen months, we have heard that profit is more important than revenue, quality is more important than profit, that people are more important than profit, that customers are more important than our people, that big customers are more important than our small customers. No wonder our performance is inconsistent!'[13]

The mass marketing of managerial techniques as a packaged goods industry has fostered superficiality as it became legitimate to accept and utilize management ideas without an in-depth grasp of their

Figure 1.4: Ebbs, Flows and Residual Impact of Business Fads. 1950–88

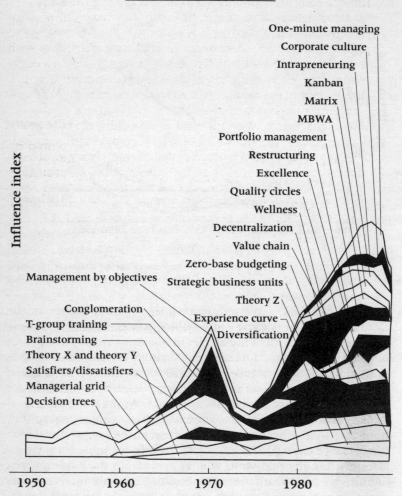

One-minute managing
Corporate culture
Intrapreneuring
Kanban
Matrix
MBWA
Portfolio management
Restructuring
Excellence
Quality circles
Wellness
Decentralization
Value chain
Zero-base budgeting
Management by objectives
Strategic business units
Conglomeration
Theory Z
T-group training
Experience curve
Brainstorming
Diversification
Theory X and theory Y
Satisfiers/dissatisfiers
Managerial grid
Decision trees

Influence index

1950   1960   1970   1980

Curves shown are for illustrative purposes. Empirical foundation of chart based upon frequency of citations in the literature. However, increased interest in business topics in the past decade tends to exaggerate amplitude of recent fads when compared to earlier decades. As a result, the author has modified curves to best reflect relative significance of trends over entire period.

Source: Pascale, *Managing on the Edge* (1990), p. 20

underlying foundation, and without the commitment necessary to sustain them. 'Not surprisingly, ideas acquired with ease are discarded with ease. Fads ebb, flow – and even change by 180 degrees.'[14]

Paradigms define substantial shifts in the knowledge and practice of management, but the concept is frequently applied wrongly to the most trivial matters: the management literature is replete with references to new paradigms, applied in every discipline, every functional area, every industry. All that is usually meant here is a slight change from the normal. Paradigms are fractured into countless, fairly meaningless fashions.

More pugnaciously, Micklethwaite and Wooldridge argue in *The Witch Doctors* (1997) that, like economics a century ago, management theory today is an immature discipline, lacks 'canonical texts and defining methodologies' and is 'bedevilled by contradictions that would not be allowed in more rigorous disciplines'. Acknowledging that management education is now a multi-billion dollar industry in the United States alone, they conclude their damning critique of contemporary management gurus with sympathy for 'the fate of managers and their pitiful predilection for magic cures'. Eileen Shapiro suggests a more satirical view of management fads, and concludes that it is up to managers themselves whether they use new theories and practice in a positive way or to create havoc:

> It's the managers who test-drive the theories and often create them themselves by virtue of the ideas they invent, borrow, steal, and transform, based on what they read, think, hear, and just dream up. Without question, striving for management theory to attain the status of a serious intellectual discipline, unfettered by internal contradictions, is an honourable goal. But aiming for an economy in which managers are willing to make decisions without the benefit of complete information or coherent theory – and are able to learn from the results – is more important by far.[15]

The Importance of Innovation

Accepting that there is an important role for management theory and research, virtually every major management thinker in the last twenty years has been drawn into the search for coherent new paradigms that might comprehend the exponential changes occurring in the economy and industry. In *The Competitive Advantage of Nations* Michael Porter addresses the 'need for a new paradigm' of national competitive advantage:

> The long-dominant paradigm for why nations succeed internationally in particular industries is showing signs of strain . . . A new theory must start from the premise that competition is dynamic and evolving. Much traditional thinking has embodied an essentially static view focusing on cost efficiency due to factor or scale advantages. Technical change is viewed as exogenous, or outside the purview of the theory. As Joseph Schumpeter recognised many decades ago, however, there is no *equilibrium* in competition. Competition is a constantly changing landscape in which new products, new ways of marketing, new production processes, and whole new market segments emerge. Static efficiency at a point in time is overtaken by a faster rate of progress . . . A new theory must make improvement and innovation in methods and technology a central element. We must explain the role of the nation in the innovation process. Since innovation requires sustained investment in research, physical capital and human resources, we must also explain why the rate of such investments are more vigorous in some nations and not others. The question is how a nation provides an environment in which its firms are able to improve and innovate faster than foreign rivals in a particular industry. This will be fundamental in explaining how entire national economies progress, because technological change in the broad sense of the term, accounts for much of economic growth.[16]

In one way or another nearly all the management writers who have engaged in the search for new paradigms have been addressing the fundamental questions posed by Porter. Peter Drucker, the most outspoken management theorist of the twentieth century, stressed *The Age of Discontinuity* (1969), and the importance of the *knowledge economy* in *Managing for the Future* (1992), and consistently examined the implications of post-industrialism for management practice.

The Age of Unreason (1989) and *The Age of Paradox (The Empty Raincoat)* (1994) by Charles Handy commented more sensitively than most management strategists on the dilemmas to be faced:

'We are entering an age of unreason, a time when the future, in so many areas, is to be shaped by us and for us; a time when the only prediction that will hold true is that no prediction will hold true; a time, therefore, for bold imagining in private life as well as public; for thinking the unlikely and doing the unreasonable'.[17] For Handy it is a period of upheaval in which only 'upside-down' thinking will connect: 'Organizations used to be perceived as gigantic pieces of engineering, with largely interchangeable human parts. We talked of their structures and their systems, of inputs and outputs, of control devices and of managing them, as if the whole was one large factory. Today the language is not that of engineering but of politics, with talk of cultures and networks, of teams and coalitions, of influence or power rather than control, of leadership not management'.[18]

People, creativity, the excitement of change, technology and speed of a response are at the centre of Tom Peters's startling contribution to management knowledge in *Liberation Management* (1992), *The Pursuit of Wow!* (1994) and *The Circle of Innovation* (1997). In his hyperactive typography Peters highlights the counterproductive effect of standardized corporate responses which bring a blight of sameness to products and services – functional, timely, customer-friendly things which are basically just boring commodities. Peter's reaction is that commoditization is not inevitable, and that companies should create 'waves of lust' for the aesthetic qualities of products and services.[19] Of course, a customer-focused strategy becomes a wish list if it is not backed up with strong core processes which deliver continuous innovation, effective operations and efficient customer service and support.

Rosabeth Moss Kanter entices lethargic companies to break free of the last vestiges of corporatism and learn to be nimble in *The Change Masters* (1983), *When Giants Learn to Dance* (1989) and *World Class* (1995). To succeed in the customer-driven global economy businesses must meet best-in-the-world standards, pioneer the best ideas and technologies, invest in their people, act as partners to suppliers and customers, and connect to networks adding reach and resources. 'World class companies are rich in the three golden intangible assets, the three 'C's of concepts, competence, and connections.'[20]

Most management writers have attempted to convey the overwhelming sense of movement and action experienced by people in industry as they tried to come to terms with markets, technology and organizations that were transforming all around them. Alvin Toffler was the first to discuss (in *The Third Wave*) the widening impact the convergence of telecommunications and computer technology would have on every aspect of work and society. Peter Senge in *The Fifth Discipline* demonstrated the intelligent response to such constant, complex and dramatic change in people's existence in creating *learning organizations* – 'organizations where people continually expand their capacity to create the results they truly desire, where new and expansive patterns of thinking are nurtured, where collective aspiration is set free and where people are continually learning how to learn together'.[21]

Many other management theorists before and after Senge wrestled with the problem of how organizations can continually adapt, change, innovate, create and network in order to survive and succeed in market environments that are quickly becoming more unpredictable, with technologies that are becoming more pervasive and integrative, with organizations that have become pliable and porous, and with people who are questioning, assertive and independent. Though most theorists refer to the new organization with different names and emphases, a common pattern may be discerned: unlocking the mystery of organizational self-renewal.[22] To be viable in the changing and demanding business environment of today organizations must be able to improve themselves continually as part of their normal functioning; to be intelligent, critical and open; and to be creative and capable of eternally transforming themselves while sustaining a sense of purpose and direction (Table 1.1). These writers focused upon particular, constructive ways in which organizations could respond to changing demands; other management writers concentrated on surfing the waves of change.

Surfing the Waves

The uncrowned king of paradigm surfers is John Naisbitt, whose original *Megatrends* (1982) proved a remarkably prescient identification of the main patterns in shifting societal trends, for which he was rewarded with sales of 8 million copies of his book worldwide. The trends he noted, including the move to decentralized, networked, high-tech information society, were surprising at the time, but now seem commonplace (Table 1.2). The world has

Table 1.1: Typology of the New Organization

A. Wildavsky (1972)	The Self-Evaluating Organization.
M. Landau (1973)	The Self-Correcting Organization.
Karl E. Weick (1976)	The Self-Designing Organization.
B. Staw (1977)	The Experimenting Organization.
Peter Drucker (1988)	The Networked Organization.
Charles Handy (1989)	The Shamrock Organization.
Peter Senge (1990	The Learning Organization.
Peter Keen (1991)	The Relational Organization.
D. Quinn Mills (1991)	The Cluster Organization.
James Brian Quinn (1992)	The Intelligent Enterprise.
W. Davidlow and M. Malone (1992)	The Virtual Corporation.
M. Hammer and J. Champy (1994)	The Re-engineered Corporation.
Russell L. Ackoff (1994)	The Democratic Organization.
Tom Peters (1994)	The Crazy Organization.
Richard D. Hames (1994)	The Appreciative Organization.
Ikujiro Nonaka and Hirotaka Takeuchi (1995)	The Knowledge Creating Company.
Arie de Geus (1997)	The Living Company.
D. Matheson and J. Matheson (1998)	The Smart Organization.

moved on, and so has Naisbitt, who has turned East. *Asian Megatrends* (1997) identifies the burgeoning influence in Asia of the ethnic Chinese business network, which is poised to take the commercial lead from Japan. Along with that will come the largest middle-class market in the world in Asia, which will retain distinctive characteristics. Asian market economies will fuel an explosion of growth and urbanization in supercities that will become economic powerhouses of high technology. Women will capture a central place in Asian enterprise, as Asia itself will once again become the centre of the world (Table 1.3). Naisbitt must be kicking himself that he did not get his Asian thesis published a few years earlier, before the gloss began to chip off the Asian economic miracle with the major collapse of currencies, stock markets and

Table 1.2: Original Megatrends

From	To
Industrial society	Information society
Forced technology	High tech/high touch
National economy	World economy
Short term	Long term
Centralization	Decentralization
Institutional help	Self help
Representative democracy	Participatory democracy
Hierarchies	Networking
North	South
Either/or	Multiple options

Source: J. Naisbitt, *Megatrends* (1982)

Table 1.3: Asian Megatrends

From	To
Nation states	Networks
Export led	Consumer led
Western influence	Asian way
Government-controlled	Market driven
Villages	Supercities
Labour intensive	High technology
Male dominance	Emergence of women
West	East

Source: J. Naisbitt, *Asian Megatrends* (1997)

the property market in a series of South-East Asian countries in the autumn of 1997. However, the trends he has observed will no doubt revive.

Another futurist, Ian Morrison, urges companies to have the courage to jump from the first curve of their traditional business base, existing organization and current revenues to *The Second Curve* (1996). The second curve is defined by adopting breakthrough technologies, offering new products and services, and searching out new emerging markets wherever they may be. This will involve a transformation of corporate marketing, organization and individuals (Table 1.4). As with all great leaps, the trick is to know the right moment to make it, or whether, and for how long, it is possible to keep a foot on both curves at once. Reaching the second curve means learning to live with paradox, with conflicting goals and technologies, absorbing new business rules and methods. There are great risks in making this jump, and comfort in staying with what you know, but this ultimately leads to stagnation and obsolescence.

Table 1.4: From First Curve to Second Curve

First Curve	Second Curve
MARKET	
Capital	Knowledge
Producer	Consumer
Atlantic	Pacific
Japan	China
International trade	Electronic commerce
Computers	Internet
Money	People
ORGANIZATION	
Mechanistic	Organic
Engineering	Ecology
Corporations	Individuals and networks
Horizontal and vertical integration	Virtual integration
Business processes	Culture
THE INDIVIDUAL	
Hard work	Hypereffectiveness
Security	Uncertainty
Current career	Future career
Faith	Hope
Loyalty	Courage

Source: Morrison, *The Second Curve* (1996), p. 15

THE EVOLUTION OF MANAGEMENT

Other theorists, while concerned with the economic and techno-logical changes sweeping through society, have focused in on the detailed implications for management and organization, and the resulting paradigm shifts. Bennis, Parikh and Lessem, in a brave attempt to balance economics, ethics and ecology, identify *Northern*, *Western* and *Eastern* paradigms of management, and suggest the elements of a path of cultural evolution to a new global paradigm (Table 1.5). Northern management is the dominant paradigm of Europe and America, of Peter Drucker, and his early work on plan-ning and directing; of Rensis Likert on teamwork and participation; of Alfred Chandler on the visible hand of hierarchical organizations; and of George Steiner on the social responsibility of business.

However, Northern rationalism is being overturned by a Western style of entrepreneurism espoused by Tom Peters; the emotively oriented shared values discussed by Deal and Kennedy are supplanting formal teamwork; Handy suggests how vertical organizations are becoming lateral; and George Gilder reawakens the spirit of enterprise. Eastern management, being part of a more corporate philosophy, is represented by companies rather than individuals, with the TQM of Toyota; the quality circles of Shigeru Kobayashi at Sony; and the concept of lean manufacturing at Honda. Finally, Robert Ozaka has emerged with an interpretation of human capitalism:

> While the westerly based management concepts remain too strongly vested with old-style capitalism, at least at a societal level, the easterly base approach remains too Japanese in form and content to become more widely spread. It is the globally based approaches that transcend the limits posed by particular cultures . . . The new paradigm-manager is by definition trans-cultural in his or her approach to developing self-mastery within him or herself; in generating social synergy across a group; in engendering organizational learning within insti-tutions, and in fostering sustainable development across the globe.[23]

Continuing with the exploration of a new philosophy of man-agement, Richard Hall contrasts the old hierarchical spirit with a

Table 1.5: The Evolution of Management

	Old Paradigms			New Global Paradigm
	Northern	**Western**	**Eastern**	
Individual manager	Effective managment (Drucker)	Entrepreneurial management (Peters)	Total quality management (Toyota)	Self-mastery
Social group	Effective teamwork (Likert)	Shared values (Deal/Kennedy)	Quality circles (Sony)	Social synergy
Organization as a whole	Hierarchical organization (Chandler)	Networked organization (Handy)	Lean organization (Honda)	Organizational learning
Economy and society	Corporate responsibility (Steiner)	Free enterprise (Gilder)	Human capitalism (Ozaka)	Sustainable development

Source: Bennis, Parikh and Lessem, *Beyond Leadership* (1994), p. 9

new *Soul of the Enterprise* (1993). Instead of companies which preach teamwork between employees, customers and suppliers, while management make decisions that profit only the owners, 'We need a more challenging, holistic view of the purposes of enterprise, something beyond balancing the conflicts between fiduciary duties for profitability, customer satisfaction, purifying the environment and the like ... which ... cannot cope with holistic considerations'.[24] Hall recognizes that all the elements within a living system are integral to the entire system's well-being (Table 1.6). Such principles are particularly resonant in knowledge-based organizations, where organizational participants are inevitably more questioning and demanding; as Bartlett and Ghoshal argue, 'unlike capital, knowledge is more valuable when those on the front line control and use it'.[25] Tom Cannon records how the failure of Anglo-US corporations to accept and internalize this perspective leads some to doubt their long-term competitiveness, including Konusuke Matsushita, founder of the Matsushita Electrical Industrial Corporation with a turnover of $61 billion in 1996 and 265,000 employees:

Your firms are built on the Taylor model, and even worse, so are your heads. With your bosses doing the thinking while the workers wield screwdrivers, you're convinced deep down that this is the right way to run a business. For you the essence of management is getting ideas out of the heads of managers and into the hands of labour. We have gone beyond the Taylor model. We realize that business has become so complex, the survival of firms so precarious, and our environment increasingly unpredictable, competitive, and dangerous that firms' continuing existence depends on their day to day mobilization of every ounce of intelligence.[26]

Table 1.6: The Old and New Soul of the Enterprise

Old	New
Profit first priority	Customer satisfaction first priority
Assets are things	Assets are people
Thinkers are separated from doers	Doers and thinkers are the same
Mass production	Lean production
Separated marketing with suppliers and customers at arm's length	Integrated marketing with partnership-based relationships with suppliers and customers
Organizations controlled by hierarchies, functional departments separated	Organizations based on teamwork, numerous cross-teams
Performance measurement for control, financially dominated	Performance measurement for improvement, broader measures
Scale economies important	Time economies important

Source: Hall, *Soul of the Enterprise* (1993), p. 281

Ways in which to manage paradox are illuminated by Tom Cannon, the chief executive of the UK Management Charter Initiative and joint-chairman of the Institute of Management's

Management Development to the Millennium (1994) study. The key paradoxes highlighted are:

- Acting now for the long term.
- Growing through consolidation.
- Building individualistic teams.
- Getting more for less.
- Thinking local, acting global.
- Simultaneous growth of economic regionalism, and economic internationalism.
- Winning through action-oriented reflection.
- Consolidating internal capabilities while re-engineering.[27]

Cannon addresses the critical choices confronting managers in *Welcome to the Revolution*: 'Some will survive by affirming core strengths and concentrating their efforts around a specialism. The role of management is to establish a framework within which the options are understood and decisions made. For managers the options are clear. Innovative business and business leaders have absorbed these choices and opted for change' (Table 1.7).

The Implications of Information Technology

Most management writers take a multi-factorial view of emerging paradigms. Some writers are more likely to attribute most casual influence to a single variable, and the most frequently singled-out factor is information technology (IT). R. D. Hames, for instance, looking at the essence of future organization, saw the shift from the industrial to the information age in terms of its impact on the design of organizations, particularly from an IT perspective.[28] One of the key emergent trends is a shift from organizational envelopes as containers of business activity to network linking between organizations.

As organizations seek value through the strength of their ties to – and networks with – other organizations, attempts at imperative managerial control become intrusive and inappropriate. Control through networks, particularly where there is considerable complexity and short span of product life-cycles, means that emergent 'windows of opportunity' require rapid and widespread sharing of knowledge. Old paradigms of management tradition and practice

Table 1.7: Management Choices

Pre-Revolution	Post-Revolution
Lifelong employment	Lifelong employability
Minimize risks from change	Maximize opportunities for change
Adversarial management	Collaborative management
Narrow view of main stakeholders	Extensive view of main stakeholders
Concentrate rewards	Distribute rewards
Emphasize administrative expertise	Emphasize technical expertise
Focus on continuity	Focus on continuous discontinuity
Separation and specialization key to success	Holistic approach to organization
Fragmented view of work and enterprise	Integrated view of work and enterprise
Stick by the old rules	Search out new rules

Source: Cannon, *Welcome to the Revolution* (1996), p. 18

become increasingly obsolete. Fulk and DeSanctis provide an over-view of the research that has begun to address issues of electronic communication and its impact upon, and change of, organizational forms.[29]

Hames stresses the emergence of the information organization centred on 'appreciative systems' which are open and adaptive, premised on learning, co-operation and flexibility, on networks of individuals rather than either individuals alone or structures alone.[30] The vision of the emergent organization that Hames advances is one that regards the drivers of change as essentially technological: it is the innovations opened up by the microchip that lead the way. Hence, for Hames, the 'rational', technological' driver at the heart of new paradigms is information technology (Table 1.8).

Table 1.8: Transition from Industrial to Information Age Organizations

Industrial Age Organization	Information Age Organization
Focus on measurable outcomes	Focus on strategic issues using participation and empowerment
Highly specialized knowledge base resulting in single-skilling	Interdisciplinary knowledge base resulting in multi-skilling
Individual accountability	Team accountability
Clearly differentiated and segmented organizational positions, roles and responsibilities	Matrix arrangement – flexible positions, roles and responsibilities
Linear input–output thinking about programmes	Holistic perspective on programming
Reactive in solving problems as they emerge – a short-term focus dominated by the 'bottom-line'	Proactive: anticipate issues before they become crises; achieving balance between short-term pragmatism and long-term purpose
Local perspective informs programming	Global perspective informs local action
Hierarchical, linear information flows	Multiple interface, 'boundaryless' information networking
Attention to quantitative differences	Attention to qualitative differences
Plant and equipment targeted for investment	Development of people targeted for investment
Achieving effectiveness through methods	Achieving superior performance underpinned by shared values
Initiatives for improvement emanate from a management élite	Initiatives for improvement emanate from all directions
Present-oriented, doing what is known now	Future-oriented, operating at the cutting edge

Source: Hames, *The Management Myth* (1994)

Common to almost all accounts is an emphasis on the role of information technology in providing the infrastructural means whereby new paradigms may be developed. The impact of IT is everywhere. Information technology specialists Tapscott and Caston identify a number of recurring business themes in *Paradigm Shift*:

- The question of the productivity of knowledge and service workers.
- Just as the productivity challenge of the industrial age was industrial, that of today is in products and services. The challenge is being met by the eclipse of the old paper-and-pen based bureaucratic systems that have survived thus far, and their replacement with source data capture, integrated transaction processing, electronic data interchange, real-time systems, on-line decision support, document management systems, and expert systems. These are leading to new high-performance work-system models.
- Quality, encompassing consistency, predictability, employee motivation, supplier involvement and performance measurement are the new hallmark of service – and knowledge-based industries, as well as those in production.
- Responsiveness: pioneered by firms like Benetton, programmes for mass customization are increasingly being applied. Computers record point-of-sale data on purchasing trends in particular markets that can be fed into subcontracted just-in-time manufacturing systems that deliver speedily to global markets.
- Globalization means the decline of protectionism, the decline of favoured 'home' markets, and the growth of twenty-four-hour trading markets.
- Out-sourcing focuses the key resources of an organization on its core value-adding processes. This is not vertical integration within an enterprise but 'vertical and horizontal integration across organizations, including alliance partners, sales and distribution agencies, key suppliers, support organizations, and other divisions within their own company'.[31]
- Partnering: hitherto independent, autonomous and unconnected businesses and government bodies are establishing alliances, partnerships and network relationships to meet specific market needs. The enterprise is becoming extended. Capacities become enhanced not by old-style growth in size, measured in terms of the number of contracts of employment initiated, but through various kinds of subcontract, partnerships and other extensional

media. These connect the organization with suppliers, customers, markets, governments and so on.
• Social and environmental responsibility: the growth of new social interests in the environment becomes reflected in new relationships with the environment, with groups 'representing' it, and with customers, suppliers and other stakeholders.

Tapscott and Caston stress the role that information technology plays in enabling hierarchies to be superseded by open networked organizations (Table 1.9). Network organization puts a different perspective on strategic learning: understanding is likely to be maximized through learning-by-doing in the network, which disseminates widely. The network can be a mechanism for fast-tracking organization learning about markets, applications and suppliers, through collaborative and open forms of decision-making that eliminate the inefficiency of traditional hierarchical styles. Instead, decisions can be based upon expertise, openly elicited and listened to in the organization, and distributed to everyone more or less immediately by e-mail.

Tapscott and Caston perceive three critical shifts in the application of IT:

From personal to work-group computing: Linking individuals so that they can work in communication as teams on common data, design and analysis from wherever they are networked.

From system islands to integrated systems: In the past each functional area that was touched by IT, such as physical plant and facility control, financial management control systems and human resource management, had their own separate systems. Not surprisingly, communication problems, conflicts and power struggles were rife between the functional departments controlling the separate islands. Each had different bits of information with which they could seek strategic advantage for their interests, as they perceived them. Common information technology architecture in an enterprise facilitates greater openness, cohesion and team development.

From internal to inter-enterprise computing: IT systems are what make global networking possible. They can link enterprises with customers, suppliers, distributors, even regulators in an electronic value chain. Early examples included the American Airlines SABRE ticketing system, but emergent technologies

Table 1.9: From Closed Hierarchies to Open Networked Organizations

	Closed Hierarchy	Open Networked Organization
Structure	Hierarchical	→ Networked
Scope	Internal/closed	→ External/open
Resource focus	Capital	→ Human, information
State	Static, stable	→ Dynamic, changing
Personnel/focus	Managers	→ Professionals
Key drivers	Reward and punishment	→ Commitment
Direction	Management commands	→ Self-management
Basis of action	Control	→ Empowerment to act
Individual motivation	Satisfy superiors	→ Achieve team goals
Learning	Specific skills	→ Broader competencies
Basis for compensation	Position in hierarchy	→ Accomplishment, competency level
Relationships	Competitive (my turf)	→ Co-operative (our challenge)
Employee attitude	Detachment (it's a job)	→ Identification (it's my company)
Dominant requirements	Sound management	→ Leadership

Source: Tapscott and Caston, *Paradigm Shift* (1993), p. 22

include 'inter-enterprise databases, voice response systems, electronic messaging, and new point-of-sale technologies'[32] as well as electronic data interchange (EDI). Through this technology a supplier can be hooked into a user in a network and each can use this access to suggest improvements, not only to their own systems, but also their partners'. Innovation is rapid and transparent and can flow instantaneously through the network.

Changing Competitive Milieus

Other writers concentrate on the impact of a changing competitive milieu upon new paradigm formation. In a special edition of the *Strategic Management Journal* on *The Search for New Paradigms* (1994)

Prahalad and Hamel define substantial paradigm shifts in strategic management in response to the driving elements of the new competitive milieu, including deregulation, decentralization, excess capacity and the rise of new competitors, increased merger and acquisition activity, increased accounting for the environment, new forms of customer sovereignty, new digital technologies and products, the constitution of regional trading blocs, and the arrival of global competition. Among the structural consequences for businesses are:

Disintermediation: The combination of the pervasiveness of information technology and consumer demands for better value means that new players can enter the market with ease. The relationships between existing businesses and organizations such as travel agencies and airline ticketing are no longer fixed.

Disintegration: The breakdown of vertically integrated structures and the emergence of virtual corporations.[33] Long-term relationships and agreements can provide companies with an alternative to vertical integration as transaction costs undergo dramatic change.

Convergence: The fusion of hitherto separate industries such as chemical and photo imaging (e.g. photo CD; computers, communications and consumer electronics). The convergence of technologies and businesses represents a breakdown of clearly demarcated boundaries.

Industry structures are no longer 'givens': they are variables to be managed by the strategic choices made by senior executive management. What were 'dominant logics' of the firm in the past will not remain so in the future: business paradigms change, and managers must recognize these changes and act on them. The focus of competition becomes more diffuse and can come from many directions: products, product lines, business units, clusters of business units within a firm, clusters of firms, a global network of firms.

Innovation in organizations will come, according to Prahalad and Hamel, from the nurturing and application of 'core competencies':

> *Core Competencies* are the collective learning in the organization, especially how to co-ordinate diverse production skills and integrate multiple streams of technologies . . . Core competence is communication, involvement, and a deep

commitment to working across organization boundaries ...
The tangible link between identified core competencies and
end products is what we call the core products – the physical
embodiments of one or more core competencies.[34]

The key thing is to know what the firm's core competencies are
and to nurture them, not to be deflected in their application in
whatever business the firm be in at the moment. Products do not
make a business; competencies do.

Competencies, in principle, can be lodged in any organization –
but some organizations are colossi that have the resources to
develop or secure competencies on a large scale. These firms are
often referred to as diversified multinational corporations, or
DMNCs for short; they are the key players in the emergent global
economy, characterized by multidimensionality and heterogeneity.

Multidimensionality: Multidimensional because they cover mul-
    tiple geographical markets, multiple product lines and multi-
    functional activities. They have multiple stakeholders both
    internally and externally, and thus multiple perspectives on
    choices and decisions. This means that they have no homogen-
    ous unidimensional hierarchical structure that ties these mul-
    tiple dimensions together in a subordinated whole.
Heterogeneity: DMNCs are simultaneously highly local and global.
    They intrude into many national and regional locales, with their
    own issues, politics, markets and prejudices overlain on their
    own multidimensionality. Hence, high variability occurs in the
    degree of 'localness' or 'globalness' as it applies to particular
    businesses and functions.

In *Competing for the Future* Hamel and Prahalad draw up the
blueprints for the *strategic architecture* that companies need if they
are to succeed in future markets (Table 1.10):

It is a view of strategy that is less concerned with ensuring a
tight fit between goals and resources and is more concerned
with creating *stretch goals* that challenge employees to accomplish the seemingly impossible. It is a view of strategy as more
than the allocation of scarce resources across competing projects; strategy is the quest to overcome resource constraints
through a creative and unending pursuit of better *resource*

leverage. It is a view of strategy that recognizes that companies not only complete within the boundaries of existing industries, they compete to *shape the structure* of future industries. It is a view of strategy that recognizes that competition for *core competence* leadership precedes competition for product leadership, and that conceives of the corporation as a portfolio of competencies as well as a portfolio of businesses. It is a view of strategy that recognizes that competition often takes place within and between *coalitions* of companies, and not only between individual businesses.[35]

Governments and companies everywhere have become increasingly concerned with the competitiveness of their industries and how to facilitate the most productive response to the new challenges. Official and business-led inquiries into the sources of comparative advantage and the future shape of successful industries have proliferated. Three recent inquiries stand out as the most inspiring and influential: in the United States the Tomorrow's Corporation series of conferences sponsored by the Polaroid Corporation in Aspen, Colorado (1992–4) brought together academics and industrialists to explore the dimensions of the new structures and operating forms of industry, which included consideration of the wide adoption of employee share ownership in US corporations. In the UK the Tomorrow's Company Inquiry (1992–5) was launched by the Royal Society for the Encouragement of Arts, Manufactures and Commerce (RSA) and funded by twenty-five leading international companies to look into 'the sources of sustainable business success'. The inquiry concluded that the *inclusive* company was of prime importance, to reflect more fully the interests of all stakeholders (see Chapter 6). The RSA was formed by a group of artisans in 1754 with the mission statement:

To embolden enterprise,
to enlarge science,
to refine art,
to improve our manufactures and
to extend our commerce . . .

Having lived through the first industrial revolution, the Fellows of the RSA will certainly have witnessed some changes of paradigm over the last 250-plus years.

Table 1.10: The New Strategy Paradigm

Not Only   **But Also**

The Competitive Challenge

Not Only	But Also
Re-engineering processes	Regenerating strategies
Organizational transformation	Industry transformation
Competing for market share	Competing for opportunity share

Finding the Future

Not Only	But Also
Strategy as learning	Strategy as forgetting
Strategy as positioning	Strategy as foresight
Strategic plans	Strategic architecture

Mobilizing for the Future

Not Only	But Also
Strategy as fit	Strategy as stretch
Strategy as resource allocation	Strategy as resource accumulation and leverage

Getting to the Future First

Not Only	But Also
Competing within an existing industry structure	Competing to shape future industry structure
Competing for product leadership	Competing for core competence leadership
Competing as a single entity	Competing as a coalition
Maximizing the ratio of new product 'hits'	Maximizing the rate of new market learning
Minimizing time-to-market	Minimizing time-to-global-pre-emption

Source: Hamel and Prahalad, *Competing for the Future* (1994), p. 24

The third inquiry was a major Australian government project, published as *Enterprising Nation: Renewing Australia's Managers to Meet the Challenge of the Asia–Pacific Century*.[36] The task force membership represented senior executives from the Australian corporate sector, academia and the public sector. The terms of reference of this task force were to 'advise on measures to strengthen management development and business leadership within Australian enterprises. To identify effective management practices in a range of areas, to raise awareness of the need for improved leadership and management skills and to foster enterprise commitment to management development.'[37] This is probably the most sustained study of shifting paradigms, and their implications, that has yet been conducted at such a senior level of policy development. All but one of the recommendations were accepted by the government of the day. Any effort to implement the report, however, was abandoned by the incoming conservative government.

At the outset of their report the Karpin Industry Task Force on Leadership and Management Skills address 'A new paradigm for management development'.[38] Three global drivers of the paradigm shift are identified: *globalization*, *technological innovation* and *customization*. The approach adopted by the task force to these drivers of change draws on Rand.[39]

Globalization: This is identified in terms of the coalescence of national into global markets, and the development of more competitive sources of labour and capital. As the task force notes, 'The world market for capital now has few barriers and manufacturing capacity is also becoming increasingly mobile. More and more enterprises are entering global markets as exporters, as multidomestics, as multinationals and as transnationals.'[40]

Technological innovation: 'In manufacturing, the number of robots working in factories around the globe is rising and some observers are predicting that intelligent systems will soon replace many workers in service industries. Whole new industries and companies have been created in the last ten to fifteen years including the personal computer industry, software, biotechnology and financial derivatives.'

Customization: This refers to the new focus on customers as the real drivers of organizations, rather than something external and ancillary to organization functioning:

Customers are the lifeblood of enterprises. As customers become more educated and affluent, and as more and more choices are made available to them, they can then demand that companies tailor products and services more accurately

Table 1.11: How to Get Your Company Ready for the Global Century

Build for Speed and Flexibility

Flatten hierarchies:
Fewer bureaucrats make for faster reaction times and freer flow of ideas. ABB has only one layer between the top ranks and the business units

Be on the lookout for joint ventures and partnerships:
They conserve capital, bring you information and technology, and get powerful local players on your side. AT&T is trying to use Unisource, a consortium of European phone companies, to break into the highly protected European telecom market

Be Global and Local

Look for global products and economies of scale:
If you are serving global customers you shouldn't have to cut dozens of separate deals in separate countries. If you can standardize components, do it. Texas Instruments has a team that combs its operations for ideas with global potential. Ford is centralizing its auto-design process to save money by standardizing parts

But don't overcentralize:
No market has a monopoly on the best ideas any more. ABB designs its tilting trains in Sweden and its locomotives in Switzerland. Intel is doing cutting-edge research in Israel. Motorola designed a new generation of pagers in Singapore

Open Up the Company

Stay open-minded:
It's up to the CEO to establish corporate culture that nurtures innovation. Keep challenging assumptions. Don't get locked into dying businesses. Andy Grove has shifted Intel's focus from memories to microprocessors to systems

Open information channels:
Install e-mail and financial-reporting systems that bring everyone into the loop

Table 1.11: (continued)

Use teams to chase new opportunities and ensure cross-fertilization: GE Appliances and Texas Instruments use SWAT teams to set up new operations. LM Ericsson used teams to beat rivals by developing digital mobile-phone systems for Europe, the United States and Japan	*Diversify management:* You are unlikely to succeed in places such as India or China without Indian and Chinese executives. But be sure these managers feel that they belong to the company and share its goals. AT&T is launching a programme that will bring young managers around the world to the United States for three-month to two-year stints

Source: After Industry Task Force on Leadership and Management Skills, *Enterprising Nation* (1995)

and cost effectively to their needs. Increased competition also serves to fuel this trend as companies look to differentiate themselves from their competitors. As a consequence many mass markets around the world have become more segmented and many new niche markets have emerged.[41]

Globalization, technological innovation and customization are opportunities, not threats; citing *Business Week*, the Karpin Industry Task Force on Leadership and Management Skills shows 'How to get your company ready for the global century' (see Table 1.11).[42]

Capability

Concentrating on global competition, the Boston Consulting Group identifies four main components of the core competencies that corporations need to build if they are to achieve success in the new global competition: business processes; strategic capabilities; strategic investments in support infrastructure; and CEOs who champion capabilities-based strategies that are able to reach down into the creative well-springs of organization members in general, rather than just those of 'top management'.[43] To achieve this strategic capability requires greater flexibility and innovation through, according to the task force, the use of:

- Cross-functional teams
- Integration of processes across organizational boundaries
- Organization around products *and* markets
- Delegating authority to lower levels of the organization
- Reducing the number of management layers.

Where these shifts are under way, not only will the language of management shift from one of command and control to one that stresses working through and with other people as members of an organizational team,[44] but the role of managers will be markedly different. The University of Western Sydney Task Force Research Team represented these changes in the form of a contrast between an old and a new paradigm (Table 1.12). In the past, while formal structures of imperative command, crystallized as bureaucracy, could aspire to control all that was within the reach of the organization, that control could never be total. The many 'vicious circles' which arose when management, in its attempts to restore a perceived power deficit, provoked only increased employee resistance are well recorded from Gouldner onwards.[45] Clearly, that control will be far weaker and attempts to achieve it far more inappropriate when the most important relations entered into by the organization are not within its grasp as a legally fictive individual. As networks expand and as markets intrude into organizations, intra-organizational hierarchies – and control premised on them – recede in importance. As organizations seek value through the strength of their ties to and networks with other organizations, attempts at imperative managerial control become increasingly inappropriate.

The Boston Consulting Group focuses on fundamental economic and social changes which will shape the new profile of senior managers (Table 1.13).[46]

Table 1.12: Old and New Paradigms of Management

Organization discipline	Organization learning
Vicious circles	Virtuous circles
Inflexible organizations	Flexible organizations
Management administrators	Management leaders
Distorted communication	Open communication
Hierarchies	Markets
Strategic business units drive product development	Core competencies drive product development
Strategic learning occurs at the apex of the organization	Strategic learning capacities are widespread
Assumption that most organization members are untrustworthy	Assumption that most organization member are trustworthy
Most organization members arc not empowered	Most organization members are empowered
Tacit and local knowledge of most members of the organization must be disciplined by managerial prerogative	Tacit and local knowledge of all members of the organization is the most important factor in success and creativity creates its own prerogative

Source: University of Western Sydney, 'Embryonic Industries' (1995)

Changes in Economic Structures

Chief amongst the changes in the economic structure within which business operates is the breakdown of regulated, national markets, under the impact of globalization. The stable business competition of the past, with known customers and competition, within a nationally regulated framework, has changed dramatically. In a world economy of open markets with floating exchange rates and unstable currencies, the only likely futures are ones of turmoil, unpredictability and instability. In such an environment, the Boston Consulting Group reported from their interviews with Chief Executives, 'successful companies would respond by placing a premium on flexibility, by shortening planning horizons and by developing a very strong external competitive focus'.[47]

Fundamental Shifts in the Nature of Business Competition

These include shifts to the following:

* Capabilities-based competition.
* IT and human resources as enablers of competitive performance.
* Relationships with suppliers and outsourcers as a basis of competitive advantage.

Capabilities-based competition describes the situation where, despite existing cost advantages, scale and brand premiums, competitors have been able to overtake existing firms in the market, such as Wal Mart overtaking KMart in the US discount retailing business. In 1979 Wal Mart had just 229 stores compared to KMart's 1,891 (and had, on average, about half the revenues). Yet during the 1980s Wal Mart grew at 25 per cent per annum and returned higher pre-tax returns than KMart, despite the greater scale, cost advantages and brand premium that the latter could command. How Wal Mart was able to do this was the subject of a *Harvard Business Review* presentation by Stalk, Evans and Shulman.[48] They identified the success factor as 'capabilities-based competition', where capabilities are exceptional and difficult-to-replicate business processes. At Wal Mart these were based on the management of IT and of supplier networks, all oriented around the key value-creating based process in a retail store: shifting product to customers from suppliers. Collaboration technologies can improve co-operative work practices and lead to more effective business activities.[49]

Table 1.13: Fundamental Economic and Social Changes Will Drive the Emerging Profile of the Next Generation of Senior Managers

Key drivers of change	Impact on business	Key challenges for the next generations of senior managers
Changes in economic structures →	Deregulation and opening up of national economies →	1. Mastering a complex, fast-changing and possibly unfamiliar competitive environment
The basis of competition →	Emergence of capabilities-based competition • time-based • process-based →	2. Managing relationships with global customers, suppliers, partners, owners, colleagues and workforces 3. Mastering the new basis of competitive success
The changing shape of business organization →	Growing importance of human resources and information technology as competitive enablers →	
	Organizing around processes	4. Leading an organization of quite different design
→	A knowledge-based workforce Business complexity Globalization Growth in flexible working arrangements Growth in women in management Increasing levels of education in the workforce	5. To work with quite new sorts of colleagues

Source: Boston Consulting Group, *The Australian Manager* (1995), p. 1227

Stalk et al. abstract four lessons for managing capabilities-based competition:[50]

- Corporate strategies should centre not on products and markets but business processes.
- Key processes must be transformed into strategic capabilities that consistently provide better value and service to customers for competitive success.
- Companies create these capabilities by making strategic investments in a support infrastructure that links together and transcends existing organization design.
- Because capabilities necessarily cross functions, the champion of a capabilities-based strategy is the CEO.

Capabilities-based competition calls for the organization to be redesigned not around the traditional hierarchies of command and control but around the horizontal and linked processes that define the workflow of the organization, connecting suppliers to customers. The focus is on teamwork arrangements, internal collaboration and the minimization of sectional interests. To do this successfully

requires local decision making and flexibility. Employees operating processes require day-to-day autonomy and freedom to continuously adjust complex processes in order to meet customer needs. They require information that has traditionally not been available to low level employees and they need to share senior management's understanding of the success factors of the business . . . Whatever the pace and effect of change, the consequences for senior management are substantial. They must learn the skills of operating in organizations in which team behaviour is as important as individual performance, where some key accountabilities are shared rather than individual. They must operate in environments where information is shared between many employees and where there are, by any traditional standards, extraordinary levels of devolution of decision-making and authority.[51]

In some respects the devolution required will not be as fraught with danger as many of the older managers might think. The workforce will increasingly be composed of knowledge workers.[52] An organization that comprises knowledge workers is one where the manager's role is to create a context in which decisions can be made rather than to make those decisions personally, because the knowledge that is essential to that decision-making simply may not be held, or even shared, by more traditional senior management. Their task, increasingly, will be to assemble and lead teams that can deal with the expansion of business knowledge, horizons, competition and complexity. Part of this expansion is encapsulated in the term 'globalization': the implications of this for business have been characterized by Ohmae in four key changes:[53]

- Management will need to be as experienced in foreign transactions, and in dealings with non-traditional customers, operations and markets, as they are with domestic ones.
- The tyranny of head office must end: senior managers will need to be located near the markets and operations they serve rather than in head office.
- As a corollary, organizations will have to develop more decentred network or amoeba-like structures, rather than ones centralized on traditional head offices.
- Additionally, such organizations will have to develop value-systems that are plural and embracing rather than exclusive and discriminatory.

Shifts in Society

There are three shifts in social structure that are likely to be of particular importance for management in the twenty-first century:

- Growth in flexible working arrangements.
- Growth of women in management.
- Increasing levels of education in the workforce generally.

The major variable affecting the nature of workforce participation in all the advanced economies in the past decade or so has been the increasing participation of women in the workforce after the birth of a child. Workplaces in the advanced societies are now being shaped by the needs of women as they seek to integrate work with their responsibilities to family and children – principally through the development of more flexible working arrangements premised on an increasing number of part-time jobs. With the rapid development of knowledge-work based on IT a growing number of part-time jobs involving teleworking at a distance, perhaps from home, will be likely to increase this flexibility further.

The enhanced participation of women in organizational life will not necessarily be brought about by flexible, part-time teleworkers: these are not likely to be jobs with much clout in either the labour market or the company. However, women are increasingly entering the workforce with a commitment to building a career for themselves as well as to motherhood, in organizational contexts that are governed by a formal adherence to principles of non-discrimination. In such contexts the pressure to ensure that the rhetoric and the reality are not too far apart will be substantial.

> The most successful businesses in the next ten to twenty years will be those that best exploit the skills and talents of their staff. The most successful of those businesses will see themselves as creating the conditions in which their employees can make best use of their talents. In our estimation, limiting opportunities for women – who will include half of the most talented and able employees – will simply not be consistent with business success in many organizations.[54]

In most organizations age- and seniority-linked assumptions about careers will have to be changed if mothers are to be able to participate on an equal footing with fathers. Affecting these assumptions will be the increased human capital that is invested in employees as knowledge-workers. On the one hand, organizations will not be able to afford to squander or fail to recognize that human capital; on the other hand, more educated employees of both genders are less likely to hold stubbornly to gendered stereotypes.

Early career placements that expose high-potential managers to ambiguous and uncertain situations will help them to develop their mastery of a complex, fast-changing and possibly unfamiliar competitive environment. Additionally, a good general education, including language studies, about the major regions of competition and partnership (such as Asian studies) will be required. High-potential managers will need to develop a sound knowledge of organization, communications and motivational psychology, as well as leadership, teamwork and communication skills. Management development programmes will need to address discrimination and diversity issues, consciously ensuring that non-discriminatory practices characterize all functions of the organization and its members. University business schools will have to see that their students are exposed to 'traditional broadening liberal arts subjects' that 'are intellectually testing and challenge paradigms and world views'.[55]

Disorganized Capitalism

Limerick and Cunnington paint a vision of the organization future driven by the emergence of a far less regulated political economy.[56] The term that they adopt from Lash and Urry is the era of 'disorganized capitalism', where economic relations are more globally competitive and less organized as an adjunct of statecraft than they once were.[57] Also, they see the emergence of a 'postmodern' society which is quite different from the 'modern' society and is characterized by a decline in the ideas of mass society, mass market and mass production. People no longer identify themselves as part of the mass: they want to express their difference through identity with subsets of the once homogenous conception. Now there are plural, multiple and niche-based sources of identity available to people, such as their sexuality, their culture, their ethnicity. Niche-based markets sustain these sources of identity. Flexible production systems mean that firms can deliver many different adaptations of a product to different markets, rather than presuming or creating a mass market.

But according to Limerick and Cunnington, it is not just a question of markets and production systems. They see 'boundaryless' organizations, based on network structures, characterized by cultures of collaborative individualism, entrepreneurship and action learning, as the new desirable order (Table 1.14). Management becomes much less concerned with the imperatives of control, and more with meaning and symbolic behaviour, reflecting the shift to networks. These are less conducive to imperative control because they are not subject to management prerogative vested in unique organizational rights of command. Consequently, skills such as team-building, negotiation and the management of politics become the central tasks as the internal economy of the firm shifts from economies of scale to economies of time, premised on 'lean manufacturing'.

Flexibility about changing needs, threats and opportunities goes together with a non-hierarchical structure and a free flow of

Table 1.14: The Essential Elements of the New Organization

Discontinuous change	Organizational change	New managerial focus	New managerial competencies
• Economic change • Disorganized capitalism $\rightarrow$ • Postmodernism • Interpersonal change • Neo-humanism	• Structure: – Networks – Boundaryless organizations $\rightarrow$ • Culture: – collaborative individualism • Strategy – entrepreneurship	• Metastrategic management • Identity, vision and operating systems of management • Management of meaning, especially during periods of discontinuity	• 'Soft' competencies: – empathy – trust $\rightarrow$ – managing symbols • 'Hard' competencies: – negotiating – politicking – contracting

Source: Adapted from Limerick and Cunnington, *Managing the New Organization* (1993)

information up as well down the organization.[58] Leadership becomes more collective, more distributed. Rather than being the prerequisite of a charismatic leader, leadership may well be something that is best nurtured by group processes. All managers may need leadership skills and vision in flattened organization structures. Leadership, as the 'new leadership studies' suggest,[59] requires a compelling vision; a 'climate of trust' based on competence, congruity and constancy; the creation of meaning and the ability to learn from mistakes; a healthy and empowering environment; and flatter, flexible, adaptive, decentralized learning systems and organizations.[60]

INTELLIGENT SUSTAINABLE ORGANIZATIONS

According to James Collins and Jerry Porras in *Built to Last – The Successful Habits of Visionary Companies*, companies that survive and succeed do not oppress themselves with the ' "Tyranny of the O R" – the rational view that cannot easily accept paradox, that cannot live with two seemingly contradictory forces or ideas at the same time. The "Tyranny of the OR" pushes people to believe that things must be either A *OR* B, but *not both*.' It makes such proclamations as:

- 'You can have change *OR* stability.'
- 'You can be conservative *OR* bold.'
- 'You can have low cost *OR* high quality.
- 'You can have creative autonomy *OR* consistency and control.'
- 'You can invest for the future *OR* do well in the short term.'
- 'You can make progress by mechanical planning *OR* by opportunistic groping.'
- 'You can create wealth for your shareholders *OR* do good for the world.'
- 'You can be idealistic (values-driven) *OR* pragmatic (profit-driven).'[61]

As demonstrated in their detailed case studies of leading US corporations that seem to have captured the secret of considerable commercial success and longevity, it is possible for organizations to liberate themselves with the 'Genius of the *AND*': the ability to embrace both extremes of a number of dimensions at the same time, to pursue A and B simultaneously and successfully, not *balance* but creative genius (Table 1.15).

Some writers would maintain that an intelligent organization is, in essence, a sustainable one. Sustainability has two meanings: one stresses the ability to keep on going, to sustain something for a long period of time, as in a long-lived business enterprise. The other stresses sustainability in the sense of renewal – for instance, where an environment exists that sustains all other activities, thus making them possible. The two uses are not disconnected: any sustainable enterprise requires access to key resources. Historically, the definition of what is key has changed over time. For de Geus, the significant paradigm shift is from a world of business 'dominated by capital to one dominated by knowledge'.[62] The argument is represented in Table 1.16.

The transition from feudalism to capitalism is familiar enough from many historical studies.[63] The transition from a capitalist society, where access to capital has the highest value, to one where access to knowledge is more prized, is a relatively recent trend.

Table 1.15: The 'Genius of the AND'

On the One Hand	AND	Yet, on the Other Hand
Purpose beyond profit	AND	Pragmatic pursuit of profit
A relatively fixed core ideology	AND	Vigorous change and movement
Conservatism around the core	AND	Bold, committing, risky moves
Clear vision and sense of direction	AND	Opportunistic groping and experimentation
Big Hairy Audacious Goals	AND	Incremental evolutionary progress
Selection of managers steeped in the core	AND	Selection of managers that induce change
Ideological control	AND	Operational autonomy
Extremely tight culture (almost cult-like)	AND	Ability to change, move and adapt
Investment for the long-term	AND	Demands for short-term performance
Philosophical, visionary, futuristic	AND	Superb daily execution, 'nuts and bolts'
Organization aligned with a core ideology	AND	Organization adapted to its environment

Source: Collins and Porras, *Successful Habits* (1996), p. 44

Through building a learning organization, enterprises are able to develop what de Geus terms 'tools for foresight'. What characterizes far-sighted, long-lived enterprises? Four key factors function as the characteristic 'family resemblances' of sustainable enterprises in the sense of being long-lived. According to de Geus, long-lived companies are:

- Sensitive to their environment: they have the ability to change and to adapt
- Cohesive, with a strong sense of identity: they have the ability to build a community of committed people in and around the firm, and to develop their own persona
- Tolerant and decentralized, thus permitting marginal experimentation through being able to build constructive relationships

Table 1.16: The Historically Changing Priorities
of Management

Era	Key resource	Exploitation of:
Feudal society	Access to land	Natural fertility, and technologies that allowed for the production, appropriation and trade in surplus produce.
Capitalist society	Access to capital	Human labour power, and technologies that harnessed, extended and appropriated the surplus value that could be extracted from people as commodities working with other assets.
Knowledge society	Access to knowledge	Systematic ingenuity, innovation and knowledge, that adds value to companies through the optimization of people as sources of creativity that develop the consistent knowledge-base of the enterprise.

Source: de Geus, *The Living Company* (1997).

with other entities, both intra-organizationally and extra-organizationally

- Conservative in financing: they have the ability to govern their own growth and evolution, and thus control their sense of direction.[64]

It is also interesting to consider what they are not:

> The ability to return investment to shareholders seemed to
> have nothing to do with longevity. The profitability of a com-
> pany was a *symptom* of corporate health, but not a *predictor* or
> *determinant* of corporate health . . . Nor did longevity seem to
> have anything to do with a company's material assets, its
> particular industry or product line or its country of origin.[65]

The findings reported by de Geus came from an internal study
conducted for the Shell organization, but find corroboration in
the research conducted by Collins and Porras that also found the
visionary companies, most of which had survived for more than
sixty years, put a lower priority on maximizing shareholder wealth
or profits, were sensitive to the environment, whether it was conceived as a natural, social or business environment, and had a
strong sense of identity.[66] These findings may seem paradoxical to
managers who, of necessity, have to manage the future from the
here-and-now. Here-and-now they are responsible to shareholders
who demand immediate and bigger returns on investments; but,
if they attend exclusively to these short-term demands then they
may well threaten the long-term viability of their companies,
investor profits and their own careers. However, de Geus suggests
that this paradox only occurs within a paradigm that is by now
obsolete, suboptimal and destructive: 'Corporate success and longevity are fundamentally interwoven, in a way that, nowadays, is
qualitatively different from the relationship between success and
longevity in the economic environment of five decades ago.'[67]

With regard to the second definition of sustainability, Maynard
and Mehrtens offer in *The Fourth Wave: Business in the 21st Century*
(1996) a highly optimistic view that just as the first wave of agriculture was superseded by the second wave of industrialization, which
covered much of the earth and continues to spread, while a new,
post-industrial third wave is gathering force in the modern industrial countries, a fourth wave is apparent. The second wave was
rooted in materialism and the mastery of man over the natural
world; the third wave manifests growing concerns for balance and
sustainability. 'By the time of the fourth wave, integration of all
dimensions of life and responsibility for the whole will have
become the central foci.' Social accounting, including the univer-
salization of capital ownership, internalization of the social and

Table 1.17: Characteristics of Second, Third and Fourth Wave Corporations

	Second Wave	Third Wave	Fourth Wave
Goals	Maximize profits	Create value	Serve as global steward
Motivation	Make money	Make money and help solve societal problems	Leave valuable legacy for the future
Values	Profit, growth, control	Creating value, trust, learning	Responsibility for the whole service, personal fulfilment
Stakeholders	Owners of business, stockholders	Stockholders, employees, families, suppliers, customers, communities, government	Stockholders, employees, families, suppliers, customers, communities, government, ecosystem, Gaia
Outlook	Self-preservation; business as a way to make a living	Co-operation; business as a way for people to grow and serve	Unity; business as a means to actively promote economic and social justice
Domain	National and local; five to ten years into the future	International; share responsibility for the welfare of local, national and global communities; decades into the future	Global; share leadership in local, national and global affairs; generations into the future

Source: Maynard and Mehrtens, *The Fourth Wave* (1996), p. 164

environmental costs of doing business, and capitalization of natural resources, will drive corporations to embrace social and environmental responsibility (Table 1.17).[68]

Hames presents a similar paradigm shift from a less to a more sustainable organizational world:[69] learning organization is extended, securing the temporal sustainability of the corporation to the anchor of a 'self-organizing system able to "learn" its way into preferred futures, in ethical reciprocity with its environment, and in ways that are "appreciative" of all stakeholders' needs, expectations and desires'.[70] The 'appreciative paradigm' begins with a familiar critique of 'modernism' (in terms of its hierarchical, exploitative, destructive qualities), before moving to an affirmation of 'appreciative praxis' premised on:

- Diversity of variety which nurtures survival.
- Optimization rather than maximization of energy usage.
- Co-operation which appears to be more conspicuous than competition in many natural systems.
- Self-regulation rather than externally imposed or controlled direction.
- Collaborative learning from experience – this is the way the young of all species develop to remain healthy and adaptive.
- Transformative change which is continuous in healthy systems.
- Connectedness – all parts of a system are interrelated in some way to all other parts.
- Equivalence – all of the roles that exist in natural systems are basically comparable.[71]

The preferred organizational model for Hames's *Burying the 20th Century* is network organization: 'What hierarchy was to the 20th century, the distributed network will be to the 21st . . . [because] the network is the only organizational type capable of unguided, or unprejudiced growth . . . the network is the least structured organization that can be said to have any structure at all.'[72] Thus it is digitalization that is driving development but, on this occasion, digitalization connected to a networked ecological consciousness. Collaborative technologies are paralleled by collaborative learning as a process of cultural evolution.

To explore what we are becoming requires addressing questions such as:

- What are the key drivers for the future?
- Should they remain the same as in the past or could other possibilities be explored? If so, what are they likely to be?
- Will these engage all stakeholders' interest and commitment in the long term?
- How will the new possibilities change choices about how the organization does what it presently does and how it will do what it will do in the future?
- What will the organization end up looking like if the driving forces change?

Such questions enable organizations to identify their key strategic determinants for future visions. Once these are determined, then the organization will need to affirm new principles and priorities to ensure that its competencies and protocols are consistent with the changed strategic intent, and that its design – symbolic, aesthetic and structural – corresponds with these changes.

At the heart of the paradigms of twenty-first-century, business will be virtual, intelligent organization networks, competing in a global, open economy, in ecologically sustainable ways, appreciative of the many stakeholders with an interest in the company's performance.

CONCLUSION

This introductory chapter has reviewed the key drivers of the current paradigm shifts:

→ Paradigm shifts as strategic responses to changing competitive milieus
→ Information technology as the technical core of current paradigm shifts
→ Innovation and learning as the central rationale of new paradigms
→ The importance of wider conceptions of stakeholders to new paradigms
→ The overwhelming need for new business paradigms to be based on sustainability.

Table 1.18: The Central Paradigm Shifts Considered

	CHANGING PARADIGMS	
FROM		*TO*
Classical/ neo-classical management orthodoxy	*CHAPTER 1* *PARADIGMS*	Multiple changing management paradigms
Local/national international	*CHAPTER 2* *GLOBALIZATION*	Glocalization/ globalization
Manual/analogue stand alone	*CHAPTER 3* *DIGITALIZATION*	Electronic/digital network
Strategic planning rational strategy	*CHAPTER 4* *STRATEGY*	Strategic thinking innovation/core competence
Taylorism/Fordism hierarchy	*CHAPTER 5* *ORGANIZATION*	Intelligent networked virtuality
Shareholders/ financial performance indicators	*CHAPTER 6* *STAKEHOLDERS*	Stakeholders/non- financial performance indicators
Profit/growth/ control	*CHAPTER 7* *SUSTAINABILITY*	Sustainable enterprise

This review prepares the broad themes to be investigated in greater detail in the subsequent chapters of this book:

Globalization: The macro-context in which the twenty-first-century futures will unfold
Digitalization: The critical technological drivers of the future scenarios
Strategy: The creative strategies of future organization
Organization: The future possibilities of intelligent organization design and practices

Stakeholders: The plurality of interests and indicators for future organizations

Sustainability: The design of future organizations that will be intelligent enough both to endure and be ecologically sustainable.

To return to the initial model of the emerging trends in the development of management paradigms, Table 1.18 relates this series of paradigm shifts to the progress through the themes of the remaining chapters of the book. Though there is plenty of room for debate and creative discovery of the detail of different paradigm shifts, the fact that the business world is changing in fundamental ways, and will never be the same again, is evident to everyone who intends to make their enterprise succeed in the approaching millennium.

Chapter 2

GLOBALIZATION

The world is slowly starting to move from an era of the wealth of
nations to an era of the wealth of the world.[1]

Since the establishment of the earliest civilizations trade has
crossed frontiers and regions. The discovery of the material riches
of distant lands has proved the spur to the greatest adventures of
history. The industrial revolution generated wealth largely by
taking raw materials from one part of the world, manufacturing
them in another and marketing the finished goods throughout the
globe. This is the pattern of exchange that has defined international
trade for 200 years. However, the concept of globalization that has
burst into prominence in the last decade implies a great deal more.
In this chapter we examine the implications for business of the
integration of all forms of economic activity on a global basis.
Investment, research and development, production, distribution
and marketing are becoming increasingly globalized in a growing
number of industries and products.

The conception of business activity as essentially based on local
or national markets, with a degree of permanence reinforced by
local standards and distinctive technology which will change only
slowly, is displaced by the paradigm shifts of globalization. The
integration of markets and technology allowed by deregulation
and facilitated by telecommunications and improved transport suddenly means that more businesses are up against world standards,
and that breakthroughs in products and processes can occur everywhere at once. As companies attempt to internationalize, they
quickly learn the paradox of globalization: that the world is
composed of many cultures. They must begin by coming to terms
with this pluralism.

Table 2.1: Paradigm Shifts

Local/National International	Globalization/ Glocalization
Separation	Integration
Protection	Deregulation
Immobility	Mobility
Technological leads	Technological diffusion
Local standards	World standards
Time lags	Simultaneity
Unitarism	Pluralism

THE INTERNATIONALIZATION OF ECONOMIC ACTIVITY

With the increased scale, speed, diversity and complexity of international business, Lester Thurow noted in *The Future of Capitalism* that 'For the first time in human history, anything can be made anywhere and sold everywhere', a concept of globalization that conveys the integration of worldwide economic activities.[2] Such integration is necessary, the argument goes, for businesses to capture expanding market opportunities by co-ordinating and controlling their operations to maximum effect. The rich promise of new and emerging global markets for business is tempered by the threat of intensified competition at home. Governments are concerned to sustain their national competitiveness and economic growth and to minimize the economic dislocation and job losses caused by the defensive restructuring of domestic industries. Both the OECD, in *Globalization of Industry* (1996), and the IMF, in *Globalization: Opportunities and Threats* (1997), have considered the policy implications of globalization as the new 'powerful motor of world-wide economic growth'.

Globalization of industry refers to an evolving pattern of cross-border activities of firms, involving international investment, trade and collaboration for purposes of product development, production and sourcing, and marketing. These international activities enable firms to enter new markets, exploit their technological and organizational advantages, and reduce business costs and risks. Underlying the international expansion of firms, and in part driven by it, are technological advances, the liberalization of markets and an increased mobility of production factors. These complex patterns of cross-border activities increasingly characterize the international economic system and distinguish it from the earlier predominance of arm's-length trade in finished goods.

National economies are becoming more closely integrated as firms spread their operations and assets across countries. This brings greater economic efficiencies and welfare, as well as more intense competition, a greater need for adjustment and more demands on national and international policy. The current challenge for many countries – in a situation of low economic growth and high unemployment – is to ensure effective adjustment while minimizing related international frictions, so that the potential welfare and efficiency gains from globalization are attained.[3]

Dimensions of Globalization

Ricardo Petrella, the director-general of the Forecasting and Assessment in Science and Technology (FAST) Commission of the European Community, has described the historical processes of internationalization, multinationalization and globalization. The *internationalization* of economy and society, a process which began with the first movement of trade, refers to the flows of exchange of raw materials, semi-finished and finished goods and services, money and ideas and people between national states.

Though the world trading system developed considerably from the sixteenth century onwards, it was only at the end of the nineteenth century and the beginning of the twentieth century that significant transnational activity emerged. This *multinationalization* of economy and society is characterized by the transfer of resources, especially capital and, to a lesser extent, labour, from one national economy to another. Typically this involves the creation of production capacities of a firm in another country through direct subsidiaries, acquisitions or various types of co-operation (commercial, financial, technological and industrial). Put simply, a multinational is a corporation whose activities have been gradually extended to other countries.

What is distinctive about the end of the twentieth century is the magnitude and pace of globalization. Petrella defines the characteristics of contemporary globalization in terms of the

- Internationalization of financial markets.
- Internationalization of corporate strategies, in particular their commitment to competition as a source of wealth creation.
- Diffusion of technology and related R&D and knowledge worldwide.
- Transformation of consumption patterns into cultured products with worldwide consumer markets.
- Internationalization of the regulatory capabilities of national societies into a global political economic system.
- Diminished role of national governments in designing the rules for global governance.

Hirst and Thompson argue that the present highly internationalized economy is not unprecedented and in some respects is less open and generalized than that which existed in the previous high-water mark of the global economy between 1870 and 1914.[4] Genuinely transnational companies are comparatively rare. Most companies are nationally based and trade multinationally on the strength of national locations and activities. Capital mobility is not producing a profound shift of employment and investment from the advanced industrial countries to the developing world. Foreign direct investment is highly concentrated among the industrialized countries, and apart from a small group of developing countries (mainly in South-East Asia), the developing world remains highly marginalized. The world economy is far from being truly 'global'. Trade, investment and financial flows are concentrated in the Triad of Europe, Japan and North America, and this dominance is likely to continue. These major G3 economic powers have the capacity, if they co-ordinate policy, to exert powerful governance pressures over financial markets and other economic activities.

While the extent of globalization varies markedly in different economies and industries, the net result is considerable. Overall, annual sales of goods and services by foreign affiliates are one and a half times the value of world exports, and a rising share of private sector GNP is accounted for by the combined value-added of foreign-based firms and the foreign output of home-based firms: over 50 per cent for Belgium, Canada, the Netherlands, Switzerland and the United Kingdom; more than 30 per cent for Australia, France, Germany and Italy; and over 20 per cent for Japan and the United States.[5]

Table 2.2 illustrates the way in which each element of globalization is experienced:

Table 2.2: Concepts of Globalization

Category	Main Elements/ Processes
Globalization of finances and capital ownership	Deregulation of financial markets, international mobility of capital, rise of mergers and acquisitions. The globalization of shareholding is at its initial stage
Globalization of markets, strategies and, in particular, competition	Integration of business activities on a worldwide scale; establishment of integrated operations abroad (including R&D and financing); global sourcing of components, strategic alliances
Globalization of technology and linked R&D and knowledge	Technology is the primary catalyst: the rise of information technology and telecoms enables the rise of global networks within the same firm and between different firms. Globalization as the process of universalization of Toyotism/lean production
Globalization of consumption patterns and cultures	Transfer and transplantation of predominant modes of life. Equalization of consumption patterns. The role of the media. Transformation of culture in 'cultural food', 'cultural products'. GATT rules apply to cultural flows
Globalization as political unification	State-centred analysis of the integration of world societies into a global political and economic system led by a core power
Globalization of perception and consciousness	Socio-cultural processes as centred on 'One Earth'. The 'globalist' movement. Planetary citizens

Source: After Petrella, 'Globalization . . .' (1996), p. 66

Globalization Today

Many enthusiastic proponents of the globalization thesis argue that business survival is increasingly about performance in the world market. Domestic markets are no longer the focus of economic activity and competition: it is competing to world-class standards that counts. Kenneth Ohmae in *Managing in a Borderless World* (1989) insists that

> On a political map, the boundaries between countries are as clear as ever. But on a competitive map, a map showing the real flows of financial and industrial activity, those boundaries have largely disappeared. People want to buy the best and cheapest products – no matter where in the world they are produced . . . We've become global citizens, and so must the companies that want to sell us things . . . Global needs leads to global products.[6]

Ohmae is a proponent of the thesis of declining state power in the face of strong globalization driven by market developments internationally. He is not alone among influential management thinkers. In *World Class: Thriving Locally in the Global Economy* (1996) Rosabeth Moss Kanter identifies four broad processes as aspects of globalization – mobility, simultaneity, bypass and pluralism. Together these reinforce each other and accelerate globalizing forces:

Mobility – capital, people, ideas: The key elements of business – capital, people and ideas – are increasingly mobile. The electronic movement of capital has vastly increased financial flows while making them more difficult to detect or regulate. The international flow of migrant professionals and knowledge workers has helped to create a global labour market in a growing number of occupations. Ideas move immediately around the world through the global media: CNN and the BBC World Service are available in 140 countries; the *Wall Street Journal* and *Financial Times* are published in European, Asian and South American editions. High-speed information transfer makes place irrelevant.
Simultaneity – everywhere at once: Globalization means that time-lags in the introduction of products and services are now declining precipitously. Time-lags before full international market

penetration in consumer electronics have fallen to six years for colour TVs; one year for CDs. With VCRs different formats have struggled on, but for the fax machine a common standard was adopted universally by 1988. Brand names are travelling the world. New products can create their own infrastructure or support, influencing practices in every country.

Bypass – multiple choices: Bypass suggests numerous alternative routes to reach and service customers, taking away the advantage of those who dominate particular channels. Cellular and satellite telecommunications systems bypass land-based systems; the Internet bypasses established sales channels. New international networks provide new opportunities and proliferating choices for consumers.

Pluralism – the centre cannot hold: Activities once concentrated in a few places disperse to multiple centres of expertise and influence. 'The centre cannot hold', predicted W. B. Yeats, and now throughout the world decentralization is occurring. In finance, telecommunications, car manufacture and a range of other industries the traditional centres of control and technology are encountering the growth of multiple centres of innovation and influence. Corporations are under pressure to disperse headquarters expertise to reflect the changes taking place in markets and industries.

For proponents of the globalization thesis it is these processes of globalization that make possible the design, production, distribution and consumption of processes, products and services on a world scale, using patents, databases, advanced information, communication and transport technologies and infrastructures. There are even global products:

> Many of the new products are geared to satisfy increasingly diversified and customized global markets regulated by 'quasi-universal' norms and standards . . . Credit cards are a typical illustration of a global service 'devised' for a specialized, high-value added world market, based on the integration of whole clusters of new technologies (data processing, materials, telecommunications etc.) and managed by globalized organizations with a growing world expertise.[7]

It is not surprising that, in the view of some theorists of globalization, the world has apparently become 'boundaryless', despite the continued existence of borders between states and all the administrative devices that maintain them.

Globalization: Winner-Takes-All Markets

However, the global economy is not just about proliferating choices, instant satisfaction and the mass enjoyment of electronic novelties. It can also be about the creation of 'winner-takes-all markets', in which comparative advantage can be exploited on a world scale, and in which only a privileged minority benefit. Ethan Kapstein of the Council on Foreign Relations in New York claims that 'rapid technological change and increased international competition are fraying the job markets of the major industrialized countries ... The global economy is leaving millions of disaffected workers in its train. Inequality, unemployment and endemic poverty have become its handmaidens.'[8]

Apocalyptical views of the consequences of globalization are not convincing, but there is evidence of increasing unemployment and widening inequality as the world economy develops and becomes a powerful force in local economies. In the 1990s unemployment grew to 34 million in the OECD countries, with at least 80 million unemployed in the developing world and a further 600 million underemployed.[9] In the United States the distribution of rewards from global competition have proved particularly skewed:

> In the 1980s all of the gains in male earnings went to the top 20% of the workforce, and an amazing 64% to the top 1%. The pay of the average Fortune 500 CEO goes from 25 to 157 times that of the average production worker. CEO salaries tripled in France, Italy and Britain, and more than doubled in Germany ... At no other time since data have been collected have American median real male wages consistently fallen for a two decade period of time. Never before have a majority of American workers suffered real wage reductions while the per capita GDP was advancing.[10]

A concern is that this inequality is not a temporary effect of occupational and industrial competitive restructuring, but a permanent feature of the unbalanced economies created by globalization. Yet the call for further liberalization of trade and investment involves governments relinquishing some of the traditional ways in which they have exercised responsibility for protecting domestic industries or vulnerable workers. Countries become caught by interdependency as they pay the price for access to larger markets. As finance, technology factories and equipment seem to move 'effortlessly across borders', Robert Reich poses the question: to what extent can a nation continue to be thought of as a society when it no longer has an identifiable national economy.[11]

The images of globalization are powerful – national cultures, national economies and national borders are apparently dissolving. However, critics of the reckless use of such images have emphasized the real limitations of emerging globalization, and the historical antecedents of the international processes that are now causing so much excitement. In a section of a World Economic Survey entitled 'From Hype to Eternity' the *Economist* insisted:

> The scale of both globalization and technological change tends to be vastly exaggerated. On some measures, economies at the turn of the century were every bit as open and integrated as they are today. Most industrial countries' trade as a share of GDP is not much larger now than it was a century ago. And whereas capital has certainly become incomparably more mobile in recent decades, net capital flows between countries were actually bigger relative to GDP in the late 19th century. Britain then invested a massive 40% of its savings abroad.[12]

Moreover, as Wade argues, the situation has shifted during the late 1980s so that the post-war trend towards greater trade integration is weakening.[13] Weiss cites a declining ratio of world trade growth to output from 1.65 in 1965–80 to 1.34 in 1980–90.[14] Wade proposes structural, rather than merely cyclical reasons for this decline related to the shift in OECD countries out of manufacturing, which boosts their share of less trade-intensive services.[15]

Globalization and the Triad

The globalization of world trade is taking place between the Triad countries: between Western Europe, North America, Japan and the newly industrialized countries of South-East Asia. Technological, economic and cultural integration is developing within these three regions, and between the three regions. The phenomenon of 'Triadization' is demonstrated in the pattern of international trade and investment flows. In the 1980s the Triad accounted for 80 per cent of all international capital flows. Similarly inter-firm strategic alliances are heavily concentrated among the companies from the Triad countries. The 'Triadization' of the world economy relates to scientific power, technological supremacy, economic dominance and cultural hegemony, and therefore the ability to govern the world into the future.[16]

There is little doubt that the major players in the continuing domination of the Triad are the multinational companies: these have acquired a new significance and assertiveness as individual nation states are apparently less able to influence economic events in the international economy. According to Petrella, multinationals, as providers of the technology infrastructure, goods and services for the world economy, have seized the initiative. These organizations alone have transformed themselves into 'global' players, operating at the most influential level of decision-making. The world economy gives top priority to technology, and to those who research, develop and produce technology – overwhelmingly the multinationals. These companies are considered to be the key actors in the production of wealth, ensuring employment and, therefore, individual and collective well-being. Multinationals are central to those arguments that stress the importance of global business and the rise of markets.

The Emergence of the Multinationals

In 1991, according to UN estimates, there were about 36,000 multinational corporations (MNCs) in the world, with 170,000 subsidiaries; their total revenues were in excess of $15.5 trillion. They accounted for about a quarter of the world's GNP, and a much higher share of the private sector input. While not all MNCs are large, most large companies in the world are MNCs. In fact about 450 companies, with annual revenues in excess of $1 billion, account for about 80 per cent of the total investment made by all companies outside their home country. The largest 100, excluding those in banking and finance, accounted for $3.1 trillion in worldwide assets in 1990, of which $1.2 trillion was outside the companies' home country. MNCs use their internal organization for cross-border transactions rather than depending on trade in an open market.[17]

Traditionally, the motivations for becoming a MNC included securing key suppliers, seeking new markets, and accessing low-cost factors of production. The emerging motivations for becoming a MNC are different and focus on scale economies, the amortization of R&D expenses, and shortening product life-cycles. Successful firms operating internationally usually have technological and organizational advantages over purely domestic ones. Foreign affiliates tend to have higher labour productivity and are more investment-intensive and trade-oriented than the average domestic firms, due to the high-technology, high-wage and capital-intensive industries in which international firms operate, their larger size, and their use of advanced production and management methods and a more skilled workforce. The share of employment in foreign manufacturing affiliates has also increased – or declined less sharply – than in domestic firms, but in part this has been due to merger and acquisition activity by foreign firms which transfers existing employment into the foreign-controlled sector, rather than generating new employment in completely new operations.[18]

Industrial globalization is changing the scope and distribution of world business and expanding the presence and influence of foreign companies in national economies. Firms and industries are being restructured and rationalized at transnational level as production factors become increasingly mobile and communication costs decline. New patterns of industrial specialization and new competitors emerge rapidly, changing the competitive position of firms and countries. At the same time, economies are being increasingly linked and integrated through the global strategies of firms.[19]

It is well known that the economic scale of the largest of these giant corporations now exceeds the gross domestic product of most countries. Unsurprisingly these companies are exclusively domiciled in Triad countries. The *FT*500 reveals the continuing dominance of US international companies – at least as measured by market capitalization. However, a very different picture emerges from the Fortune 500, which grades companies according to their sales: here, Japanese and European companies predominate. A different league again appears when the number of employees is the criterion (see Appendix p. 434).

Multinationals: Size and Uncertainty
The corporate giants of the present may be in a very different position in the future, and few of the present US leaders were in this league (or even existed) in 1962, when Berle and Means last assembled data on the largest manufacturing corporations

measured by asset size. John Kay has cautioned against extrapolating from the present to the future or assuming that large-scale firms are able to persist in the market because of the competitive advantage conferred by their size.[20] Too many examples from business history, such as PanAm, fail to sustain that proposition. Size is predominantly the result of competitive advantage, not its actual cause.

What was true in the past concerning competitive advantage has become a more pressing fact in the present with the speed of technological discovery and application, the increasing intensity of productivity, and the rapidly shifting nature of markets. This has created a more uncertain business world in which the largest companies have to be as fast on their feet as the leanest, and continual innovation is necessary for survival. As Bowman and Kogut argue:

> The most remarkable fact in the economic history of this century has been the increasing concentration of production by the largest corporations in the industrialized countries. It has been the sheer rapidity of this corporate growth that has spelled the limits of its continuation. The labour forces of corporations today are vastly more productive than before. The rising productivity of labour has outpaced the growth of the value of output by the largest firms. Large corporations require increasingly smaller workforces to maintain a high level of productivity and service. There is . . . a more fundamental change occurring . . . in which the historical advantage of large corporations is no longer assured. The uncertainty of markets, the importance of niches and innovations in increasingly wealthy societies, the creation of new flexible technologies and telecommunications systems, and the growth of well-educated workers and managers have created a major break in the organization of work and in its division among large and small firms . . . A revolutionary break with the design principles of mass production and economies of size. Competitive pressures are forcing large companies to redesign how work and management are organized in order to be more flexible, quicker, and market oriented.[21]

THE GLOBAL ECONOMY

The most prominent features of globalization are:

• New aspects of international trade.
• International direct investment.
• International inter-firm collaboration.
• International capital flows and financial instruments.

Globalization is not a totally new phenomenon. Quantitative evidence of national indicators such as the share of exports as a percentage of GDP, or the share of foreign investment in total investment flows, suggest the internationalization of economic activity has not changed greatly since the beginning of the century. The internationalization of trade, production and finance have fluctuated dramatically since then, collapsing at the end of the 1930s and only recovering in the 1950s. However, globalization now is both quantitatively and qualitatively different from before. Though faced with a slowdown in growth, governments have now accepted the necessity to maintain open markets in spite of the cost, whereas in the 1930s countries built high tariff walls to keep competition at bay. Moreover, the deregulation of financial markets has unleashed new forces not previously seen in the tightly regulated financial institutions of the recent past.[22]

What changed through the 1980s and 1990s is that firms have used new combinations of international investment, trade and collaboration to expand internationally and to achieve ever greater efficiencies:

Composition: The growth in international trade has been outstripped by the growth in the flows of international direct investment (despite the downturn in the early 1990s) and in the number of international collaboration agreements.
Geographical diversification: Cross-border operations are still largely concentrated in the OECD area, but have involved an increasing number of firms from OECD source and destination countries. Outside the OECD area, the Dynamic Asian Economies (DAEs) and China have increasingly been involved in the process of globalization.
Functional pattern: The pattern of cross-border transactions

linking firms to raw materials and final markets has been reshaped by international intra-firm and inter-firm operations focused on specific intermediate functional areas of operations: technological development and co-operation, different phases of production, and external sourcing and intra-firm trade in intermediate outputs.[23]

International Trade

International trade presently has three principal components:

- Intra-regional trade.
- International sourcing of intermediate inputs.
- Intra-firm and intra-industry trade.

Total OECD trade expanded during the 1970s at an annual average of nearly 20 per cent in nominal terms, bringing trade flows to 20 per cent of total OECD GDP. During the 1980s trade expanded more slowly with the deceleration of GDP growth; after slowing further between 1991 and 1993 trade has picked up again. Over the last thirty years the largest increases in world shares of imports has been in the European Community (EC) and the newly industrialized economies (NIEs: Taipei, Hong Kong, Korea, Singapore), with Japan importing slightly more. Increases in export shares have been recorded for the EC, Japan and the NIEs. The most significant change is the increase in US imports to 20 per cent of the total, combined with a decline in exports from 22 per cent to 18 per cent of the total. In the same period exports from Japan double to over 11 per cent of the total (Table 2.3).

Much of this trade is within the regions concerned. Intra-regional trade in Europe (the share of intra-European imports in total European imports) climbed from 55 per cent in the mid-1960s to 70 per cent in 1989. Asian intra-regional trade doubled to over 40 per cent at the end of the 1980s, while trade between Canada and the United States fell from around 40 to 30 per cent.[24] Import penetration – the share of imported manufactured goods in total domestic demand – reveals the exposure of economies to foreign competition: since 1970 it has grown in all industrial countries, but most rapidly in the United States. The lowest import penetration is found in Japan, then the US, followed by the larger European

Table 2.3: Percentages of World Imports and Exports
1966–8 and 1987–9

	Imports 1966–8	Exports 1966–8	Imports 1987–8	Exports 1987–8
North America	19.1	22.0	20.1	17.8
Japan	4.4	5.7	5.5	11.3
European Community	38.7	39.2	44.9	45.6
NIEs	1.8	1.1	5.1	5.5

Source: OECD, 1996a, Table 1.2, p. 23

countries; it is highest in the smaller European countries with the most internationalized economies, which also export a high percentage of their production.

Interestingly, export coverage (exports as a share of production) is lowest in Japan and the United States, where exports account for only around 10 per cent of production. The relatively low share for Japan reflects the concentration on a few competitive sectors (computers, consumer electronics, cars) and low exports in other sectors. Over 70 per cent of Japanese exports in 1970 were in cars, electronics and other machinery.[25]

In the industrial countries there is higher import penetration in high-technology industries, followed by medium-technology industries, with domestic production satisfying demand in low-technology industries – with the exception of clothing and footwear. High-wage industries are therefore more heavily represented in imports, which contradicts the view that the imports of the industrial countries are largely composed of low technology, low-wage goods. Industrial countries increasingly specialize in high-technology industries, which consequently feature more prominently in both their imports and exports.

International sourcing of parts and materials is a major feature of global production systems and accounts for a large part of total trade. International sourcing is linked with international investment: when companies invest internationally they are more likely to source internationally. Direct imports of parts and materials account for more than half manufactured imports in the large industrial countries. The ratio of imported to domestic sourcing is

35–40 per cent for France, Germany and the UK, 13 per cent for the United States and only 7 per cent for Japan.[26] International sourcing is more prevalent in oil refining, textiles, apparel and footwear, motor vehicles, computers, aerospace, and communications equipment and semiconductors. The US sources from Japan, the European countries from each other, and Japan from the United States and Asia, where significant Japanese investment has been made.

With increasing globalization, intra-firm trade grows, as firms move components and parts to the location of final assembly and finished products to the final market. Intra-firm trade (IFT) refers to products which stay within a multinational enterprise. IFT is the replacement of market transactions by internal transactions within firms operating internationally. Market imperfections and high transaction costs provide an incentive for firms to internalize international transactions of goods which embody firm-specific knowledge and expertise. Over one third of US trade is intra-firm trade. Between 1983 and 1992 on average 43 per cent of merchandise trade between the US and Europe was IFT, with multinationals from both countries contributing approximately equally. IFT made up 71 per cent of all US–Japanese trade on average, and over 90 per cent of this was conducted by Japanese multinationals.[27]

Despite the premise of world trade negotiations that global free trade is the goal of international commerce, the liberal view is at odds with the way countries and companies do business. A 1993 study by McKinsey claimed that only 13 per cent of Japan's economy was competitive. If all protectionist measures were removed and consumers free to choose products from anywhere in the world, Japanese unemployment would soar.[28] In a paper on *Paradigm Crisis in International Trade Theory* (1991) Winifried Ruigrok presented a rough outline of the real division of global trade:

- Approximately 25 per cent takes place inside global companies. Intra-company trade is not subject to arm's length market transactions.
- Another 25 per cent is bilateral trade organized by preferential trade agreements such as found in the European Community and North American Free Trade Agreement.
- Yet another 25 per cent is barter trade where goods and services are exchanged against other goods and services rather than

money. A country rich in resources but poor in manufacturing will sell a fixed amount of wheat or zinc, for example, for major machinery and equipment.

- Finally, at most only 25 per cent can be considered free trade governed by GATT rules. Even here, there are many exceptions. Services, textiles, and agriculture are not subject to GATT, but are regulated by special side agreements or not at all.[29]

Economic orthodoxy continues to insist that liberalization of markets is the best way to increase prosperity. There was a sharp rise in living standards in the West following trade liberalization after 1945. However, in recent decades there has been a slowing of growth in the advanced industrial countries, combined with a virtual exclusion from further economic development in much of the rest of the world. The gap between the rich and poor countries is widening, not narrowing. International trade is booming, but for some the link between trade and prosperity is hard to distinguish. Can global trade be *fair* as well as *free*?

Tariffs and the WTO
Ten years ago two thirds of the world's people lived in economies protected by barriers of culture, politics, geography and import tariffs. Today 122 countries have joined the World Trade Organization, with twenty-eight more countries applying to join. Trade can be a route to prosperity as long as it operates fairly, and distributes its benefits widely. However, untrammelled free trade may simply make the rich richer, by enabling them to strike unreasonable bargains with weaker trading partners. Renato Ruggiero, director-general of the WTO has said, 'Globalization will not go away ... Policymakers could not stop the process even if they wanted to ... The only real question is whether or not we accompany its advance with domestic policies which will help us to adapt to the reality of change without unbearable social cost. Internationally, the choice is whether this inevitable process will take place within a system based on agreed rules or simply on power.'[30]

The goal of the World Trade Organization is 'open, fair, and undistorted competition'. In January 1995 the WTO was established as successor to GATT (the General Agreement on Trade and Tariffs), but it is not a world government of trade; it is a consensus-based organization in which all members must agree mutually beneficial rules for international trade which are intended to create maximum openness, fairness and transparency. Every member of the WTO is supposed to open its markets to every other member of the WTO on equal terms. A foreign-owned company operating in a member state has to be treated in the same way as a domestic company. WTO members commit themselves to further opening of markets and no 'backsliding'. When countries negotiate a reduction in trade tariffs, they are encouraged to commit themselves to a tariff binding, and to agree not unilaterally to increase the tariff in the future without providing compensation to their main trading partners. A high proportion of tariff bindings increases the stability of the world's trading environment. The Uruguay Round of talks increased bound product lines to 99 per cent for developed countries, 98 per cent for transition countries, and 73 per cent for developing countries.

Dumping, subsidies and non-tariff barriers (such as local content requirements) are practices which can affect the fairness of trade competition. Countries may introduce laws to protect health and safety and the environment, so long as such laws are not intended as barriers to trade. The WTO recognizes the need to help poorer countries and allows discrimination in their favour through the generalized system of preferences. Developing countries are given longer periods to implement WTO measures, and are allowed to maintain higher tariffs on certain goods.[31]

The most prominent country queuing to join the WTO is China, the fourth largest industrial economy in the world at purchasing power parity estimates. WTO conditions for joining include:

- End of subsidies to state-owned enterprises.
- Market access for agricultural products.
- Market access for financial services.
- Phasing out of non-tariff barriers for cars and other industries.
- End of restrictions on trading activities of Chinese and foreign-owned companies.

WTO membership would speed up the process of economic reform in China. By dismantling the state-controlled foreign-trading system and allowing all firms established in the country to import and export goods freely within three years, China is accepting one of the basic principles of the WTO. China has started to provide more information on its quotas and licensing arrangements, state pricing system, export duties and customs inspection standards. A

50 per cent reduction in tariffs on 5,000 products was announced in October 1996. The WTO wants a transition to its conditions within five years; China is looking for fifteen years.

The World Bank estimates that China's imports would jump by 55 per cent and exports by 40 per cent as a result of WTO membership. This estimate is based on a reduction in China's average import tariff to 16 per cent, which China agreed to implement in 1994. The reduction in tariffs could be greater: the European Union wants China to reduce average tariffs to 7 per cent from the current 23 per cent. Tariffs on manufactured goods in international trade have fallen dramatically as a result of successive rounds of GATT negotiations – from 40 per cent in 1950 to under 5 per cent in 1996. However, non-tariff measures have become more prevalent as countries seek other ways to protect their domestic industries.[32]

Foreign Direct Investment

The growth of trade as a measure of globalization is becoming replaced in significance by the rapid expansion of international foreign direct investment (FDI). Such figures need to be interpreted with a degree of caution. In 1995 OECD foreign direct investment inflows exceeded $200 billion and outflows exceeded $250 billion. Inflows grew by 50 per cent and outflows by 40 per cent, as a result of unprecedented investments made by American, British and German firms.

These figures confirm the role of foreign direct investment as one of the primary vehicles for further international economic integration. Although firms have been investing abroad for well over a hundred years, never before have so many firms invested in so many countries. A growing number of firms now view overseas expansion through direct investment as a necessity rather than as an expensive luxury reserved for only the largest firms. The aim is often to achieve more effective access in markets where the investor is presently under-represented. Growing awareness of the need to invest abroad is matched by a keen competition among the host countries to attract firms. While there remains ample scope for further liberalization in many countries, the changes which have arisen so far represent a watershed in attitudes towards

foreign investment within the domestic economy. Most countries now permit inward investment, and many actively court
foreign firms.[33]

Foreign investments by the United States doubled in 1995 to reach
$97 billion, as shown in Table 2.4 (an amount as great as the total
world foreign investment in 1986). $50 billion of this investment
went to Europe, and $3.2 billion to Japan (despite Japan reporting
only $37 million inward investment in that year). Inward invest-
ment into the United States reached $75 billion in 1995, $65 billion
coming from Europe. Outflows from Japan peaked in 1990 with $48
billion, and in 1995 were $22 billion, largely as a result of more
restrained activity by the Japanese banks and insurance companies,
and a drop in the purchase of foreign real estate. In manufacturing
half of Japanese affiliates in Europe were unprofitable in 1994. The
greatest increase in Japanese overseas investment has occurred in
China and other ASEAN economies.[34]

Table 2.4: Direct Investment Flows in OECD Countries ($ Million)

	INFLOWS			OUTFLOWS		
	1993	1994	1995	1993	1994	1995
France	12142	10995	12156	12167	10895	9582
Germany	240	3003	9012	19557	14587	34890
Japan	86	888	37	13714	17938	22262
Netherlands	6507	4371	5889	10993	11502	7929
UK	14536	11066	29910	25697	29721	37839
US	41107	49448	74701	72601	49370	96897
Total all OECD countries	126661	138517	189788	189532	187550	242890

Source: Derived from OECD, 'Recent Trends in Foreign Direct Investment', in
Financial Market Trends 64, June (1996), p.38, Table 1

Mergers and Acquisitions

A large part of foreign direct investment takes the form of mergers and acquisitions. According to KMPG, cross-border mergers and joint ventures increased by 17 per cent in 1995 to reach $229 billion. German firms were particularly active, mostly in the US and UK and, to a lesser extent, in China. Japanese firms also increased their foreign takeovers by 50 per cent. In many sectors industries are in a state of flux: with enhanced competition, technological change and deregulation, firms look to strengthen their position by overseas mergers or foreign acquisitions. This strategy allows for cost reduction and geographical diversification. In recent years major mergers and acquisitions have occurred in pharmaceuticals, telecommunications, investment banking, electric, gas and water utilities, and in the food sector.[35] Such mergers and acquisitions often grew at the expense of investment in new business areas: often they were a form of paper entrepreneurialism, involving portfolio purchases of existing assets. Portfolio investments, such as bonds and mutual funds, rose 28 per cent in the OECD between 1981/2 and 1991/2,[36] while total FDI declined from 21 to 18 per cent of total long-term transfers from the thirteen major OECD countries.

In pharmaceuticals, companies can no longer automatically pass on higher prices to the consumer: governments are now concerned at the spiralling cost of health care, and traditional markets have become saturated in the absence of major drug launches. A result has been a series of large-scale mergers and acquisitions in order to achieve greater economies of scale in production or research and development or to expand sales. In telecommunications a combination of deregulation, the demand for cheaper and more efficient phone services, and technological change has put pressure on telecommunications companies to become more efficient. Telecoms acquisitions in Europe are anticipated in the run-up to liberalization in 1998, and further telecoms privatization has increased the scope for FDI.

Mergers and acquisitions tend to be the dominant form of foreign investment within the OECD: 91 per cent of foreign investment outlays by foreign MNCs in the United States in 1994 involved the acquisition of existing firms. However, FDI figures do represent the aggregate sum of thousands of foreign acquisitions, joint ventures and green-field investments.[37]

Explaining the behaviour of multinational companies the OECD suggests:

To some extent, globalization is simply the sum of its parts: more firms in more sectors in more countries are investing abroad, and those which are already multinational are doing more of the same. The theme which unites these myriad investments is market access. Much as firms agglomerate within domestic markets in order to be closer to customers or suppliers, so too are their foreign investments driven in part by the dictates of economic geography. Firms invest abroad chiefly to be represented in each of their major markets, whether at a national or a regional level. In many cases, the investor is content to remain within his own geographical region. Faced with slow growth or intensified competition in the increasingly deregulated home market, firms are looking abroad as a strategy of geographical diversification, the alternative of industrial diversification having fallen into disrepute.[38]

Small firms are also making international investments as they are faced by strong currencies and rising foreign production by their industrial customers. FDI is arising in more non-industrial sectors, particularly service sectors, such as banking. Foreign markets are becoming an attractive alternative to expansion at home, often through the acquisition of local companies. Privatization has encouraged major inward investment, as former state utilities are quickly acquired by international companies. And for the first time, companies which have been privatized are looking abroad for investment opportunities, particularly in other countries where privatization is taking place.

The Growth of FDI

More countries are becoming engaged in international investment. In 1980, eight countries (the US, UK, Germany, Netherlands, France, Canada, Switzerland and Japan) accounted for 92 per cent of the total outward stock of FDI. By 1994 these countries accounted for 80 per cent of the total, and other countries, including Belgium, Sweden, Italy and Australia, had become prominent outward investors. The number of places to invest has become limitless, together with their capacity to absorb investment. Singapore has received $20,000 per capita in inward direct investment. Asian and South American countries in particular have lifted restrictions on foreign investment, this encouraging development strategies which rely heavily on the participation of foreign MNCs, with policies of privatization, deregulation, demonopolization and liberalization.[39]

Japan and Germany have both enhanced their foreign investment strategy recently. Japan increased its Asian share of investment to reflect the growth prospects and sales potential of Asia as a whole. German investment overseas has increased markedly, partly due to high production costs at home, though only half this investment is by manufacturing companies. The primary aim of German overseas manufacturing investment is to achieve market access. 'Foreign production by German firms, to the extent that it replaces exports from Germany, substitutes for future, rather than existing output of factories located in Germany.'[40] Nor are foreign firms shunning Germany because of the high labour costs. Between 1984 and 1993 foreign firms reported investing $72 billion in Germany, compared with foreign inflows of $22 billion recorded by the Bundesbank.[41]

International expansion of firms has increased the relative importance of foreign ownership in OECD countries. The annual sales of goods and services by foreign affiliates are one and half times the value of world exports, and a rising share of private sector GNP is accounted for by the combined value added of foreign-based firms and foreign output of home-based firms: over 50 per cent for Belgium, Canada, the Netherlands, Switzerland and the UK; more than 30 per cent for Australia, France, Germany and Italy; and over 20 per cent for Japan and the United States.[42] Wide differences remain in the share of output and employment of foreign-controlled firms in the different OECD countries, as Figures 2.1 and 2.2 reveal, and in most countries the share of foreign subsidiaries remains below 20 per cent. Why then has foreign ownership come to be seen as a much more important factor than it evidently is? The answer lies in the sectoral incidence of foreign subsidiaries. Foreign ownership is most evident in high-technology industries such as computers, chemicals, pharmaceuticals, automobiles and electronics – industries which attract a great deal of public attention. Foreign enterprises account for a large share of production in most of these industries in the major OECD countries, with the important exceptions of Japan and the United States (Table 2.5). In Japan it has been difficult for foreign capital to become established in productive investments. The United States attracts substantial amounts of overseas investment but this still

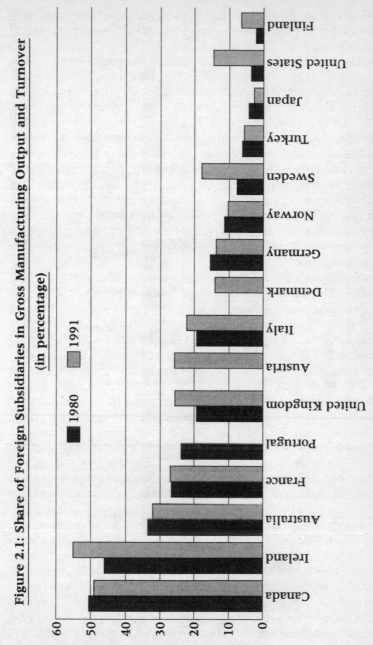

Figure 2.1: Share of Foreign Subsidiaries in Gross Manufacturing Output and Turnover (in percentage)

Legend: ■ 1980 ▨ 1991

Countries (left to right): Canada, Ireland, Australia, France, Portugal, United Kingdom, Austria, Italy, Denmark, Germany, Norway, Sweden, Turkey, Japan, United States, Finland

Note: Figures for 1980 and 1991, or nearest year

Source: OECD, Industrial Activity of Foreign Affiliates data bank

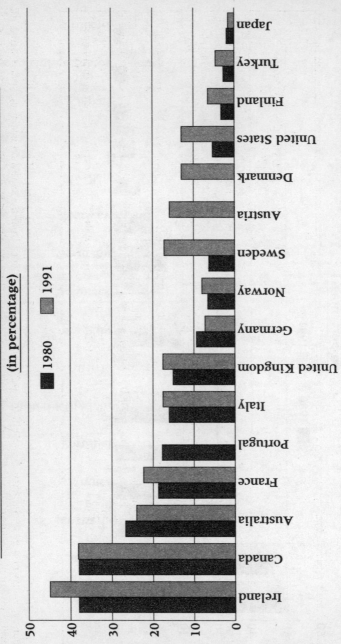

Figure 2.2: Share of Foreign Subsidiaries in Manufacturing Employment (in percentage)

■ 1980 ▨ 1991

Note: Figures for 1980 and 1991, or nearest year

Source: OECD, Industrial Activity of Foreign Affiliates data bank

Table 2.5: Industrial Sectors with the Highest Share of Production by Foreign Enterprises*

Percentages

Canada 1987	France 1990	Germany 1990	Italy 1989	UK 1990	US 1989	Japan 1989
Motor vehicles 85	Computers 74	Computers 82	Computers 78	Computers 78	Other manufacturing 30	Chemicals 11
Chemicals 76	Chemicals 45	Chemicals 43	Electronics 55	Motor vehicles 60	Non-metallic products 29	Machinery/ equipment 2
Non-metallic products 55	Electronics 31	Food/beverages 23	Chemicals 30	Chemicals 36	Chemicals 27	Basic metals 1
Machinery/ equipment 44	Non-metallic products 26	Motor vehicles 24	Food/beverage 15	Electronics 26	Basic metals 22	Other manufacturing 0.6
Other manufacturing 35	Machinery 28	Basic metals 21	Machines 12	Basic metals 21	Electronics 19	Paper/printing 0.5

* Production from foreign-owned enterprises and enterprises with foreign participation as a share of production in industry in each country. Values may be overestimated if small firms (<20 employees) are excluded from the census on which figures are based, as small firms are predominantly domestic. Production refers to turnover, output or sales, depending on the source. For Japan, only 2-digit ISIC data available.

Source: OECD, DSTI, Industry Division

represents only a small share of the largest national economy in the world.

It is likely that the dramatic growth of foreign investment flows will continue for the foreseeable future; however, even enthusiastic proponents of further internationalization, such as the OECD, harbour some doubts:

> There remains the possibility of a backlash against this process. Host countries might perceive that the economic results from inward investment have not lived up to their expectations. The structural adjustment engendered by increasing global economic integration may cause resentment among those groups in particular countries that are adversely affected. In spite of all the hyperbole about the unstoppable juggernaut of globalization, countries retain the power to prevent inward investment – albeit at an increasing cost. Fewer and fewer countries make use of a screening mechanism for inward investment, but most retain restrictions or even prohibitions in certain sectors. Furthermore, even when governments have no overall restrictions, a number of impediments to inward investment might arise such as through public control of local enterprises or the private practices of local firms themselves.[43]

The developing countries are becoming players in foreign investment themselves. Foreign direct investment from non-OECD countries amounted to $40 billion in 1994. The largest MNCs in the developing countries originate principally in Brazil, South Korea, Hong Kong and Taipei. These latter are, in a sense, only the tip of the iceberg. Many of the MNC conglomerates in South-East Asia are controlled by Chinese owners even when they come from countries such as Malaysia, Thailand and Indonesia that are not themselves 'Chinese' countries. These firms were responsible for 80 per cent of the total pledged foreign investment in China in 1994. However, dozens of countries are not receiving any significant foreign direct investment, and there is a strong and continued concentration of FDI in a handful of countries. 'As of 1991, a good 81 per cent of world stock of FDI was located in the high-wage – and relatively high-tax – countries: principally the US, followed by the UK, Germany, and Canada. Moreover, this figure represents an increase of 12 points since 1967. Indeed the stock of FDI in the UK and the US exceeds the stock in Asia and the entire South' (Table 2.6).[44]

Political instability, poor market prospects and severe debt-servicing problems in some parts of Latin America, almost all of Africa and parts of the Middle East are still excluding them from membership of the globalization club. In contrast, South-East and East Asia have experienced an inward investment boom, with a doubling of investments between 1980 and 1991 (although this has to be seen less in comparison with their past than with the present situation in the US and Europe). In Latin America extensive privatization of major public industries has kick-started inward investment, with, for example, 80 per cent of the inflows into Argentina resulting from the acquisition of shares in privatized firms.[45]

Table 2.6: The Most Important Host Countries for FDI
Based on cumulative flows, 1985–94 (US$ million)

United States	402445
United Kingdom	172277
China	**92761**
France	85474
Spain	72570
Belgium-Luxembourg	63041
Canada	51409
Australia	49298
Netherlands	45292
Singapore	**44057**
Italy	32521
Mexico	31292
Malaysia	**25213**
Sweden	24349
Argentina	**19780**
Germany	18779
Hong Kong	**14868**
Switzerland	14714
Thailand	**14568**
Brazil	**13499**

N.B. Definitions of FDI differ greatly across countries.

Source: OECD (1996e), p. 54

The Transfer of Technology

What is crucial to any country is not the total quantity of foreign investment, but its *quality*. The total value does not indicate the actual benefit to the country concerned. Government policies play a vital role in ensuring that the domestic economy benefits from overseas investments by developing localization of sourcing and of staffing. The transfer of technology is the crucial benefit which inward investment can bring (or that outward investment can secure).

Technological advantages are a major component of the international strategies of firms, and there are differences between the distribution of R&D capabilities and the commercial application of technology. According to the OECD, among the factors which determine the location of R&D are:

Centralization: The economies of scale in R&D, and its strategic importance, favour centralization of R&D as a headquarters function.

Diversification: The development of distinct Asian, European and North American regions encouraged globalized firms to establish R&D in each, to gain access to complementary high-quality research resources, R&D staff and institutions, to develop new products and processes and adapt products and technology to local conditions in large markets, and spread risks.

Entry strategies: International acquisitions of high-technology firms are often aimed at capturing R&D resources (for example the acquisition of biotechnology companies in the United States).

Country-specific factors: Firms from smaller countries (such as the Netherlands, Sweden and Switzerland) perform more of their R&D in foreign countries because of limited domestic resources, and the need to draw on the developments in the major R&D performing countries. In contrast, Japan and Korea perform less of their R&D away from home. (Though if R&D is broadened to include market research, the Japanese have invested considerably in this, particularly in the United States.)[46]

The diffusion and application of new technology, particularly process technologies, are rapid in the subsidiaries of international firms, resulting in higher labour productivity and greater efficiency in foreign firms than domestic firms. However, R&D intensities

(R&D as a share of production or turnover) are generally lower in foreign subsidiaries than in domestic firms. Where the domestic R&D intensity is low, foreign subsidiaries may perform comparatively more R&D. In the United States the inward investment boom resulted in the concentration of R&D by foreign firms in a few high-technology sectors: pharmaceuticals, industrial chemicals, and audio, video and communications equipment. This is often due to the acquisition of R&D-intensive US firms by European companies.

Firms are often reluctant to transfer R&D outwards; however, US firms have significant R&D activities in Germany and Japan, suggesting a Triad approach to R&D operations, building on strong technology bases. Though Japanese firms have invested in R&D in electronics in the United States and other countries, this represented only 2.5 per cent of group R&D expenditures in 1992–3.[47] On average the share of business R&D financed directly from foreign sources (excluding domestic financing) is still below 3 per cent of total R&D spending.[48]

Non-Manufacturing Investment

In many countries the flows of FDI have been into the real estate, tourism and leisure sectors. In Australia, for instance, relatively little FDI goes into the manufacturing sector. Most comes from Japan and most goes into speculative ventures in real estate. When one calculates the extent to which Japan's FDI is manufacturing-driven, it is interesting to note that only one third of its 1995 FDI went to the manufacturing sector,[49] and this was principally within the Triad: in off-shore lower-wage manufacturing within the Japanese-dominated East Asian bloc, in the European bloc, securing entry principally through the UK, and in the US, ensuring access to the market there.

What is Driving Globalization?

Globalization is driven by the strategic responses of firms as they exploit market opportunities and adapt to changes in their technological and institutional environment, and attempt to steer these changes to their advantage. The OECD groups the factors shaping globalization into four general categories, which are inter-linked:

Firm Behaviour

→ Strategic, pre-emptive and imitative behaviour
→ Exploitation of competitive advantages: use of superior technology, organization, production or marketing
→ Consolidation of competitive advantages: gain access to highly skilled people, advanced technological and commercial infrastructure, lower labour costs, and raw materials
→ Organizational changes; adoption of lean production methods and more horizontal internal and external organizational structures, including greater local and international outsourcing.

Technology Related Factors

→ Declining computing, communication, co-ordination, and transport costs
→ Increasing importance of R&D, coupled with rising R&D costs
→ Shortening product lives
→ Shortening of imitation time lags
→ Rapid growth of knowledge-intensive industries
→ Increasing customization of both intermediate and finished goods
→ Increasing importance of customer-oriented services.

Macro Economic Factors

→ Availability of key production factors
→ Productivity differentials
→ Fluctuations in exchange rates
→ Differences in the business cycle
→ Catching up by lagging economies.

Government Policies

→ Liberalization of international trade and capital movements
→ Promotion of regional integration
→ Inward investment incentives
→ R&D, technology, small firms and related industry policies
→ Intellectual property rights and effective patent life
→ Competition policies.[50]

THE STAGES OF GLOBALIZATION

More companies are becoming increasingly international in their operations and interests, though few companies have reached the stage of being truly global concerns. The progress towards internationalization can be typified in a number of ways: the OECD suggests a series of stages that could resemble the life-cycle of growing companies as they stretch their wings from the domestic to the international market:

Purely domestic: Companies with domestic operations only, but with supply to foreign firms in the home market increasingly common – for example small-scale parts manufacturing firms.

Export oriented: Companies becoming interested in exports through foreign intermediaries or marketing affiliates, some international licensing, few foreign employees – for example, most small- and medium-sized firms.

Overseas production: Companies engaged in final assembly in foreign markets. Design, development, key component manufacture are retained in the home country. Domestic and foreign production are increasingly integrated into international supply networks and goods and services sourcing – for example, firms in the clothing industry.

Integrated overseas production: Companies that integrate foreign production, including key components. Design and development, finance and other corporate functions begin to be distributed among affiliates. Intermediate inputs are sourced globally, with significant intra-firm trade, and substantial foreign employment – for example, large firms in the motor vehicle industry.

Global companies: Companies with integrated international operations in all major regions, including management, financial control, product and process R & D, production and marketing. Extensive inter-firm trade in intermediates and final products, high sales by affiliates in foreign markets, and high flows of international investment – for example, firms in the computer industry.[51]

Strategic Approaches to Globalization

Initial reasons for going overseas evolve over time as managers develop different objectives for their international activities. Bartlett and Ghoshal identify four different strategic approaches as management thinking changes:

International
MNC managers see overseas operations as distant outposts, the main role of which is to support the domestic company with sales, raw materials or component supplies. This conforms to the product life-cycle theory that products are developed for the domestic market, and only subsequently sold overseas.

Multinational Infrastructure
Plants are often built for local marketing advantage or to improve political relations rather than to maximize production efficiency. Similarly a proliferation of products designed to meet local needs also contributes to a general loss of efficiency in design, production, logistics, distribution and other functional tasks.

Global
In an operating environment of improving transportation and communication facilities and falling trade barriers, some companies adopt a different approach to international operations. These companies, many of them Japanese in origin, think in terms of creating products for a world market and manufacturing them on a global scale in a few highly efficient plants. This classic global strategic thinking views the world as its unit of analysis. The underlying assumption is that national tastes and preferences are more similar than different, or that they can be made similar by providing customers with standardized products with adequate cost and quality advantages over those national varieties that they have been used to. Theodore Levitt suggests that, in the future, successful companies will be those that make and sell the same things, in the same way, in one global market.[52] For this approach to business to succeed requires more central co-ordination and control than earlier stages of development. It is associated with an organization structure in which various product or business managers have

worldwide responsibility. R&D, strategy and manufacturing are managed from headquarters.

Transnational

Throughout the 1970s and 1980s many of these global companies seemed invincible. In a globalizing environment they had overwhelming victories, not only against local companies, but other multinational competitors. Their very success, however, created and strengthened a set of countervailing forces of localization. Many host governments viewed these global companies as a more powerful and threatening version of the earlier companies which had exhibited an unsophisticated, unresponsive stance in their international strategies. In an era when many countries faced crushing interest burdens on their foreign debt and mounting trade deficits, the global company's focus on home-country exports and centralized control caused concern. In response, many governments increased both the restrictions and the demands they placed on global companies, requiring them to invest, transfer technology, meet local content requirements, and so forth. Customers also contributed to this strengthening of the localized forces by rejecting homogenized global products and reasserting their national preferences – albeit without relaxing their expectations of the high quality levels and low costs that global products had offered. Finally, increasing volatility in the international economic and political environment, especially the rapid changes in currency exchange rates, also undermined the efficiency of such a centralized global approach. Local responsiveness and global efficiency are simultaneous if sometimes conflicting demands. Dispersed resources can be integrated into an interdependent network of worldwide oper ations in which transnational management will become more responsive to local needs, while also retaining global efficiency, as Bartlett and Ghoshal suggest [53]

Multinationals inevitably take political risks in operating across the sovereignty of multiple host countries. Working as they do across so many different national rules of so many complex competitive games, they have to be political. Being political goes hand in hand with flexibility, particularly when they are threatened by fluctuating currencies. Consequently, MNCs need organizational structures and management systems for product, functional and geographic diversity.[54]

Sectoral Strategies for Globalization

There are a wide range of possible strategies for international expansion, though there are common features among distinct sectoral groups of industries. The OECD analysed the impact of globalization for eight industries: pharmaceuticals, computers, semiconductors, motor vehicles, consumer electronics, non-ferrous metals, steel and clothing (Table 2.7).[55] These eight industries can be distributed into four groups of industries: pharmaceuticals, computers and semi-conductors are science-based since their commitment to R&D activities is far above the manufacturing average. Motor vehicles and consumer electronics are part of the scale-intensive group, characterized by increasing returns to scale. Non-ferrous metals and steel are included in the resource-intensive group, as raw materials processing industries. Clothing is labour-intensive, where the share of labour costs in total costs is well above the average for manufacturing.

Globalization in Science-based Industries

In science-based industries (pharmaceuticals, computers and, to a lesser extent, semiconductors) the predominant mode of expansion is based on the internationalization of *firm-specific advantages*. Foreign investment is high and foreign affiliates have a large share of sales in host markets. International trade in these industries is largely intra-firm, because of the specialized characteristics of inputs into final products. International collaboration agreements focus on technology, because of the prime importance of product innovation. Pharmaceuticals is somewhat more market-oriented in international collaboration and is more intensive in international investment.

Globalization in Scale-intensive Industries

Motor vehicles and consumer electronics are scale-intensive industries based on the assembly of components into complex final consumer products. The pattern of expansion has been more trade-oriented, with high levels of trade in components, and high and increasing intra-regional trade in components and/or finished products as lean production methods are more widely applied. Foreign direct investment has been less important in the past, except for US producers, but has increased rapidly, and intra-firm

Table 2.7: Sectoral Globalization

Industry aggregation	Industries in the survey	Major competitive challenge	Major reshaping force	Features of globalization	Common policy issues	SMEs presence
Science-based	Pharmaceuticals Computers Semiconductors	Capability to bring results of R&D and product development to the market	Steep rise in the R&D threshold	Limited to the Triad area, with little trade	Technology base. IPRs	Few and very technology-focused
Scale-intensive	Motor vehicles Consumer electronics	Capability to coordinate complex production processes	Diffusion of the 'lean' production system	Mainly in the Triad area, with high and increasing trade regionalization	Local content, standards	Numerous as subcontractors
Resource-intensive	Non-ferrous metal Steel	Capability to reduce costs, optimize production-location and market-location	Substitution of materials by users	Worldwide, with high trade regionalization	Competition Environment	Increasing in upstream-end operations and recycling
Labour-intensive	Clothing	Capability to provide quality and/or price competitive products	Decrease in the importance of labour costs	Worldwide, with increasing trade regionalization	Tariffs and quotas	Dominant

Source: OECD, DSTI, Industry Division

trade is relatively important for vertically integrated producers. Both industries are highly concentrated, so there have been few mergers and acquisitions, compared with pharmaceuticals, and international agreements are focused on production.

Globalization in Resource-intensive Industries

The third set of industries comprises steel and non-ferrous metals. They are resource-intensive and have high intensity in intermediate inputs. Their intra-firm trade is low, and although, for example, energy costs determine the location of aluminium-smelting operations, firms in these particular industries are increasingly oriented downstream towards final markets and away from their intermediate inputs.

Globalization in Labour-intensive Industries

The labour-intensive clothing industry is characterized by high levels of trade in finished clothing, and high levels of international sourcing of textiles as inputs, although trade in clothing parts is not significant. It has little international investment, little intra-firm trade and few international collaboration agreements outside sourcing arrangements.

Generic Global Strategies

Dunning suggests three conditions for the existence of global multi-national enterprise:

- The location-specific advantages of overseas markets must provide the requisite motivation for the company to invest there.
- The company must have strategic competencies to counteract the disadvantages of the relative unfamiliarity with foreign markets.
- The company must also have some organizational capabilities so as to get better returns from leveraging its strategic strengths internally rather than through external mechanisms such as contracts and licences.[56]

Whatever the economic, technological and competitive factors pushing companies towards further internationalization of their activities, whether they succeed will depend on the effectiveness of their international business strategies. For Alfred Chandler in

Scale and Scope (1990), the evolution of the global corporation is the final stage in the transformation of industries in search of economies of scale, economies of scope and national differences in the availability and cost of productive resources.

Economies of Scale
In many industries, including fine chemicals, automobiles and oil-refining, production-scale-economy volumes exceeded the sales levels individual companies could achieve in all but the largest countries, forcing them to become international or perish. The minimum efficient level for capital-intensive plants is 80 to 90 per cent of capacity, in contrast to labour-intensive industries. The costs and profits of capital-intensive industries are determined by plant utilization and throughput, rather than by the simple amount produced.

Economies of Scope
Less capital-intensive industries are less affected by scale economies. But opportunities exist for scope economies – worldwide communication and transportation networks. Trading companies handling the products of many companies achieve greater volume and lower unit cost. Later, as producers broaden their range of products, marketing and sales networks are established, such as consumer electronics service networks or auto dealerships.

Factor Costs
With changes in technology and markets came requirements for access to new resources at lower cost. European and US oil companies were attracted by the Middle East's 'sweet crude' – low-cost easily refined oil. Less capital-intensive industries such as textiles, clothing, shoes, etc., turned to international markets as a source of cheap labour.

Cheap Labour
It is misleading to assume that the search for cheaper labour is in itself the central driving force of the increasing internationalization of many industries. In most industries there are more important factors than labour costs, including access to markets, technology and other resources. Increasingly industry requires more highly skilled labour, and the possession of relevant skills is more immediately important than the price of labour. Of course, there are labour-intensive industries in which reducing the cost of the labour input

to the barest minimum is a primary motivation. However, the international search for cheap labour is a short-term strategy, as the conditions which create cheap labour are gradually being eliminated.

> The increased costs of transportation and logistics management were more than made up for by much lower production costs. However, many companies found that once educated, the cheap labour rapidly becomes expensive. Indeed, the typical life cycle of a country as a source of cheap labour for an industry is now only about five years. This forced companies to chase cheap labour from Southern Europe, to Central America, to the Far East, and now to Eastern Europe.[57]

No country will ever build a competitive advantage based on cheap wages, even if, for a short time, some companies that operate in it might do so.

Innovation

The most important competitive force in the new world economy is the capacity for innovation, a thesis powerfully illustrated by Michael Porter in *The Competitive Advantage of Nations* (1990). Porter correlates the advance of knowledge, achievement in innovation and national competitive advantage. In his search for a new paradigm of national competitive advantage he starts from the premise that competition is dynamic and evolving, whereas traditional thinking had a static view on cost efficiency due to factor or scale advantages. But static efficiency is always being overtaken by the rate of progress in the change in products, marketing, new production processes and new markets.

A new paradigm sees improvement and innovation in methods and technology as central. The question then becomes: why do industries in some countries invest in innovation more vigorously and successfully than others? Firms do not simply maximize within fixed constraints but 'gain competitive advantage from changing the constraints'. The crucial issue for firms, and nations, is how they 'improve the quality of the factors, raise the productivity with which they are utilized, and create new ones'.[58] Elsewhere Michael Porter maintains that:

> As the basis of competition has shifted more and more to the creation and assimilation of knowledge, the role of the nation

has grown. Competitive advantage is created and sustained through a highly localised process . . . Ultimately nations succeed in particular industries because their home environment is the most forward looking, dynamic and challenging. Companies achieve competitive advantage through acts of innovation . . . Innovation can be manifested in a new product design, a new production process, a new marketing approach, or a new way of conducting training. Much innovation is mundane and incremental, depending more on accumulation of small insights and advances than on a single major technological breakthrough . . . It always involves investments in skill and knowledge, as well as in physical assets and brand reputations.[59]

The capacity to successfully innovate on a worldwide basis becomes the key defining competency of leading international companies.[60]

The Transition to Transnationality

In the emerging international environment more and more businesses are driven by simultaneous demands for global efficiency, national responsiveness and worldwide innovation.

Multinational firms in a transnational industry find it increasingly difficult to defend a competitive position based on only one dominant capability. Worldscale economies of standardized products are not adequate or appropriate in most industries. Companies build global efficiency through a worldwide infrastructure or through distributed, but specialized, assets and capabilities that exploit comparative advantages, scale economies and scope economies simultaneously. Flexibility in rearranging product designs, sourcing patterns and pricing policies in order to remain responsive to continually changing national environments becomes essential to survival. Exploiting centrally developed products and technologies is no longer enough. MNCs must now be able to learn from the many environments to which they are exposed and to translate the benefits of such learning through their global operations into transnational innovations. What results is a three-dimensional competitive game of remarkable complexity and scope.

Companies building and defending profit sanctuaries that are impenetrable to competitors, leveraging existing strengths to build new advantages through cross-subsidizing weaker products and market positions, making high risk pre-emptive investments that raise the stakes and force out rivals with weak stomachs or purse strings, and forming alliances to isolate and outflank competitors. These and other similar manoeuvres must now be combined with world scale economies to develop and maintain global competitive efficiency.[61]

Globalization and Firm Structures

As companies elaborate more sophisticated business strategies to capture the advantage in international competition, their corporate structures change over time to meet the new demands. Stopford and Wells and Malnight adopt a life-cycle or evolutionary approach to MNC forms, in which more complex structures emerge as the significance of international activities develops.[62] Mark Hanna highlights the structural differentiation that can occur in MNCs:

Organization Forms with Simple Structures
These are small- and medium-sized enterprises, which are export-oriented but have few staff, simple structures and minimal co-ordination and control mechanisms.

The functional form offers an appropriate structure early in the organization life-cycle. Activities are grouped into functionally specialized areas like marketing, accounting, finance and production; they might also be grouped by knowledge or skills. It is possible to have a worldwide functional form as the company becomes more international if operating in stable market environments. Another possibility is to have autonomous subsidiaries.

More Complex Co-ordination and Control Structures
In ascending order of development these include:

Holding company: One firm owns a number of functionally separate subsidiaries.

Multidivisionals: Each division is a semi-autonomous profit-centre and usually has a functional organization structure. Conglomerates are multidivisions with unrelated product strategies. The HQ is responsible for strategic planning and monitoring, and the division is responsible for day-to-day operations. The HQ allocates cash to each division on its ability to yield further profits. The emphasis is upon decentralization, adaptability, product or geographic perspective.

Hybrid: The firm has both functional and multidivisional components. The functions important to the product or market are put with the division. The functions important to economies of scale are centralized in the HQ.

Matrix: An organizational structure where there are two reporting relationships – one vertical and one horizontal. It can be a permanent matrix or a shifting matrix as projects, markets or people change.[63]

Mother–daughter structures: These are a hybrid between a domestic functional form and an international holding company. Many of these structures have so many companies associated with them that they resemble internal markets. These forms prevailed in Europe until the 1960s, but had no internal controls like a multidivisional; the subsidiaries simply reported to the chief executive. Companies tended to switch to a multidivisional form – mostly worldwide product forms.

Keiretsu: Thousands of companies in Japan are organized like this, but only around fifty are global. The firm forms part of a sourcing, marketing, financing and information grid. These organizations are frequently only the trading arm of an industrial group – for example, Mitsubishi, C. Itoh and Sumitomo. In some cases Japanese industrial groups do not consist of diversified companies, but of vertically related suppliers and buyers. Toyota is an example of such an organization, but it is a lot smaller than GM.

Networks and hierarchies: A network form seems to be better able to handle the uncertainty of the market and to profit from the co-ordination of activities among business units and countries. While there is agreement that co-ordination of a network is valuable,[64] there are different views regarding the overall trends. Bartlett and Ghoshal suggest that multinational networks are characterized by assigning different functions to country subsidiaries depending on the resources of the location and their own competence.[65] Prahalad and Doz advocate the notion of a lead country subsidiary, where the subsidiary that has developed a specialized competence in an important market takes on global responsibilities.[66] In fact, many firms, such as Asea Brown Boverie (ABB), IBM and Procter and Gamble, have moved some or many global product responsibilities to diverse country locations. The advantage of this lead country form is that it gives initiative to so-called foreign subsidiaries to build on what they do best for the benefit of the global corporation.

Heterarchy: An extreme argument is that the structural hierarchy of the firm is giving way to what Gunnar Hedlund has called a heterarchy.[67] Unlike the traditional form, the heterarchy consists of multiple centres. Co-ordination and control relies heavily on long-term careers and shared values, rather than on financial yardsticks of performance. The price of this kind of organization is redundancy; the benefit is its encouragement of flexibility and exploration of new markets and ideas. Hedlund distinguished the structural hardware from the psychological software of the heterarchy. The heterarchy is unlike the matrix in that it has more mixed and flexible dimensions and does not culminate in an apex top manager. Conflicts are resolved with arm's-length-bargaining or conflict-resolution techniques based on shared perspectives. The human resource aspects of heterarchies include rotating personnel, developing the capacity for strategic thinking among a broader range of people, and encouraging the willingness to take risks and experiment.[68]

Each of these structures developed fairly naturally out of the corporate and national practices of the countries and regions concerned, with the structures of multinational enterprise in Europe often appearing the most traditional. Hanna concludes:

> It is interesting that there has been a change in the conventional wisdom regarding the backwardness of the European form of organization. In fact, the mother–daughter form appears to be well suited as a platform from which to develop a network organization. Perhaps because the structural form is more fluid, there is a need to develop operating systems by which to support co-ordination and flexibility. It may well be no coincidence that European firms, such as ABB, are often held up as the current standard of what constitutes the future design of multinational firms.[69]

Measurement and Performance

Consideration of *what* the international structure of a company is means little without knowledge of *how* it operates. The neatest organizational structure will not succeed if it does not connect with the strategy of the company, and strategies will not succeed without effective operating and performance-measurement systems. The linkages between structure and performance in the multinational require a proper fit between organizations, strategy and environment. As Farley and Kobrin argue:

> What matters most in the design of the global corporation of today is the architecture of process, of measurement, and of co-ordination. Organizing the multinational firm for performance means the proper design of operating systems more than simply the artwork of an organization chart ... Structure is just one aspect of design. What may well matter are the hidden operating systems of measurement, process, and co-ordination. Being global is above all the co-ordination of dispersed activities, and co-ordination demands the appropriate operating and control systems.[70]

Farley and Kobrin conclude their consideration of the problems of organizing the multinational enterprise with four specific recommendations:

- Organization does matter but it needs to be seen as contingent on strategy.
- It is important to locate, train and keep talented, knowledgeable and competent people.
- It is essential to establish a high-performance, goal-setting programme.
- As firms become global and dispersed while simultaneously becoming more locally differentiated, it becomes important to use corporate culture – vision, values, beliefs, attitudes and norms – to co-ordinate and control employees.[71]

Jack Welch, the chief executive of General Electric, who has many spent years building a corporate vision that has now become part of the folklore of contemporary multinational management, is quoted by Farley and Kobrin: multinationals, he says, must strive to:

- Be customer driven.
- Be number 1 or 2 or get out of the line of business.
- Work on speed and agility.
- Achieve quality.
- Maintain ownership.
- Manage continual change.
- Show respect for others.
- Be boundaryless.[72]

Of course, only those companies that have come to dominate their industries internationally in the way that General Electric has can ever work to a principle such as '*be number 1 or 2 or get out*'.

STRATEGIC ALLIANCES

Most companies striving to succeed in fast-moving markets need to collaborate frequently in order to compete. Hence the importance of building strategic alliances. Strategic alliances are sometimes likened, not without good reason, to 'sleeping with the enemy'. 'The more a company becomes globalized, the more it is likely to lose its own identity within a tangle of companies, alliances and markets.'[73] As Bleeke and Ernst put it,

> In businesses as diverse as pharmaceuticals, jet engines, banking and computers, managers have learned that fighting long, head-to-head battles leaves their companies financially exhausted, intellectually depleted, and vulnerable to the next wave of competition and innovation. In place of predation, many multinational companies are learning that they must collaborate to compete ... Multinationals can create highest value for customers and stakeholders by selectively sharing and trading control, costs, capital, access to markets, information and technology with competitors and suppliers alike. Competition does not vanish ... Instead of competing blindly, companies ... increasingly compete only in those precise areas where they have a durable advantage or where participation is necessary to preserve industry power or capture value ... Managers are beginning to see that many necessary elements of a global business are so costly (like R&D in semiconductors), so generic (like assembly), or so impenetrable

(like some of the Asian markets) that it makes no sense to have a traditional competitive stance. The best approach is to find partners who already have cash, scale, skills or access you seek.[74]

Almost all these alliances are within and between companies based in the Triad economies. Many thousands of strategic alliances now exist, and they are continually being created, particularly in high-technology industries. If once multinational companies apparently attempted to pursue strategies independently, controlling markets by exploiting the vulnerability of competitors and striving to capture key resources, by the late 1980s, according to Bartlett and Ghoshal, they had accepted that they needed to pursue multiple sources of competitive advantage simultaneously:[75] building interdependent and integrated network organizations within the company as well as building collaborative relationships externally with governments, competitors, customers, suppliers and a variety of other institutions. Rising R&D costs, shortening product life-cycles, growing barriers to market entry, the increasing need for global economies and the expanding importance of global competition all stimulate interests in, and the attractiveness of, collaboration. Through collaboration business organizations seek to achieve 'leverage' for their core resources: that is, they seek to add value to their basic resources by coupling them to other resources that they do not possess.

Globally Leveraging Advantage

Managers of MNCs realized that, alone, they might not have all the human, financial or technological resources necessary to respond effectively.

This led many to shift their strategic focus away from an all encompassing obsession with pre-empting competition to a broader view of building competitive advantage through selective and often simultaneous reliance on both collaboration and competition ... Instead of trying to enhance their bargaining power over customers, companies began to build partnerships with them, thereby bolstering the customers' competitive position and, at the same time, leveraging their own competitiveness and innovative capabilities. Instead of challenging, or at least accommodating the interest of govern-ments, many MNCs began actively pursuing co-operative relationships with government agencies and administrators.[76]

Even companies in apparently powerful positions in their industry increasingly make use of strategic alliances, either to strengthen specific elements of business systems, or to create strategic tools with which to make stringent changes to the structure of an indus-try (Figures 2.3a and 2.3b).

Alliances are defined by Yoshino and Rangan as 'co-operation between two or more independent firms involving shared control and continuing contributions by all partners'.[77] They identify the major strategic objectives of alliances as: maximizing value; enhancing learning; protecting core competencies; and main-taining flexibility. Two managerial dimensions must be taken into account by an alliance-seeking firm: co-operation and compe-tition. The task when managing an alliance is to optimize these two dimensions. Yoshino and Rangan offer a typology of strategic alliances based on the possibility of co-operative inter-action and conflict potential, yielding four types of alliance – pro-competitive, non-competitive, pre-competitive and competitive (Figure 2.4).

Global Pro-competitive Alliances
Vertical value-chain relationships form within and between manu-facturers and their suppliers and distributors. These relationships were once managed at arm's length but they are now accorded more attention as their strategic nature is recognized. Firms work closely to develop or improve products or processes, but this requires low levels of organizational interaction. Firms tend not to be rivals and, as in the case of Toyota, rely on a federation of alliances to compete against their market rivals.

Global Non-competitive Alliances
These tend to be intra-industry links between non-competing firms – for example, General Motors and Isuzu jointly developing a small car that both will sell. The level of interaction in this co-operative effort is high, as joint development calls for close contacts in mul-tiple functions (for example, design, engineering, manufacturing,

Figure 2.3a: IBM Uses Alliances to Strengthen Specific Elements of Its Business System

IBM

Partner	Subject	Goal
Ferranti	Installation of IBM PCs in Ferranti computer	Penetrate markets for PS/2 operating system
Toshiba	Development of LCDs	Share development costs / Access Toshiba technology
DEC, Apollo, HP	Joint development of operating system for workstations	Build competitive position against Sun and AT&T
Siemens	Development of 64 MBit DRAM	Share development costs
Microsoft	Joint software development	Improve competitive position in PC business

Figure 2.3b: GEC Uses Alliances as 'Strategic Tools' to Aggressively Change the Industry Structure

GEC

Partner	Subject	Goal
General Electric (USA)	Construction of gas turbine with GE know-how	Break up Rolls-Royce monopoly position
CGE	Merger of power generation and distribution divisions	Build largest power-plant manufacturer in Europe
Alsthom	Power plant installation	Restructure industry
General Electric (USA)	Home appliances	Restructure industry
Philips*	Medical technology	Build strong competitive position against Siemens

*Negotiation terminated

Source: Krubaski and Lautenschlager, 'Forming Successful Strategic Alliances' (1993), p.61

Figure 2.4: Typology of Alliance

		Low	High
Conflict potential	High	Pre-competitive alliances	Competitive alliances
	Low	Pro-competitive alliances	Non-competitive alliances

Extent of organizational interaction

Source: Yoshino and Rangan, *Strategic Alliances* (1995), p. 19

marketing). Since the firms' competitive universes meet only occasionally, neither views the other as a major rival.

Global Competitive Alliances

These are similar to non-competitive alliances in terms of the extent of joint activity, but critically different in that the partners are apt to be competitors in the final product market. Examples include Siemens and Philips, jointly developing a one-megabyte chip, Motorola and Toshiba, jointly planning to manufacture microprocessors in Japan, and Ford and Nissan, manufacturing vans in the United States. Such co-operation calls for intense inter-action between the partner firms, even though they are direct rivals with an implicit potential for conflict. In such alliances the protection of core strategic competencies is uppermost in the minds of collaborating managers.

Global Pre-competitive Alliances

These bring together firms from different, often unrelated industries to work on well-defined activities of mutual interest, such as new technology development. Du Pont and Sony's development of optical memory storage products is an example. Working together, the two firms, neither of which possesses the technological or the market know-how to succeed alone, expect to develop a product that they will subsequently manufacture and market independently. The joint activity is well-defined, involving only a limited interaction between the firms, largely confined to research.

One type of strategic alliance can develop over time into a different kind of relationship:

> IBM's pre-competitive alliances with Intel and Microsoft are examples of such a transformation. The alliances that brought together IBM on the one hand, and the world's dominant chip maker and the largest software company on the other, helped popularize and standardize the personal computer industry. But with success came mounting conflict. The erstwhile partners began to compete, each trying to cast itself in the role of the standard setter. IBM's loss was its former partners' gain. The *Wall Street Journal* called the IBM-Intel link one of 'high technology's most tangled relationships'. As one of IBM's senior executives put it, 'Our relationships include customer, supplier, partner, and competitor.'[78]

Why Form Strategic Alliances?

The term strategic alliances is used to describe a variety of different forms of inter-firm co-operation agreements which are becoming increasingly dense and complex:

- Shared research in developing products and processes in R&D-intensive industries.
- Non-equity contractual agreements in production and marketing.
- Minority equity participation.
- Formal joint ventures.

The full range of potential inter-firm links is suggested in Figure 2.5, stretching from contractual agreements to different kinds of equity arrangements. The appropriate structure, whether it is simply a licence, technology alliance or fully fledged joint venture, will depend upon what is required. Each form allows different possibilities, including developing product markets, sharing upstream risks, sharing development costs, leapfrogging product technology, exploiting economies of scale, filling product gaps or penetrating new markets (Figure 2.6).

Figure 2.5: Range of Interfirm Links

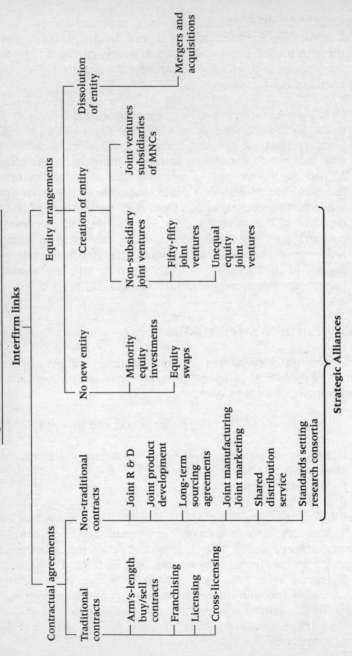

Source: Yoshino and Rangan, *Strategic Alliances* (1995), p.8

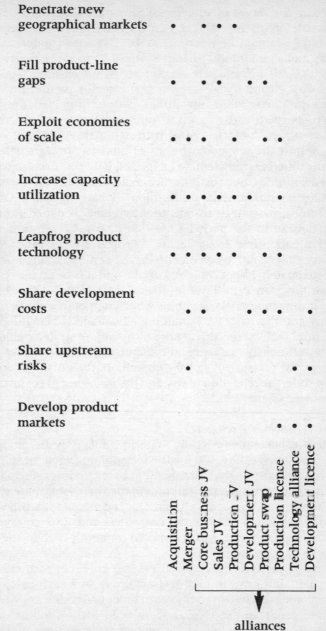

Figure 2.6: Many Alliance Options are Available

Note: Figures for 1980 and 1991, or nearest year.

Source: Krubasik and Lautenschlager, 'Forming Successful Strategic Alliances' (1993, p. 60)

The current waves of strategic alliances are different from the traditional foreign investment joint venture. Joint ventures are traditionally formed between an MNC HQ in an industrialized country and a junior local partner in a less developed country. The primary goal is to gain new market access for existing products. In this classic contractual agreement the senior partner provided existing products, while the junior partner provided the local marketing expertise, the means to hurdle protectionist barriers and the government contacts to deal with national regulations.

In contrast the scope and trends of modern strategic alliances are quite different: they tend to be formed between firms in industrialized countries, and focus on the creation of new products and technologies, rather than distribution of existing ones. Of the 4,200 inter-firm strategic co-operation agreements signed by enterprises globally in the period 1980–89, nearly 92 per cent were between enterprises from Japan, Western Europe and North America. Collaborative agreements have been increasing at a rate of approximately 10 per cent per annum, and this trend runs parallel with the growth in flows in direct investment.[79] Alliances are forged during industrial transitions when competitive positions are shifting, and the basis for rebuilding advantage is being defined. The central motivations driving the formation of strategic alliances include technology exchange, the impulse towards industry convergence, the pressure of global competition, the pursuit of economies of scale, the reduction of risk and the influence of government policies (see Figure 2.7).

Global Technology Exchanges

The R&D collaborative need to share technology resources is the single most powerful reason for the formation of modern strategic alliances. Breakthroughs in innovations based on inter-disciplinary and inter-industry alliances blur boundaries between formerly discrete industry sectors and technologies. Technology-intensive sectors such as telecommunications, computers and office equipment, electronics, pharmaceuticals and special chemicals become the central focus of agreements.

There are more technology sources and potential partners than in the past, and firms in high-technology sectors each co-operate to complement their own resources in order to develop knowledge-intensive goods and services, and to reduce the time for innovations to reach the market. Companies face a technological

Figure 2.7: High-tech Alliances Are Driven by Economic Factors

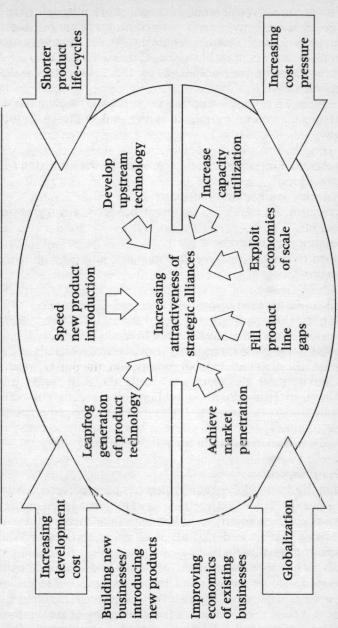

Shorter product life-cycles

Increasing cost pressure

Develop upstream technology

Increase capacity utilization

Speed new product introduction

Increasing attractiveness of strategic alliances

Exploit economies of scale

Leapfrog generation of product technology

Fill product line gaps

Achieve market penetration

Increasing development cost

Building new businesses/ introducing new products

Improving economics of existing businesses

Globalization

Source: Krubasik and Lautenschlager, 'Forming Successful Strategic Alliances' (1993), p. 56

environment of accelerating change, shortening product life-cycles, small market windows (limited pay-back period) and multiple vertical and lateral dependencies for market success. Essentially co-operation has been stimulated by escalating R&D costs; at the same time declining communication costs make co-operation easier.

As Table 2.8 reveals, according to the OECD, the main motives for setting up technology-related agreements in the 1980s focused upon:

- Searching for technological complementarities to extend R&D capabilities.
- Reducing innovation time-spans.
- Increasing efficiency to get new products and processes to markets.
- Gaining market access.
- Restructuring in mature technologies and slow-growth industries.[80]

Global Industry Convergence
High-technology industries are converging – for example, computers and telecommunications are becoming integrated, bio and chip technologies are intersecting, and advance materials and aerospace/autos manufacturing are working more closely together – and new technologies emerge which in the early stages involve enormous investment without an immediate return. For example, High Definition Television (HDTV) is beyond the resources of any single company: as a result there is both a Japanese consortium, and a European consortium for HDTV.

Global Competition
During the 1990s global competition has been perceived as something that takes place between teams of players aligned in strategic partnerships. Particularly in industries where there is a dominant worldwide market leader, strategic alliances and networks allow coalitions of smaller partners to compete against the leading companies rather than each other. MNCs face a dual challenge: to compete in global markets and to produce tailored solutions. In this context strategic alliances help to transfer technology across borders. Access to new markets is facilitated by using the complementary resources of local firms, including distribution channels

Table 2.8: Motives for Technology-based Strategic Alliances, Sectors and Fields of Technology, 1980–89

Fields of Technology	Number of alliances	High cost/ risks	Lack of financial resources	Technology complementarity	Reduction innovation time span	Basic R&D	Market access/ structure	Monitoring technology/ market entry
				Percentages				
Biotechnology	847	1	13	35	31	10	13	15
New materials technology	430	1	3	38	32	11	31	16
Information technology	1,660	4	2	33	31	3	38	11
Computers	198	1	2	28	22	2	51	10
Industrial automation	278	0	3	41	32	4	31	7
Microelectronics	383	3	3	33	33	5	52	6
Software	344	1	4	38	36	2	24	11
Telecom.	366	11	2	28	28	1	35	16
Other	91	1	0	29	28	2	35	24
Total database	4,182	6	4	31	28	5	32	11

Source: MERIT/CATI, Hagedoorn and Schakenraad, 'The Role of Inter-firm Cooperation Agreements' (1991)

and product-range extensions. Sometimes inter-firm co-operation is a second best option to direct investment, particularly for smaller companies, allowing them to explore market opportunities which may be approached later with more elaborate market strategies.

Global Economies of Scale and Reduction Risk

When partners pool resources they benefit from economies of scale, and from an increased rate of learning. Alliances allow partners to leverage their specific capabilities and therefore save costs of duplication.

The Influence of Government Policies

Apart from the direct promotion of international collaboration – in European Community programmes, for example – government policies may indirectly favour co-operation in the same way as they stimulate direct investment. Where there are limits imposed on local participation of foreign companies, joint ventures and minority equity participation become prevalent. Where there are national differences in intellectual property, environmental standards and other regulations, inter-firm agreements may make products acceptable to local regulatory authorities. Finally, competition policy limiting collaboration in the home market may encourage firms to seek foreign partners and thus expand internationally.

Risks and Costs of Collaboration in the Global Economy

Bartlett and Ghoshal argue that in the mid-1980s a large number of MNCs rushed into polygamous relationships (partly under the influence of Ohmae's concept of 'Triad Power' and Peters and Waterman's injunction to 'stick to the knitting' – i.e. companies should stay with their core competence). Companies saw strategic alliances as a way of developing Triadic power while focusing investments, efforts and attention only on those tasks which the company did well. All other activities were out-sourced either through alliances or subcontracting.

Another way of looking at virtual companies, alliances and joint ventures is as the out-sourcing of risk, allowing organizations at arm's length from parent companies to take risks more freely,

Figure 2.8: Finding the Right Degree of Centralization

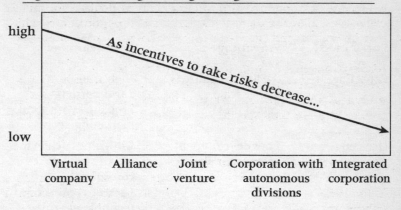

high

As incentives to take risks decrease...

low

| Virtual company | Alliance | Joint venture | Corporation with autonomous divisions | Integrated corporation |

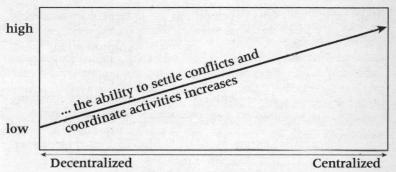

high

... the ability to settle conflicts and coordinate activities increases

low

Decentralized   Centralized

Source: *Harvard Business Review*, January–February 1996

something which the parent firms wish to avoid. The cost of this is, of course, felt by the parent firms when they are called upon to settle conflicts and co-ordinate activities among loosely connected partner companies (Figure 2.8). Every market entry mode has associated benefits and disadvantages: the latter arise from high transport costs, problems with local marketing agents, difficulties in controlling technology with licensing, in achieving quality control with franchising, in controlling joint ventures, and in assuming the entire risk with wholly owned subsidiaries (Figure 2.9).

The explosive growth of alliances helped to highlight the risks of collaboration, the competitive aspects of these relationships, and the high levels of strategic and organizational complexity of managing co-operative relationships. One partner may use the strategic

Table 2.9: Advantages and Disadvantages of Different Entry Modes

Entry mode	Advantage	Disadvantage
Exporting	Ability to realize global scale economies	High transport costs Tariff barriers Problems with local marketing agents
Licensing	Low development costs and risks	Difficulties achieving global strategic co-ordination Lack of control over technology
Franchising	Low development costs and risks	Difficulties achieving global strategic co-ordination Problems of quality control
Joint ventures	Access to local partner's knowledge Sharing of development costs and risks Political acceptability	Difficulties achieving global strategic co-ordination Lack of control over technology
Wholly owned subsidiaries	Protection of technology Establishment of tight control necessary for achieving global strategic co-ordination	Assumption by company of all costs and risks

Source: Yoshini and Rangan, 1995

alliance to develop a competitive edge over the other, so that the benefits become asymmetrical. One partner may seek to extract the core competence of another. One partner may learn the other's skills and then discard it, or one company may keep control over critical investments in the domain of product development, manufacturing, marketing, or wherever the most valuable part of the business is located.

The vast majority of cross-company collaborations are founded on a basis of trust and shared commitment. But even the most carefully constructed alliance can become risky. Often strategic alliances become short-term solutions that mask deeper deficiencies in the companies concerned, and these cause problems later when the company is still vulnerable. Inter-firm collaboration may also carry the cost of strategic and organizational complexity. Different companies have different priorities – for example, in US and UK companies, which are very stock-price oriented, there is an emphasis on accounting. By contrast Japanese, Dutch and Swiss companies are indifferent to stock price.

Making Global Alliances Work

Strategic alliances today are broader than the joint ventures of the past; they may cover product development, manufacturing and marketing. Forging alliances is one thing; making them work is quite another: strategic and environmental disparities between partners, a lack of common experience and perception, difficulties in inter-firm communication, conflicts of interest and priorities, and personal differences among individuals managing the interface make strategic alliances exceptionally difficult to manage.

Building co-operative ventures requires careful partner selection. The physical assets of the intended partner have to be assessed, including the condition and productivity of plant and equipment. The less tangible assets of partners have to be gauged, including the strength of brands, quality, customer relationships, levels of technological expertise and organizational competence. A common experience is a sometimes unanticipated but escalating commitment – 'The thrill of the chase blinds pursuers to the consequences of the catch' – particularly when the selection management and the practical alliance management are undertaken by different people. The key operating managers should be involved in the implementation stages of the alliance, and in pre-decision negotiation processes. This creates continuity and long-term understandings.[81]

It is often best to aim for simplicity and flexibility in the scope of the alliance, rather than for a broad and all-encompassing equity participation. The key to success is simple and focused partnerships. Three factors make for complexity:

- Complicated cross-holding and equity.
- Cross-functional coordination and integration needs.
- Breadth and scope of joint activities.

At each stage negotiators should ask whether something is absolutely necessary. In managing the boundary there are different ways in which the interface can be structured:

- As an independent legal entity.
- Managed by both or one of the parent companies.
- Simple administrative mechanism of a joint committee.

If the alliance is manufacturing and marketing a new product on a worldwide basis then an independent entity is required. But if the partners are simply aiming to market each other's existing products, then a few simple rules determining the marketing parameters will suffice. Irrespective of the objectives of the alliance, the process of collaboration creates flows of information across boundaries of competing companies. Precise arrangements and understandings are necessary to ensure full exploitation of knowledge-sharing, and to prevent outflow of knowledge each company wishes to retain.

Alliances, unlike acquisitions, are premised on the equality of both partners. But forming committees and management structures based on parity often will lead to deadlock, rather than dynamism. It is better to negotiate on the basis of integrative rather than distributive co-operation. When attempting to build successful co-operative ventures it is important to avoid easy-but-not-best solutions, and not to enter alliances as the second-best option. It is useful to remember that alliances need not (and are usually not!) permanent. Finally, flexibility is the key, both in making the relationship work and in allowing an exit if it cannot be made to work.[82] Of course, sometimes it is best not to go into a joint venture in the first place: political pressures to form joint ventures are diminishing even in developing countries, and it may be possible to launch a wholly owned enterprise. 'Chinese officials are proving more concerned about what outside investors bring to the country

– in terms of jobs, technology, and foreign exchange – than how their deals are structured.'[83]

Alliances are essentially an intermediate strategic device, and part of a web that includes many other transactions. Around half of all cross-border strategic alliances terminate within seven years, and so it is important for managers to have a good idea of what comes next. Most alliance businesses are finally purchased by one or other of the partners, and termination of the alliance does not mean failure. But the prevalence of early terminations suggests that it is important to consider whether parties are likely to be buyers or sellers. Understanding the sequence of likely future transactions is necessary since alliance partners will be competitors in future, and it is best to avoid what the Chinese refer to as 'two partners in the same bed with different dreams'.[84]

Localization and Globalization

Impulses to form international strategic alliances occur as a part of the seemingly irresistible pressure towards further globalization of corporate strategies. As Barlett and Ghoshal put it,

> Global chess . . . could only be played by companies that managed their world-wide operations as interdependent units, implementing a co-ordinated global strategy. Unlike the traditional multinational strategic approach that was based on an assumption that each national market was unique and independent of others, these global competitive games assumed that a company's competitive position in all markets was linked by financial and strategic interdependence . . . In industry after industry, companies that operated their local companies as independent profit centres found themselves at a disadvantage to competitors playing the global strategic game of cross-subsidizing markets. Companies that found no economic, technological, or market reason to manage their businesses globally were suddenly finding the urgent need to do so for reasons of competitive strategy.[85]

Globalizing business strategies often gain support from assumptions that they constitute a universal force of unilinear dimensions. Levitt's insistence that 'the world's desires have been irrevocably homogenized . . . no one is exempt and nothing can stop the process' is a case in point.[86] If such a proposition were true this homogenization of taste and consumption would inevitably lead to standardization of products, manufacturing, marketing and trade. This saturation of markets, with a few common products gaining enormous profit, is manifested in the 'cola culture'. Coca-Cola is the world's most famous expression (after OK), has the world's most famous brand name (worth an estimated $39 billion), and is sold in almost 200 countries. According to the *Guardian*, 'Coca-Cola invested billions of dollars into soft drinks infrastructure. Selling soft drinks requires little capital, produces superb returns, demands minimal reinvestment and yields huge cash flow.'[87] There is no end to the profit aspirations of such companies. Another similar example is McDonald's, which, having reached the stage of feeding 0.1 per cent of the US population every day, sees no reason whatsoever why it should not feed a similar proportion of the world. However, standardization has its limits, and there are important cultural, political and economic forces for local differentiation that have emerged powerfully in recent years to question the logic of globalization.

In a sense this dilemma is the traditional global/local one facing managers as their enterprises become increasingly international. Farley and Kobrin suggest that

> A global strategy should be conceptualized as a continuum of choices balancing pressures to respond locally with pressures to integrate across borders, and strong pressures to respond to local market differences . . . In reality more multinational firms respond to both sets of pressures simultaneously; it is their relative intensity that varies. The critical strategic problem facing managers is balancing or trading-off pressure to respond to local differences with those to integrate across borders; to deal with the costs and risks of technology, for example, by selling relatively standardized products in a large number of markets while responding adequately to differences in national regulation or standards.[88]

The concept of global corporations as roaming stateless organizations, staffed by functionaries who are global citizens, working out of a laptop while living in identical hotel bedrooms in whatever part of the world they happen to be in today, is somewhat wide of the mark. 'Companies can out-source; they can decentralize operations; they can relocate. But when all is said and done, even multinational giants have to put down roots and build strong ties with communities if they expect to excel.'[89] Understanding that even multinational corporations have a well-defined national identity highlights the importance of winning acceptance in foreign markets.

The Japanese corporations which had successfully ridden the waves of globalization were among the first to appreciate the urgent need to become more sensitive to host-country economic and political forces: 'If the strategic implications of the globalizing trends have dominated management thinking in the West, the cultural and political forces for *localization* have become the preoccupation of top-level executives in Japan'.[90]

Multinational enterprise relationships with national governments have experienced something of a sea-change. To host governments MNCs often represent important external sources of investment, technology and knowledge that may further national priorities, including regional development, employment creation, import substitution and export promotion. To the MNC the government offers access to local markets or resources, and opportunities for profit growth, as well as improved competitiveness. However, a fundamental tension exists between national governments and MNCs in their operating objectives. The multinationals want unrestricted access to resources and markets throughout the world and freedom to integrate manufacturing and other operations across national boundaries, as well as an unimpeded right to co-ordinate and control all aspects of the company on a worldwide basis. Thus, governance of the corporation, especially as a taxable entity, can frequently cut across government of the territories in which it operates, especially as a taxing authority.[91]

These objectives do not always appear compatible with government priorities to develop prosperous national economies that can hold their own in world competition. The difficulty is that governments conceive of capturing global competitiveness within the national economy, and MNCs think of it in terms of the global system. Governments and MNCs are motivated by very different aims: the MNC has a bottom line to which it can reduce costs and benefits, while governments have a far more complex and ambiguous set of social and political priorities to deal with.

During the 1980s rising import penetration was seen as a serious threat to national economies and even those governments which advocated free trade, such as the United States, began to negotiate voluntary restraint and orderly trade agreements. At the same time the industrial policies of governments became more sophisticated. They sought to prevent the use of 'screwdriver plants' – simple assembly lines of products essentially manufactured overseas – to evade trade restrictions. Such plants offered low-skilled employment, with little local value added, and minimum new technology. Some governments applied investment regulations which defined specific levels of local content, technology transfer and a variety of other conditions, in an effort to make MNCs increase the extent of their local activities.

At the same time MNCs were beginning to realize that there were limits to the homogenization of worldwide tastes; consumers seemed inherently to prefer a degree of aesthetic and cultural distinction. The arrival of flexible manufacturing systems, including computer-aided design and manufacture, enabled the cost-effective pursuit of smaller, more highly differentiated market niches wherever they appeared. Flexible manufacturing technologies mean that MNCs can begin to respond more effectively to local consumer preferences and national government restraints, while sustaining productive efficiency.

The Strength of Local Specialization

A paradoxical consequence of increasing globalization is the concentration in different local economies around the world of clusters of world-class expertise in special industries. This significant local dimension of the globalization phenomenon consists of local economies built upon inter-linked networks of relations among firms, universities and other institutions in their local environment.[92] Early specialization is reinforced by the growth of similar firms and institutions to create highly competitive industrial and service clusters. Local geographic concentrations of three broad groups of industrial and service activities have been noted:

• Highly competitive traditional, labour-intensive industries, which are highly concentrated, including textiles and clothing in some areas of Italy and the Unites States, furniture production, shoes, etc.

- High-technology industries where there has often been a clustering around new activities. Well-known examples include biotechnology in San Francisco, semi-conductors in Silicon Valley, scientific instruments in Cambridge (UK) and musical instruments in Hamamatsu (Japan).
- Services, notably financial and business services, which are concentrated in a few big cities, such as advertising, films, fashion design and R&D activities.

The rationale for the local concentration of specialist economic activity is explained by the OECD in the following way:

> There are advantages of being in the same location as similar firms, specialized suppliers and contractors, knowledgeable customers, a good technological infrastructure, and specialist institutions; where a highly skilled labour force is available; and where specialization within firms enables extensive outsourcing (vertical disintegration) and encourages similar new firms to be set up in the location (horizontal disintegration).[93]

Globalization increases the competitiveness of these local economies by attracting international firms with their own specific advantages, and enhancing established sourcing and supply relations. Local firms individually may respond to heightened competition through improving their innovative performance. Innovation may be extended through the development of greater interactions between firms, suppliers, users, production support facilities, and educational and other institutions in local innovation systems. Additionally, firms may adopt leaner production methods, more efficient management techniques, greater local out-sourcing and local production network use, to increase efficiency and spread risks and costs by taking advantage of local specialization in regional networks and industrial districts. Through building these they can improve production and service links with international companies investing locally. Local firms, particularly if they are highly specialized, will co-operate with international firms seeking complementary resources in the specialized assets of small firms.

The OECD studied the extent to which inward international investment increased or decreased the pattern of specialization and concentration of economic activities. Foreign direct investment has been directed to prosperous regions in the United States, France,

Germany and the Netherlands, and more urbanized and core regions in Canada and Spain.[94] It was only in the United Kingdom that manufacturing located in peripheral regions attracted above average investment. Globalization measured by incoming foreign investment therefore tends to reinforce regional specialization, accentuating the development of special local economies and enhancing the clustering of similar activities.

Small and Medium-sized Enterprises and Globalization

Globalization is associated with giant corporations, yet in most industrial countries over the last twenty years the share of small- and medium-sized companies (SMEs) has been increasing, as has their general significance to economic activity. SMEs have been more important in generating employment in services such as construction and transport, and in traditional manufacturing industries. Most SMEs are not very active in international markets, and only about a quarter have any foreign operations. SMEs connect with the international economy through exports, often acting as suppliers and subcontractors for large global companies in the electronics and car industries. The OECD acknowledges that there will be increasing globalization of SMEs with strong internal capabilities, competing on non-price factors such as R&D, innovation, quality, flexibility, specialization and a strong customer base in new areas of goods and services.

Globalization Policy Issues

As MNCs reorganize their strategic, production and marketing activities by using new combinations of international investment, trade and collaboration, several policy issues are raised: how, for instance, should national economies respond to globalization? For the OECD these processes are part of the creation of efficient, highly co-ordinated international industrial systems:

> International expansion has been driven by firm strategies based on their technological and organizational advantages shaped by a number of factors and government policies. Technological factors driving expansion include the rapid growth of knowledge-intensive industries which are foreign investment intensive, use intra-firm trade intensively and

collaborate externally in development, the need to recoup growing R&D costs, find highly trained and skilled workers, and organize production more efficiently, underpinned by declining communications and transport costs. Macroeconomic factors include availability of production resources and differences in growth potential and market development in different countries and regions. Government policies significantly influence firm strategies by liberalizing capital, investment and trade flows, promoting regional integration and promoting competitiveness. Trade policy and the liberalization of trade and investment are enabling factors which have driven global expansion and increased the integration of production and markets.[95]

The present context for business is one of heightened competitiveness due to better location of production and greater firm efficiencies – particularly for intermediate inputs and components – more foreign investment and trade in domestic markets and increased competition in foreign markets; overall there are more operations by all kinds of foreign firms in all national markets. Though this economic activity is for the moment concentrated in the advanced industrial countries, firms from the developing world are increasingly competing on the basis of the same high quality inputs, and are becoming closely linked to the existing industrial markets, through international investment, contracting and supply networks in high-technology industries, as well as in traditional industries.

The OECD suggests that, to meet the new international competitive challenges, businesses need to improve their performance by increasing global efficiency, using communications and computing capabilities to co-ordinate development, production and marketing.[96] Both internal and external R&D collaboration and contracting will require expanding. New organizational methods such as lean production, out-sourcing of production and services, workforce reorganization and training will also be necessary, as will co-ordinating production with marketing, and with R&D and design, to respond more flexibly to changes and fluctuations in demand.

Governments throughout the world have struggled with the policy implications of dealing with such dramatic and seemingly perpetual industrial restructuring caused by the impact of globalization. The OECD records a broad shift by member governments by the end of the 1980s away from general investment, short-term crisis aid, and subsidies for sectors facing over-capacity and structural problems. Industry support expenditure by governments has become more strategic and has shifted towards R&D, trade and foreign expansion. There was an increasing focus on improving the operating conditions for companies and supporting intermediaries who deliver services to business.

As for the future, the OECD recommends the implementation of a series of economic and technical policy measures if countries are to make an adequate response to the competitive pressures of globalization. These policies consist of improving business operations, improving access to international markets, and improving the environment and infrastructure within which business operations exist. Business performance will be enhanced by: improving investment incentives in intangible assets, particularly human capital; promoting international co-operation in long-term generic research; helping innovation by diffusing new product technologies and new production methods; encouraging incentives for the flow of finance to small firms; and attracting investments in the service infrastructure. Additionally, the OECD recommends the adoption of international best practice; improving management performance; and promoting industrial modernization with targeted programmes for problem areas to help deal with lack of skills, poor technology and financing barriers.

The policy frame within which the OECD makes its recommendations focuses on 'widening and deepening liberalization on all fronts'.[97] What happens to countries and companies that, despite their best efforts, for reasons beyond their control, are less able to compete, at least at the present time? It is doubtful that the older 'industry policies' premised on protection will be useful. The collapse of the East Asian economies during 1997 underscores this point. Today, protectionist remedies are less effective than they may have seemed in the past. As the OECD argues:

> Production and trade in technology and investment intensive components and sub-assemblies have become increasingly important, raising backward and forward linkages among firms along the production chain. In many cases an 'imported' product contains a higher proportion of local content (intangible and tangible) than a competing 'domestic' product. For this reason attempting to tilt playing fields in favour of

'domestic' firms through discriminatory measures such as antidumping duties, voluntary export restraints, bilateral safeguard actions or preferential treatment, aside from being more complicated to carry out, may well become arbitrary and, sometimes, even harmful to the economic interests of the country imposing the measure. In addition to the origin of products, the nationality of corporations has become more difficult to ascertain in the wake of investment and capital market liberalization . . . The relative economic importance of national versus foreign firms for the host country – the 'who is us?' issue – is also much less clear-cut than in the past.[98]

THE LIMITS OF GLOBALIZATION?

Winners and Losers

'In an increasingly interdependent world we must all recognize we have an interest in spreading the benefits of economic growth as widely as possible and in diminishing the risk either of excluding individuals or groups in our own economies, or of excluding certain countries or regions from the benefits of globalization.'[99] Bayer and Drache also pose the question: is social disintegration the price of economic integration?[100] There appear to be two primary casualties of globalization: firstly, low-skilled workers in traditional manufacturing countries, who either see their jobs slip away overseas or experience a painful slide in their wage rates as their employers strive to reduce costs. Secondly, and more seriously, whole countries and regions, which find they have been sidelined by the forces of international trade and investment, and instead of experiencing a growing involvement and benefit from the global economy, may encounter a greater sense of dependence and isolation. Particularly vulnerable are the relatively unskilled and undereducated, especially in labour market systems like that in the USA, where labour market policies are not very active or interventionist.

In 1979, the average American male college graduate earned 49% more than a high-school graduate; by 1993 the gap had widened to 89%. The lowest paid 10% of American men have seen a drop in their real wages of almost 20% since 1980 . . . Wage inequality in America has undeniably increased. And

many blame information technology and globalization ...
Over the past decade, America has allowed its minimum wage
to fall in real terms to 34% of the median wage (though it is
about to raise it). In France, by contrast, the minimum wage
is close to 60% of the median.[101]

Wood believes that trade with developing countries is the prime
cause of the increase in inequality *within* industrial countries. He
estimates that it has reduced the demand for low-skilled workers
in rich economies by more than a fifth. In evidence, he points to
figures showing that 'between 1970 and 1990 those countries
which saw the biggest increase in manufactured imports from
developing countries also suffered the sharpest drop in manufacturing's share in total employment'.[102] However, most jobs are
clearly non-tradable. A shortage of truck-drivers in America cannot
be relieved by unemployed truck-drivers from China. And even
for the 16 per cent of American workers who make their living in
manufacturing, the overlap of production with low-wage countries
is relatively small. America's main competitors in most sectors are
other high-wage countries, as is true of most OECD states.

More jobs and skills are entering the tradable sector. As the
prospects for those without skills diminish, the opportunities for
those with highly specialized skills suddenly become global.

Winner-take-all markets are spreading to more and more
occupations, such as lawyers, doctors, bankers, academics and
chief executives. In such jobs the market pays individuals not
according to their absolute performance, but to their performance relative to others ... What has changed is that new
technology and globalization have expanded the market for
skills from a local into a global one, increasing the opportunity
for the rich to become even richer.[103]

Super-competitiveness

Classical trade theory assumed that capital and technology were
not readily mobile between countries. As a result developed countries made capital-intensive, high-tech products, while developing
countries were confined to low-tech, labour-intensive activities.
But a global capital market has given poor countries better access to

capital, and technology has become more transferable. Information technology allows knowledge to be codified and diffused across borders more rapidly, making it easier for developing countries to catch up. Intelligent organization is no longer just the preserve of clever countries:

> On the surface ... the mix of lower wages and first-world technology would appear to make third world economies super-competitive. It is inevitable, goes the argument, that there will be a massive shift of production and jobs from high-wage countries to low-wage countries ... The only solution, argue people such as Ross Perot, Pat Buchanan and James Goldsmith, is for rich countries to close their borders to imports from developing countries ... But the idea that low-wage countries with access to the latest technology will be able to undercut workers in almost every industry in developed countries is based on two misunderstandings. The first is about the link between wages and productivity. International trade tends to equalize labour costs per unit of output, so differences in wages between countries reflect differences in average productivity in their traded sectors. Low wages in developing countries currently go hand in hand with lower productivity. A study by Stephen Golub (1995) found that in 1990 wages in manufacturing in Malaysia were only 15% of those in America; but then average productivity in manufacturing too, was only 15% of America's. In part this reflects simpler machinery (because labour is cheap relative to capital), but inferior infrastructure and education in poor countries also play an important part. Differences between countries in average unit labour costs are much smaller than differences in wages alone suggest.[104]

The Economist, at least, still has confidence in the virtues of the trade theory of comparative advantage:

> Even if China could make everything more cheaply, America would, by definition, still have a comparative advantage in some products. So long as some differences between countries persist, such as the skill of labour forces, which unlike technology cannot easily move abroad, the law of the comparative advantage continues to hold. China's comparative advantage

will tend to lie in low-skilled, labour-intensive industries and America's in knowledge-intensive products that take advantage of its relative abundance of skilled labour.[105]

However, this comparative advantage of the developed countries may well be slipping away in significant sectors of service employment. Some people fear the new supercompetition because the growth of information technology and intelligent organization 'allows previously untradable services to be traded just like steel or shoes. This is because the increasing codification of knowledge reduces the need for physical contact between producers and consumers. Any activity that can be conducted through a screen and a telephone, from the writing of software to running a secretarial service, can be carried out anywhere in the world'. Routines can be cheapened further by greater routinization of existing tasks; the re-engineered tasks can then be moved to places where wages are cheaper. The transaction cost associated with doing so does not appear to be great: satellites and computers can ensure virtual linkage. According to *The Economist*, 'Firms in the rich world have out-sourced all manner of things to developing countries – from computer programming and airline revenue accounting to processing hospital patients' records and insurance claims. More than 100 of America's top 500 firms buy software services from firms in India, where programmers are typically paid less than a quarter of the American rate.'[106]

Despite the attention drawn to the wages issue, and the associated cost of taxes, by journalists and politicians, the truth is that MNCs do not, by and large, invest where wages and taxes are lowest. If they did the theory of comparative costs would work far better than it does. The reasons are self-evident: wages are often a minor cost-factor in MNC calculations; greater transaction costs are associated with the presence or absence of densely embedded networks for business in particular locales. Additionally, domestic institutional linkages frame businesses in embedded relationships with universities, financial institutions, government institutions, and so on. Government–business relations typically have an exclusive rather than an open character and can be an important component in building national competitive advantage.[107]

Competitive advantage increasingly depends on knowledge. While rich industrial economies continue to enjoy an advantage in knowledge-intensive industries through the depth of institutional embeddedness of their industries in complexly interdependent business systems, the location of these industries as a 'first world' preserve is drawn increasingly into question. So is the presumed distribution of skills. In newly industrialized countries such as South Korea and Taiwan R&D as a share of GDP shadows OECD averages, but is developing faster (albeit from a lower base). As *The Economist* concludes, 'In future, workers with intermediate skills in rich countries' knowledge intensive industries will also face fiercer competition from the Asian tigers as they move upmarket in response to increased competition from cheaper countries such as China.'[108]

An emerging danger is that competitive advantage in the future will open up the possibility of global domination more rapidly than it was ever achieved in the past. Brian Arthur argues that in a growing number of industries there is a natural tendency for the market leader to get further ahead, causing a monopolistic concentration of business.[109]

New knowledge-based industries tend to have several things in common: high fixed costs, such as R&D, but low variable costs. Pharmaceutical industries, for example, are heavy on know-how, but light on material resources. Such industries have network externalities: for instance, the more widely an operating system is used the more likely it is that the software will become the industry standard. Strong leading firms have a firm grip on the market and a lock-in effect on customers. Increasing returns magnify the market leader's advantage. By cutting its price the leader can grab a bigger share of the market, earn bigger profits and spend more on R&D than its rivals, sharpening the edge still further. While economists have been aware of the possibility of increasing returns for a long time, they have believed them to be rare in practice. However, information technology, and the general shift in economies from processing tangible goods to processing information and ideas, now introduce increasing returns to scale in a growing number of industries, according to Brian Arthur.[110]

What Happens to the Losers?

If the aim of international competition is to win, only a few can be winners. A real danger is that the losers are excluded and abandoned to their situation. The winners come together and increasingly integrate with one another. Where such processes

occur within societies they may lead to increased poverty,
unemployment, alienation and crime. But the consequences are
even more serious when the processes of exclusion and alienation
involve countries and whole regions of the world:

> A new divide in the world appears, coinciding with the emerg-
> ence of globalization. De-linking is the process through which
> some countries and regions are gradually losing their connec-
> tions with the most economically developed and growing
> countries and regions of the world. Rather than participating
> in the processes of increasing interconnections and integration
> that are constructing the new 'global world', they are moving
> in the opposite direction. De-linking concerns almost all coun-
> tries of Africa, most parts of Latin America and Asia (with the
> exception of countries from South East Asia) as well as parts
> of the former Soviet Union and Eastern Europe.[111]

The share of world trade in manufactured goods of the 102 poorest
countries of the world was 7.9 per cent of world exports and 9 per
cent of imports in 1986. Ten years later these shares had fallen to
1.4 per cent of exports and 4.9 per cent of imports. Conversely,
the share of the three regions of the Triad increased from 54.8 per
cent to 64.0 per cent of world exports and from 59.5 per cent to
63.8 per cent of world imports. Petrella characterizes these trends
in terms of a process, occurring over the last twenty years, that
has gradually reduced 'the exchanges between the richest and
fast-growing countries of North America, Western Europe and
Pacific Asia and the rest of the world – Africa in particular'. What
is alarming, he suggests, would be if this trend were to extrapolate
into an equivalent period into the future, because 'the share of
Africa, the Middle East, Latin America, Russia and Central/Eastern
Europe (39.2 per cent of world trade in 1970 and 26.4 per cent in
1990) would be reduced to 5 per cent in 2020'. Such an occurrence,
should it materialize, would be a 'de-linking' of the less from the
more developed world. The Triad would compose the core of an
increasingly globally integrated world economy from which the
countries outside the Triad blocs would be excluded. One can only
speculate on the political consequences of such a new global division: they are unlikely to be integrative for the world system as
a whole.[112]

Death of the Nation State?

At the very time when political action may be necessary to remedy some of the more destabilizing impacts of globalization on the world system the significance of the nation state has been considerably weakened. The largest twenty multinational corporations have a turnover in excess of the GNP of most nation states. The onset of globalization raises profound questions about the traditional role and viability of the nation state. National institutions no longer represent a genuine shared community of economic interests in such areas as public finance, trade policy, wealth creation and civil rights. Ohmae insists that the nation state 'has become an unnatural, even dysfunctional unit for organizing human activity and managing economic endeavour in a borderless world . . . it defines no meaningful flows of economic activity'.[113] The reasons for this are evident in the seeming triumph of markets over politics: according to Drache, 'Efficiency has become the universal belief of all major corporations and most leading industrial powers. In their view, capital has to be free to move across national boundaries if the world economy is to recover its past *élan*. Firms have to reorganize their production to take advantage of the new opportunities. People are expected to accept new employment conditions to accommodate to a world where business is no longer bound by national borders.'[114] This is the underlying belief of those who argue for free trade. Bhagwati defines this as a covenant between governments and markets such that 'the logic of efficiency has to determine the allocation of activity among all trading nations'.[115]

In a world where the rules of international trade are being redefined, and traditional protectionism is not an option, states have to make a choice between the prospects of free trade with associated costs, or developing the conditions for managed trade. Many countries have sought to join a trade bloc, whilst building a regulatory environment which offers incentives for economic growth through institutional arrangements that protect national economies from international economic disorder.[116] Meanwhile businesses seeking to change cost structures in order to compete internationally want to dismantle existing social programmes in the advanced industrial countries. Governments find it difficult to reconcile their existing social programmes for health, education and retirement with the demands of footloose business to make their economy more competitive. What is in danger of being lost is, in Drache's words, 'any viable notion of social responsibility – the institutional capacity for the achievement of a more equitable society'.[117] Also at risk are those many fibres of a civil society, its 'social capital', that enable a market economy to operate efficiently.

The pressure to down-size the state seems universal. However, even after the great waves of privatization that have swept the world, as Drache contends, 'it is premature to announce the death of the nation state. Countries remain in charge of the essential part of their national sovereignty: law making and jurisprudence; macro-economic policy, including money, finance and taxation'.[118] Can these pressures for a smaller state be associated simultaneously with a responsible rethinking of the role of the state in a global economy? Most of the social and economic programmes of national governments, although subject to severe efficiency drives and a transformation in management, resourcing and method of delivery, are still in existence. Considerable evidence, from many different countries, suggests the emergence of a new paradigm of public management, which is results-oriented rather than inward-looking, and sees the state as an enabler rather than a provider.[119] We are witnessing not the death of the state but the decline of politics as compared to markets, and the increasing incursion of the former on the latter. Additionally, the claims made on state resources by some of the losers, such as the unemployed and the poor, may be diminishing, but other claims remain strong. As Petrella claims, among the willing clients of national governments are the multinational corporations themselves which, despite employing the rhetoric of enterprise, demand rather a lot from the state. They expect states to cover the costs of the infrastructure of basic and high-risk research – universities and vocational training systems – and to promote and fund the dissemination of scientific and technical information and technology; to provide tax incentives for investment in industrial R&D and technological innovations, as well as to guarantee that 'national' enterprises from the given country have a stable home base as well as privileged access to the domestic market via public contracts (defence, telecommunications, health, transport, education, social services). Some multinational firms – particularly those in the high-technology strategic sectors (defence, telecommunications, data processing) – require industrial policy to protect designated sectors of the domestic market from international competition; they also demand support and assistance (regulatory, commercial, diplomatic and political) for local companies in their efforts to survive in international markets.

Often these expectations will be represented in terms of a logic of capital mobility. That is, if the local state does not provide the required sweeteners, mobile capitalism will simply exit the scene and set up where the benefits sought can be ensured. The thesis is overstated because, in terms of the important criteria of share of assets, ownership, management, employment and the location of R&D, home bases remain important. Very few firms are genuinely transnational in these respects.[120] With Petrella and Weiss we can conclude that the proponents of the thesis that strong globalization erodes state capacities oversell the proposition: they emphasize the extent and the novelty of international investment while underrating the capacities of states to adapt and to innovate around their specific national institutional frameworks.[121] Globalization is itself in part a consequence of these adaptations and innovations, especially when the most successful countries of East Asia, such as Japan, implement internationalization strategies as a state initiative. These are particularly evident in the development of global financial markets.

Global Financial Markets

International financial flows and foreign currency exchanges now dwarf the value of international trade in goods. The global financial system has become extremely volatile and very complex. The implications of this for the global economy are enormous, because financial services are circulation services: they are fundamental to the operation of every aspect of the economic system. Each element of the production chain depends upon certain levels of finance to keep the chain in operation. This is not just true of manufacturing but of all intermediate and consumed services in the system.[122] The intensified competitiveness of international financial markets is due to four interacting forces:

Market saturation: From the late 1970s in both the commercial banking and retail sectors it was clear that market saturation was being reached in the mature economies.

Disintermediation: With rising inflation accompanied by rising interest rate charges corporate borrowers became more inclined to make investments or raise capital without going through the intermediary channels of the traditional financial institutions, preferring the commercial paper market for short-term funds, and the bond market for long-term financing.

Deregulation of financial markets: The close regulation of financial markets by national governments was abandoned and led to the opening-up and liberalization of new geographical markets and new financial products, and changes in pricing policies.

Internationalization of financial markets: The growth in international trade increased the demand for commercial financial services on an international scale, and the spread of multinational operations has created a demand for other international financial services. Finally, increased institutionalization of saving creates an enormous pool of administered investment capital seeking the best return on an international basis.[123]

The progressive deregulation of financial services is the most important development in the internationalization of the financial system, playing a major role in eliminating distortions and reducing ineffective controls. This process is a fundamental part of the changes associated with the strengthening of regional trading blocs. The European Commission's proposals for integrating financial services are intended to ensure the free flow of capital between all member states, with free trade in all financial services within the community, and the standardization of banking technology. The UK 'Big Bang' of 1986 removed the barriers which had previously existed between banks and securities houses and allowed the entry of foreign firms into the Stock Exchange.

Innovations in telecommunications and processing technologies have transformed the operation of financial services and promoted a wealth of financial product innovations: 'the number of financial markets has proliferated in the 1970s and 1980s as "financial engineering" (the invention of new financial instruments) has become an important art form of the late twentieth century'. New forms of intangible financial product are created, new markets emerge, such as 'those in options and futures (which trade in forward contracts in commodities, money and shares) and equities (which trade in stocks and shares) have taken their place alongside the Eurodollar and Eurobond markets as important global markets'.[124] The array of new financial instruments, providing new methods of lending that facilitate greater spreading of risk, increase the diversity of international financial markets. The global integration of financial markets becomes possible, as time and space collapse and the potential for virtually instantaneous financial transactions is created in loans, securities and more innovative financial instruments.[125]

The deregulation and internationalization of financial markets creates a new competitive environment:

> Deregulation and financial innovation . . . became a condition for survival of any world financial centre within a highly integrated global system, co-ordinated through instantaneous telecommunications. The formation of a global stock market, of global commodity (even debt) futures markets, of currency and interest rate swaps, together with an accelerated geographic mobility of funds, meant, for the first time, the formation of a single world market for money and credit supply.[126]

The global integration of financial markets brings many benefits to the participants, in terms of speed and accuracy of information flows and directness of transactions. However, instantaneous financial trading means that shocks felt in one market communicate immediately around the world's markets, making the global financial system sensitive and volatile as a result of the telecommunications revolution, as demonstrated by the stock market crash of October 1987, or by the South-East Asian monetary collapses of late 1997. How near to the 'edge of chaos' the international financial system has moved is an open question.[127] The speculative basis of much of the system suggests that such protective mechanisms as are in force have simply rescheduled a global financial crisis rather than prevented it.[128]

What matters is not so much the concentration of power in financial institutions as the explosion in new financial instruments and markets, coupled with the rise of highly sophisticated systems of financial co-ordination on a global scale. Harvey suggests that 'the financial system has achieved a degree of autonomy from real production unprecedented . . . carrying . . . into an era of equally unprecedented financial dangers'.[129] The Eurodollar financial market in 'stateless' money expanded from $50 billion in 1973 to

$2 trillion by the time of the 1987 crash, thus approaching the size of the money aggregates within the United States. Harvey notes how the economy of whole cities has been transformed: 'New York lost its traditional garment trade and turned to the production of debt and fictitious capital instead ... The biggest physical export from New York is now waste paper.' It was this financial speculation and fictitious capital formation, much of it unbacked by any real growth in production, which President Bush from time to time described as 'voodoo economics'.[130] Even the Japanese industrial system, which created the strongest economy of the late twentieth century, was not powerful enough to withstand the damaging collapse of speculative activity in the Tokyo Stock Exchange, which saw 60 per cent of the value of the Nikkei wiped out between 1990 and 1995.[131]

The increasing powers of co-ordination possessed by the world's financial system emerged to some degree at the expense of the power of nation states to control capital flows, and hence their own fiscal and monetary policy. The breakdown in 1971 of the Bretton Woods Agreement, whereby the price of gold and the convertibility of the dollar were fixed, acknowledged that the United States was no longer able to control world fiscal and monetary policy single-handedly. The inflation-budgeting it used to fund the Veitnam War turned the world's largest creditor nation into a debtor. The subsequent adoption in 1973 of the flexible exchange rate system was a response to massive speculative currency movements against the dollar that occurred after the collapse of the Bretton Woods Agreement and during the death throes of US involvement in Vietnam. Since 1975 the major industrial powers have sought, through the IMF or through collective agreements, to intervene in financial markets, winning back a degree of collective state control lost by individual countries.[132] However, it is clear that, despite such agreements, on many occasions since, states have been at the mercy of the financial discipline of international capital flows, and many governments have had quickly to rewrite their political programmes in the face of strong capital flight from their country. Despite lectures from national leaders like Malaysia's Mahathir, it has become evident that when confidence in a national currency is tested the weaker nation state will no longer be able to hold the line.

The domination of US firms in the expansion of transnational banking during the sixties and seventies was a reflection of the focal role of the country in the post-war international financial and trading system. But European, and later Japanese, banks have increasingly internationalized their operations. In Japan the rise of banks, like other areas of economic activity, has been dramatic, as the nation accumulated financial surpluses. In 1985 the Japanese replaced the Americans as the largest holders of international assets and by 1987 held $1.4 trillion compared with the $630 billion held by the US.[133] However, the banks were damaged by the bursting of the speculative bubble in Japan, and they were heavily exposed in the South-East Asian collapse at the end of 1997. Their continuing losses suggest that they have not been entirely successful in finding a new role in the international financial community.

Meanwhile the structural dislocation of the international financial system from the international economic and production system that, ostensibly, it is there to service, proceeds relatively unchecked. During the 1980s there was an explosion in asset-backed lending in the UK, particularly in commercial property and personal mortgages, as people sought to gain short-term profit supported by asset-price inflation. Lending to the property sector rose 800 per cent in real terms, while that to manufacturing increased by only 50 per cent.[134] In the United States there was a similar lack of supportive relationships between investors and industry, as Michael Porter has observed in a research project on corporate investment, sponsored by the US Council on Competitiveness. It is possible that as pressure mounts for US capital investors to become involved in industry like their Japanese counterparts, the reverse is occurring in the Japanese investment system, as Carl Kester has recently revealed (see Chapter 5).

Corporate International Financial Manoeuvres

In the absence of any reform to the structure and operation of the capital investment market for industry, and as companies become integrated into international financial operations and structures as a necessary consequence of engaging in international trade, it is unsurprising that a large proportion of corporate activity becomes concerned with international financial manoeuvres, making it increasingly difficult to tell where commercial and industrial interests begin and strictly financial interests end. As David Harvey argues:

This confusion has been particularly associated with the growth of what is now called 'paper entrepreneurialism'. Tremendous emphasis has been put in recent years on finding ways other than straight production of goods and services to make profits. The techniques vary from sophisticated 'creative accounting' through careful monitoring of international markets and political conditions by multinationals, so that they can profit from relative shifts in currency values or interest rates, to straight corporate raiding and asset stripping of rival or even totally unrelated corporations. The 'merger and take-over mania' of the 1980s was part and parcel of this emphasis upon paper entrepreneurialism, for although there were some instances where such activities could indeed be justified in terms of rationalization or diversification of corporate interests, the thrust was more often than not to gain paper profits without troubling with actual production. Small wonder, as Robert Reich (a Harvard economist, formerly President Clinton's Labour Secretary) observes, 'that paper entrepreneurialism now preoccupies some of America's best minds, attacks some of its most talented graduates, employs some of its most creative and original thinking, and spurs some of its most energetic wheeling and dealing'. Over the last fifteen years, he reports,the most sought after and most lucrative jobs to be had in US business lay not in the management of production but in the legal and financial spheres of corporate action.[135]

The global economy has in many ways become dominated by an economy of signs representing capital flows, rather than an economy of things. Of course, manufactured and other tradable products and services are important, but at the core of the key decision-making in the contemporary globalized economy are intangibles, such as trust in a currency's future value, and bets hedged against those judgements of trust. What makes these possible are the instantaneous representational possibilities afforded by a wired world.

CONCLUSIONS

Attitudes towards the overwhelming political and economic forces for globalization range, as Thomas Friedman of the *New York Times* noted, from enthusiastic integration to determined isolation, and from a belief that the free market will resolve all resulting tensions to a commitment to comprehensive social, economic and environmental regulation (Figure 2.10). The continuing impulse of markets and technology to integrate the world will require a considered response. Elements of each of the diverse motivations noted by Friedman may be found in the ideologies and practices of companies as well as governments. Representing the integrationists are liberal international organizations such as the IMF, the World Bank, the WTO and OECD, which stress the inevitability of further globalization and the significance of the role of international agencies in fostering understandng and agreement. On the isolation wing Ross Perot and others – particularly US business

Figure 2.9: Responses to Globalization

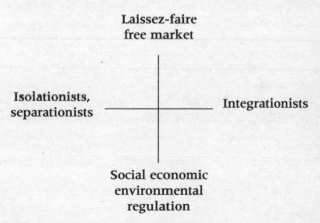

The political response to how open markets and technology are combining to integrate the world

Laissez-faire
free market

Isolationists,
separationists   Integrationists

Social economic
environmental
regulation

people – who yearn for the days of national self-sufficiency and international trade supremacy, are simply failing to recognize that the world has moved on. Among the optimists are those such as Ohmae and *The Economist*, who are seduced by the opportunities of winner-take-all global markets, if only free trade can become a reality.

Finally there are political bodies like the European Union and more enlightened organizations and companies, which acknowledge the irresistible force and many attractions of further internalization, but insist on a considered range of regulations to sustain communities, economies and the environment against the most damaging effects of globalization. This response to globalization seems to be the most acceptable in the face of such dramatic economic and political changes at the turn of the millennium. Taking advantage of the enhanced international opportunities for competition involves improving investment in internal and collaborative research and development, investing in human capital, and creating world-class processes and state-of-the-art products and services. Such opportunities bring new responsibilities, and respect for international social and environmental regulations, and for the integrity of different cultures, is an essential prerequisite in a global corporate citizen.

Chapter 3

DIGITALIZATION

The importance of information as a key resource of business has long been recognized. The development of information and communication technologies has provided the means to process and transmit vast amounts of information; effective information management is now seen as essential if information and knowledge is to be used productively and intelligently by companies. However, the compounding convergence of information and communications is creating a digital world of business activity that is at the forefront of the development of new products and processes.

This phenomenon of digitalization represents a series of profound paradigm shifts for business. Economic activity is no longer fundamentally about transforming materials into goods: increasingly, what is crucial both to the process of transformation and to the finished goods and services themselves is the information and knowledge embodied in them. Intellectual capital is the critical resource of the knowledge economy as organizations, processes and products become more knowledge intensive. In every avenue of industry, from cars to fashion goods, from advertising to medicine, the intelligent use of information and knowledge is transforming processes and adding value to products.

In this chapter we examine how, increasingly, knowledge and information is created and used as binary digits and transported electronically, rather than in physical forms. Hardware, once the central medium of processing, is being replaced by software, and companies that once based their functions and fortunes on their hardware move increasingly into information-based activities. Ultimately digitalization creates new structures of electronically networked business, replacing the individual, market-based relations of the past. The structures of business come to resemble the technologies upon which they are based.

Table 3.1: Paradigm Shifts

Manual/analogue stand alone	Electronic/digital network
Atoms	Bits
Physical	Electronic
Hard copy	Digital
Mainframe	Modular
Hardware	Software
Single function	Multimedia
Stand alone	Networks

FROM ATOMS TO BITS

'The change from atoms to bits is irrevocable and unstoppable.'[1] Negroponte's essay on the transformation of the world of atoms into a world of binary digits powerfully suggests the paradigmatic shifts implicit in the new information and communications technologies. The microchip, computer and telecommunications revolutions involve the creation of new products, services and markets, the transformation of organizational forms and activity, and the restructuring of whole industries: '. . . These are not ordinary technologies in any sense of the word. To appreciate their true significance, these technologies must be seen as generic and fundamental to the way businesses, the economy and our society are structured and organized, and the way they operate'.[2]

The economic implications of information technology are closely connected with the impulses towards globalization. 'The two are intimately linked. By reducing the cost of communications, IT has helped to globalize production and financial markets. In turn, globalization spurs technology by intensifying competition and by speeding up the diffusion of technology through foreign direct investment. Together, globalization and IT crush time and space.'[3] This has contributed to a convergence of industrial activities worldwide, and a fusion of economic systems: 'Products are becoming digital. Markets are becoming electronic'.[4]

University of Glamorgan
Learning Resources Centre - Treforest
Self-Service Receipt

Customer name: MS NINA SADLOWSKY
Customer ID: ******0522501

Title: Changing paradigms : the transformation of
management knowledge for the 21st
ID: 7311895721
Due: 30/05/2007 23:59

Title: knowledge link : how firms compete
through strategic alliances
ID: 7310386718
Due: 30/05/2007 23:59

Total items: 2
Balance: $0.00
23/05/2007 17:29

Thank you for using the Self-Service system
Diolch yn fawr

The new business dimensions attainable are illustrated in Figure 3.1. Suddenly, with information technology, it is possible for the company to reach anyone, anywhere, and for anyone to reach the company. The range of this interaction extends from simple messages to data access, complete transactions or co-operative work. This model has been perfected in airline reservation systems, and by some financial services companies; but in most businesses multiple, incompatible databases distributed among disparate functions and remote departments limit the scope of such a universal facility. However, innovations in business processes and information technology are carrying all information- and transaction-based industries in this direction. The 'Information Superhighway', as it is termed in the United States, or the 'Information Society', as the European Commission describes it, confers 'the ability to access immense quantities of information and entertainment on demand, to interact with and manipulate large quantities of data, to transact remotely and to communicate while on the move'.[5]

The precipitous rise of the information-technology industries have proved a major driver of economic growth, stimulating the innovation of new products and processes in all other branches of industry, promoting structural change throughout the economy, and constantly facilitating the development of new service sectors. The OECD assessed the impact of the information revolution upon the economy in the following terms:

Information technology (IT) is arguably the most pervasive technology of our time. It not only comprises a major, growing branch of economic activity in its own right – a branch which has been a major 'driver' of economic growth in the post-war period – but also generates a flow of product and process innovation in other branches. These encompass both rational izing (productivity enhancing) innovations and growth promoting ones which enable new types of economic activity. Their impact spans manufacturing, services and government (including defence). More broadly, IT enables structural changes to take place in the economy. Rapid growth in IT alters the relative size of industrial branches. Improved computational capabilities allow larger organizational entities to be managed and permit management to span more complex portfolios. Improved communications capabilities permit centralized control of multinational corporations. Thus, IT helps

Figure 3.1: The Business Dimensions of the Information Technology Platform: Reach and Range

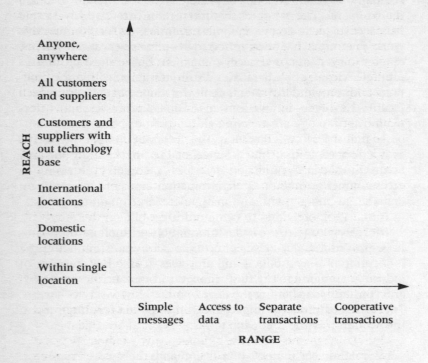

Source: Keen and Knapp, *Every Manager's Guide to Business Processes* (1996)

firms grow larger, more complex and to operate globally – tending to undermine the power of nation states and to increase the need for new forms of international organization on the side of the government. Further, the growing opportunities for information-handling generated by IT permits these to develop into separate industrial sectors. New service sectors thus appear, leading some economic activity (classically the writing of computer software) to be reclassified from 'manufacturing' to services'.[6]

This process is continually accelerating: the power and capacity of integrated circuits doubles every eighteen months, in line with Moore's Law (named after the co-founder of Intel). The tiny laptop is many times more powerful than the $10-million mainframe of the 1970s. In 1970 there were around 50,000 computers in the world: by 1996 it was estimated there were 140 million, and this figure is rocketing upwards. Information technology is different from earlier technologies and will have more profound economic consequences. It is distinguished by its pervasiveness and can be applied in every sector of the economy, but unlike electricity, information technology may transform every function within the company. This provides the basis for a new structure of industry, which Estabrooks defines as *electronic capitalism*, 'a capitalism that is electronic, optical . . . and therefore instant and global as well'.[7]

Among the more remarkable aspects of the new technology is that it allows knowledge to be developed more readily, and stored, accessed and distributed more easily. This simplifies business transactions and allows them to be conducted remotely:

> Perhaps the most important characteristic of IT is that it deals with knowledge. More and more knowledge can now be codified: information, whether in the form of numbers, letters, pictures or voice can be reduced to digital form and stored in computers as a series of zeros and ones. This allows knowledge to be diffused more rapidly and so makes it easier for developing countries to catch up. Codification of knowledge and low transmission costs also make services more tradable by eliminating the need for direct contact between producers and consumers; and it makes production more footloose, allowing firms to base different parts of their business in different countries and connect them by computer networks.[8]

This profound change in the technological infrastructure of business enterprises suggests an equally significant transformation of organization and management. Hierarchical and centralized organizations of functional specialists applying standard procedures to deliver mass-produced goods and services efficiently give way to flatter, more decentralized firms with flexible arrangements by professionals who rely on real-time information to mass-customize products for specific markets or customers (Figure 3.2). Organizations then depend more heavily upon informal commitments and networks, flexible teamwork and a customer orientation to achieve co-ordination. Information technology is central to each stage of this transformation, potentially enabling global co-ordination of

Figure 3.2: Impact of Information Systems on Business Structures

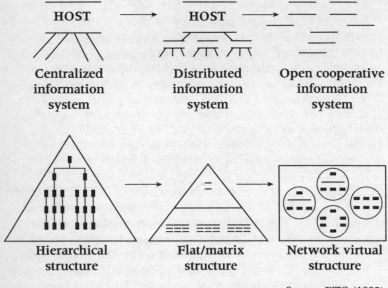

Centralized information system	Distributed information system	Open cooperative information system

Hierarchical structure	Flat/matrix structure	Network virtual structure

Source: EITO (1995)

enterprise networks, distributed processing, portable work and constant access (Table 3.2):

CHANGING TECHNO-ECONOMIC PARADIGMS

Technological change is in one sense an enabling agent: it makes possible new structures, new organizational arrangements, new products and new processes. Innovation has become a major determinant of business success, and a key factor in the raising of living standards and quality of life. Innovation was the subject of much of the early chapters of Adam Smith's *The Wealth of Nations*, but it has emerged again in recent decades as a vital competitive weapon: as technology delivers the possibility of distributed processing power, computer-integrated manufacture or global communication networks, these are immediately put to use in pursuit of further techno-

Table 3.2: Information Technology and Organizational Transformation

Information Technology	Organizational Change
Global networks	International division of labour: the operations of the firm are no longer determined by location; global reach is extended and costs of global co-ordination decline
Enterprise networks	Collaborative work and teamwork: the organization of work can be co-ordinated across divisional boundaries; a customer and product orientation emerges; emphasis upon workgroups with lower management costs
Distributed computing	Empowerment: individuals and work groups have the information, knowledge and responsibility to act; business processes are streamlined; the costs of hierarchy and centralization decline
Portable computing	Virtual organizations: work is no longer tied to particular geographic locations; information can be delivered wherever needed; and work becomes portable
Graphical user interface	Accessibility: everyone in the organization, including senior executives, can personally access information; workflows can be the result of co operative efforts from remote locations

logical advance. Just as 'normal science', in Kuhn's phrase, is 'the actualization of a promise' contained in a scientific paradigm, a tech-nological trajectory is the pattern of normal problem-solving activity or progress on the ground of a technological paradigm.[9]

Most technological change passes unnoticed; it consists of the progressive modification of products and processes. Then there are radical innovations – discontinuous events which may drastically change products or processes. More significant still are changes in technology systems, which not only affect many parts of the economy but may also generate total industries. Freeman suggests that the following five 'generic' technologies have created such new systems:

- Information technology.
- Biotechnology.
- Materials technology.
- Energy technology.
- Space technology.[10]

The fourth category of technological change is what Freeman terms 'changes in the techno-economic paradigm'. These are large-scale revolutionary changes,

> The 'creative gales of destruction' that are at the heart of Schumpeter's long-wave theory. They represent those new technological systems which have such pervasive effects on the economy as a whole that they change the 'style' of production and management throughout the system. The introduction of electric power or steam power or the electronic computer are examples of such deep-going transformations ... Not only does this fourth type of technological change lead to the emergence of a new range of products, services, systems and industries in its own right – it also affects directly or indirectly almost every other branch of the economy ... the changes involved go beyond specific product or process technologies and affect the input cost structure and conditions of production and distribution throughout the system.[11]

Long Waves of Economic Transformation

The notion that global economic growth occurs in a series of long waves is associated with the work of the economist Kondratiev (prefigured earlier in the work of van Geldren, who used the metaphor of spring tides of rapid expansion, followed by ebb tides of relative stagnation and depression, with each complete cycle lasting about half a century). Figure 3.3 is a simplified picture of four

Figure 3.3: Long Waves of Economic Activity and Their Associated Major Technologies

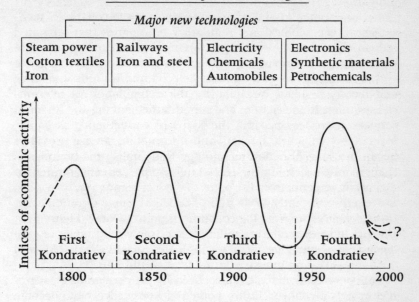

Source: Dicken, *Global Shift* (1992), p. 99

K-waves: each appears to be divided into four phases – prosperity, recession, depression, recovery. Every wave tends to be associated with significant technological changes, around which other innovations – in production, distribution and organization – cluster and ultimately spread through the economy. For such diffusion of technology to stimulate economic growth the appropriate demographic, social, industrial and financial circumstances have to be present.

In explaining the periodic waves of scarcity and abundance different theories have emphasized the importance of innovation and entrepreneurship; the accumulation of capital; and employment and skills.[12] The fifth Kondratiev cycle, which appears to have begun in the 1980s, is associated primarily with the first of the five new generic technologies: information technology. However, it is the convergence of communications and computer technology which is most significant for the development and internationalization of the economy. These innovations impact upon other technology clusters and product innovation from the remaining generic technologies, stimulating the transformation of whole industries.

The phenomenon of convergence involves the collapse of technological, geographical and regulatory boundaries that separated industries in the industrial age, forcing a restructuring of entire economies. In the seventies and eighties the focus of convergence was upon the merger of computers, telecommunications, and office and factory systems, precipitating the deregulation of telecommunications. In the eighties and nineties the banking and financial services sector has become the focus of convergence as banks, insurance companies, retailers and information service providers began to use information technology to demolish the boundaries that separated their industries.[13] Many companies concentrated on digital convergence from the point of view of technology providers: however, in the early 1990s John Sculley of Apple Computer pictured convergence from the consumer's point of view (Figure 3.4). Distinct industries offering different services would move to take advantage of emerging digital technologies such as CD-ROMs and virtual reality, and industry boundaries would blur.[14]

This new economy is characterized by an accelerating pace of technological change: 'Entire bodies of knowledge have become or are becoming outdated and obsolete in shorter and shorter periods of time. Many of the technologies, machines and ideas and even some of the institutions that have served us so well for the greater part of this century are either outmoded or obsolete altogether'.[15] Information technologies are more sophisticated than any previous industrial technology. In order to facilitate economic production processes, mechanical technologies employed physical means – cogs, gears, wheels, pistons. The industrial economy depended on physical motion and enormous amounts of energy and materials to operate. In contrast, the intelligent technologies of today are digital, programmable entities, capable of capturing and processing information and communications in many forms, with universal applications. They operate by the manipulation of electrons and photons, inside materials rather than outside, using a minimum of physical resources and energy.[16]

This qualitative difference of knowledge-based industries means that they are not constrained by scarce physical resources in the way earlier industries have been, and in principle this provides limitless opportunities for innovation and growth. 'The fundamen-

Figure 3.4: John Sculley's Vision for Digital Convergence

Info Industry, 2001: Fusion powered

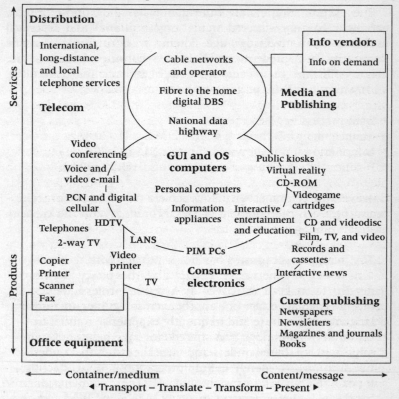

Source: Adapted from a presentation by John Sculley at Harvard University,
Program on Information Resources Policy (1991)

tal economic laws of the evolving virtual economy recognize that the basic factors of production are no longer land, labour, and capital or even energy and matter at a more fundamental level. Ultimately, the only real factors of production and the only real limits to economic growth and prosperity are knowledge, creativity, imagination, and intelligence.'[17]

The Evolution of Information Management

The evolution of the new information-based techno-economic paradigm has encountered many organizational and technical problems, often involving huge expense without any measurable improvement in productivity. Keen has chronicled some of the major difficulties in the management of information technology in organizations through four distinct eras:

- Data processing (DP) (1960s).
- Management information systems (MIS) (1970s).
- Information innovation and support (IIS) (1980s).
- Business integration and restructuring (BIR) (1990s).

However, the central problem for each era was the structural dislocation between the potential of the technology and the capacity of organizations to achieve this.

> The management process has not kept pace with technology – its users and pervasive impact and the policy decisions needed to make it effective. As a result, professionals and business managers face one another across a gulf of unfamiliar language and culture and frequently experience mutual frustration trying to bridge it. A shared language helps, but more important is a shared understanding of the issues that underlie the decisions. To merely define integration and architecture, for example, gives little insight into what these elements mean for the planning process or business managers' contribution to it.[18]

Earl has identified this dislocation with the technical, organizational and philosophical shift from the data-processing approach of the 1960s to the more strategic application of information technology adopted by many companies by the early 1980s (Table 3.3):

Table 3.3: Paradigm Shifts in Information Management

Distinctor	DP Era	IT Era
Financial attitude to IT	A cost	An investment
Business role of IT	Mostly support	Often critical
Applications orientation of IT	Tactical	Strategic
Economic context for IT	Neutral	Welcoming
Social impact IT	Limited	Pervasive
MIS thinking on IT	Traditional	New
Stakeholders concerned with IT	Few	Many
Technologies involved in IT	Computing	Multiple
Management posture to IT	Delegate abrogate	Leadership involvement

Source: Earl, *Management Strategies* (1989), p. 21

The Data Processing Era

In the 1960s large, expensive mainframe computers were installed in commercial organizations that were hardware driven, and required software application programs to be individually written. The automation of large-scale clerical activities proceeded, but applications projects often overran budgets, failed to perform satisfactorily or were abandoned. The legacy of this era includes unwieldy centralized systems and unintegrated peripheral personal computer systems established in resistance.

The Management Information Systems Era

The focus of attention shifted to building reporting systems for management, though useful information was often confused with huge computer printouts. The breakthrough of time-sharing for the first time allowed flexible, *ad hoc* access and processing of multiple tasks. The next stage was a distribution of tasks between personal computers and mainframes or servers with central databanks. This *client–server* sharing of resources is the basis of contemporary information technology. The 1970s saw the arrival of packaged software, which helped to stimulate decision-support systems, and end-user computing. The principal achievement of the management information systems era was the shift from transaction processing to data-base management. In this era greater professionalism developed in the management of IT resources, but just as the control of central resources was achieved, the personal computer revolution of the 1980s took off.

The Information Innovation and Support Era

Resources and processing power became diffused, with PCs, telecommunications and software packages widely available. As prices rapidly fell, extravagant claims about what information technology could do for any business proliferated; many people were disappointed to discover that IT could not replace business vision and capability. By the mid-1980s advances in telecommunications were achieving more dramatic transformations than those in computing, and local area networks, fibre optic cable and satellite technology, combined with the increasing array of devices that carried microprocessors, began to provide powerful resources around which to build businesses. The convergence of computers and communications, and greatly improved connectivity, allowed shared data resources, computer-integrated manufacturing, just-in-time inventory systems, and changed the meaning of customer service. The emphasis of information systems shifted from control to coordination and support services, and, as a result, managers became computer literate.

The Business Integration and Restructuring Era

The great potential of IT to allow different departments and functions to work interdependently was increasingly recognized, and in many organizations this had led to a fragmentation of technologies and approaches around local networks. Incompatibility of software, computers and systems undermined networking capability and provoked a determined search for open systems interconnection. In the 1990s, standards, open systems and integration moved to the top of the IT agenda. The driving force was no longer technology integration but business integration, as companies attempted to co-ordinate all their operations. Tapscott illustrates how

- People become more effective in their work and learning with personal multimedia.
- Teams perform better through clearer processes possible with workgroup computing.

Figure 3.5: Business Transformation Through the New Media

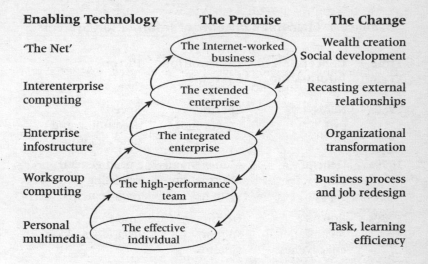

Enabling Technology	The Promise	The Change
'The Net'	The Internet-worked business	Wealth creation Social development
Interenterprise computing	The extended enterprise	Recasting external relationships
Enterprise infostructure	The integrated enterprise	Organizational transformation
Workgroup computing	The high-performance team	Business process and job redesign
Personal multimedia	The effective individual	Task, learning efficiency

Source: New Paradigm Learning Corporation (1996); Tapscott, *The Digital Economy* (1996), p. 75

- The integration and transformation of enterprises proceeds through new information structures.
- The enterprise extends, recasting external relationships through inter-enterprise computing.
- The business becomes inter-networked with greater potential value-generation through network technology (Figure 3.5).[19]

'Business process re-engineering' were briefly the most laboured buzzwords. This movement viewed IT as an enabler of new forms of organization relationships and processes, a means to streamline and eliminate work rather than simply automating it. As organization forms and information technology change rapidly, the IT industry has transformed into an entirely new set of business, products and markets.[20]

The encounter with constantly improving information technology has promoted changing conceptions of the role of information systems, and what was originally regarded as an impenetrable device of limited utility has become the main strategic resource upon which business operations and strategy are founded (Table 3.4):

Table 3.4: Changing Concepts of Information Systems

Time Period	Conception of Information	Information Systems	Purpose
1960s	Necessary evil	Specific programmes	Speed accounting and data analysis
1970s	General purpose support	Management information systems	Speed general reporting requirements
1980s	Enhance organizational effectiveness	Decision support systems	Improve decision-making
1990s	Strategic resource for competitive advantage	Strategic systems	Promote survival and prosperity of organization

INTELLIGENT INFRASTRUCTURE

In developing the uses of information technology, individuals and companies all over the world are pushing microchips, computers, optical fibre, satellite and wireless communication systems, software, multimedia and robotics along an evolutionary course that leads them to converge and coalesce into a single *intelligent technology*, with multifunctional processing, communications and artificial intelligence capabilities:

Viewed from a Schumpetarian perspective, all manufacturers and suppliers of software and service and business users are engaged in a process of creative destruction on a grand scale to engineer, integrate, and synthesize all of these technologies into a kind of infrastructure to mediate the design, development, and production of all products, equipment, and machinery, the trading and exchange of all goods and services, as well as the all-important information-processing, communications and decision-making activities that are so integral to the way organizations, economic systems, and society operate and are structured.[21]

The vertiginous decline in the cost of computer processing power (falling by an average of around 30 per cent per annum in real terms in recent decades) is accompanied by an acceleration in product life-cycles, with 70 per cent of the computer industry's revenues coming from products that did not exist two years ago. The result of this is a constantly escalating commitment on the part of most organizations to investment in information technology. 'Over the past two decades, America's investment in computers has risen by 20–30% a year in real terms. The share of IT in firms' total investment in equipment jumped from 7% in 1970 to 40% in 1996. Add in the billions of dollars that companies spend on software, and spending on IT now exceeds investment in traditional machinery.'[22]

In theory this investment should have increased profitability and boosted growth. In fact productivity gains have slowed markedly in the established industrial economies. Growth in total factor productivity (output per unit of labour and capital combined) has slipped from an average of 3.3 per cent in 1960–73, to 0.8 per cent since then. (In many services it is hard to define the unit of output, and higher output is often in the form of quality improvements.) Economists call this apparent failure of new technology the 'productivity paradox'. Helpfully, *The Economist* suggests: 'Spending a lot of money on IT is not enough; businesses also have to learn how to use it efficiently. When computers first appeared in offices in the 1970s, they were used to automate existing tasks such as typing. It took time for managers to understand that computers not only allowed them to do the same thing differently, but also to do completely different things.'[23] The broad-ranging potential of information technology to make a profound impact upon organizational activity is indicated in Table 3.5. The fact that the implementation of these systems did not always provide the expected organizational benefits provided a great boost to the business-process re-engineering movement in the early 1990s.

Table 3.5: IT Capabilities and Their Organizational Impacts

Capability	Organizational Impact/Benefit
Transactional	IT can transform unstructured processes into routinized transactions
Geographical	IT can transfer information with rapidity and ease across large distances, making processes independent of geography
Automational	IT can replace or reduce human labour in a process
Analytical	IT can bring complex analytical methods to bear on a process
Informational	IT can bring vast amounts of detailed information into a process
Sequential	IT can enable changes in the sequence of tasks in a process, often allowing multiple tasks to be worked on simultaneously
Knowledge management	IT allows the capture and dissemination of knowledge and expertise to improve the process
Tracking	IT allows the detailed tracking of task status, inputs and outputs
Disintermediation	IT can be used to connect two parties within a process that would otherwise communicate through an intermediary (internal or external)

Source: Davenport and Short, 'The New Industrial Engineering' (1990)

Estabrooks insists that the most distinguishing feature of the new economy is the presence of microchips and computers in millions of devices, equipment and household products. (It is sometimes suggested that a well-equipped saloon car of today has more processing power than the *Apollo* spaceship used in the moon landing.) Microcomputers serve as the brains of telephone switches and banking transactions, securities and commodities trading systems, as well as in the optical fibre and satellite and radio communications networks that connect them all together. 'Offices are literally being transformed into a distributed network of multimedia computers and communicating machines that allow people from all over the world to work together and communicate, co-operate, and interact with another. State-of-the-art factories are dominated by intelligent, programmable robots, flexible manufacturing systems, and automated guided vehicles.'[24]

Developing the Infrastructure

In 1946 the first fully electronic digital computer, the Electronic Numerical Integrator and Computer (ENIAC), was invented at the University of Pennsylvania. ENIAC had 19,000 vacuum tubes, weighed thirty tons, and took up 1,500 square feet of floor space. Developments in solid-state physics and semiconductor technology led to the invention of the transistor, then the integrated circuit, followed by the microchip and the microprocessor and, eventually, the microcomputer and personal computer. Innovations in microelectronics – cramming more and more circuitry and functionality into a single chip – overwhelmed the existing computer industry.

In 1971 the first microprocessor, the Intel 4004, was announced, and soon afterwards the microcomputer appeared. According to Estabrooks, 'these were revolutionary developments because for the first time they put individuals as users rather than large corporations in control of the computer revolution'.[25] In 1976 Apple Corporation was formed by Steven Wozniak and Stephen Jobs, and in 1980 IBM devised a new strategy to enable it to keep up with smart, nimble competitors. Instead of developing everything – hardware and software – in-house, IBM purchased microprocessors from Intel and a programming language from a small company, Microsoft Corporation, and it chose to retail through popular suppliers. In 1981 the IBM PC was launched; over 100 million were sold in less than ten years. The PC revolution was also a software revolution, and by the mid-1980s robust integrated software became available, incorporating word processing, spreadsheet, database, graphics and communications software. At this point the computer industry went into overdrive:

IBM's strategy worked well until the mid-1980s when it began to encounter fierce competition from clone makers, and its share of the PC market went into sharp decline. By then the weaknesses of its PC strategy were becoming increasingly evident. By turning to outsiders for its critical hardware and software components – to Intel for its microprocessors, Microsoft for its operating system, and retailers for its distribution – IBM had created an industry that was for all intent and purposes beyond its control.[26]

In 1992 Microsoft and Intel soared on the New York Stock Exchange, while IBM's share of the PC market fell below 16.4 per cent and both IBM and DEC were fighting for their lives. IBM lost 65,000 staff and split into thirteen separate companies. The new race was to develop the next generation of multimedia computers that could handle video and voice as well as data and text. In 1991 IBM, Apple and Motorola announced a joint venture to create the next generation of PowerPC computers, launched in 1994; in 1993 Microsoft announced a new operating system, Windows NT. Oracle, Sun Microsystems and IBM sought to stem the irresistible rise of Microsoft by replacing the PC with the network computer, revitalizing the market for network software (Oracle), servers (Sun) and mainframes (IBM).[27]

A series of major shifts in both the design paradigms of the computer industry and the uses computers were being put to was taking place. Tapscott and Caston define the critical technology shifts on the route to open systems and network computing (Figure 3.6).[28] Baldwin and Clark term the essential design shift a movement from the *mainframe paradigm* to a *modular paradigm*. Modularity is a design principle in which complex systems are broken down into independent modules, linked together through standard interfaces. A product may be modular in production, modular in design, or modular in use:

The benefits of modularity-in-production are scale and scope economies and the reduction in complexity of manufacturing and materials handling systems. The benefits of modularity-in-design are mix-and-match flexibility and efficient innovation, arising from the fact that all parts do not have to be redone to improve one element. The benefits of modularity-

Figure 3.6: Eight Critical Technology Shifts

	Era I	Era II
Network Computing		
Processing	Traditional semiconductor →	Microprocessors
System	Host-based →	Network-based
Open Systems		
Software standards	Vendor-proprietary →	Vendor-neutral
Information forms	Separate data, text, voice, image →	Multimedia
Vendor–customer relationships	Account control →	Multivendor partnerships
Industrial Revolution in Software		
Software development	Craft →	Engineered
User interface	Alphanumeric character set →	Graphical
Applications	Stand-alone →	Integrated

Source: Tapscott and Caston, *Paradigm Shift* (1993), p. 19

in-use are the ability to achieve customized designs and ease of maintenance, reliability, and piecemeal upgradability.[29]

Modularity exists in the mainframe paradigm in which the central processor, memory, printers and terminals that made up the product system were all modular in design and use. Although IBM's hardware systems were highly modular from the 1970s onwards, the mainframe software was not, with proprietary operating systems and compilers that translated high-level languages. Though customers could freely develop their hardware base, the software core locked them into their existing systems. In contrast, companies engaged in the modular paradigm produce systems that use standard software and interfaces, and assemble systems made of components supplied by specialist firms.

Up until this point the way in which computers were used was driven by technology and specific applications, and had little impact on the organization of companies. Computer systems were designed to serve the particular needs of individual departments. But as the personal computer revolution developed, local area networks connected people and integrated their activities, enabling them to share information and resources, and to transform business processes. The connection of local area networks to global communications networks was the next stage in building an intelligent infrastructure, in which the role of telecommunications technologies has become crucial:

The operation and organization of the evolving intelligent economy will depend on where this intelligence resides, what functions and functionalities it performs and how much access and control users, telephone companies and third parties exercise over it.

. . . Local telephone companies, long-distance carriers, and equipment manufacturers have been incorporating as much intelligence as possible into their public networks as a matter of strategy to enable them to extend their control over transmission and switching into the evolving markets for network management and enhanced communication services. The computer and office equipment industries, on the other hand, led by IBM, have designed as much intelligence and network functionality as possible into all their equipment and systems

Figure 3.7: A Client–Server Architecture

Enterprise-wide communications (via: hubs, bridges, routers, leased lines, switched digital facilities, ISDN, frame relay, and cell relay communications)

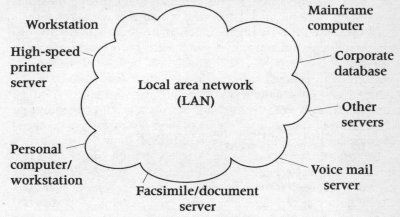

Workstation

Mainframe computer

High-speed printer server

Corporate database

Local area network (LAN)

Other servers

Personal computer/ workstation

Voice mail server

Facsimile/document server

Source: Estabrooks, *Electronic Technology* (1995), p. 147

since the early 1970s to enable them to protect their markets and supply these same new services.[30]

The predominant architecture of computer networking in the 1990s is based on the *client–server* concept of dedicating computers to specialized functions in the network, such as number-crunching, database management and e-mail (Figure 3.7). These servers provide services to individual PCs or workstations, including data and file management, printing and communications. This occurs over a network in which each server does the tasks for which it is best suited; meanwhile users can access easily and directly without knowing where the particular network resource is located. The next stage is to connect the local area networks (LANs) to a wide area network (WAN), where external servers and value-added services may be accessed (Figure 3.8).

The shift to personal computers and powerful workstations in the client–server systems of enterprise networks created greater competitive conditions in the computer industry. As the commodification of the microchip and computer industries proceeded, a

Figure 3.8: Wide Area Network Technology Platform

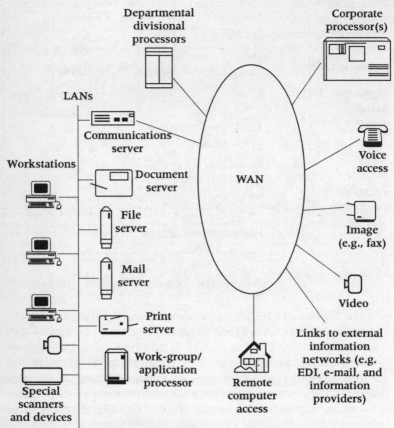

Conceptual technology architecture

Source: Tapscott and Caston, *Paradigm Shift* (1993), p. 253

great shakeup in the computer industry claimed a number of victims among the leading players, including Wang in the United States, ICL in the UK, Groupe Bull in France and Nixdorf in Germany.

Following deregulation, scale economies and developments in technology a new pattern is now emerging: firms in the computer and consumer electronics industries are moving from a vertical

Figure 3.9: The 'Old' Computer Industry

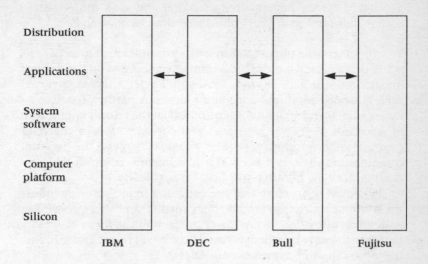

Source: Adapted from Intel documents and *The Economist*; Baldwin and Clark, 'Competition Within a Modular Cluster' (1997), p. 18

orientation, where all components are made in house and sold to customers as a complete package, to a horizontal model, where competition is largely between component firms (Figures 3.9 and 3.10). Andy Grove, the CEO of Intel, argued that the winners in this new model were firms with a dominant market share within a particular horizontal layer (for example Intel). Growing scale economies force companies into horizontal layers where they must work with other complementary firms to deliver a product to the final customer:

> The economics that drive the horizontal structure are compelling: in active-matrix LCD screens, approximately $400 million is required to build just one high-volume, state-of-the-art factory; in microprocessors, it typically takes three years to develop a new generation of chips and then costs roughly $2 billion to build just one high-volume, state-of-the-art plant; and it costs approximately $500 million, and several years, to build a state-of-the-art operating system. Few firms can justify

these types of expenditures if they are serving only a vertical, captive market. Microsoft's Windows 95, for instance, has roughly eleven million lines of codes, and took more than four thousand man years of elapsed time to develop.[31]

Whether the same phenomenon will occur in telecommunications is still being decided, though government insistence on the vertical integration of telecommunications is no longer a factor. In 1995, AT&T divided itself into telecommunications hardware, telecommunications services, and computers. Given the critical importance of standards, common interfaces and co-ordination in the telecommunications industry, problems that still bedevil the personal computer industry, it is likely that the fragmentation of the telecommunications industry will occur more slowly.

The radical restructuring of the computer manufacturing industry continues as hardware becomes smaller and more powerful, with greater functionality at lower prices, and the focus of activity moves to the new knowledge-based frontiers of the software industry. According to Rappaport and Halevi,

> The future belongs to the computerless computer company. Value derives from scarcity. In the computer industry, scarcity now resides in the gap between power – what computers and their underlying semiconductor technologies are capable of doing – and utility – what human imagination and software engineering are capable of enabling computers to do. But virtually all of these (high value-added applications) . . . represent software challenges rather than hardware challenges . . . By the year 2000, the most successful computer companies will . . . leverage fabulously cheap and powerful hardware to create and deliver new applications, pioneer and control new computing paradigms, and assemble distribution and integration expertise that creates enduring influence with customers.[32]

The ascendancy of software companies like Microsoft, Oracle, Novell and Computer Associates (CA), and the decline of big hardware companies like IBM and DEC in the ranks of America's largest industrial corporations is indicative of the growing importance of software to the new economy. Altogether the worldwide information and communications market value exceeded £800

Figure 3.10: The 1995 Computer Industry Fragmented, Horizonal Competition

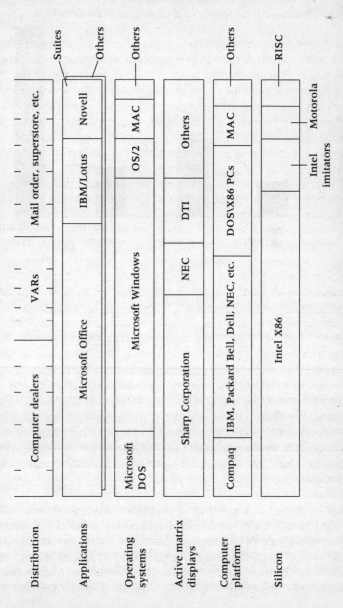

Source: Adapted from Intel documents: *The Economist*, and Department of Defense, *Building US Capabilities in Flat Panel Displays* (October 1994); Baldwin and Clark, 'Competition Within a Modular Cluster' (1997), p. 19

Figure 3.11: Worldwide Growth in ICT Sectors, 1994–6

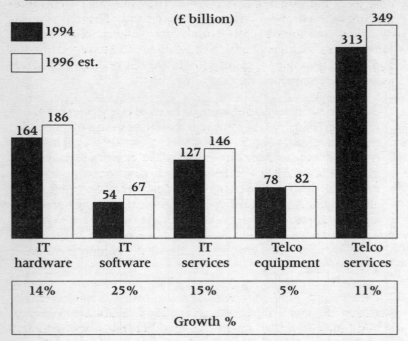

Source: IDC, EITO (1995); Spectrum, *Development of the Information Society* (1996)

billion by 1996, with Japan dominating in the supply of hardware and consumer electronics, and the United States dominating the supply of software and content.[33] By 1996 the combined global sales of information technology software and services together had a higher revenue than hardware, and the growth in the software market was strongest (Figure 3.11). (The software market receives an unanticipated boost from the enormous investment necessary to reprogram computers for the year 2000, which in the US alone is estimated to involve $50 billion of new software.)[34]

Though Apple is known as a hardware company its greatest strength is its software: the Apple operating system and its graphical interface rank among the most important innovations in computing. IBM had to make the most drastic changes in its strategic corporate direction to cope with the transition from mainframe to PC and network-based computing, and other technical changes.

It has downsized, reorganized and reoriented, giving more autonomy to its individual operating units. IBM has put systems integration, software and services at the focal point of its new strategic directions and forged joint ventures and strategic alliances with former rivals, including Lotus, Apple Computer, Motorola, Borland and Novell. Computer manufacturers are reinventing themselves as software companies:

> Software has become the strategic focus of every player in the computer industry . . . Software is a strategic source of much of the added value in hardware products and systems . . . Software is an economic commodity quite unlike any other in terms of its intellectual labour intensity and because once produced, its cost of electronic distribution is almost zero. Software can also be continuously upgraded in sophistication, functionality, and efficiency, semi-independently of the hardware. Software is both a factor of production and an end-product in itself. It represents the new form of capital of the computer-based, intelligent economy.[35]

The inexorable shift from hardware to software is fundamentally changing the character of the information technology industry; in the future it will go on to change other industries, including manufacturing. Knowledge-intensive design companies will contract out production to manufacturing establishments (rather than the other way round, as at present). A model of software-based industries is provided by the niche software companies of the United States such as those in Silicon Valley. In contrast to the large-scale, traditional information technology companies, they are highly focused, depend entirely on technical and creative skills, and search for new applications that in very short-life cycles can generate phenomenal revenues (Table 3.6).

THE KNOWLEDGE ECONOMY

The application of the intelligent infrastructure of information and communication technologies with immense information processing and communications capabilities has transformed the structure and operation of all businesses, and the meaning and concept of organization in the knowledge-intensive economy. J. K.

Table 3.6: Comparison of Investment Dynamics in Hardware and Software

Traditional development characteristics of ICT hardware	Emerging development characteristics of ICT software
• Large amounts of capital • Significant expertise and technological resources to test and develop • Long development time building incrementally on specific technology precepts • Internal development within dominant ICT company • Anticipation of long life-cycle and subsequent benefits • Dependent on patenting for security • Non-standard interface to secure software content royalties	• Low total capital requirements • Dependent on combination of technical and creative skills (often not stimulated by large company environment) • Limited technical resource requirements • Low barriers to entry, therefore many small companies or individuals pursuing the 'killer application' • Unclear end point (i.e. undefined Information Society) • Many potential routes to success (or failure) • Short probable life-cycle • Inability to patent or secure • Highly dependent on venture capital

Source: Spectrum, *Development of the Information Society* (1996)

Galbraith was one of the first to recognize the profound organizational implications of the knowledge economy in his prophetic reference to the arrival of a lumpen technocracy made in *The New Industrial State* in 1967:

> In an economy where the organized intelligence is the decisive factor of production, the selection of the intelligence so organized is of central importance ... In the past, leadership

in business organization was identified with the entrepreneur – the individual who united ownership or control of capital with the capacity for organizing the other factors of production for innovation. With the rise of the modern corporation . . . the guiding intelligence – the brain – of the enterprise . . . [has passed to] a collective and imperfectly defined entity . . . [which includes] senior officials . . . white and blue collar workers . . . [and] embraces all who bring a specialized knowledge, talent, or experience to group decision-making. I propose to call this organization the Technostructure.[36]

A report by the OECD on *The Knowledge Based Economy* (1996) estimates that more than half total GDP in the rich economies is now knowledge-based, including industries such as telecommunications, computers, software, pharmaceuticals, education and television. High-tech industries have almost doubled their share of manufacturing output over the past two decades, to around 25 per cent, and knowledge-intensive services are growing even faster. By one reckoning *knowledge workers* – from brain surgeons to journalists – account for eight out of every ten new jobs. All these knowledge workers tend to be employed in smaller, more focused establishments, and are likely to produce ideas or information rather than things:

Production is increasingly in the form of intangibles, based on the exploitation of ideas rather than material things. The fashionable talk is about the *weightless* economy or dematerialized economy. As production has shifted from steel, heavy copper wire and vacuum tubes to microprocessors, fine fibre-optic cables and transistors, and as services have increased their share of the total, output has become lighter and less visible. In a speech in 1996, the Federal Reserve's Alan Greenspan pointed out that America's output, measured in tonnes, is barely any heavier now than it was 100 years ago, even though real GDP by value has increased twentyfold. And as production becomes lighter, it also gets easier to move. The average weight of a real dollar's worth of American exports is now less than half that in 1970.[37]

The Weightless Economy

It is argued that the shift from material goods to intangibles is the defining feature of the new economy.[38] Not only have services such as finance, communications and the media multiplied in size, but even tangible goods have more and more knowledge embedded in them. According to one estimate, the value of America's stock of intangible investment (R&D, education and training) overtook the value of its physical capital stock during the 1980s. The tangible benefit of these intangibles often remains elusive to statistical measurement and economic analysis:

> Economic theory has a problem with knowledge: it seems to defy the basic economic principle of scarcity. Knowledge is not scarce in the traditional sense – the more you use it and pass it on, the more it proliferates. It is different from traditional goods in that it is, as economists put it, 'infinitely expansible' or 'non-rival' in consumption, meaning that however much it is used, it does not get used up. It can be replicated cheaply and consumed over and over again: if you use a software package, you are not stopping millions of other people using it too. But scarcity has not gone out of the window altogether. What is scarce in the new economy is the ability to understand and use knowledge.[39]

The impact of the knowledge economy is penetrating every aspect of business activity. The convergence of computing and telecommunications capabilities is encouraging the convergence of manufacturing and services.[40] Manufacturing is becoming more like services: customer service is increasingly important, and products are being tailored to the needs of individual customers.

Intelligent Manufacturing Infrastructure

The new manufacturing infrastructure is implanting more intelligent technologies at every stage in the production process. Computer Aided Design (CAD) permits concurrent engineering to speed project development. In 1994 the Boeing 777 was the first jetliner designed entirely using concurrent engineering and paperless design techniques, with contributions from designers all over the world. Similarly Ford and other car manufacturers develop new products with design studios scattered across the globe. Manufacturing Resources Planning (MRP) is the computer-based resource used by companies to manage inventory and streamline and improve the efficiency of operations and customer service. Computer Integrated Manufacturing (CIM) involves master computer schedules integrating an entire plant, including all equipment, inventory and personnel, by means of which all activities can be co-ordinated to ensure that customized goods are produced on schedule in the most efficient way.

MRP II allows managers to view and manage production activities of all divisions of a multidivisional manufacturing plant from a single centralized point, so that they can optimize their operations to achieve maximum profitability, efficiency, timeliness and customer satisfaction. And when the goods leave the plant, telecommunications tracking systems such as Global Positioning Systems (GPS) for ships and trucks allow continuous monitoring of the delivery to customers. In 1990, in search of even greater manufacturing capability, Japan launched a ten-year, $16-billion research programme into intelligent manufacturing systems, and similar research is being conducted in the United States and Europe to develop a twenty-first century manufacturing enterprise strategy.

Seeing the way the wind was blowing, major companies have not remained content to apply the new technologies to the manufacture of their existing product range, but have increasingly diversified into the manufacture of higher technologies and associated software businesses. General Motors has a growing presence in telecommunications, and is one of the leading manufacturers of satellite systems. General Electric has built a strong world position in satellite communications, broadcasting and information and financial services, and also features in aerospace and telecommunications technologies. In addition General Electric's financial services organization is so big that, if it was classified as a bank, it would rank eighth largest in the United States.[41]

The biggest consumer electronic companies in the world are diversifying into the new software and information and communication services economy. They appreciate that the revenues in their business will increasingly fall to the content providers (Figure 3.12). Sony created the Sony Software Corporation, with music, film and electronic publishing interests. Philips own Polygram, one

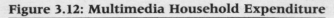

Figure 3.12: Multimedia Household Expenditure

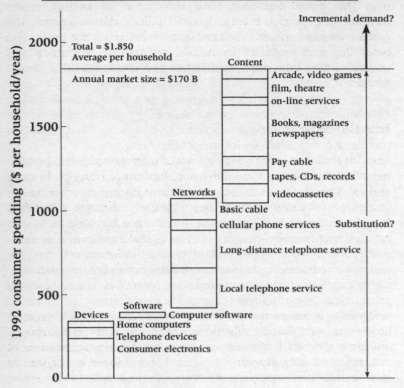

Sources: EIA; Morgan Stanley; Bear Stearns; Mercer Analysis; Collis, Bane and Bradley, 'Industry Structure' (1977), p. 164

of the world's top three producers of recorded music, and Polygram Films, which has acquired one of the largest film libraries.

One of the biggest prizes of all will be the PC-TV, with multimedia information and entertainment software. The core component of the new intelligent economy is the electronic publishing industry. Multimedia has evolved from developments in data processing, word processing and electronic publishing, and now incorporates developments in computer graphics, computer simulation, computer animation, image processing, digital photography, speech synthesis and recognition, computer-generated music and synthesized sounds, teleconferencing, artificial intelligence and virtual reality. In the profusion of new media it is helpful to remember that 'The central and common element of all of the new media technologies ... is the computer, all that it stands for, all that contains it, and all that is contained in it, connected to it, and controlled and mediated by it. The computer is the intelligent engine of all of the new information and communication media devices'.[42]

Intelligent Services

The information and telecommunications revolutions became inextricably linked to the internationalization of trade in services, and to the escalating significance of the service industries: 'Information and communications and banking and financial services may be regarded as constituting the central intelligence of the economy. Sectors responsible for mediating the production, collection, processing, and communication of information, money, securities, and wealth, as well as essential transactions of accounting, payment, and settlement processing which are integral to the operation of the market economy'.[43]

Banking and finance are essentially concerned with information processing and communications, and are very transactions-intensive. For Karl Marx money was the universal medium of exchange, but this medium has now been reduced to a series of electronic digital impulses that travel around the world at the speed of light – a digital market trading digital money. The global banking and financial services industries are based on an intelligent communications infrastructure. Ultimately the automation of global trading systems will lead to the globalization of much of the banking and financial services sector, including the securities industry. Already the leading currency, commodities and securities options and futures exchanges are becoming geared to programmed trading, which contributed to the stock market crash of 1987, though since then some of the programmes have been rewritten to attempt to minimize crises rather than compounding them.

The influence of information and communications technology as the basis of their operation is seen most clearly in companies like Reuters, Knight-Ridder, Dun and Bradstreet, Dow Jones and McGraw Hill, which provide electronic information services. Reuters began life as an international news service and diversified

Figure 3.13: The Converging Information Society

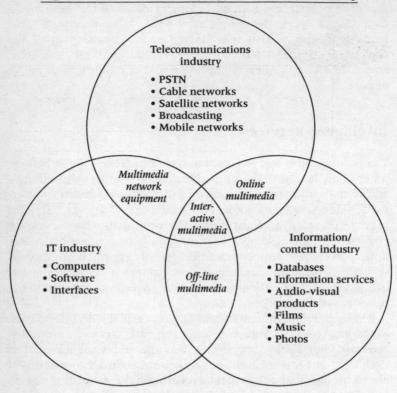

Source: OECD, 'Information Infrastructure Convergence and Pricing' (1996); Devotech, 'Développement d'un environnement multimedia en Europe' (1996)

into international stock market quotations, international business and economic information, and currency, commodity and securities trading services, reaping spectacular profits for its former UK newspaper owners. Similarly some of the biggest retailers are offering information and financial services with smart cards replacing cash.

Companies from diverse industries are attempting to secure as much control as possible over electronic networks in order to govern the supply of content (Figure 3.13). This is driving deregulation and structural change and eroding industrial, institutional and legal boundaries between industries. It has implications for regulatory

Figure 3.14: Evolution of Information Society Infrastructure

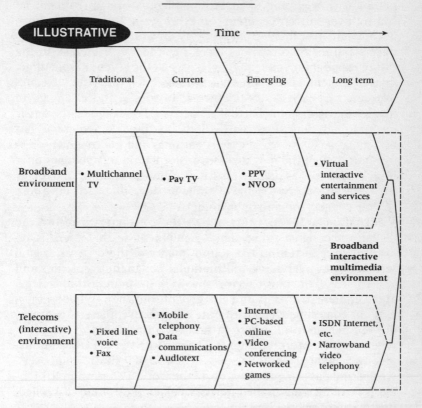

Source: Spectrum, *Development of the Information Society* (1996)

and anti-trust policies in the telecommunications, broadcasting, and banking and securities industries – and therefore for governments. The globalization of media industries is proceeding rapidly, with News Corporation, Bertelsmann, Time Warner and Pearson leading the way. This is part of the breakdown of the traditional barriers separating five of the world's largest industries – computing, communications, consumer electronics, publishing and entertainment, and their transformation into a dynamic whole.[44] A new broadband and telecoms interactive environment is already emerging (Figure 3.14).

The most valuable core of the new information, communication and media industries will be intellectual property. However, digitalization is beginning to make it difficult to retain commercial control over software content, and throws up insistent questions of copyright over intellectual property, in which both original producers and media companies have a considerable interest. In the future copyright revenue may well exceed the revenue from direct sales of content. Lash and Urry have suggested that 'The "irreducible core" of each of the culture industries is the exchange of finance for rights in intellectual property.'[45] For example, the music business has flourished, particularly in the UK, where it has become a major source of export earnings and international prestige, but though the new digital transformation technologies offer huge possibilities as the vectors for distribution multiply and diversify (interactive services, digital audio broadcasting, etc.) they pose serious dangers for copyright holders.

Digital audio broadcasting allows the consumer to record the digital audio signal using digital equipment so that there is no discernible reduction in the sound quality of the original. Digital technology is overtaking international copyright regulation and governance of the music sector, throwing the administrative, legal and corporate structures into a degree of confusion. What is emerging is a contest between corporate and creative interests concerning the definition of copyright and the distribution of copyright revenue (the Performing Rights Society (PRS) in the UK administers 16.5 million works on behalf of 750,000 music composers, writers and publishers from around the world). This example highlights the difficulties in the international administration of intellectual property rights.

The arrival of the new digital technologies presents significant problems to the international copyright-collecting societies concerning the definition of rights: who should administer them, and who should benefit from them? There will clearly be major changes in the organization of copyright-collection societies around the world, reflecting the technological transformation of the media industries. The 1993 GATT negotiations resulted in the TRIPS Agreement (Trade Related Aspects of Intellectual Property Rights), which set out more effective measures and sanctions against piracy. Though almost all countries are signatories of the Berne Convention on copyright, piracy is facilitated by the new technologies, and has become a significant industry in many developing countries.[46]

Network Universe

The internationalization of services, intelligent manufacturing systems and the knowledge-based economy is sustained by constant advances in networking capability that freely allows intra-company and inter-company flows of information and communications, co-ordination and decision-making. Customers, suppliers, markets and competitors are all becoming connected up. The launch of digital satellite services questions the importance of fixed telecommunications infrastructures. Satellite capacities have increased, and satellite systems have become accessible and affordable for companies. The Intelstat VI satellite series, which began operation in 1989, has the capacity for 24,000 voice circuits and three television channels, and the Intelstat VII can carry 90,000 two-way voice circuits. In 1998, BSkyB set up an Astra satellite television service with 200 channels. Cellular telephones have spread like a contagion around the world, and the rapid development of wireless technology, along with the proliferation of laptop computers, promises an era of mobile data communications.

Optical-fibre technology is transforming the world's telephone services, and video-on-demand and other tele-services are waiting for a media-saturated public to catch up (cable TV companies are planning 500-channel television, made possible by digital compression). Negroponte suggests that digital compression research will soon enable one optical fibre capacity to deliver gigabytes per second: 'a fibre the size of a human hair can deliver every issue made of the *Wall Street Journal* in less than a second. Transmitting data at that speed, a fibre can deliver a million channels of television concurrently – roughly 200,000 times faster than copper twisted pair wire'.[47] The broadband infrastructure of the twenty-first century has been laid in national optical-fibre networks in the major industrial countries. Japan, at a projected cost of $250 billion, has an ambitious programme to create a fully national broadband infrastructure by the year 2015. In the United States the High Performance Computing Act (1991) was supplemented by the Communications, Competitiveness and Infrastructure Modernization Act (1991) 'to advance the national interest by promoting and encouraging the more rapid development and deployment of a nation-wide, advanced, interactive, interoperable, broadband telecommunications infrastructure on or before 2015'.

The adoption of the same target year for the installation of broadband nationally by the two leading industrial powers could hardly
be a coincidence.

Doubts are emerging about the necessity of comprehensive
broadband infrastructures; however, all the industrial countries are
aiming to have fully digitalized telecommunications networks by
the year 2000. Meanwhile competitive access providers (CAPs)
are offering high-speed, high-capacity digital transmission services
to companies, and companies can secure private networks on
public telecommunication services. By 1993 asymmetrical digital
subscriber line (ADSL) technology was making it feasible to offer
digital data services and video over the copper wire of existing
telephone companies. Estabrooks makes sense of this confusion of
wires:

> All networks are becoming increasingly interconnected and
> integrated with one another, and competition and co-
> operation are growing on an intramodal and intermodal
> basis ... What is emerging is a network of heterogeneous
> networks that compare and complement one another to sup-
> ply all of the information and communication needs of indi-
> viduals, homes and businesses ... The outcome will have a
> profound effect on the evolution of post-industrial society in
> the 21st century. Convergence and creative destruction are
> accelerating across all segments of the rapidly expanding
> information and communications economy, affecting not only
> the computer, telecommunications, cable television, and
> broadcasting industries but the information, publishing, bank-
> ing, securities, and retail insurance, real estate and entertain-
> ments industries as well.[48]

Intelligent multimedia telecommunications will have a profound
impact on the organization of work, travel, energy and the environment. They will form the basis for more flexible and co-
operative enterprises, while blurring the boundaries between
individual firms and industries. However, in order to capture the
possible synergies, organizations will need to develop extensive
electronic and contractual relationships with networks of suppliers,
customers and partner companies, with a growing variety of linkages along the value chain. Finally it is essential to remember that
the intelligence created in these systems comes from people, as

Tapscott emphasizes: 'It is not simply about the networking of technology but about the networking of humans through technology. It is not an age of smart machines but of humans who through networks can combine their intelligence, knowledge, and creativity for breakthroughs in the creation of wealth and social development. It is not just an age of linking computers but of internetworking human ingenuity'.[49]

The Internet: The Embryonic Network of Networks
The Internet burst upon the computer world with all of the intensity of spontaneous combustion. Apparently overnight, and without any specific significant investment, it has become regarded as a working model of the global networks of the future, with immense commercial and information potential. One estimate of the Internet's achievements suggests:

- The Internet has introduced a sophisticated communications language transmission control protocol/internet protocol (TCP/IP), allowing personal computers from anywhere in the world to communicate with each other seamlessly across networks.
- The technology of the Internet is accessible to anyone with a PC and modem from the office or at home, inexpensively replicating the sophisticated communications of major corporations.
- The Internet houses a multitude of services, communications, access to databases, electronic transaction, marketing and interest groups, training and education. It is multi-functional, allowing the downloading of data, pictures, voice and video.
- The business of the Internet is growing rapidly, creating a strong supply side that will generate substantial revenues. To business, consumers, individuals and government the Internet presents new, inexpensive, communication opportunities.[50]

In March 1997 the OECD held a major conference on *Gateways to the Global Market. Consumers and Electronic Commerce*, in which it was emphasized that an electronic commercial revolution had already begun, based on the Internet and the World Wide Web.

The Internet began as a US Department of Defense experiment to demonstrate the feasibility of interconnecting computing devices. Four computers were interconnected in 1969; by 1984 this had risen to 1,000; in 1995 it had reached 10 million, at which time the Internet encompassed 70,000 computer networks worldwide.

Figure 3.15: Four Stages of Compounding Internet Activity

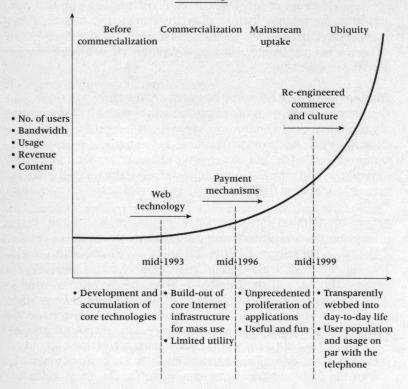

Source: Hambrecht and Quist, 'The Internet', (1995); Spectrum, *Development of the Information Society* (1996)

Users of the Internet exceeded 100 million by 1998. Estimates vary of the continued exponential growth in the number of users of the Internet, because it is developing in such an unpredictable way, but Don Tapscott guesses that 1 billion people will have access to the Net by the new millennium.[51] In the course of its unplanned development the Internet has made some startling technological breakthroughs which will help define communication standards for the twenty-first century (Figure 3.15).

TCP/IP emerged as the standard networking protocol in 1973, allowing every computer to connect regardless of its operating system. This protocol is the basis of all Internet services, including e-mail, Internet relay chat (IRC), file transfer protocol (ftp), and Hypertext Markup Language (HTML), the language of the World Wide Web. The World Wide Web (WWW) arrived in 1989, and Mosaic, the first Web browser, was launched in 1993 by Marc Andreessen, a University of Illinois student. The browser software could be downloaded for free from the university, and by 1994 there were 3 million users. When Mosaic was introduced there were only fifty known Web servers; by the end of 1995 there were 100,000. In one of the most spectacular marketing coups in the history of commerce, Andreessen then launched the Netscape browser as a commercial venture and developed a customer base of 20 million users by the end of 1996.[52]

The Internet is rapidly becoming an everyday substitute for the telephone, and in addition offers many publishing, distribution, transaction and marketing services. It promises to replace static marketing with more interactive relationships between producers and customers. However, the Internet has its problems: it is at present chaotic and poorly maintained, and no match for proprietary networks such as Reuters. Some input is needed if the Internet is to be robust and secure enough to become a fully effective alternative transactional medium. Meanwhile Intranets, private company networks using the TCP/IP standards of the Internet, are becoming widespread. Netscape predicts that Intranet usage will exceed external Internet usage by the year 2000. Intranet technology is attractive because:

- It is independent of hardware platforms.
- It can be integrated into the Internet, allowing access to data outside the company.
- Outsiders can be prevented from gaining access to company information.
- Internal web sites can give easy access to databases and company information.
- Browser software is cheaper than PC-based software.
- Internet usage fees are cheaper than building and maintaining wide area networks.[53]

Scott McNealey of Sun Microsystems estimates that Sun's 13,000 employees send or receive on average about 1.8 million e-mail messages a day, each person receiving a daily average of 135.[54]

Morgan Stanley estimates that in the first fifteen years of its life the PC industry generated revenues of £160 billion in net shareholder value, and believes the Internet industry will create more value: revenues from Internet business are likely to be around £3 billion in 1995, growing at 40 per cent each year to reach £23 billion by the year 2000. The Internet industry is quickly segmenting into the supply of infrastructure and equipment (networks, PCs, TVs); the supply of services and software (Netscape, Microsoft) and the supply of content.

Increasing bandwidth is a critical factor to be resolved if the Internet is to continue to grow: at the moment bandwidth constrains both the number of users and the speed at which content can be accessed. (Users in Europe have learned to do their web-surfing early in the morning before the 70 per cent of total users based in the United States switch on.) As Spectrum Strategy consultants point out, this fundamental problem with the Internet will not be readily resolved:

> Unlike a public telephone network where capacity is most often controlled by a single entity and carefully planned, the *ad hoc* development of the Internet from many connected networks has led to difficulties with bandwidth, network capacity and interconnect . . . There are many points in the Internet that can cause a bottleneck: the speed of the end user's modem, the bandwidth in the local loop, the number of modems at the Internet service provider (ISP), the ISP's connection to the core Internet backbone, the content server's connection to their ISP. Freeing up one point with a faster modem or fatter pipe does not ensure the overall capacity is increased.[55]

Such factors could signal a shift away from the Internet to better-maintained, closed and fully self-controlled networks. This would be sad because despite its chaotic switching, routing, bandwidth allocation and traffic management, there is something spontaneous, democratic and ingeniously creative about the Internet which will be difficult to replicate commercially.

CONCLUSIONS

The digital convergence of network telecommunications, multimedia and software promises for Estabrooks 'the building of a seamless infrastructure to interconnect and integrate the economies of the world'.[56] Though astonishing advances have been made in this direction, it is sobering to realize that according to the UN International Telecommunications Union 80 per cent of the world's population have no access to a telephone, let alone a computer. The race to connect the world up has several decades yet to run. But will this make the world a better, more prosperous place? *The Economist*, which has taken a close interest in the implications for business of the development of the new information and communication technologies, displays a touching faith that this may well bring the dream of perfect competition a little closer:

> Neither IT nor globalization overturns the basic rules of economics. Indeed IT does the opposite, by making economies work rather more as the textbooks say they should. The theory of perfect competition, a basic building block of conventional textbook economics, optimistically assumes abundant information, zero transaction costs and no barriers to entry. Computers and advanced telecommunications help to make these assumptions less far-fetched. IT, and the Internet in particular, makes information on prices, products, and profit opportunities abundant, serving it up faster and reducing its cost. This in turn makes the market more transparent, allowing buyers and sellers to compare prices more easily. At the same time, advances in telecommunications have brought down transaction costs by slashing communications costs between far-flung parts of the globe and by allowing direct contact between buyers and sellers, cutting out the middlemen. IT has also lowered barriers to entry by improving the economics of smaller units. In other words, the basic assumptions of perfect competition are starting to come true. Better information, low transaction costs and lower barriers to entry all add up to a more efficient and competitive market. By helping to ensure that resources are allocated to their most productive uses, this should in the long term boost economic growth.[57]

Of course, IT will make markets faster and more pervasive in their impact, but it takes something of a leap of faith to assume that competition will become fairer, rather than continuing to benefit predominantly those who are better equipped technologically.

Even in the information and communications industries themselves, behind the appearance of greater competition, forces for concentration are often immense. There are indications that Microsoft could potentially become more dominant in critical sectors of technology than IBM ever was, as witnessed in US court cases concerning internet software.[58] Regulation is therefore necessary, firstly to ensure competition survives in the provision of infrastructure and services; secondly to encourage international interoperability between different systems and services; and, most importantly, to extend the principle of universal access (currently mandatory only for telephony and terrestial television) to other essential emerging information services and products.

Similarly the implications of information technology for organizational life in the future are not yet clear. For some the prospects are inspiring:

> The virtual corporation could be the predominant form of organization a generation from now. It will have no pre-established boundaries, and it will be conspicuous by the absence of hierarchy. It will be a completely horizontally structured and geographically distributed organization. The majority of people will likely be working in small cluster groups that are distributed throughout the world in network-intensive, computer mediated, interactive environments.[59]

Many would find this future attractive, if challenging. Lars Groth lucidly presents a less sanguine, and probably more accurate, perception of the human emotional and organizational implications of information technology.[60] A more direct outcome is the continual acceleration in the rate of obsolescence of organizations' and individuals' knowledge base and skills. To effectively counter this there will have to be provision for the continual upgrading of skills and life-long learning. The success and very survival of companies and national economies will depend on how well they respond to the unceasing imperative in an intelligent economy to acquire and expand knowledge through the effective use of information and communication technologies.

Chapter 4

STRATEGY

Fundamental structural changes in a wide range of industries driven by forces of globalization, digitalization, changing customer expectations, and new social and environmental demands have made the business environment more turbulent and unpredictable than ever before. Managers feel the strain of attempting constantly to improve their performance in circumstances that are becoming more competitive – for example, striving to develop quality at a time when product life-cycles are shorter and shorter. The expansive confidence and certainties of the 1960s, when corporate planning enjoyed a wide acceptance, has gone and was replaced in the early 1990s by more immediate concerns about the means of survival. Neither the certainty of strategic planning nor the immediacy of survival management offers business a productive way forward.

In this chapter we examine how different approaches to corporate strategy have attempted to understand the changing and uncertain competitive environment, and the strengths and weaknesses of different strategy models. The main methods of implementing strategies of rationalization, quality improvement, business process re-engineering, and change management are presented. The more promising pursuit of innovation and corporate entrepreneurship is considered. In the search for the new corporate resources of capability and competence there is the potential for reinventing whole industries and releasing the productivity of knowledge.

Table 4.1: Paradigm Shifts

Strategic Planning/ Rational Strategy	Strategic Thinking/ Creative Strategy
Strategic plans	Strategic architecture
Assets	Resources
Certainty	Doubt
Technology/skills	Core competence
Reactive	Proactive
Re-engineering processes	Re-engineering industries
Asset productivity	Knowledge productivity

CREATING OPTIONS FOR THE FUTURE

There was a constrained quality to much of corporate thinking and management practice in the 1990s:

> Humbled by new global competitors, managers were consumed with TQM, re-engineering, downsizing, teamwork and employee empowerment. Managerial preoccupation was with *catching up* with the best of breed among their competitors. Issues of strategy seemed either remote, unimportant or uninteresting to many. The key words were *implementation* and *execution*. Strategy, some managers seemed to assume, was easy; implementation was the hard part.[1]

Management consultancies which had specialized in strategy, such as McKinsey and Boston Consulting Group, were overshadowed by the meteoric growth of re-engineering consultancies such as CSC Index, and responded by refocusing around efficiency- and time-based competition.

In the increasingly competitive environment of the last thirty years corporate boards have frequently been confronted by three rather stark possibilities, according to Hamel and Prahalad.[2] Faced with declining profitability they could abandon R&D budgets and significant investment programmes, restructuring the portfolio and downsizing headcounts in order to improve the return on investment. This is described by Hamel and Prahalad as *denominator* management: it is much easier to cut costs than to find ways of raising

Figure 4.1: The Quest for Competitiveness

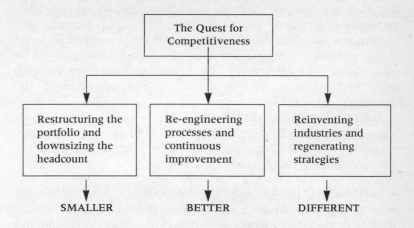

Source: Hamel and Prahalad, *Competing for the Future* (1994), p. 15

revenue. The defence for this approach is that it aims at asset productivity, but Hamel and Prahalad claim it simply amounts to 'selling market share profitably'.[3] Recognizing that restructuring downwards is ultimately a negative strategy, executives have adopted business process re-engineering and continuous improvement to point the company in the direction of customer satisfaction and total quality, and to improve balance sheets.

However, Hamel and Prahalad suggest that the most successful companies are the ones capable of fundamentally reconceiving their objectives, regenerating core strategies and reinventing the industry (Figure 4.1). Companies that have been able to create new options for the future by reinventing their industry are more often found in Japan, the US and Europe; however, there are examples in every industrial country. In the UK companies that have achieved significant transformation include British Airways, ICI/Zeneca, Reuters and Vodaphone. All show in different ways how strategic innovation can succeed. Of course, these are all large companies, and the most profound innovativeness may be found in the expanding small-and-medium-sized company sector.

The turmoil in the field was reflected in considerable academic doubts concerning the viability and validity of strategic planning. Mintzberg questioned the usefulness of the planning process, and the basic approaches to strategic analysis which had been the basis of thinking for thirty years.[4] The emphasis upon learning and evolutionary adaptation seemed to suggest that quicker response times to changing environmental circumstances were more useful than thinking about strategy. With profound questions hanging over the basic tools and concepts of strategic management, the search for new paradigms began.

Is strategic management about reacting or anticipating? Is strategy created or does it emerge? Hamel and Heene pose fundamental questions which remain unresolved by both academics and practitioners in the field of strategic management:

- Is the process of strategy top-down, bottom-up or middle-out?
- Is strategy more about doing or more about thinking?
- Is it *content* that matters in strategy-making, or should the emphasis be put on the *process* by which strategies are created?
- Is strategy prospective or retrospective?
- Is strategy about positioning within an extant industry structure or about redrawing industry boundaries for one's own advantage?
- Is the essence of strategic management the creation of sustainable advantage or the continuous discovery of new sources of advantages as old advantages lose their potency?
- Does the dynamic of strategy derive from the search for *fit* between the firm and its environment or from a *deliberately created misfit* between resources and aspirations?
- Is devolvement and decentralization the key to strategic vitality or does vitality stem from the clarity of strategic direction emanating from the top of the company?
- Are corporate winners the products of Darwinian selection or purposeful action?[5]

These questions are likely to endure, and any attempt to resolve them will offer a richer and more diverse set of strategic paradigms for management thinking. This will be no bad thing, as the simplicity and absolute certainty that buttressed earlier strategic management concepts may have helped to enhance consultancy opportunities, but they probably did less to prepare companies for the future. For example, Whipp identifies the 'predominance of list-building, the rush to prescription and the statements of the obvious found in key strategy texts'.[6] And Kay reflects on thinking in the field of strategy: 'the inability to distinguish sufficiently clearly between taxonomy, deductive logic and empirical observation is responsible for the limited progress which has been made in the development of an organized framework for the study of business behaviour.'[7]

The Changing Competitive Environment

Prahalad and Hamel highlight the forces impacting upon the business environment, changing the economics of industries in unpredictable ways, undermining many of the assumptions of traditional strategy models and therefore necessitating a radical rethinking of strategy and strategic development (Figure 4.2).

Deregulation
Deregulation of airlines, telecommunications, financial services and utilities has had a major impact in the United States and the UK, and the wave of deregulation has extended to other European countries, Japan and large parts of the developing world. This has had serious consequences for the profitability of major companies, the pattern of competition and market opportunities. In turn this impacts on related industries, including logistics and retailing. The pattern of further deregulation and privatization of the primary infrastructural industries seems likely to continue for fiscal, technological, commercial and political reasons, and is transforming the former command economies of Eastern Europe.

Structural Changes
Technology and customer expectations are transforming many industries – for example, the computer and wider information technology industry. IBM, Fujitsu, Hitachi and Bull were all vertically integrated. The new computer industry is more competitive and fragmented. Intel and Motorola dominate in components, Compaq and IBM in hardware; Microsoft dominates in operating systems, and Lotus and many others feature in software applications. In this decentralized, fragmented, competitive environment it is much easier for new firms to emerge and challenge dominant players very quickly.

Figure 4.2: The Inevitability of Industry Transformation

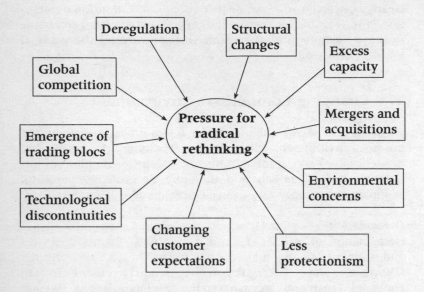

Source: Prahalad and Hamel, *'Strategy as a Field of Study'* (1996), p. 7

Excess Capacity

Problems of excess capacity once hit only mature industries such as bulk and commodity chemical companies. Governments would be drawn into worldwide negotiations to restructure excess capacity, determining the time-frames, cost-benefits, competitive consequences and social impact of such restructuring. However, from the 1980s onwards it became increasingly clear that a wide range of industries, from consumer electronics to automobiles, were beginning to experience severe excess capacity. As industries struggle to come to terms with excess capacity, additional capacity comes on stream, particularly from developing countries such as India and China. Global restructuring of excess capacity is a critical unresolved dilemma to be faced by international trade negotiations and corporate strategy.

Mergers and Acquisitions

Mergers, acquisitions and strategic alliances have rap̶
for market and technological reasons, but also as a ɪ
with excess capacity through rationalization. In tele̶
tions, financial services and the utilities, mergers and a
have been a way of accessing restricted markets. Merger a̶   ̶ui-
sition activity in industries that are highly sensitive to governments
inevitably provokes a series of strategic questions involving anti-
trust, technology integration and product rationalization.

Environmental Concerns

Suddenly the impact upon the environment of industrialization
has become a very real public concern. Demands to reduce emissions, to recycle, to accept stewardship of environmental resources
are all pressing upon an increasing range of industries around the
world. The imperative to be environmentally responsible will have
a growing impact upon all aspects of business, from the conception
and design of products and services to their use and subsequent
disposal by customers.

Less Protectionism

Successive rounds of GATT negotiations are dismantling the formal restrictions on global trade. Countries and regions are still able
to protect their industries with an array of implicit restrictions,
but such attempts at protectionism are becoming less viable. The
national industries that were protected in the past, such as telecommunications, services, power and agriculture, are unprepared for
the challenge of meeting world standards.

Changing Customer Expectations

The emergence of the knowledgeable, discerning and aggressive customer has had a dramatic effect upon business. The demands for high
quality, improved price-performance relationship and immediate
delivery have changed companies' strategies and operations.

Technological Discontinuities

Technological transformation impacts upon existing industries as
well as inspiring new industries. New product and service configurations are constantly occurring – for example, in information
technology cellular phones, distance learning, personal printers,
fax machines, and on-line information services.

mergence of Trading Blocs

The emergence and strengthening of regional trading blocs, including the European Union, NAFTA and ASEAN, will change the basis and pattern of world trade. These regional interests will significantly affect the location of investments, the nature of logistics and the basis of networks.

Global Competition

Global competition is becoming pervasive and affects a wide range of industries, from semiconductors to telecommunications, from management consultancy to office cleaning. Distinctions between domestic and international sectors of business are becoming irrelevant, and the boundaries of opportunity and competition have changed.[8]

Summarizing the environmental transformation of the last twenty years, Michael de Kare-Silver suggests that strategy development has to take into account the following:

- Power has shifted firmly to the customer.
- Scale is not necessarily an advantage.
- Borders and boundaries have collapsed, geographically and industrially.
- Technology is ever more quickly copied.
- There is a constant stream of new, low-cost competitors.
- Information technology has revolutionized what can be accessed and achieved.
- Globalization makes it more difficult for corporate headquarters to manage.[9]

COMPETING PARADIGMS

In strategic management it is possible to discern significant contrasting and competing paradigms and paradigm shifts. The structure of industry is dynamic and diverse, with different sectors at various stages in their evolution and business cycle at any one point in time, which means that these paradigms tend to co-exist in an uneasy tension rather than replacing each other.[10] Hamel and Heene emphasize:

The task of coming to an agreement on what strategy is, or should be, is complicated by the fact that the phenomena under study are changing faster than they can be described . . . Where is the theory that can help companies make wise strategic choices in perpetually undefined industries like financial services and telecommunications? . . . Strategy academics should make no apologies for devoting as much time to the development of new paradigms as to the testing of existing ones. If there is a shortage of anything in the strategy field, it is not of well-tested theory, but of administratively sophisticated, contingency-sensitive and operationally subtle theory. If we have learnt anything about strategic management it is that strategy is about contingencies, trade-offs, paradoxes and uncertainty. Why should we expect to find a grand unified theory of competitiveness? Diversity and variety in paradigms is less a sign of confusion than of the multifaceted phenomena of corporate success and the limited usefulness of any single strategy dictum. The problem comes when strategy choices and perspectives are posed as dichotomies: centralization versus decentralization; competition versus collaboration; emergent strategy versus designed strategy, and so on. What is needed is subtlety, balance and perspective.[11]

Paradigms, it is important to remember in the context of strategic management, are both a means of understanding the world and a basis for informing action. Joyce and Woods are concerned with paradigms which accept that it is possible to plan and act rationally, and that managers can use this ability to improve organizational performance. They suggest three distinct paradigms of strategic management: modernist, postmodernist and new modernist; and consider each paradigm along six dimensions:

- The role of top management.
- The nature of successful change.
- Expectations about others at lower levels.
- Attitude to planning.
- Attitude to chance events.
- Organizational requirements.[12]

Modernist Paradigm

The dominant rationalist paradigm of strategic management of the sixties and seventies was exemplified in the work of Ansoff's *Corporate Strategy* (1968). This approach concentrates on strategy formulation as a process of analysing hard data in order to make a decision about the business the company should be in. It is intended to provide analytical justification for strategic decisions, and depends on techniques of listing, classifying, rating and evaluating. Strategic decisions are assumed to be the prerogative of senior executives, who devise a strategic plan by which the destiny of the company is guided: 'the corporate future is programmable because the future is knowable and organizational change is controllable'.[13] Since planning and implementation are separated the main problem is to secure general commitment to a policy devised by the strategists. It is normally accepted that plans seeking to close the gap between current position and future objectives require refining over time to give more precise results.

Postmodernist Paradigm

This approach promotes diversity and prefers emotional rather than formally rational strategic responses. Peters and Waterman's *In Search of Excellence* is seen as a pioneer of this paradigm, even though their emphasis upon the importance of shared values and experimentation does not accord with postmodernist spontaneity. Peters and Waterman pointed out that old management paradigms were not working, and called for the empowerment of other organizational participants. Some elements of the postmodern approach are found in the work of Mintzberg and Stacey, who reject the positivist dictation of strategy.[14] All top managers can do is create the conditions in which the creativity of others will be exercised and supported. Discovery of strategic direction in periods of chaos occurs through intuition. In this context the capacity to learn quickly becomes the key to survival.

New Modernist Paradigm ~~(complexity)~~

New modernists see managers as proactive and purposeful, but do not accept that they are guided by the rational-analytical systems of strategic planning.[15] Hamel and Prahalad, in their inspired path-breaking *Competing for the Future* (1994), insisted that managers must pursue industry leadership in envisioning the future. In a later work Ansoff himself accepts the impact of turbulent

Table 4.2: Environmental Turbulence, Strategic Intervention and Necessary Response

Scale of Turbulence	Strategic Intervention	Response Necessary
Surprising	Creative	Flexible
Discontinuous	Entrepreneurial	Strategic
Changing	Anticipatory	Marketing
Expanding	Reactive	Production
Repetitive	Stable	Custodial

Source: Derived from Ansoff and McDonnell,
Implanting Strategic Management (1990)

environments and discontinuities which make organizational responses more difficult (Table 4.2).[16] The new modernist paradigm works *with* a situation to craft an emerging strategy, rather than programming a strategy like the modernists, or discovering one, as in postmodernist approaches. Managers must nurture and develop strategies, and successful change involves learning from experimentation. Quinn accepts incrementalism as a purposeful technique of strategy formulation,[17] and Mintzberg suggests that organizational members can be included in the sense of commitment.[18] Hamel and Prahalad emphasize the resource significance of capabilities or competencies needed to become industry leaders (Table 4.3).[19]

In a robust defence of a rational, new-modernist strategic management Gaddis resists attacks from four directions. Firstly, the development of the science of complexity and chaos theory which has cast doubt on the certainty that any corporate system can be guided towards a preconceived future. Secondly, the constraints of cultural heritage, which may encourage passivity. Thirdly, resurgent incrementalism and emergent strategy, as identified with Mintzberg. Finally, persisting short-termism that undermines strategic thought. Gaddis contrasts 'proactive purposefulness' with 'reactive powerlessness'; a kinder comparison might be with 'creative responsiveness' (Figure 4.3).

Table 4.3: Three Paradigms of Strategic Management

Dimensions	Modernist	Postmodernist	New Modernist
Top management role	Decision-making élite	Back successful initiatives by lower level managers	Responsible for intellectual leadership
Successful change	Programmable	Discoverable	Based on foresight and experiment
Expectations about those at lower levels	To be committed to proposals and to implement strategic plan	To show diversity, difference and spontaneity (empowerment)	To have their own agendas – but agendas which can be included
Attitude to planning	Planning is a core activity	Proactive planning is impossible	Planning is emergent
Attitude to chance events	Need to plan for flexibility	Require chaotic action in response	Chance events can be opportunities
Organizational requirements	Operational management to be shaped by strategy	Anti-hierarchy culture – support for informality	Organizational readiness – commitment and competence – which have to be developed

Source: Joyce and Woods, *Essential Strategic Management* (1996), p. 49

Strengths and Weaknesses of Existing Strategy Models

One survey of senior executives' views on strategy tools and frameworks discovered that 68 per cent found them too theoretical, superficial and confusing; 38 per cent found them inapplicable to their business situation; and over 25 per cent said they were not helpful in today's competitive environment. A majority agreed a new strategy model was required, and that such a framework must be customer and market driven rather than driven by a company's

Figure 4.3: A Comparative Time Line: Proactive Purposefulness Versus Creative Responsiveness

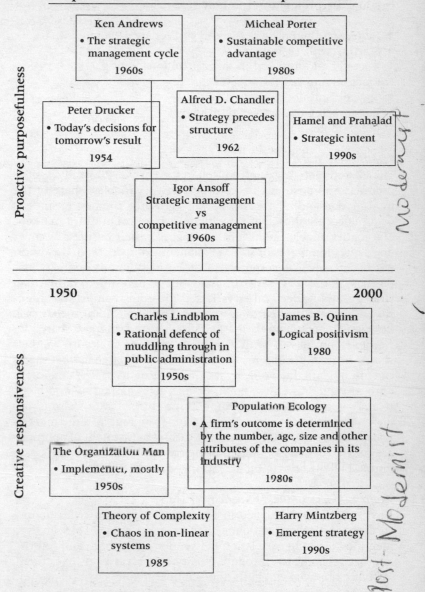

Source: Adapted from Gaddis, 'Strategy Under Attack' (1997), p. 41

own strengths.[20] Michael de Kare-Silver, responding to this, assessed the strengths and weaknesses of some of the major strategy tools according to seven criteria:

- Reflecting the business realities of the late 1990s.
- Starting with customers.
- Rooted and immersed in market understanding.
- Practical and not too theoretical.
- Specific and not too superficial.
- Encouraging of a longer-term view.
- Measurable.[21]

The Boston Matrix

The Boston Matrix was introduced in the early 1970s, and classifies products and businesses according to two variables: share of the total market and rate of the market's growth. The best businesses or products are those with the highest shares of buoyant markets. The matrix enables managers to categorize their business as cows, dogs, question marks or stars, to facilitate comparison of the different businesses in a corporate portfolio or different products in a business portfolio. Clearly this is a guide to investment rather than strategy, and neglects other variables, including competitive intensity, advantage and customer needs. The implication is that cash flow will depend upon market growth and market share: for example, businesses with dominant shares of mature markets should be cash-generating. Yet businesses with large market shares can often retain them only by major investments in R&D, maintenance of capital-intensive plant, or energetic marketing and being treated as cash cows would undermine this. Market share is also difficult to define as some products are dominant in some markets and weak in others, thus requiring careful adjustment of appropriate courses of action in different markets. Finally, the matrix says nothing about how to build a stronger market position.

Profit Impact of Market Strategy (PIMS)

PIMS was also developed in the early 1970s, and relies upon a substantial database of financial and market data. PIMS analysis identified a strong correlation between market share and returns, and between relative product quality and return on investment. With the renewed emphasis upon competitiveness market position was seen as a central element in strategic decision-making; quality was recognized as a key ingredient in Japanese success, and most markets moved up the quality spectrum. PIMS highlighted the relative competitiveness of products and services, laying the groundwork for Michael Porter's conception of competitive advantage. However, the original framework for the PIMS analysis became dated, and changing market conditions question some of the basic assumptions of the framework. For example, the assumption of a profit impact of market share rests upon the belief in economies of scale, although there are increasing numbers of companies which have lower market shares but higher profitability, like low-cost Asian producers. More specific guidance concerning sources of competitive advantage is necessary, and PIMS provides only an incremental approach to the predetermined drivers in existing markets.

Michael Porter's Five Forces and Three Generic Strategies
Though it was developed in the early 1980s Porter's framework remains the most popular tool of strategic management. The five forces model of buyers, suppliers, industry competitors, potential entrants and substitutes is still useful to companies attempting to assess the dynamics and trends of their industry (Figure 4.4). The three generic strategies of lowest cost, differentiation and focus illuminated meaningful strategy options. Finally, Porter expanded understanding of the value chain, encouraging inspection of where in the chain a company can add value better than rivals.

However, Porter now accepts that cost is no longer the factor it once was, since scale cannot guarantee lowest cost, and prices are often manipulated to secure competitive advantage regardless of cost. Moreover, he has begun to blur the distinction between focus and differentiation, focus being differentiation in one market segment. Porter's research was completed before the onset of the consumer revolution, and could stress the assets of manufacturers rather than the demands of customers in determining generic strategy.

Core Competencies
Prahalad and Hamel's concept of core competency launched a new wave of strategic thinking about learning in the organization, co-ordinating diverse skills and integrating multiple streams of technology, thus building on the collective strengths of the company. Developing core competencies opens avenues of opportunity for companies encouraged to play to their strengths. This concept

Figure 4.4: Porter's Five Forces Model of
Competitive Markets

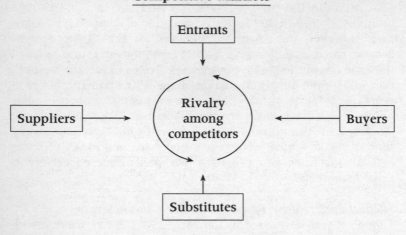

Source: Based on Porter, *Competition in Global Industries* (1986)

helped to break down boundaries within organizations, translating combined competencies into product leadership. It contrasts considerably with the view of the company as a portfolio of independent businesses representing a set of financial assets (Figure 4.5). Core competencies are seen as the *real* resources of the firm; the problem is how they can be leveraged in multibusiness companies. 'The real sources of advantage are to be found in management's ability to consolidate corporate wide technologies and production skills into competencies that empower individual businesses to adapt quickly to changing opportunities.'[22]

Though inspirational, the framework merely cites examples of companies that have successfully discovered their core competencies; it does not suggest how an organization's core competencies can be defined (Table 4.4).

Without a greater emphasis on what customers want, rather than the capability of the company, it is possible that a focus on core competencies can lead to a neglect of other essential skills. For example, Goold, Campbell and Alexander cite Texas Instruments, which had an effective competence in semiconductor technology but failed in the consumer electronics business because it did not know enough about the market segments it was entering.[23]

Figure 4.5: Competence-based Strategy

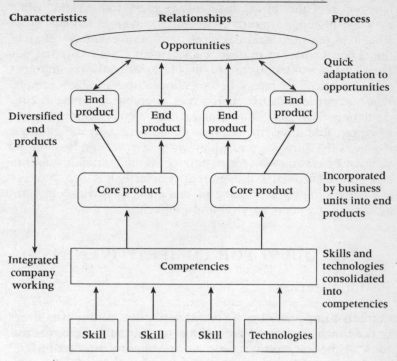

Source: Joyce and Woods, *Essential Strategic Management* (1996), p. 163

Table 4.4: Examples of Core Competence

Company	Core Competence
Canon	Optics, imaging, microprocessor controls
Citicorp	Operating systems
Honda	Engines
3M	Substrates, coatings, adhesives
NEC	Digital technology
Sony	Miniaturization

Source: Adapted from Prahalad and Hamel, 'The Core Competence of
the Corporation' (1990)

Metastrategy?

It is apparent that all strategic management frameworks, while they may illuminate in certain circumstances, are potentially problematic in practice. Makridakis refers to the weaknesses of all of the major theories of strategic management (Table 4.5). There is some evidence of serious corporate failures when the commitment to one particular strategy becomes too absorbing: for example, Hanson's portfolio matrix approach as it became an unwieldy conglomerate. Even companies that have apparently achieved excellence can find it a very transient phenomenon, as did all but a couple of the thirty-six companies declared to be 'excellent' in the study by Peters and Waterman: 'Strategy is not monolithic nor can it be reduced to a series of steps, recipes or analytical tools. Strategy is a frame of mind, a thinking process concerned with long-term adaptation, therefore survival and well being'.[24]

THE QUEST FOR COMPETITIVENESS

Rationalization

Continual rationalization by what were once leading companies in the United States and Europe was one of the most dismal features of the last twenty years: downsizing, overhead reduction, portfolio rationalization and defensive restructuring. The strategy was to regain efficiency and corporate strength in order to rejoin the competitive struggle with new, dynamic companies from Japan and other parts of the world. Hamel and Prahalad are understandably vituperative on this corporate vandalism masquerading as management science:

> As important as these initiatives are, their accomplishment cannot restore a company to industrial leadership, nor ensure that it intercepts the future. When a competitiveness problem (stagnant growth, declining margin, and falling market share) finally becomes inescapable, most executives pick up the knife and begin the brutal work of restructuring. The goal is to carve away layers of corporate fat, jettison underperforming businesses, and raise asset productivity. Executives who don't have the stomach for emergency room surgery, like John Akers at IBM or Robert Stempel at GM, soon find themselves

Table 4.5: Major Theories (Approaches on Strategy)

Strategic theory	Brief description	Problems or unrealistic assumptions
Decentralization	Decision-making is placed in the hands of functional managers	Without effective co-ordination, decision-making can become ineffective
Diversification	To maintain high growth, companies must diversify into promising industries or new markets	Difficulty in accurately forecasting promising industries/ markets
Conglomerates	Acquiring dissimilar businesses under a single corporation	By definition the most conglomerates can achieve is average returns
Long-range planning	Extrapolate long-term trends in sales, demand etc. and plan capital investments and other expansions accordingly	The established growth in sales, demand etc. cannot be guaranteed in the future
Strategic planning	Go beyond long-range planning by avoiding the disadvantages of extrapolation when trends change	Strategic planning is not possible without reliable predictions about the future
Portfolio matrix	Products or business units are classified as dogs, cows, question marks and stars. The objective is to get rid of dogs and to promote stars, financing them with cash generated from cows	It assumes futures stars can be identified, it ignores synergies, it can drop profitable products, it disregards competitive action and learning

Table 4.5: (continued)

Strategic theory	Brief description	Problems or unrealistic assumptions
Experience curves	As production doubles, nondirect costs decrease by a constant percentage	It might work for mass production, but bureaucracy can wipe out economies of scale
PIMS	An empirical database containing company-supplied information whose purpose is to discover the relationship between profitability and other factors	Too many methodological problems and tautologies to make the result reliable and useful
Centralized corporate strategy	Strategy must be formulated at the top, where the whole picture of corporate goals and long-term visions is available	Individual managers have little or no say in determining the strategy for their units/departments
Searching for excellence	Through empirical research, identify the factors common to excellent companies and use them to become excellent too	Past excellence cannot be used to achieve excellence in the future
Restructuring	Getting rid of unprofitable businesses or those that do not fit the corporate identity	The challenge is to know which businesses to get rid of

Table 4.5: (continued)

Strategic theory	Brief description	Problems or unrealistic assumptions
Competitive strategies	Analyse the competitive situation in your industry and learn to read competitive signals	The challenge is to predict future competition, not analyse that of the past or present
Strategic alliances	Form alliances (if necessary even with your arch-rival(s)) to improve your competitive position	Long-term effects can be detrimental, as they provide a false sense of security
Global rationalization	The market place is the world. Thus, production, marketing, finance and R&D decisions must be made with such a view in mind	How do you know future conditions? A change in exchange rates, for instance, can make all plans useless
Core competences	Special skills or technologies which provide lasting competitive advantages to firms	Core competences can change and be a disadvantage to firms that do not recognize the change
Delayering/ restructuring	Reduce the layers of middle management and fire workers/ employees through improvements	Losing valuable people whose experience, knowledge and skills may be needed, either now and/or in the future
Horizontal organizations	Flat, non-hierarchical organizations where information is shared to facilitate functional co-ordination	No problem as long as appropriate computer networks, open-minded management and educated workforce exist

Table 4.5: (continued)

Strategic theory	Brief description	Problems or unrealistic assumptions
Competing for the future	By identifying forthcoming opportunities (while also avoiding emerging threats) a firm can create new markets and expand its activities beyond traditional products/ services	Pioneers are often not successful (e.g. Microsoft vs. Apple or Lotus, or lately Netscape)

Source: Makridakis, 'Metastrategy' (1997), p. 130

out of a job. Masquerading under names like refocusing, delayering, decluttering, and right-sizing (one is tempted to ask why the 'right' size is always smaller), restructuring always has the same result: fewer employees ... 'Make this company lean and mean'; 'make the assets sweat'; 'get back to basics'. Return on capital employed, shareholder value, and revenue per employee become the primary arbiters of top management performance. Although perhaps inescapable and in many cases commendable, the resulting restructuring has destroyed lives, homes, and communities – to what end? For efficiency and productivity. Although arguing with these objectives is impossible, their single-minded – and sometimes simple-minded – pursuit has often done as much harm as good.[25]

Rationalization was pursued most vigorously by managers in the United States and Britain: 'they can downsize, declutter, delayer, and divest better than any managers in the world',[26] but the result was higher asset productivity, smaller companies, smaller market share and less prospects for the future. One analysis by Mitchell and Co., interestingly revealed that the value of shares in companies that had downsized was 26 per cent lower than the share value of similar organizations that had not.[27]

Achieving Change

Companies led by more far-sighted managers attempted to engage in more positive and productive approaches to change. Managing change is about effectively pursuing some improvement in the company. The change may be to the company structure, operation or performance:

> No company can escape the need to reskill its people, reshape its product portfolio, redesign its processes, and redirect resources. Organizational transformation is an imperative for every enterprise. The real issue is whether transformation happens belatedly – in a crisis atmosphere – or with foresight – in a calm and considered atmosphere, whether the transformation agenda is set by more prescient competitors or derives from one's own point of view about the future; whether transformation is spasmodic and brutal or continuous and peaceful.[28]

Hence two broad types of change can be recognized:

Proactive change: Involves attempting to anticipate the future, by forecasting what is likely to occur, and drawing up strategic plans, timetables and targets to meet the anticipated changes. Being proactive provides the opportunity to get things right before the competition, but it is hazardous.

Reactive change: Involves responding as efficiently as possible to change in the business environment that has already occurred. It is easier to work out what the company should do in these circumstances, but there is less time to do it properly as other companies may have got there first.

The Art of Anticipation

All companies are engaged in process of planned change and reactive change simultaneously, and it is a case of achieving the right balance. Many commentators have argued that organizations spend too much time in reactive change, and do not make enough effort to plan change programmes to cope with future contingencies, anticipating shifts in products and markets, and creating capabilities to provide options. Peters and Waterman's *In Search of Excellence* and Rosabeth Moss Kanter's *The Change Masters* emphasized that to minimize the disruption of reactive change organizations should be more proactive and creative in their response to uncertainty.

The Management of Change

The real difficulty in implementing change strategies as opposed to conceiving of them has led to a voluminous literature on how to manage change.[29] The well-known barriers to change include, at the organizational level, an excessive focus on costs and a failure to see the potential benefits; a heightened perception of the risks involved; lack of co-ordination and co-operation in the change process; and attempting to integrate incompatible systems. Personal obstacles to change include the overwhelming desire to reduce uncertainty, and the fear of loss of skill, position or profession (Table 4.6).

Table 4.6: Common Barriers to Best Practice Implementation

Internal focus	Organizations either fail to find or reject ideas and information from the outside: 'Not Invented Here' syndrome.
Lack of credibility	Information sources, recommendations, and reports are perceived as political or biased and not taken seriously. Decisions are viewed by those in the organization as political and biased.
Secrecy	A needs-to-know culture prevents people from developing a general perspective on important decisions and denies access to information required for specific situations.
Lack of proper skills	The people involved in the best practice implementation are assigned with little regard

to training or skill. There is little training or support from experienced people.

Lack of resources	Attempts to implement best practices are made without providing adequate resources. People are asked to do things 'in their spare time'.
Lack of discipline	Management will not kill projects; the process to choose among projects is inconsistently applied; there are many 'special cases'. In this last instance, many decisions are made outside the normal decision process.
Lack of strategy	Corporate strategies are vague vision statements or over-specified long-term plans. Neither provides much guidance. The result: conflicting priorities, and general confusion.
Metrics are misused	Predictions are turned into commitments. Uncertainties are represented by misleadingly precise forecasts. Historical measures are used for punishment rather than learning.
Tendency to oversimplify	We face increasingly complex situations and systems and less time for really understanding them and developing perspective. Faced with too much data and not enough information, people tend to oversimplify to deal with overload.
People are reluctant to change	The new practices upset the *status quo*; people move to protect their positions and interests Making a change leads those who built the current system to feel that they did a poor job.
Power and politics	Loud advocates, fear of accountability, resistance to relinquishing control, fear of being seen as disloyal, and lack of trust all conspire against best practice implementation.

Source: Matheson and Matheson, *The Smart Organization* (1998), p. 89.

There are many approaches and techniques of change management aimed at eliminating these obstacles, including careful, collective diagnosis of the need for change; enlisting senior management support in the change process; employing focus groups to explore the implications of change; fully investigating the viable options; finding ideas that fit; incremental rather than shock implementation; ensuring alignment with the needs and goals of users; and throughout placing a premium on communication, education, training, participation and involvement.

Gareth Morgan offers some sage advice on the skills necessary for those contemplating change management:

- An ability to manage tensions between present and future, so that one can position for the future while avoiding collapse in existing operations. This ability is particularly important in achieving major strategic transformations, and requires the development of managerial attitudes and structures that aid rather than hinder transition.
- An ability to develop 'change experiments' that can test the feasibility of different lines of development and thus create a range of opportunities for large-scale change through an incremental 'trial-and-success' approach that does not place the entire organization at risk.
- An ability to achieve 'good timing' in relation to the introduction of new technologies and entry into new markets, because in times of rapid change timing often spells the difference between success and failure.[30]

Total Quality Management (TQM)

The success of Japanese companies in winning significant market share in major product sectors had a more positive stimulus upon Western management: it rekindled an interest in the importance of quality. The quality movement has represented the most consistent effort to achieve organizational change and improvement in a continual, systematic, patient and consistent manner. This movement reached its height with the widespread adoption of Total Quality Management. TQM is an organization-wide effort to improve quality through changes in structure, practices, systems and attitudes.[31] Over the last twenty years Japanese companies have shown a remarkable commitment to attaining the highest possible quality in important product areas such as consumer electronics and cars, and it is often assumed that TQM was a Japanese innovation. However, it was originally developed in the USA in the 1950s and 1960s.[32] TQM is a potent force for organizational change but, as with other change management approaches, effective implementation is the hard part.[33]

A recent research project on excellence in quality management, conducted by a group of German McKinsey Company consultants, examined 167 companies in the worldwide automotive supply industry, where quality is measured very strictly and objectively by the direct customer. The study covered trends from 1987 to 1991, with forecasts up to 1997, and dealt with business units and individual operating companies.[34] In order to establish world-class benchmarks of overall quality the study looked at two components:

Design quality: The quality of design is a company's ability to develop products that meet the demands of the customer as closely as possible.

Process quality: Process quality is a company's ability to manufacture and deliver a product to the specifications agreed with the customer, with the lowest number of defective parts per million (ppm).

In the analysis of their data they were able to do distinguish high-quality companies with around 72 ppm defects; quality companies with 302 ppm; average companies with 890 ppm; and lower-quality companies with 4,820 ppm. They investigated the different qualities of management in these four categories of company and discovered an ascending ladder of performance, with each level of quality associated with a more intensive approach (Figure 4.6):

Level I – inspection: Companies at this level achieve quality primarily by interim and final inspection followed by the elimination of defects. The quality function works separately from other functions and is almost solely responsible for quality. These companies' products are prone to significant levels of defects: their ppm is 4,800, their reject rate is over 5 per cent, and their rework rate is over 3 per cent.

Level II – quality assurance: The quality objectives are mainly focused on production, which is also the function driving the

Figure 4.6: Four Levels of Quality

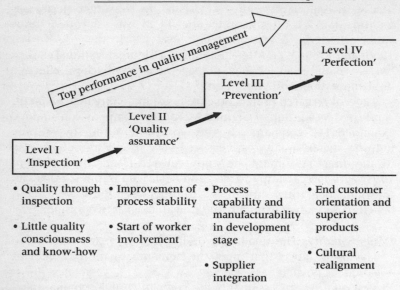

* Quality through inspection
* Little quality consciousness and know-how

* Improvement of process stability
* Start of worker involvement

* Process capability and manufacturability in development stage
* Supplier integration

* End customer orientation and superior products
* Cultural realignment

Source: Rommel et al., *Quality Pays* (1996), p. 5

optimization and stabilization of the processes. The ppm is about 900, and reject and rework rates about 3.1 per cent and 2.7 per cent respectively.

Level III – prevention: At this third level product design interacts with product processes ('robust design'), and for the first time a clear customer orientation emerges in the product features. The proportion of competitively superior products rises to 25 per cent, the ppm falls to 302, and reject and rework rates are 1.5 per cent and 1.7 per cent respectively.

Level IV – perfection: The ultimate quality company has internalized a culture that generates quality in all areas. Every employee is aware of the importance of quality for the success of the company, and searches for opportunities to improve products, striving for perfection and zero-defects. A prerequisite for this is a good relationship with internal customers and suppliers. The consistent orientation towards external customers helps employees to recognize added value and translate it into practice through superior product design. Over 35 per cent of their products are superior to other producers, their ppm rate is less than 100, and reject and rework rates are less than 0.8 per cent.

Of course, the automotive parts industry is one unusually suited for such quality techniques and measurement, but companies in many other sectors of industry are pursuing 'perfection' in the products and services they offer, and making appropriate organizational and cultural changes to encourage a commitment to total quality. This *kaizen* or continuous improvement was not fast enough for many companies impatient for quicker and more radical solutions to their business problems; for them business process re-engineering promised more dramatic performance improvement.

Business Process Re-engineering (BPR)

BPR became the management vogue of the early 1990s, in the way quality had been in the 1980s, and strategy in the 1970s. The concept of business process re-engineering was introduced by Michael Hammer in a provocative article, 'Re-engineering Work – Don't Automate, Obliterate', published in the *Harvard Business Review* (July–August 1990) and followed by the book by Hammer and Champy, *Re-engineering the Corporation: A Manifesto for Business Revolution* (1993). The cover of the book carried the bold injunction from Peter Drucker: 'Re-engineering is new, and it has to be done'. What then has to be done? 'Re-engineering is the fundamental rethink and radical redesign of business processes to achieve dramatic improvements in critical, contemporary measures of performance such as cost, quality, service and speed.'[35] This emphasis upon asking fundamental questions such as '*Why* do we do what we do? And why do we do it the way we do it?' distinguished BPR from more gradual and continuous modes of improvement (Table 4.7).

Hammer and Champy insist that companies should concentrate on processes rather than functions as the central focus for the design and management of business activity. A *process* is considered to be 'a collection of activities that takes one or more kinds of input and creates an output that is of value to the customer'.[36] Examples of business processes include:

Table 4.7: The Transformational Scope of Business Process Redesign

	Continuous process improvement	Business process redesign
Change	Incremental	Quantum leap
Focus	Current practice	Start again
Frequency	Continuous	One shot
Scope	Narrow within function	Broad, cross-functional
Participation	Bottom-up	Top-down
Risk and rewards	Low to moderate	High
Type of change	Work design	Structure, culture roles
Role of IT	Incidental	Key enabler
Aids	Ideas and suggestions	Methods and tools

Source: Earl, *The New and Old of Business Process Design* (1994), p. 11

- Developing a new product.
- Refining some materials.
- Issuing an insurance policy.
- Fulfilling a customer order.

In contrast to business processes, business *functions* are the task- or skill-based departments into which most work activities, such as manufacturing, finance, sales and distribution, are presently organized.

Horizontal Processes and Vertical Authority Structures

The *customer* is interested in the end-to-end process which produces the good or service (the horizontal process linkages). The *organization* itself is often focused inwardly and on the vertical chains of command through which it manages departments. Since work inevitably flows across departmental divides, each hand-off to the next department is potentially a source of delay. If there is a lack of trust or limited training, people will not be allowed or not be able to move work forward, and will be forced to wait for inspection or authorization. Therefore a key challenge of re-engineering is *empowerment*:

- Giving staff the training to perform a variety of roles within a process, therefore improving flexibility and continuity.
- Extending areas of responsibility for decision-making on behalf of the organization without seeking managerial approval.
- Investing the authority to fulfil those responsibilities and a supportive environment which allows staff to learn from mistakes.

Empowerment requires a redesign of structures and relationships to achieve sustainable improvements and is not possible without fundamental changes in mindset.

There is a re-engineering spectrum (Figure 4.7) extending through:

Process improvement: Improvements within particular functions rather than of the entire process.
Process re-engineering: The redesign of an end-to-end process intended to produce significant improvements in cost, quality or cycle time which may start with the question, 'Should we be doing this at all . . . ?'
Business re-engineering: The redesign of the entire business architecture across all processes.
Transformation: The attempt to 'reinvent the business' by questioning why the business exists, and what it is trying to achieve.
Ongoing renewal: Recognizes that the process of organizational renewal and industrial reinvention is continuous.[37]

BPR involves looking at the business from the outside in, and concentrating on processes that serve customers. This highlights the way in which the current structure detracts from the creation of value, by retarding attempts to introduce change, and causing unresolved cross-functional friction which diverts energy. The emphasis should be on sustainable leaps in performance, as grand ideas are often scaled down in the face of constraints, and result in disappointment. Such major enterprises lead to greater pressures on all concerned, and personal ambition can lead to rival initiatives. A balanced and holistic solution is required, for which the resources, people and training have been put in place to achieve sustainable change.

Figure 4.7: The Re-engineering Spectrum

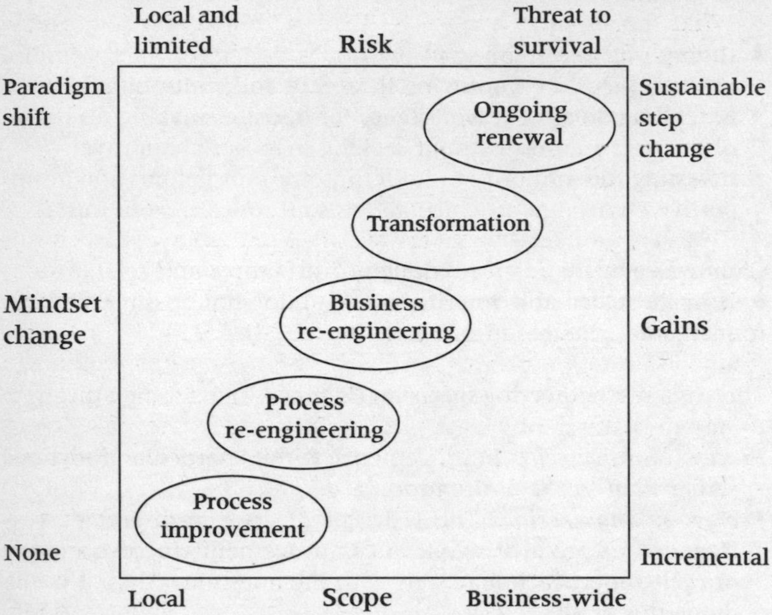

Source: Coulson-Thomas, *Business Process Re-Engineering* (1994), p. 43

Though the rhetoric is of empowerment, open cultures and support for innovation; old-style managers, risk avoidance and fear still dominate the industrial scene. People empowered to do their jobs are often not invited to become involved in developing or even understanding the goals of the enterprise. A fundamental mindset change requires managers to jettison the intellectual baggage of the past, to elaborate and communicate shared understanding of the organization's preferred future, and to create an environment that promotes learning and allows imagination.

BPR essentially requires a total rethink of business strategy, processes and management around very basic questions.

Business Strategy

- Would we do things differently if we were starting the business again?

- What are the core competencies of the company; how can they be developed; how easily could they be replicated?
- What face-to-face contact is there with customers (possible through focus groups, etc.)?
- How great is the organizational capacity for continuous learning and innovation?

Business Processes

- How to eliminate unnecessary tasks and reduce any delays introduced by multiple authorizations and inspections.
- How to ensure process roles can be performed by multiple staff, and staff are trained to perform multiple roles.
- How to concentrate responsibility for end-to-end tasks into single roles or small works groups.
- How to reduce the amount of paper handling and rekeying of data through electronic communications, both internally and with customers and suppliers.
- How to create a balanced set of performance measures.
- How to build staff understanding of business objectives and critical performance measures.
- How to equip staff with the tools and techniques to take responsibility for the continuous review and refinement of the processes they work on.

Business Management

- How to increase staffing flexibility by creating a multi-skilled workforce.
- How to reduce duplication of effort and investment by:

  forming strong partnerships with customers and suppliers
  - sharing key information (e.g. point-of-sales data)
  - undertaking joint developments
  - responding quickly to eliminate multiple storage points in a supply chain

- How to improve cross-functional communications to speed up issue resolution and development of new products and services.
- How to give staff the freedom and authority to execute their responsibilities.

- How to encourage the continual challenging of non-value-adding tasks, out-sourcing those which divert time and resources from critical business activities.
- How to encourage the acquisition of new knowledge by all staff.[38]

The proponents of BPR stimulated considerable hopes, if not of the miracle breakthrough in efficiency promised, at least of significant performance improvements. One survey in 1995 discovered that 38 per cent of executives interviewed saw re-engineering as the main source of profit growth over the next three years.[39] An American Management Association survey of 700 corporations a year earlier confirmed this view.[40] However, despite the executive obsession with re-engineering in the 1990s, it did not live up to its high expectations, as many surveys revealed. A Watson Wyatt survey on the effectiveness of re-engineering, and the results secured, reported that only 22 per cent of managers said they had been able to hit targets, less than half the companies surveyed had succeeded in increasing their operating profits, and only 2 per cent saw any increase in employee morale.

Such poor results suggest that the problems of implementing BPR are greater than the slogans which accompany it might imply. James Champy's response was to focus on the need for *Re-engineering Management* (1995), if re-engineering work was to succeed. A major difficulty is the assumption that information technology can be part of a magical solution towards improving business efficiency. Now it is realized that technology alone cannot resolve business problems, and there is a major shift in emphasis towards *business driven* solutions. There are many IT problems, among them late delivery of essential systems, under-functional systems, and costs far exceeding original estimates. But there were more fundamental difficulties inherent in the BPR approach to streamlining business processes, including:

- Loss of technical expertise.
- Loss of functional expertise.
- Lack of retraining, loss of morale.
- Lack of flexibility.
- Loss of personal relationships.
- Loss of personal intuition.
- System hierarchy replacing command hierarchy.
- Lack of explanation and preparation.

- Lack of consultation over new process
- Lack of motivation.
- Lack of 'unfreezing' stage (loosening the
- Struggle between process teams and line m
- Re-engineering does not work well in non-l

Disillusion with BPR reinvigorated the search for
solutions to business problems. The focus had a   ed
towards more broadly defined innovation than the p   s focus
of BPR, and in the late 1990s, with the great surge of new products
and services, the vital importance of innovation was more apparent
than ever.

INNOVATION

Innovation is the collateral of human creativity: it is the capacity to
create options for the future. Strategic innovation involves assembling new combinations of resources which create productive possibilities for a sustained period of time.[41] Peter Drucker in his book
Post-Capitalist Society (1993) argues that 'The productivity of knowledge is going to be the determining factor in the competitive position
of a company, an industry, an entire country. The only thing that
will increasingly matter . . . is management performance in making
knowledge productive'. Improving the productivity of knowledge
involves, more than anything, innovating new products, processes,
organizational structures, markets, companies and industries.

The present interest in innovation in the West has partly been
stimulated by a sense that innovation is occurring more rapidly in
Japanese companies; 'And if Western managers were once anxious
about the low cost and high quality of Japanese imports, they are
overwhelmed by the pace at which Japanese rivals are inventing
new markets, creating new products and enhancing them.'[42]

The imperative of innovation applies not simply in fast-moving,
high-technology industries in which research and development is
paramount, such as pharmaceuticals and consumer electronics.
Innovation applies equally well in all industrial and organizational
contexts. According to Baden-Fuller and Stopford in their book on
Rejuvenating the Mature Business (1992), 'There is no such thing as
mature industries . . . only mature firms'. Successful industries are
populated by imaginative and profitable firms. Firms faced with

decline in demand for their product or service have
more innovative to survive (creating new products or
ces, or diversifying using existing competencies). It is often
assumed that innovation correlates closely with organizational size,
that the giant companies with huge R&D budgets will account for
most new ideas. The recent history of innovation suggests otherwise. Size alone does not guarantee success in innovation. As John
Kay argues in *The Foundations of Corporate Success* (1993):

> A common error in looking forward is to think that current
> performance and above all current size are important
> elements in future success. A very little knowledge of business
> history demonstrates that size offers no long term protection
> for those who have no competitive advantage. And lack of it
> provides no obstacle to those who genuinely do have competi-
> tive advantage ... size is mostly the result of competitive
> advantage, not its cause.

With state-of-the-art equipment now available even to very small
firms just starting up, the opportunities are greater now than in
the days when capital intensity decided everything: 'Small firms
with limited resources can challenge the leaders: it is the capacity
to learn and innovate that is vital'.[43]

There are many types of innovation and invention is not just
about the R&D of new products. Innovation can be about:

- Discovering a multitude of ways of adding value to existing
  products and services.
- Large organizations finding ways to act like small, flexible, cost-
  effective organizations.
- Manufacturing firms adopting computer-integrated manufacturing technology.
- Service firms adopting new forms of information and communications technology.
- Implementing structural and operational changes, such as the
  adoption of self-managed teams or network structures.
- Extending marketing into new countries or sectors.

The challenge is to sustain constant innovation in changing
business environments. Organizations must run fast to keep up
with the changes taking place all around them; they must modify

not just from time to time but all of the time. Just like the smallest amoeba, large corporations must constantly adapt to their environment or die. In high-technology firms this process of innovation and change is even more rapid. One company in Silicon Valley modified its structure twenty-four times in four years to keep up with changes in the environment. Companies facing decline must shift to an innovative frame of mind and release the creativity of employees if they are to survive.

Companies increasingly tackle gaps in their innovation capability by using networks to link multiple partners on an international basis; this means that they are able to cover the escalating costs of R&D, to exchange knowledge, to develop new products, to share production technologies, and to combine in distribution and marketing. These co-operative interrelationships are now so developed that, it has been argued, 'Given the pervasiveness of alliance formation in nearly every important industry today, our present understanding of the firm as an independent agent may lose much of its current meaning'.[44]

Innovation can involve very radical transformation in response to sudden shifts in the market environment, but it often means a consistent process of incremental change (Table 4.8).

Table 4.8: Incremental and Radical Industrial Change

INCREMENTAL CHANGE	RADICAL CHANGE
Continuous progression	Frame breaking burst
Maintain equilibrium	Research new equilibrium
Effect organizational part	Transform entire organization
Through normal structure	Create new structure
New technology	Breakthrough technology
Product improvement	New products create new markets.

Innovations often represent quite modest advances, but can improve every aspect of the organization:

Technology: Improved production processes, more efficient, greater output, better work methods, improved equipment, smoother work flow.

Product or service: Small adaptations of existing products, new product lines.

Structure and system: Improved organization structure, strategy, reward system co-ordination, information system, accounting and budgeting.

People: Improved skills, abilities, higher expectations, supportive culture, problem-solving, better communications.

Innovation may involve much of the unpredictability of other forms of creative endeavour; however, the rational sequence of innovation is often portrayed as:

Need: A perceived problem of lack of performance, prompts consideration of possible innovations.

Idea: A model, concept or plan of how to do something. It may be a new machine, product or technique. It is evaluated and proposed for adoption.

Adoption: If the decision is to go ahead with an innovation, it is adopted for implementation.

Implementation: When new equipment, a new idea or technique is brought into service, with investment and training. This is often the most difficult step to achieve.

Resources: Time, effort and money are required to succeed with innovation.

Dussauge and his colleagues explore why many technology-based companies appear similar in structure but perform differently in the marketplace, exhibiting tremendous variation in technology development, new product development, growth and profitability. Neither a high level of R&D expenditure, nor the adoption of a particular organizational structure seem to guarantee success:

To explain these differences, we must dig below the surface, to the level of group and organizational processes. Innovative, fast-cycle companies demonstrate particular patterns of leadership, vision, communication, decision-making, and culture. 'Research' is concerned with the creation of new knowledge whereas the purpose of 'development' is to apply scientific or engineering knowledge, different processes appear to be required ... Fast-cycle companies move beyond the dominance of their functions and divisions to develop strong cross-functional linkages. Relationships among the various functions and areas of specialization are strongly interactive in innovative firms ... [There are] three keys to new product innovation – leadership, teamwork, and simultaneity ... Well developed teams with differentiated roles aimed at a common vision are key to rapid product innovation. Speed is achieved, however, through the simultaneous accomplishment of what used to occur in sequence ... Two processes are critically important to achieving simultaneity: collapsing the stages of development and fostering 'multilearning' among programme participants through intensive communication.[45]

Innovative organizations tend to exhibit characteristics that nurture a culture of creativity: they are organic, free flowing, flexible; they empower employees, have few rigid rules, and emphasize bottom-up innovation (Figure 4.8). Mechanistic organizations devoted to increasing output have different emphases: they are geared to efficient production, routine procedures and products, in a stable environment. Since most organizations require innovation *and* efficient output, they may often become ambidextrous, switching emphasis and even structures as the need arises, or evolving separate structures and cultures for 'creative' departments such as R&D and design.

Corporate Entrepreneurship

Successful innovating companies have a good understanding of customer needs and make effective use of outside technology and outside advice, even though they may do more work in-house. Top management support is often critical. A pattern of *horizontal linkages* has been developed tailoring innovations to customer needs and making effective use of technology, but with influential support. This is *collective entrepreneurship*, the most formidable paradigm of innovative organizations, as Robert Reich eloquently explains:

Workers in such organizations constantly reinvent the company; one idea leads to another. Producing the latest generation of automobiles involves making electronic circuits that

Figure 4.8: Innovation Comes from All Directions

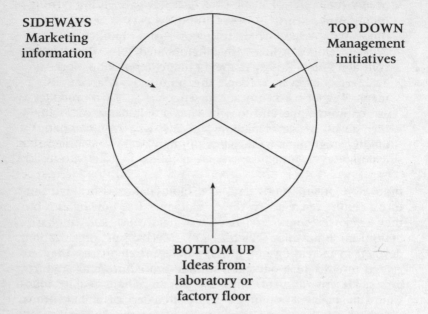

SIDEWAYS
Marketing
information

TOP DOWN
Management
initiatives

BOTTOM UP
Ideas from
laboratory or
factory floor

govern fuel consumption and monitor engine performance;
developments in these devices lead to improved sensing
equipment and software for monitoring heartbeats and moist-
ure in the air. Producing cars also involves making flexible
robots for assembling parts and linking them by computer;
steady improvements in these technologies, in turn lead to
expert production systems that can be applied anywhere.
What is considered the 'automobile industry' thus becomes
a wide variety of technologies evolving toward all sorts of
applications that flow from the same strand of technological
development toward different markets. In this paradigm,
entrepreneurship isn't the sole province of the company's
founder or its top managers. Rather, it is a capability and
attitude that is different throughout the company. Experimentation and development go on all the time as the company
searches for new ways to capture and build on the knowledge
already accumulated by its workers. Distinctions between
innovation and production, between top managers and production workers blur. Because production is a continuous

process of reinvention, entrepreneurial efforts are focused on many thousands of small ideas rather than on just a few big ones. And because valuable information and expertise are dispersed throughout the organization, top management does not solve problems; it creates an environment in which people can identify and solve problems themselves.[46]

Collective entrepreneurship places great stress on creating an effective organization and improving performance through the development of people. This aims to promote trust, an open confrontation of problems, employee empowerment and participation, the design of meaningful work, co-operation between groups, the breakdown of hierarchical approaches, a regard for internal relationships and processes, and team-building.

The Search for Strategic Resources

The resource-based view of the firm and management strategy is becoming the most influential contemporary theoretical paradigm, though the definition of key resources stretches across competence, core competence, invisible assets, strategic assets and skills as the essential strategic components, as Bogaert, Martens and Van Cauwenbergh lucidly argue.[47] According to Barney, company resources include assets, capabilities, organizational processes, firm attributes, information and knowledge, which enable the firm to conceive and implement strategies to improve its performance.[48] These resources are divided into three categories: physical capital, human capital and organizational capital; and not all resources are strategically relevant. Other writers distinguish *having* (what the firm owns) from *doing* (what the firm can do). Hall makes the distinction between *assets* (things which a firm owns) and *skills or competencies* (the knowledge of employees and other stakeholders, and their collective aptitudes) (Table 4.9).[49]

There is a distinction between resources and capabilities. Amit and Schoemaker define *resources* as stocks of available factors owned or controlled by the firm as inputs into the production process (capital equipment, skills of individual employees, patents).[50] *Capability* refers to the capacity of the collected resources to perform some task or activity.[51] Capabilities become firm specific through complex interactions among resources – for example,

Table 4.9: A Chronological Overview of Concepts Used in the Resource-based Perspective

Author(s)	Main concept(s)	Description or additional concepts
Wernerfelt (1984)	Resources	Resource position barriers
Itami (1987)	Invisible assets	Information-based resources/dynamic resource fit
Dierickx and Cool (1988)	Strategic assets	Stocks accumulated through investments (flows)
Aaker (1989)	Assets and skills	• Asset: something a firm possesses superior to competition • Skill: something a firm does better than competitors
Akerberg (1989)	Competence	Organizational competence depends on individual competences
Prahalad and Hamel (1990)	Core competence	• Strategic architecture • Collective learning: production skills and technologies
Klein *et al.* (1991)	Metaskills	• Metaskills: generate core skills
Barney (1991)	Firm resources	All assets, capabilities, processes, attributes, information, knowledge controlled by a firm
Grant (1991)	Resources	• Resources: inputs to the production process • Capability: capacity of resources to perform some task
Hall (1991, 1992)	Intangible resources	• Skills or competences: e.g. the know-how of people • Assets: things which are owned

Table 4.9: (continued)

Author(s)	Main concept(s)	Description or additional concepts
		• Intangible resources may be linked with a functional, cultural, positional or regulatory capability
Stalk *et al.* (1992)	Capabilities	• Capability: more broadly based than core competence
		• Key business processes
Amit and Schoemaker (1993)	Resources	• Stocks of available factors owned/ controlled by the firm
	Capability	• Capacity of firm to deploy resources using organizational processes, to effect desired end
	Strategic assets	• Set of difficult to trade, imitate, scarce and specialized resources and capabilities

Source: Bogaert, Martens and van Cauwenbergh 'Strategy as a Situational Puzzle: The Fit of the Components' (1994)

manufacturing flexibility, responsiveness to market trends, or highly reliable service. Dierickx and Cool distinguish between *stocks* (technological expertise, brand loyalty), which are accumulated over time by progressive investments, and *flows* (R&D spending, advertisement spending).[52] Flows can be adjusted quickly but stocks require time and effort to build.

Invisible or intangible assets are believed to be crucial to business success. *Invisible assets* are resources such as consumer trust or brand loyalty,[53] or other information-based capabilities. Invisible assets are difficult to accumulate, and may have simultaneous multiple uses. *Intangible assets* range from intellectual property, through contracts, patents, subjective resources such as network, culture and reputation.[54]

According to Barney, strategic assets have four attributes:

- They are valuable (exploit opportunities and/or neutralize threats in the firm's environment).
- They are rare among the firm's current or potential competitors.
- They are not readily imitable.
- No equivalent substitutes exist.[55]

In other words strategic assets are specialized and scarce. Advantage can evolve from recognizing the distinctive capabilities of an organization, and investing in them heavily, looking for a long-term return.[56] Firms need to find a balance between the exploitation of existing resources and the development of new ones.[57] Strategic management is concerned with maintaining and developing strategic assets and skills, with selecting strategic and competitive arenas to exploit those assets and skills, and with neutralizing competitors' assets and skills.[58] Itami insists that 'effective strategy in the present builds invisible assets, and the expanded stock enables the firm to plan its future strategy to be carried out. And the future strategy must make effective use of the resources that have been amassed'.[59] Prahalad and Hamel suggest that a strategic architecture is needed, 'a road map of the future that identifies which corporate competencies to build and their constituent technologies'.[60]

Reinventing Industries

In their article on 'The Core Competence of the Corporation' (1990), which became the *Harvard Business Review*'s most reprinted article ever, and in *Competing for the Future* (1994), the book that followed, Hamel and Prahalad succeeded in re-engineering much of strategic management. For both academics and managers, the emphasis on competence and synergy ahead of cash flow and control was a welcome inspiration. The concept of core competence has four key components:[61]

Corporate span: Core competencies span across businesses and products within a company, and can support all of them.
Temporal dominance: The products and services offered by a company are but a momentary expression of the core competencies

which evolve over time and will outlast products, and inspire new products.

Learning-by-doing: Collective corporate endeavour enhances competence: 'core competencies are the collective learning in the organization, especially how to co-ordinate diverse production skills and integrate multiple streams of technologies. Core competence may not diminish with use . . . competencies are enhanced as they are applied and shared.'[62]

Competitive locus: Product market competition is merely the superficial expression of a deeper competition over competencies. 'Conceiving of the firm as a portfolio of core competencies and disciplines suggests that inter-firm competition, as opposed to inter-product competition, is essentially concerned with the acquisition of skills.'[63]

One way of thinking about core competence is to regard it as an expression of the resource-based view of the firm which emerged as a counterpoint to the market-structure emphasis of competitive strategy. The resource-based view suggests that competitive advantage is not dependent upon industrial structure, but on the possession of unique skills, knowledge, resources or competencies: 'Prahalad and Hamel have taken the resource-based point of view even further and have been even bolder: their concept of core competence admits a proactive construction of competence, sees competence as spanning multiple businesses, and, most importantly, sees competition as being over the acquisition and development of competence'.[64]

The central argument of Hamel and Prahalad is that companies cannot be complacent about present market leadership, but must exercise their core competencies in order to assume leadership ten years from now. This involves a fundamental assessment of what customers might want in the future, what channels will be used to reach customers, which companies will be competitors, and what skills and capabilities will be required. 'Although process re-engineering dominates the top management agenda in many companies . . . to create the future, a company must also be capable of "re-engineering" its industry. The logic is simple: To extend leadership a company must eventually reinvent leadership, to reinvent leadership it must ultimately reinvent its industry, and to reinvent its industry it must ultimately regenerate its strategy'.[65]

Competencies are the core attributes of a company: they may

develop unanticipated products and services, invent and shape
consumer demand and help the company to enter new markets
rapidly and successfully. Core competence enables firms consistently to claim first mover advantage. *Strategic architecture* is designed
to stretch the imagination and capability of the organization:[66]

It is a view of strategy that is less concerned with ensuring a
tight fit between goals and resources and is more concerned
with creating *stretch goals* that challenge employees to accomplish the seemingly impossible. It is a view of strategy as more
than the allocation of scarce resources across competing projects; strategy is the quest to overcome resource constraints
through a creative and unending pursuit of better *resource
leverage*. It is a view of strategy that recognizes that companies
not only compete within the boundaries of existing industries,
they compete to *shape the structure* of future industries.[67]

Visionary Companies

Hamel and Prahalad have firmly rejected dichotomized thinking
which, for example, creates a division between *unrelated diversification* and *core business*. Growth *and* diversification can be achieved:
'*Core competencies* are the connective tissue that holds together
seemingly diverse businesses. Core competencies are the *lingua
franca* that allows managers to translate insights and experience
from one business into another'.[68] Organizational choices need not
be restrictive, but may be synthesized without exchanging one set
of problems for another (Table 4.10).

Collins and Porras develop this insight in their highly popular
book *Built to Last – Successful Habits of Visionary Companies*. For them
it was not necessary for companies 'to oppress themselves with
what we call the "Tyranny of the OR".'[69] Their study of (mainly
American) companies with a long track record of making a significant impact upon the industrial world found that these companies
were not constrained by their core beliefs, but used them as a
springboard for greater achievement. Collins and Porras describe
these leaps of imagination in the most creatively exciting companies as *Big Hairy Audacious Goals* (BHAGs) (Table 4.11).

Table 4.10: Higher Level Synthesis of Organizational Choices

Thesis	Antithesis	Synthesis
Corporate	Business units	Interlinkages
Centralized	Decentralized	Collective
Bureaucratic	Empowered	Directed
Clones	Renegades	Activists
Technology-led	Customer-led	Benefits-led
Diversified	Core business	Core competence

Source: Hamel and Prahalad, *Competing for the Future* (1994), p. 293

For example the Boeing 747 was an incredibly risky adventure but along the way Boeing maintained its core value of product safety and applied the most conservative safety standards, testing, and analysis ever to a commercial aircraft. Merck, in keeping with its core value of imagination, sought pre-eminence primarily by creating new breakthrough innovations, not by creating me-too products. Jack Welch at GE made it clear that attaining number one or number two in a market at the expense of integrity would be unacceptable . . . Motorola never abandoned its basic belief in the dignity of and respect for the individual throughout all of its big, hairy, self-selected challenges.[70]

Collins and Porras advice is to 'Try a Lot of Stuff and Keep What Works' and to appreciate that 'Good Enough Never Is'. In the 1960s Pierre Wack worked for Shell where he developed the art of scenario-planning. He suggested the critical elements were:

- Taking the existing mental models of the decision-makers as the starting point.
- Reframing the issues involved, through the introduction of new perspectives.
- Changing the mental models of decision-makers.
- Understanding predictability and uncertainty.

Table 4.11: Sustaining the Core While Stimulating Progress

Core to Preserve	Company	BHAGs to Stimulate Progress
Being on the leading edge of aviation; being pioneers; risk-taking	Boeing	Bet the pot on the B-17, 707, 747
Tapping the 'latent creative powers within us'; self-renewal, continual improvements, honourably serve the community via great products	Motorola	Invent a way to sell 100,000 TVs at $179.95; attain six-sigma quality; win the Baldridge Award; launch Iridium
Elevation of the Japanese culture and national status; being a pioneer, doing the impossible	Sony	Change the worldwide image of Japanese products as poor quality; create a pocketable transistor radio
Preserving and improving human life; medicine is for the patient, not for profits; imagination and innovation	Merck	Become the pre-eminent drug-maker worldwide, via massive R&D and new products that cure disease

Source: Adapted from Collins and Porras, *Successful Habits* . . . (1996), p. 113

For Wack strategic vision involved a clear logic: business success would be achieved by building the profit potential of the company through developing a reservoir of potentialities. This included a commitment to excellence in a number of capabilities combined into a strategic vision of what the company wants to be. Scenario-planning allows a perception of the world beyond the traditional business models, and provides a language in which new theories of action can be jointly developed.[71]

Value Creating Cultures

Matheson and Matheson urge companies to think more about the quality of their decision-making, and to create a culture which might stimulate a commitment to continuous value-creation. The vital elements of this creative culture are:

Value creation culture: Value creation is the compelling argument for change.

Creating alternatives: Multiple alternatives are created and evaluated.

Continual learning: Improvements are continually identified and acted on.

Embracing uncertainty: Uncertainty is understood, communicated and managed.

Outside-in strategic perspectives: Meaningful information is available from the outside.

Systems thinking: People understand complex cause-and-effect relationships.

Disciplined decision-making: Systematic decision processes are used routinely.

Alignment and empowerment: A common understanding of strategies for value creation co-ordinates the organization.

Open information flow: People have unrestricted access to information.

CONCLUSIONS

There is an important distinction between the ability to make good strategic decisions and the ability to carry out those decisions effectively. The emphasis of management in recent decades has been on the implementation side, manifested by the fascination with performance improvement through TQM, benchmarking, just-in-time, re-engineering, and so forth. This is all part of the huge corporate effort to 'do things right', which has distracted companies from the question of whether they 'are doing the right things'. 'A long list of companies (IBM, Kodak, Rank Xerox, International Harvester, the entire American robotics industry, to name a few) urgently pursued efficiency . . . while their business slipped away because of obsolescent strategy.'[72]

As the business environment becomes increasingly turbulent and technological change becomes more rapid it will pay companies to think more about whether they have the right strategic intent before they set about implementing it. If the preconceived strategic plans of the past are no longer appropriate, strategic thinking should not simply be abandoned. Creative and responsive strategic thought is stimulated by developing the capabilities and knowledge that allow proactive approaches to change, based on transferable skills, even if this involves the rethinking of whole businesses and industries.

Chapter 5

ORGANIZATION

What characterizes 'intelligent organizations'? Until quite recently the answer to this question might have involved looking at manufacturing concerns in the automobile industry, such as Toyota. The 'lean production' associated with Toyota would seem to be the very model of ultra-modern and intelligent management. Today, as the industrial age of the automobile is overtaken by the information age of software, we might look instead at a firm like Microsoft, and the many smaller, more innovative software houses that are developing in its wake. The shift in focus from the hardware of the car industry to the production of software leads to many important changes in organizational paradigms.

In this chapter we look at the organizational implications of the move from mass production to flexible manufacturing and quality production. There is a new emphasis on the importance of skill acquisition. This involves the dedication to continuous improvement only possible in cultures committed to quality. Finally, we explore the way in which bureaucratic control and imperative communication have been superseded by an emphasis on learning and forms of virtual organization. Together these changes make it possible for organizations to employ the whole of the potential of their employees rather than some fraction of it.

ORGANIZATION DESIGN

In the past, rational organization design was characterized by a focus on a hierarchical structure, imperatively co-ordinated; communications were governed by managerial fiat and plans were tied to the mass production of a relatively standardized product, in long and inflexible production runs. The epitome of this was the

Table 5.1: Paradigm Shifts

Taylorism, Fordism hierarchy	Intelligent, networked virtuality
Mass production	Quality production
Long production runs	Flexible manufacturing
De-skilling of labour	Skilling-up of teams
Employee resistance	Continuous improvement
Inspection-based culture	Quality-based culture
Bureaucratic control	Learning
Imperative communication	Virtual organization

automobile industry, where Henry Ford's innovation of the production line, together with Frederick Taylor's stress on scientific
management, produced a highly bureaucratic organization focused
on the technology and workflow of the line.

Characteristically, work was dumbed-down into small cycles,
sometimes as short as fifteen seconds, at an intensity dictated by the
management in setting the speed of the line. Typically, employees
resisted this dehumanization of their labour. The creativity of
employees resided more in imagining how they could resist managerial authority than in how they might improve processes and
products.

The picture changed dramatically during the 1980s and 1990s.
Learning from Japan became the watchword. In some respects
Japanese organizations seemed to do things very differently. While
they were still bureaucracies, they were a different kind of bureaucracy – a learning bureaucracy dedicated to the continuous
improvement of quality. Rather than inspecting for acceptable
levels of defects after production they sought to build a commitment to quality into the production process. Quality, considered
both in terms of internal customers in the workflow, and in terms
of the final consumer, was at the heart of process improvement.
This was accompanied by new approaches to mass production,
through the use of flexible specialization in work skills, premised
on teamwork rather than individual work, along with an appreciation of the productivity gains that innovative machines could
make. Using smart machines, Japanese companies tried to create

smarter workers to make better products. Where this was not possible they sought to robotize the more routinized aspects of the workflow. At the same time, there was a widespread application of smarter manufacturing with subcontractors. Rather than being ruled by price-competition, automobile firms sought to develop relational contracts with subcontractors, based on the same philosophies of continuous improvement as were applied in manufacturing. Once more, quality was at the core. Intensified global competition and the development of new digital technologies became the drivers that saw the lessons from Japan become widely distributed in existing industry, especially in the United States and Europe, by the end of the 1980s. However, as this chapter will go on to argue, some of the same lessons were being absorbed in new industries, such as software: there was even greater potential for organizational innovation in these 'virtual' organizations.

The Model of Modern Management

Modern management theory is founded on Weber's account of bureaucracy. In its day it was enormously influential in shaping the thinking of management researchers.[1] According to Weber, bureaucracies were the inevitable design for rational organization. Such organizations would be:

- Differentiated into discrete areas subject to unified functional control.
- Governed internally and linked as a unity through a hierarchy of offices, with clear responsibilities and duties attached to them.
- Managed on the basis of a detailed knowledge of 'the files'. Each functional area would have a staff whose job was constantly to update these records.
- Comprised of roles where individual duties and actions would be defined 'without regard for persons': hence, everyone was to be treated in accordance with the rules rather than in accordance with their social identity or status.
- Staffed by competent individuals, formally and certifiably trained to do the tasks of the bureaucracy, with opportunities to make their career in the service of the bureaucracy, slowly moving up through its ranks.[2]

In many ways Weber foresaw one element of the modern paradigm of organizations: bureaucracy. In addition to bureaucracy, F. W. Taylor and Henry Ford contributed two other key elements:

- Highly differentiated and consciously designed jobs, de-skilled along Taylorist lines.
- A system of semi-automatic assembly-line production, referred to as 'Fordism', based on intensive, divided labour linked together mechanistically.

Taylorism is well known: it was the adoption of a systematic measurement and redesign of tasks to make their execution as simple, efficient and controllable as possible. The system of conveyors and handling devices ensured the movement of materials to the appropriate workstation. A semi-automatic assembly line organized work into a linear flow of sequential transformations applied to evolving raw materials. Workers became adjuncts to the moving line, repeating a few elementary movements in a predetermined workflow designed by engineers.

The pyramid of control was designed in a classically bureaucratic fashion. Authority resided in individuals by virtue of their incumbency in office and/or their expertise. Employment was based on specialized training and formal certification of competence, acquired prior to gaining the job. Individuals in the managerial chain of command held an office – both figuratively and literally. These offices were organized hierarchically; instruction was expressed in terms of universal fixed rules that legitimated imperative command – 'managerial imperative' – or 'giving orders'. Direct surveillance and supervision, as well as standardized rules and sanctions, were the norm for ensuring work was done according to plan.

Fordism was a system of mass production. Work occurred in large, spatially concentrated organizations. Real wage and productivity growth were linked in this system, and the higher real wages encouraged demand for standardized consumer goods because mass workers were also mass consumers with families and homes in the new suburbs.

For the managers under Fordism, management constituted a career in which either seniority or achievement might be the basis for advancement. Impersonality, where relations would be role based, segmented and instrumental, was the ideal, as Weber recommended. Incentives, arranged in a career ladder with differential rewards related to the hierarchical level, were the primary sources of motivation. Motivation of employees was principally through the wages system, the manipulation of bonus rates, and the extensive number of job classifications used. Prestige, privilege and power would be consistent with one another in the hierarchy.

Division of labour was extreme. Intellectual work of design, conception and communication distinguished its practitioners, the managers, from those who did manual work. The latter were so many interchangeable 'hands' executing and making possible superordinate designs, in a high specialization of jobs and functions and an extensive differentiation of roles. Production was planned against inventories of stock and raw materials. In those countries, such as the USA and the UK, that had vestiges of occupational craft unionism, these classifications became the basis of union organization and the defence of 'relativities' and 'occupational monopoly', leading to frequent demarcation disputes – about which trade is allowed to do what.

Parts and components were brought into huge warehouses in the plant by contractors who had bid the lowest price for the contract, usually secured for one year at a time. The market supplied and the company stockpiled. Customer service was secondary to shipping product.

By the 1970s this model had begun to falter. A slowdown in productivity growth, fierce international competition and upward pressures on wages squeezed profits. As productivity slowed down a process of 'internationalization' took hold, along with the associated 'deindustrialization' of areas and enterprises that had previously been strongholds of Fordism. Companies decentralized standardized production to new, dispersed localities – initially within the industrialized nations, later to newly industrializing countries – but kept managerial and financial functions within head offices in existing large metropolitan areas.[7]

The goods manufactured by this system were shunned by customers, who began to express dissatisfaction with low quality. Workers were also dissatisfied: acts of sabotage (sometimes the source of quality problems), frustrated outbreaks of truculence at work, sometimes tipping into industrial militancy, and increasing turnover and diminishing productivity became widespread. Consumers began to choose new imported products from Japan – a story that played out across diverse fields such as consumer electronics and automobiles.

Something was afoot. Not only were these Japanese products cheaper and more reliable; management writers were claiming that this was because their manufacturers followed a different paradigm in their production. By 1990 this had become known as 'lean production', based on developments at Toyota.

Lean Production: More Intelligent Organization?

One element of the model for 'modern organizations' began in the auto industry; its most popular successor was also nurtured in the industry – by Toyota in Japan. The Toyota system developed from a visit by Sakichi Toyoda to the Ford plant in Detroit in the early 1950s during the post-war reconstruction of Japanese industry. He saw much to admire there, but realized that much could be – and would have to be – done differently in Japan.[4]

What were some of the differences?

- The Japanese market was not characterized by a demand like that in the US for a small range of relatively large cars produced in vast quantities.
- The domestic market in Japan demanded many different types of cars. A more flexible manufacturing system would be required to deliver this variety.
- Not only was there a greater variety of models; they were produced in smaller batches than was typical in the USA.

Toyota responded to these market differences with innovations such as new techniques of die-changing that speeded up work processes. Fiercely competitive tendering between many suppliers was superseded by long-term relationships on the basis of mutual benefit. Suppliers became involved in design decisions with the firm. Toyota implemented their management systems in suppliers but did not vertically integrate to minimize transaction costs. Instead, they used 'just-in-time' (JIT) systems.

JIT systems establish complex market relations with component subcontractors to ensure that supplies arrive where they are needed at the appropriate time. Large inventory stocks are dispensed with, and the circulation of capital in 'dead' buffer stock minimized. Large JIT production complexes are spatially organized so that subsidiary companies, suppliers and subcontractors exist in close relationships with each other.

A number of distinct advantages flow from the JIT system. Wage costs relocate from the more expensive core workforce to the cheaper peripheral workforce; stable long-term relations develop with suppliers, opening up multidirectional flows of information between the partners in the subcontracting network. Personnel as well as ideas are freely exchanged. Innovations accelerate through the system.

Closely linked to the JIT system is *jikoda*, the principle of designing a machine with automatic defect-detection, triggered by an immediate shut-down when a fault is detected. Inspection is built into the machine. When this is combined with JIT systems it ensures defect-free production. Additionally, it eliminates the need for machine-watching: the machine runs only so long as everything is satisfactory. Hence, one worker can mind several machines simultaneously. As a team member, he is even more flexible. Employee teams acquire multi-functional skills so that they can work on different machines and processes.

Along with these technological innovations Toyota introduced management innovations. During the post-war recovery period management yielded to union pressure and introduced lifetime employment for core employees and pay based on seniority, tied to company profitability. The effects were apparent: employees had a considerable stake in the success of the enterprise and considerable incentive to stay within the enterprise. On the basis of these conditions Toyota developed the skills of its core members in the course of their employment. The firm provided the context for the entire career; the firm rewarded career-workers through the seniority wages system. Consequently production workers learnt a range of skills denied to those in the Fordist system. These skills were partly intellectual in character,[5] involving tasks such as problem-diagnosis and responsibility for taking remedial action to fix problems. And, after time in the system, the core employees (invariably men) were well remunerated.

The Toyota system, while it was a more intelligent organization than its Fordist counterparts, was still fundamentally based on many of the same principles and retained the precepts of the Taylor system, stressing both a horizontal and a vertical division of labour, together with hierarchical control structures. However, the differences were important. The skill basis was greatly enhanced. The development of multi-functional skills tied in with the definition of work tasks in terms of standardized competencies. Precise analysis of competencies available in teams, and the graphic display of these on the shop-floor, meant better management of any areas of relative scarcity. The lean production system increased both the quantitative range of skills and their distribution, even if skill-ranges did not increase in all dimensions. Less strict specialization meant that first line supervisors, 'foremen', were replaced by working team leaders. It was the teams that became responsible for the quality of their work, rather than a separate, and essentially reactive-to-failure inspectorate; this nurtured a more proactive attitude to quality.

Manufacturers are accorded more trust both by employees and by customers in this system. With buyers, dealers develop 'relationship marketing'. They guarantee that the cars they supply will pass the comprehensive and strict three-year compulsory tests in Japan. For employees, the line was not subject to arbitrary 'speed-ups' that exhausted workers at times of increased demand, nor to 'slow-downs' at times of diminished demand, though the pace of the production line was rapid enough to make it a place only for younger people.

Continuous improvement rather than speed-up was the creed. When new methods improved productivity, workers were not made redundant but moved to other areas: the remaining pool of workers were expected to maintain the same level of intensity and productivity of work. Japanese work organization used self-managing teams rather than workers straining against each other under an individualistic and competitive bonus payment and production system. Within self-managing teams, work roles overlapped with continuous, rather than discontinuous, task structure, in which workers allocated tasks internally. Work skill content was not inexorably simplified as it was in the classical modernist organization under Fordism.

Work teams changed the pace of production by adding or removing workers. Management and team members experimented with different configurations. Workers often moved with the production line and work groups performed routine quality control. Management focused on non-routine aspects of quality control, such as advanced statistical measurement or work redesign. Work groups detected and corrected mistakes quickly, saving considerable rework and scrappage. Quality control and shopfloor problem-solving were integrated.[6] Workers were expected to make improvements in work processes to make them faster or smarter. This is where quality circles come in.

Quality circles include both operatives and staff specialists such as engineers in the same circle, oriented not only towards reducing the wastage rate, but also to improving technological and process improvements. Much of the routine preventative maintenance is done by the operatives who use the machines. It is a total approach to quality, often termed total quality management (or TQM), where, in Ishikawa's terms, 'quality means quality of work, quality of service, quality of information, quality of process, quality of division, quality of people, including workers, engineers, managers, and executives, quality of system, quality of company, quality of objectives etc.'.[7] At the base is the quality of people, as Imae stressed: 'The three building blocks of a business are hardware, software, and "humanware".'[8] Only after humanware is squarely in place should the hardware and software aspects of a business be considered. Building quality into people means helping them become *kaizen* (continuous improvement) conscious. It is easy to see why, compared with Fordism, this way of working might appear to produce a more 'intelligent organization':

- It doesn't treat employees as interchangeable cogs, as did Fordism at its worst: workers are more skilled and they develop abilities to work together, and learn together, in teams, through 'quality circles'.
- The model does not assume that customers take whatever they are offered. It seeks to ensure quality.
- It involves suppliers and components manufacturers in the production cycle; it diminishes the amount of dead capital tied up in stock and warehousing, and it improves the quality of components for final assembly.

Most notably, *kaizen* consciousness relates to a flexibly specialized production system that can foster 'lean production'.

Flexible Specialization

Flexible specialization based on IT is the hallmark of flexible manufacturing systems, where small batches can be rapidly set up and
produced, and equipment rapidly reconfigured to start manufacturing another set of small batches. The 'flexible' aspect refers to
the restructuring of the labour market and the labour process,
while the 'specialization' aspect refers to the ascendancy of niche
or specialist markets and marketing, as opposed to mass markets.
It is the 'push' of the latter which is seen to require the response
of the former. More differentiated consumption triggers production
changes away from organizations based on tight managerial control
through external surveillance, de-skilling and mechanization to a
quality paradigm premised on self- and team-surveillance, multi-
skilling and continuous improvement.[9]

Small Business Flexibility
Initially, it was Charles Sabel who proposed the thesis of flexible
specialization producing a 'high-technology cottage industry'
where craft forms of production would be enveloped by new forms
of technology, and craft-skills would be greatly enhanced to
provide sources of competitive advantage through continuous
improvement.[10] In the Italian cases that he studied the IT innovations were fostered by local state initiatives. The Benetton-type
models of Emilia-Romagna provide the paradigm case. Later, in
collaboration with Michael Piore, he extended the focus to include
not only high-technology cottage industry but also the restructuring of mass-production industry through the adoption of new technologies and new practices.[11] Thus, Piore and Sabel shifted focus
from small and medium enterprises in Northern Italy to the
restructuring of large US corporations.

Big Business Flexibility
Large US corporations, such as Boeing, General Electric, GM and
Ford, sought to restructure by learning from Japan. Flexible
specialization enabled market-responsive manufacturing to be
based on generalist skills and technologies rather than ones which
were highly differentiated. Engineering and production changes
alone were insufficient, however. Katz and Sabel and Piore identified major impediments to the realization of a restructured system

in existing labour institutions: these had to change to accommodate the new production systems.[12] In order to be flexible enough to respond to changing market conditions organizations have had to develop a core of committed and flexible employees. Employers invest heavily in training costs and, as a corollary, core workers develop company-specific skills. Employers protect these as an investment through offering core workers security, frequent re-training, and every opportunity to integrate into the organization culture. Peripheralized workers, by contrast, remain less skilled with none of the benefits of those in the primary sector.

Flexible Neo-Fordism?

Critics have claimed that what is occurring is a further twist on Fordism: they call this neo-Fordism. Neo-Fordism appears to solve contradictions which the previous Fordist regime could not. The major contradiction was that the Fordist regime had reached the limits of its ability to increase productivity: it ran up against the obstacle of its own design. This became apparent as labour productivity began to slow down. It was in those countries that developed enhanced commitment by the workers, notably Japan, that productivity increases were gained. The reintegration of the active consent and knowledge of the workers back into the production process proved to be the centrepiece of lean production.

Of course, this poses some old problems in a new guise: if more 'intelligent organization' empowers workers and their team-based enterprise, how do we determine whether their newly encouraged 'intelligence' is exercised in line with managerial objectives, focusing attention on the management of organization cultures?

Corporate Culture

Corporate culture is manifest in patterns that simplify company decisions and individual decisions and behaviour, so that it becomes unnecessary to make judgements for every event. Unlike routines produced according to a formal rule, there is more scope to innovate and establish experimentation around the norms. The interaction of members in a group makes it possible to exchange information on successful practices. Under these conditions groups formulate similar patterns of perception, similar interpretations of certain subjects, and similar evaluations of alternatives. There is an adaptation function whereby groups arrive at successful results to satisfy their needs. By following the norms of the group, people gain acceptance from the group. Acceptance by a group signifies affiliation or cohesiveness.

From the corporate viewpoint, corporate culture aids adaptation to an outside environment. 'Quality first' is an example. If members accept such a slogan and internalize it, it can become a pattern for decision-making. Corporate culture may also integrate the decisions of individuals and groups with the goals of the organization, so that members do not resort to tradition as a bastion against innovation. Sharing values and having similar perceptions and assumptions will tend to result in harmonious activities.[13] Such a view seems to suggest a corporate culture dreamscape where resistance and conflict have been eliminated in favour of boundless creativity – a picture that rarely corresponds with empirical evidence on the implementation of quality programmes. Research by Sewell and Wilkinson[14] and Lewchuck and Robertson stresses that the corporate culture associated with quality initiatives is, however, more likely to introduce 'management by stress' as behavioural surveillance of quality takes hold under the electronic kanban: 'Workers are employed in jobs which offer them little real control over working conditions and at tasks that can be learned in a very short period of time. Most workers lack any real control over how they work, how fast they work, or when they work. Workloads are high and increasing, health risks are high and increasing, work is stressful and becoming more stressful'.[15] More may be produced, better, more rapidly, but if the surveys that register this do not at the same time register the human consequences, the real costs will never be accounted: 'If a particular company, for example, had the highest throughput in the industry but also had the fastest line speed, the higher incidence of RSIs (repetitive strain injuries), the highest accident claims, and the most problems with the placement of injured workers, then its status as best-in-class around throughput would have to be offset against these other measures'.[16] Wise management would insist on an audit that was as broad-based as possible. Companies need to know what gets continuously improved, under whose agenda. Of course, continuous improvement can be achieved in the indicators that management wants to attend to. But what if there are other indicators that management does not learn about?

The World that Changed the Machine

MIT discovered Toyota's use of 'lean production' as a new paradigm in the course of a research project known as the 'International Motor Vehicle Programme', conducted at the Toyota plant in Toyota City, Japan, which focused on flexible specialization.[17] Womack and his colleagues speculated that lean production, as it was emulated by firms seeking to acquire 'world's best practice', would create 'plants . . . populated almost entirely by highly skilled problem solvers whose task will be to think continually of ways to make the system run more smoothly and productively'.[18]

Once discovered in Japan, it was not long before reports of the first sightings of the lean production paradigm in the USA and the UK came in, although the export model underwent modifications that took account of different social structures, according to Oliver and Wilkinson and Morris and Wilkinson.[19] Management that followed the lean production model of just-in-time (JIT), flexible manufacturing, quality circles and *kaizen* could share in the economic success of Japan. The paradigm provided a model for translation, irrespective of context. It boiled down to some simple precepts: 'Lean production is lean because it uses less of everything compared with mass production American style', as the Swedish management writer Bengt Sandkull puts it.[20]

The circumstances in which 'lean production' triumphed have to be considered. At the outset Japanese cars sold well in overseas markets dominated by high-cost models produced locally. During the 1970s and well into the 1980s Japanese manufacturers, whatever other advantages they gained from 'lean production', certainly expended less of one vital ingredient – wages – and received more of another – labour time.[21] Japanese wages were about half those in the US and employees worked several hundred hours a year more than their American counterparts. By the mid-1990s the wage disadvantages had disappeared and the increasing value of the yen placed great pressure on costs.

Japanese auto firms today are much like their competitors in Europe. They have a high break-even point and a high need for cost reduction, usually through opening up plants overseas, in lower-labour-cost economies with a high propensity to import components and ready-mades for assembly in the inwardly-invested sites. This describes Japanese investment in Asia as well as that in the USA or UK and puts into question the 'special advantage' attaching to the 'lean production' problematic, with its methods of just-in-time (JIT), *Jikoda*, flexible manufacturing and quality circles.[22] Additionally, while once the talk may have been of the 'Japanese challenge', newer, cheaper cost production centres have come on stream in countries such as South Korea, premised on cost-reduction strategies similar to those which once characterized Japan, but with much more traditional, militaristic-style bureaucracies under state-directed financing and control.

In the late 1990s many commentators think that the Japanese miracle has evaporated. The yen became overvalued; the frailty of the Japanese credit system and the exposure of the banks to property-related debts that demand impossible p/e ratios to sustain them threatens the intersection of state, bureaucratic and private interests that created Japan, Inc. The laxness of governance structures that allowed weak controls and corrupt practices to flourish, and bureaucrats, politicians and criminals to prosper from them, has been exposed with successive finance-house bankruptcies. Not only did the West learn from Japan; so too did their immediate rivals in East Asia, meaning that the model bred new competitors and new competition. In the wake of the fiscal meltdown of currencies elsewhere in the region during 1997, the future looks as if it will be even more ferociously competitive, as these new competitors will be able to unload product at prices up to 50 per cent less than those that prevailed before the currency crises. The 1992 currency crisis in Britain produced a more competitive manufacturing sector after the first effects were absorbed and some restructuring occurred, and one might now anticipate the same scenario in East Asia.

THE QUALITY PARADIGM

In the 1980s, when learning from Japan was the fashionable thing to do, competitors everywhere learnt one word more than any other: *quality*. Management must focus on improving organizational systems to provide superior customer value – this has become a mantra for many managers involved in the quality movement. The quality movement traces its origins back to the pioneering work of writers such as Deming and Juran, work that had an enormous impact in Japan, especially during the immediate period of post-war reconstruction.[23] At the basis of the quality movement is a: managerial philosophy that seeks to increase organizational flexibility enabling companies to adapt to changing market conditions and rapidly adjust operations to meet the requirements of on-going and emerging programmes of change. Lowering costs, gaining employee commitment and ensuring continuous improvement in the delivery of services and/or the manufacture of products to meet changing customer expectations, are all part of the modern corporate push for quality management.[24]

The proponents of quality are inordinately fond of lists that articulate their rules and principles for achieving quality.[25] From such lists, and from empirical research into *The Transformation of Japanese Corporate Cultures*,[26] we have abstracted the gist of what, prescriptively, is seen to characterize quality organization.[27]

Prescribing Quality

Customers, both internal and external, will be sovereign, because quality is defined by the customer. The customer will be at the centre of the quality strategy, and all management and organization systems will be oriented to serving both internal and external customers. Consequently, organization design should reflect the importance of the customer: unnecessary buffers between organization members and customers should be reduced. Hence, organization vision, strategy, structure and job design should all be built around a customer focus. Vision will be long-term in outlook: strategy will be focused on how the organization will do what it does, better, in variably projected foreseeable futures. Organizations that achieve quality will do it through instilling customer concern as the main emphasis throughout the company: customer service tasks and solutions will be central, and so organizational structure processes and jobs will be designed to serve the customers. Quality organizations will be egalitarian organizations, according to the research reported in Kono and Clegg.[28] Separate styles of dress for managers and other employees, separate entrances, dining rooms, washrooms and other signs of symbolic differentiation will be consciously minimized.

Strategic HRM systems will stress positive public recognition of innovation through either symbolic or remunerative rewards, even when initiatives are not successful, in order to foster an 'enterprising spirit'. Employees should understand clearly that their performance and their rewards are closely related. Transparency will be the key. The HRM system will be strategic in that it is tailored to the individual in the organization, rather than the organization's need for a standardized system. Corporate cultures will be vitalized and empowered teams will be focused on customer-oriented innovation. Information systems will be designed to monitor and predict what customers actually, or might conceivably, want. The spaces between customers and core organizational processes will be minimized, and organizational reward systems will be designed so that customer service excellence is rewarded.

Organizations will link rewards to quality to ensure that this is maintained through the on-going education and training of all employees. Without this training the analytical skills required for continuous improvement will not be achieved. Thus, such organizations will be premised on full participation: quality will be the accountable basis for everyone's work. Practising management by analysis rather than by individual performance ratings will encourage management to adopt more imaginative analytic techniques than the usually dysfunctional measurement of performance at the employee level. The definition of 'who the organization is' will be widened so that it involves every member of an organization, including outside suppliers, with whom partnership development should be practised. The quality of the business will reside in the quality of its long-term partnering networks with other firms and with customers, who should also be seen as stakeholder members of the organization. Quality organizations will be exemplars of civic responsibility, where corporate citizens abide by good citizenship rules and regulations.

Distributed and networked technology should allow quality to be managed at the lowest levels of subsidiarity. This requires widespread use of information technologies such as intranet, Internet, expert systems, distributed database systems and multimedia. IT is the technical-rational core of the intelligent, quality-focused organization. Change and improvement oriented to quality must be continuous and all-encompassing, premised on rapid improvement prototyping and benchmarking on best-in-class organizations, characterized by reduced cycle time. 'Do it better; do it faster' will be one maxim; another will be conformance to standards that aim to produce zero-free defects. Understanding and reducing variation in every process is essential, as is getting it right first time by focusing on prevention rather than detection: For any of these to be achieved, continuous technical training will be vital.

The Quality Movement and TQM

In general, as we have argued, the rise of the quality paradigm in the West grew out of a desire to emulate and catch up with Japan which, from the late 1970s onwards, was seen as the number one threat to the US competitive terms. During the early 1980s Japanese competitive advantage came to be seen not so much in terms of a unique national advantage that attached to Japanese culture *per se* as in terms of more specific aspects of the country's corporate cultures and their transformation in the post-war era. The reasoning went that if the Japanese, through a commitment to quality, could restructure their organization cultures, then so could enterprises in other countries, by building similar commitments to customers, making use of teamwork rather than competitive individualism, and following the practices of continuous improvement. The quality paradigm of TQM appeared to offer an opportunity to beat Japan by adopting Japanese managerial methods.

While the recent adoption of TQM looked to Japan, its roots were elsewhere. The focus on quality derived from Quality Assurance (QA) systems based on nationally or internationally documented standards, designed initially to ensure that military procurements met Defense Department guidelines in the US and widely used during the Second World War. Having been used to place statistical controls on quality, the method developed to monitor Total Quality Control (TQC), from customer requirements through to product delivery. Increasingly, quality has become associated less with achieving 'conformance to requirements'[29] and more with progressive, continuous improvement achieved through involving employees (and customers, suppliers and end-users) in group problem-solving of processes. Thus, there was an irony attendant upon the initial reception of the Japanese challenge in the United States.

The quality movement really gathered pace after the Second World War in Japan, where the work of early pioneers such as Demming and Juran was not only well received and understood, but became the basis for indigenous innovation in approaches to quality, such as *kaizen*. While the Japanese developed the lean production system in part by refining ideas introduced by the US during the period of post-war occupation, the US had lost its focus on quality in all areas except defence contracting. Thus, in the early 1980s the Americans relearnt from Japan something that they had first taught it: the importance of quality.

Today there are many different emphases in approaches to quality, depending on which guru's influence is most keenly felt, but rather than dwelling on these as 'sects' (for such is their devotion to doctrine), it makes more sense to look at the common characteristics of the 'broad church' of quality, known as Total Quality Management. The work of Dawson and Palmer is useful for such an overview because it identifies seven main elements of the quality movement:

- A management philosophy of change.
- An emphasis on continuous improvement.
- Application of appropriate quality control techniques.
- Group problem-solving of process operations.
- A focus on 'internal' and 'external' customer-supplier relations.
- A commitment to employee involvement.
- A climate of trust and co-operation, and a non-adversarial system of industrial relations.[30]

Total Management

TQM involves a total management approach to quality improvements, one that seeks to involve all employees, customers and suppliers in quality issues. It is a holistic approach to quality management that builds change management into its frame rather than seeking to ensure quality assurance only through conformance with standards or through shop-floor initiatives somewhat disassociated from the organization's management:

> In essence it is a management philosophy of change which is based on the view that change is a necessary and natural requirement of organizations wishing to keep pace with dynamic external business market environments and continually improve existing operating systems. Those organizations embracing this new management philosophy support an ideology of participation and collaboration through involving

employees in certain managerial decision-making processes. The philosophy based on an approach to quality incorporates the skill and expertise of employees in a group decision-making exercise which has the backing and commitment of senior management. The total approach requires the involvement of chief executive officers (who are expected to strongly endorse the programme and align themselves with the objectives), other managerial groups, supervisors and shopfloor, branch level personnel. In other words, it is a philosophy of change which centres on the management of continual improvement through involving employees in group problem-solving of processes, rather than end-product quality issues.[31]

But a proclamation by top management introducing total management approach to quality does not make it happen. Dawson and Palmer's research suggests that, empirically, some managers do resist an approach that may diminish their symbolic and actual power. The 'empowerment' element of TQM may give more discretionary control to team members; power may move from supervisors to the supervised – hardly something with which front-line supervisors, in particular, feel relaxed and comfortable. Not surprisingly, Dawson and Palmer found that management sought to retain control by limiting the empowerment of their employees;[32] hence, the widespread use of empowered teams does not seem to be a popular aspect of the implementation of quality, where that empowerment affects managerial imperative. Interestingly, the managerialist aspects of the quality paradigm make assumptions about the unitary nature of the culture at work, but it is the evidently plural and sectionalist reality of that culture that often undermines the unitary assumptions.

Continuous Improvement
This is the second hallmark of the quality paradigm, with its emphasis on the importance of incremental, as opposed to radical, innovation. The management seeks to cultivate throughout the organization the expectation that small changes can improve processes; existing attitudes see such minor adjustments and changes as a threat to entrenched attitudes and identities, and therefore resist them. To get to this point may take a major, symbolically transformational change of organization culture, where that

culture has in the past been premised on adversarial 'shopfloor versus management' (us and them) attitudes. To expect this to occur because management has suddenly found an enthusiasm for quality would be naive in the extreme. We are not suggesting that transformation cannot occur but that it is rarely likely to do so because senior management wishes it. Far more concrete changes, in many areas, over a considerable period of time, will be necessary. Dawson and Palmer's case studies in Australia, as well as those of Kono and Clegg in Japan, investigate organizations which invest heavily in training, team building and staging activities designed to create a 'vitalized' culture.[33] As Dawson and Palmer elaborate, achieving this in a multicultural and complex context, such as exists in many Australian organizations, makes the transformation very much more difficult to realize than in the far less multi-culturally complex Japanese case: Kono and Clegg point to the specifically Japanese aspects of the larger culture in sustaining many Japanese organizational transformations, as well as the organization level variables involved.

Quality Control

A third aspect of the TQM paradigm is the application of appropriate quality control techniques, not after the production process, as quality inspection, but as a constitutive part of it, premised on shopfloor workers exercising this control by means of various statistical tools applied to process operations. There is evidence to suggest that measurement fetishism can accompany TQM initiatives.[34] The symbolic aspects of measurement are easily sold as a package over which consultants have mastery that can be trained into others. In the majority of cases the statistical competencies that were promised rarely seemed to become widely distributed; instead, they would often be adopted by one or two people who felt comfortable with the techniques; thus they were developed as a resource-base of personal power rather than becoming a transparent device of collective empowerment.

Group Problem Solving

Such approaches are integral to TQM. Many specific techniques – such as brainstorming – are used to raise general topics that can then be focused on more selectively, and their complexity mastered by flow-analysis. Data may then be collected to measure various aspects of these processes; further brainstorming analyses problems and issues raised by interpretation of the data, which is followed by further analysis. At this stage the problems should be traced back to root causes, perhaps using the model known in Japan as the 'fishbone'. For groups to function effectively as problem-solving communities presumes relatively undistorted communication unhindered by any systematic barriers to entry into the quality dialogue. While none may be seen or even presumed to exist by management, there may be a lack of cultural capital, such as ability to communicate effectively in a common language. Dawson and Palmer found that in multicultural workplaces group problem-solving techniques were severely limited in their effectiveness because not everyone could communicate effectively or with confidence in the same language.[35] Additionally, where permanent night-shifts were in operation there was an important cultural divide that TQM could rarely overcome.[36]

Customer–Supplier Relations
Integral to the TQM paradigm is the assumption that every stage in any process is always supplying a product or service to a customer, whether that customer is the next in line in the formal organization cycle or an actual end-user. Hence there is an explicit focus on 'internal' and 'external' customer-supplier relations. First, customer needs require clarification through frequent, regular communication. Once it is known what is wanted and what is not, in terms of quality, then appropriate steps can be taken to raise quality to meet expectations. Where customer expectations are vague, ambiguous or unrealistic – a problem often more apparent with final or end-users – then steps must be taken to build links with them in order to clarify requirements. Demanding customers, both internal and external, are a vital element in the quality paradigm: through them communication is encouraged not only within the organization but also with suppliers and external customers, all of whom can become participants in various organizational dialogues oriented towards quality control. Establishing long-term networks with suppliers can introduce elements of bureaucracy into what were previously more market-oriented relations. Standards are often much more closely monitored and controlled in tied-suppliers than they are in those contracted on the spot-market. Project teams that span contracting organizations, whose job it is to implement and monitor standards in the supply chain, are not unusual.

Employee Involvement

A sixth element of the TQM paradigm stresses commitment to employee involvement, to be implemented through a strategic human resources management approach that emphasizes training programmes, continuous education, multi-skilling, the use of multi-function project teams, and cross-career development. Empirically, the association of the quality paradigm with a particular or distinct set of personnel practices remains unproven.[37] Evidence exists that quality initiatives can coexist with various HRM practices and that a variety of inconsistent HRM practices may be introduced under the banner of the quality paradigm. As in most other areas of quality, the rhetoric and the realities are a variable gap, depending on the contingent and contextual circumstances. Many human-resource management academics address the HRM implications of the new paradigm; Burack, Burack, Miller and Morgan do so in terms of a new, quality paradigm that relates directly to the MIT studies; these 'featured themes centre on the continuing high commitment and high performance of their members . . . mutual trust and commitment, management credibility, blending long- and short-term approaches, participative management and a shared clear vision of the enterprise's future niche, organization and managerial approaches . . . [emphasizing] contingency approaches best suited to their circumstances.'[38] The empirical occurrence of these themes are evidence of a new 'psychological contract' located in 'new paradigm organizations', defined in terms of Table 5.2.

Burack et al. see these new paradigm organizations as drawing selectively on these elements, while at the same time recognizing 'interdependencies between life and work' that find 'tangible expression in flexible working arrangements, dual career policies, daycare facilities, and support of community projects'.[39] Hence, new paradigm organizations, of which Hewlett-Packard is held up as a model, seem also to be workplaces that accept an enhanced range of stakeholders, making them, for instance, more family-centred and parent-friendly, as they seek to cater to a wider range of employee identities than just those of 'employee'. Other key stakeholders are communities and supplier-partners.

High-trust Relationships

The TQM paradigm stresses the building of high-trust relationships, and the development of non-adversarial systems of industrial

Table 5.2: The New Paradigm of Organizations

Cost-effective structures
Enduring quality, value and service
Blending long- and short-term approaches
Vision clear, focused and shared
People second 'bottom line'
   Management credibility
   Participative management and employee involvement
   High-achievement focus
   Mutual trust and commitment
   Combines group and entrepreneurial approaches
Managing paradox
Adaptive and learning environment
Strategic fit – external and internal environment,
organization
Employment relations: reflect new realities and limitations of
   firm due to competition, complex and uncertain change

Source: Burack et al., 'New Paradigm Approaches' (1994), p. 145

relations. In large part, the enhanced communication, and the common focus on customers and quality, is assumed to encourage this anyway. However, it has to go hand in hand with a restructuring of industrial relations away from adversarialism and centralization towards a more participative and enterprise-based system. Management aims to incorporate unions as partners in quality whose support will be essential for the success of the TQM paradigm; without this the enterprise may not prosper and survive, and no one will win, a claim that unionists often regard with some scepticism.[40] Of course, a call for trust and commitment will not gain credibility in an atmosphere marked by other strategic initiatives that threaten job security, such as 'downsizing'.

Some observers claim that TQM spearheads a 'marketization' of corporate hierarchies, and thus regard the quality paradigm as 'anti-bureaucratic'. However, while the introduction of a market consciousness premised on customer service may have this effect, other aspects of the quality paradigm run counter to this. Psychological contracts and the commitment to 'statistical fetishism' can be another means of developing workflow bureaucracy.

Notionally, it is highly critical of bureaucracy: the aim, after all, is to reform the organization through a focus on customers and internal and external markets rather than the pre-existing structures of organization design and process. But, in so far as these reforms proceed through standards-articulation they do so in a way that conforms with the earlier engineering traditions of scientific management. Where they differ is in the involvement of employees in developing these standards: they are no longer the resistant subjects of a design conceived elsewhere by the engineering department as the 'one best way' to work. Employees, through the philosophy of continuous improvement, have a continuing active role to play in TQM.

Politics and TQM

The politics of organizations under the quality paradigm are also likely to differ. If the seven principles of the philosophy propounded by Dawson and Palmer are implemented there should be a transition from organizational power premised on the defence of existing positions and resources, to power that seeks to facilite transformation in the name of quality.[41] As we have seen, this implies major changes for industrial relations systems. Empirically, a great deal depends on the precise manner in which the quality paradigm is introduced and implemented, as Dawson and Palmer stress by contrasting less successful with more successful strategies.[42] But the strategies are always situationally specific and embedded in local context: it seems unlikely that the lists of general principles can be refined for faultless implementation. Better to realize that all such quality paradigm strategies will involve complex politics that are situationally specific.

The political elements are many: broadband skill formation, multi-skilling, job enrichment, enlargement and empowerment all help to increase the numbers of multi-skilled employees who are less committed to the defence of pre-existing craft-based control of specialized knowledge; however, they do not guarantee its abandonment, especially where greater status and resources are associated with the defence of previous privilege. The stress on markets and customers in the paradigm may be seen as political, introducing the market into spheres of organizational life previously immune to 'new right' conceptions, while at the same time helping to overcome the 'excessive individualism' that management observers since Elton Mayo have seen as one of the costs of the

Taylor system.[43] But highly individual managers skilled in the use of managerial imperative may well have difficulties in accepting that the imperative that marks the boundaries of their symbolic power and difference should be surrendered to a collective wisdom emanating from an empowered shopfloor.

A politics of IT is also associated with the quality paradigm. IT is used extensively to make performance and quality standards visible and accountable to employees in the organization. Large-scale video screens can express quality-related information in a simple code that all can understand, alerting people to their degree of success in meeting these standards. Two aspects of this are important. First, everyone is encouraged to become a self-regarding subject: employees' view of themselves will be affected by the way in which the kanban represents the work that they are responsible for; that is, as adjuncts to quality, to which they must hold themselves accountable and to which others, including superordinates and colleagues, will hold them accountable. Such self-regarding behaviour helps to ensure that the need for external surveillance and exercise of power is minimized, as the functions of control become internalized. A part of this concerns the strategic human resource management adjuncts of the quality paradigm: these frequently seek to break down both collective strength (the power of the union as an adversarial organization in the workplace) and individual isolation. The union function of articulating plural and countervailing power in the workplace becomes less of a problem when the union, either directly or indirectly through its members, is formally involved in the quality process. Everyone is assumed to have an interest in quality; thus, to oppose it could only be construed as bloody-minded opposition to the interests of employees whose jobs depend on continually improving quality. IT also offers flexible options to organizations and their employees rather than binding them all to one architecture determined by the central task-flow of the production line.

ORGANIZATION LEARNING

The quality paradigm was a central focus of the 1980s, when, in many countries, governments and management associations institutionalized a concern with quality.[44] Hodgetts, Luthans and Lee provide a perspective that sees the quality paradigm blending

Figure 5.1: World Class Organizations

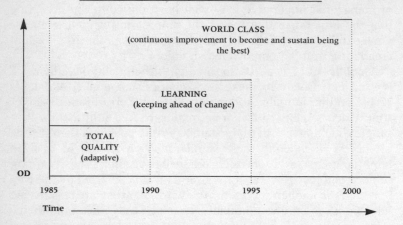

Source: Hodgetts, Luthans and Lee, 'New Paradigm Organization' (1996)

into the learning organization, which, in turn, they see morphing into the 'world-class' movement (see Figure 5.1), as the concerns of OD (Organizational Development) shift. We shall consider organization learning first.

Although the notion of organization learning has been around for some time it really gained widespread market acceptance when Senge's book on *The Fifth Discipline*, promoted to a fanfare from *Fortune* magazine, hit the bookstores in 1992. *'Forget your old, tired ideas about leadership. The most successful corporation of the 1990s will be something called a learning organization'*, said the cover. Beyond the hype, what Senge's book did, in a readable and accessible format, was to popularize ideas that had long been familiar in social systems theory, particularly in the contributions of Donald Schon and Chris Argyris, and relate them to the everyday experience of management. Senge, Schon and Argyris all derive from the most influential approach to learning in management circles, but the 'cybernetic wing' of the organization learning literature is not the only approach: 'The metaphor of organizational learning is constructed on the basis of analogies with two different entities: the cybernetic system and the human mind. Fundamental to the former conception is the notion of information. Like other natural or social systems, the organization can be conceived as an evolving information model whose most interesting aspect is its capacity for self-design.[45]

In cybernetic terms, learning may be 'single-loop' or 'double-loop'.[46] Single-loop learning feeds back on to present competencies and routines of knowledge and their application in order to remove obstacles to their functioning. It is based on four principles:

- Systems must be able to perceive, monitor and seek out significant features of their environment.
- Systems must be able to connect the information thus acquired with the operational norms that guide systemic behaviour.
- Systems must be able to identify significant deviations from these norms.
- Systems must be able to take corrective action when these deviations are detected.[47]

However, these organizational processes are only possible because the organizational system as a whole is normatively oriented. Adaptation to environment changes is made possible by norms, standards of variability and information systems. To go beyond single-loop learning requires the acquisition of new norms, their elaboration, development and diffusion throughout the organization. When this occurs we may refer to it as 'double-loop learning'. The hallmark of the latter is its fundamentally recursive character: learning transforms the existing stock of organizational know-how contained in existing normative routines and competencies. Organizations need both, although the evidence suggests that learning which is 'double-loop' is far more difficult to achieve.[48] For one thing, it demands a shift away from cybernetic analogies to ones that are more individual-oriented and focused on the second source of the metaphor of organizational learning: the human mind. Within this particular framework 'learning is no longer . . . objectified in norms, procedures, routines and standards. Rather it is the cognitive activity which produces images, representations, causal links, and which is sensitive not only to human passions but to the social and organizational conditioning of thought as well.'[49]

Learning can take many forms: it may involve accelerating learning curves through the institutionalization of personal knowledge into widespread organizational knowledge, through the quality circle. It may involve introducing behavioural change through trial and error, where actions are checked against their outcomes in order to make subsequent adjustments to the actions in order to improve quality or reduce cycle-time, through continuous improvement. Enhanced adaptation to stimuli in the organizational environment may occur through attention to end-user and customer concerns that are incorporated into changed search rules, attention rules and organizational goals. Existing managerial cognitive maps may also be modified in the light of new information.

Many scholars of organization learning agree in their emphasis on the role of environmental adaptation, the distinctiveness of organization (as opposed to individual) learning, and the identification of culture, strategy, structure and the environment as the major sources of innovation that create and reinforce learning. For larger organizations, the rapidly accelerating pace of technological change may demand learning because of the strategic complexity of new product development processes.[50] Product life-cycles shorten and 'lean production' emerges,[51] based on alternative East Asian – particularly Japanese – forms of organization using JIT, MRP, TQM, etc.[52] Research suggests that it is the differential ability of smaller firms to learn quickly, particularly about technological opportunities, that has been responsible for a changing pattern of competitive relationships between large and small firms in favour of the latter.[53] Not that large firms do not, or need not learn. That way lies failure, as was demonstrated by companies like PanAm, Rootes, Hanson and many others which failed to modify their strategy, change their structure, revitalize their culture or adapt to their environment. The existence of so many corporate failures indicates that it is not easy to translate the signals which suggest that learning may be necessary.

Organization learning must be the result of learning by individuals and must be institutionally embedded in the procedures of an organization. Otherwise the learning will remain at the individual level rather than being translated into organization learning. This requires a culture that is conducive to it. Hayes, Wheelwright and Clark develop the parameters of what they call 'continual learning', which we have referred to as double-loop learning – learning to do different things in different ways.[54]

There are two distinct ways in which organizations can strive for this advantage: through exploitative or through exploratory learning. Different emphases in the literature favour each of these two modes.

Exploitative Learning

The model of exploitative learning emerges from detailed research conducted by Adler, and Adler and Cole, into continuous improvement based on knowledge-workers at NUMMI, a joint Japanese–American venture in automobile manufacturing in the USA which has emerged as an aspirational benchmark for many firms.[55] Adler and his associates clearly share a fascination for the 'lean production' paradigm in which a detailed prescription of the task is the best basis for learning, constituted principally in terms of production efficiency: knowledge-based workers learn as they work and thus enhance the organization.

Exploitative learning displays its origins in quality management techniques. At NUMMI, where teams of four or five workers perform tasks of relatively short duration, are highly specialized, have detailed work procedures and a modest degree of job rotation, the emphasis is on quality through continuous improvement. The system lends itself to rapid learning. Workers at NUMMI learn from making an explicit model of what they already know, applied to relatively short, focused tasks, in quality circles. Explicitness about rules and routines facilitates learning.

Adler and his colleagues identify knowledge-workers as those who work in rule-enabling organizations rather than rule-constraining ones. The NUMMI case is thus an example of 'enabling' rather than 'coercive' rule setting. In rule-enabling settings continuous improvement develops through the structuring of desire, understanding and trust:

- Workers learn to share with managers a 'desire' to achieve excellence and to work towards a job well done.
- Workers come to 'understand' that their jobs depend on the competitive success of the organization and that the best way to protect their jobs is constantly to improve the way that they do them, and thus continuously to improve the competitive position of their employers.
- Managers and workers develop 'trust' in each other and this trust is amplified through the commitment shown by the workers.

Exploitative learning such as that stressed by Adler contrasts with exploratory learning, highlighted in the work of James March.[56]

Exploitative learning is typical of the learning that occurs in more bureaucratic organizations, where learning develops from existing routines. It is associated with defining, measuring and improving performance. It advances through redefining work in terms of systematic reasoning, improvements to existing capabilities and technologies, and cost-reductions. It refines existing capabilities, forcing through standardization and routinization. Generally, exploitative learning is risk-averse. Its benefits are relatively immediate and fairly predictable. Exploitative learning tends to continue existing trends, perhaps accelerating them slightly.

While the exploitative learning model suggests that all members of an organization should learn, it is clear that some learning is more strategic than others. Usually located at the organization apex, in top management, is interpretative strategic learning. Rhetorically, strategic management increasingly has more affinity with the activities of listening, learning and launching conversations rather than commanding, controlling and communication imperatives. The clear leadership that is vital is likely to accord with the three major leadership roles of communicator, integrator and planner,[57] which combine with the symbol-laden aspects of the management of meaning and organization *realpolitik*.[58]

How do communication, integration and planning combine to produce strategies for organization learning? Highly successful new firms maximize the circulation of learning throughout the 'clever company'. Organizations engaged in innovation need to devote resources to intelligence-gathering as an aspect of learning. They need to scan their environments broadly, regularly and actively as 'test-makers'.[59] Such management needs to *enact* interpretation, particularly where radical technological innovation has creatively destroyed or marginalized existing competencies: many traditional tasks of management will be then undertaken by computer-based technologies and diagnostic, interpersonal, creative and systems thinking skills become the order of the day.

Exploratory Learning

Exploratory learning allows for a different type of learning: it is no longer a question of simply learning from routines; it is associated with complex search, basic research, innovation, variation, risk-taking and more relaxed controls. The stress is on flexibility, investments in learning and the creation of new capabilities. It may be thought of in terms of coaching and cajolery, and their articulation as training, advice and recommendations: think of a sports team and the role of the coach in continuously improving both individual and team performance. Exploratory learning characterizes more intelligent organizations, where innovation, rather than refining what already exists, produces creative discontinuities. Exploratory learning offers distant time horizons and uncertain benefits as its vision. It offers the chance of increasing performance levels significantly beyond trendlines; of course, if risky ventures fail, these may fall.

Typically, exploratory learning comprises fleeting, flexible moments within the overall orderly flow. Take humour: its role in relieving tension in organizational settings, or of expressing criticism in a way that is socially acceptable, is well-known, but it can also be an occasion for learning. Humour disrupts the routines of everyday seriousness; it expresses criticism, contradiction, ambiguity and contrary worldviews. Humour is a classically improvisational form: unscripted, contextualized, creative and potentially code-breaking. Improvisations can pose unique opportunities for insight and innovation as they break through the structure of routines. Action-oriented organizations in the heat of action, like firefighters or combat units.[60] provide an organization model of improvisation sometimes in harmony, sometimes in counterpoint, with the script that steers normalcy. All organizations have moments of improvisation; not all organizations seem capable of capturing these and making them work for their future. In many, structure strives to overwhelm novelty rather than feel the shock of the new.

The premises from which Adler and his associates begin, as well as the specifics of the NUMMI case, favour the 'lean production' model of clear and detailed standardization. According to Weick and Westley, Volvo's Uddevalla plant offered a contrast as the conditions were more craft-like.[61] Adler and Cole suggest that in craft circumstances that lack clear structure it is more difficult to learn.[62] Here, individuals learn more than the organization does: the lack of structure in the latter means that little of what is innovated is incorporated; it does not shift from the individual's skill-set to that of the organization. Within a two-hour work-cycle, for example, it is hard to spot the improvements that produce a positive effect:

The Volvo model is a concept of characterizing the willingness of Volvo, when new production facilities are about to be planned (either completely new or renewed), to allow people in project groups to develop new production systems not necessarily located in the body of mainstream ideas. The result is that people's unique creativity has been left free, and recurrent innovations have been made when new plants are built. The Volvo-model concept thus implies a company's trust in the project group's abilities. This implies flexibility and an orientation towards trying out new solutions to production-related problems.[63]

In contrast to the stress on routines in exploitative learning by Adler and associates, Weick and Westley suggest that attention should focus on the unexpected, the idiosyncratic and the serendipitous that flies in the face of tight control: these are the harbingers of exploratory learning. 'If moments of balance between exploration and exploitation are transient, then researchers need to look at uncommon, often inconspicuous events to spot learning. And practitioners need to be less enamoured with large-scale training programmes and campaigns of transformation and more alert to places and moments where canons and dogma become suspect.'[64] A new plant in a new site is an organizational opportunity to achieve the type of learning that Weick and Westley propose. The Volvo plants of Kalmar and Uddevalla provided such occasions:

In such new factories there are no immediate signs of inertia where human manners, habits and values are taken for granted. Newly recruited people are open-minded regarding their opinions of work content and organization, at least if they have not been employed in the same company before. They are creating the culture of the new plant, a culture which will be the basis for the new traditions. These newly shaped traditions will obviously differ from the traditions of the older plants.[65]

The extent of the innovation in work practices at Uddevalla can be seen from Figures 5.2 and 5.3, which are the original blueprints of the layout of the plant. Automated vehicles carried the chassis and parts to the workgroups, who in teams of eight assembled all of several vehicles in their shift, becoming, with training, quite skilled mechanics.[66] The Uddevalla plant was born out of the profits of the mid-1980s' boom in the European market, and closed with the downturn in the early 1990s. Today it is a joint venture producing specialist vehicles, but the work organization developed there will be a prototype for much production work in the twenty-first century.

The moral is clear: there has to be a strategy for linking exploratory learning to exploitative learning. Levinthal and March propose that the survival of any organization depends upon being sufficiently exploitative as to ensure current viability and sufficiently exploratory as to ensure its future viability.[67] Too much exploitation risks organizational survival by creating a 'competency trap', where increasingly obsolescent capabilities continue to be elaborated. Too much exploration insufficiently linked to exploitation leads to 'too many undeveloped ideas and too little distinctive competence'.

Strategies for Organization Learning

Strategies for achieving the linkage between exploratory and exploitative learning characterize the latest developments in the lean production system. Rawlinson and Wells provide an example.[68] Under lean production work teams problem-solve, but the learning from the problem solved does not stay within the team. Manufacturing engineers, as in Taylorism, take suggestions for making work smarter or faster and recode them into standard job sheets or operating procedures. This becomes the benchmark for work within the plant. But the process does not stop there.

The benchmark, once achieved within one team and one plant, can be virtually circulated throughout the entire organization, worldwide. The interlinkage of plants by Electronic Data Interchange (EDI) allows for the learning to be distributed globally, immediately, virtually. Imagine an improved process being exploratively innovated in a plant in the UK. How could management make it virtual, distribute it freely and widely? This is a technical problem with two dimensions: portability and embeddedness.

The first dimension, that of portability, must meet three criteria if it is to be achieved. First, the exploratory learning be standardized, made more exploitative. This means that the moment of

Figure 5.2: The Volvo Uddevalla Plant Layout

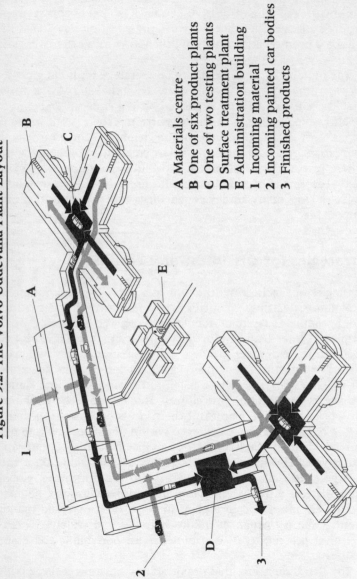

A Materials centre
B One of six product plants
C One of two testing plants
D Surface treatment plant
E Administration building
1 Incoming material
2 Incoming painted car bodies
3 Finished products

Source: Volvo Motor Company, 1988

Source: Volvo Motor Company, 1988

Figure 5.3: The Volvo Uddevalla Plant Layout

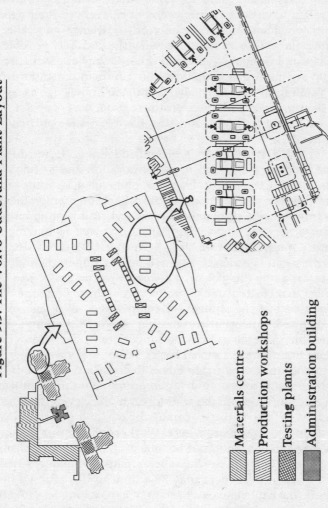

Materials centre

Production workshops

Testing plants

Administration building

insight – disorder in the orderly routine – must be codified into standardized terms that all can understand. Second, standardized information must be commodified. The dependence of the exploratory insight on the individuals who produced it must be eliminated by commodifying tacit knowledge. It must be rendered as something that any person could so, rather than something that one person might have done. If management can reduce their dependency on individuals as the bearers of knowledge and skills by translating these into computer-based artifacts, it is possible to manipulate and combine them with other factors of production in ways that are impossible if they remain a human possession. This means a shift from the knowledge-worker to knowledge as a pure factor of production. Third, abstract properties need to be developed for the phenomenon that has been standardized and commodified.

The second dimension, that of embeddedness, flows directly from the properties of the digitized corporation and technologies such as EDI. Exploratory learning embedded in innovation becomes tangible when embedded in a computer program. It is easy to transmit this throughout the world. But a program may not capture the tacit knowledge that is involved in making the exploratory innovation work. It is here that EDI can assist. The work process can be videoed, scanned on to computer and downloaded instantly by the globally networked corporation. The tacit knowledge that created an exploratory breakthrough in one plant becomes a part of the strategy of competitive advantage of the global, digitized, intelligent corporation. As Rawlinson and Wells conclude, 'the pace of work is no longer controlled and defined on a plant basis but on a global basis'.[69]

The implications of portable embeddedness are massive in the age of the smart machine. Innovation premised on the tacit learning and embedded skills of the workforces of the cleverest countries can rapidly be standardized, commoditized and abstracted into organizational processes anywhere. Workers with lower standards of schooling and education can be tooled up by their organization to match the competencies of more creative employees in the cleverest of countries. There may be a limit to this process, however. While the exploitative utilization of exploratory learning that occurs in a sophisticated system may be generalized as a portable standardized, commodified and abstracted process, the sociotechnical conditions that gave rise to the exploratory learning in the first place, by definition, cannot. They are unique and highly contingent upon the sophisticated system conditions that produced them. Global firms should thus ensure that portable processes have not cut them off from initial sources of exploratory learning. Important socio-technical system properties attach to these exploratory opportunities: certain systems of education and training, and education/training/work articulation, will offer greater opportunities for exploratory creativity to develop. (The typical schooling system of rote learning characteristic of much of East Asia, continued into tertiary education, is hardly the socio-technical system that one would require in a system that is to produce considerable exploratory innovation. Throughout East Asia this is a matter of considerable policy concern.)

The implications of these developments are substantial for those organizations that can achieve exploratory and portable exploitative gains. They are even more substantial for the national system of governance within whose administrative frameworks such exploratory breakthroughs may occur. Being a clever country is no longer a sufficient basis for ensuring national competitive edge: it is not so much nations, but firms, that are competing globally, and they are able to ensure that better learning is no longer the preserve of nationally superior systems. Indeed, it may be the lot of the cleverer countries in the new paradigm to provide the infrastructure for exploratory learning that rapidly disseminates through the global firm in such a way that the competitive advantage of nations is undermined. Under conditions of globalization the dynamic system properties of capitalism as a world system will be enhanced.

World Class Organization

Recent commentators such as Hodgetts, Luthans and Lee see the next step in the development of organization learning as the emergence of what they call the 'world-class organization' paradigm: 'Some companies have managed to go beyond the learning organization stage to become world-class organizations . . . described as being the best in its class or better than its competitors around the world, at least in several strategically important areas'.[70] Being world class is premised on being 'best-in-class' in areas already familiar from the organization learning literature, such as customer-based focus, continuous improvement, creative HRM, egalitarian climate, and technological support. The continual learning paradigm makes some rhetorically normative assumptions about people as members of organizations. It assumes that all employees are responsible, thinking adults who inherently want to do their best, and that human resources are too valuable to waste or to leave untapped; that there is no monopoly on creativity – creative talents and skills may be widely distributed at all levels of an organization and employees will raise important problems and concerns if they feel the organization will respond appropriately; that work is more interesting when people are challenged in performing it; that people take pride in training others; that better performance occurs when artificial differences between people are removed; that real responsibility motivates high performance; and that people make better decisions and implement them better when they work together. We can see, prescriptively, how these assumptions play out in an approach to organization learning that seeks to orient organizations towards the aspirational benchmark of being 'world class' in the work of Burack et al.[71] This approach begins with the recognition that more than one path leads to the new paradigm organization, depending on the contingency-base from which the organization starts. One path presumes the further consolidation of corporate excellence, as may be seen in organizations such as Hewlett-Packard. The other path is taken by organizations who realize that they have to change to survive; that otherwise they will cease to trade. The paths are outlined in a 'prescriptive model' in Table 5.3.

The prescriptive model is quite clear, and does not require further text to elaborate it. It demonstrates that TQM is a strategic intervention that in theory touches on all aspects of an organization, with perhaps the greatest impact on organizational bureaucracies, and political processes and cultures. The notion of 'psychological contract', for instance, is clearly cultural, while the review processes are bound to be political, as interests vested in existing bureaucratic structures are threatened.

Learning implies both outcomes and processes. The notion of virtuous learning circles suggests comparative improvement in efficiency, however one chooses to measure it and in whatever stakeholder terms: profits; quality of working; supply of jobs; consumer satisfaction; environmental impact or macro-economic outcomes. Vicious learning, by contrast, implies diminished

Table 5.3: Employee Relationships: A Prescriptive Model

Poor Employment Relationships	Good to Excellent Employment Relationships
Step 1	
Shaky financial foundation	Financial foundation reasonably stable
• Establishing survival situation; importance of financial conditions	• Ongoing dialogue with people about structural change to assure continuous quality, value and service improvement, cost-effectiveness
• Open up communication lines so employees are informed	• Open meeting type of internal communication
• Seek to foster understanding and support	• Continued top management reinforcement of employee support systems
Step 2	
Recognition of malfunctioning organization structure design	Rendering of new organization structure design
• Reorganization and downsizing actions to strengthen costs, financial picture	• Strengthen long-term outlook
• Movement from short-term reliance to longer-term view	• Global structure
• Narrow view of industry and world markets enlarged slowly	• Increased vigilance relative to external threats and opportunities
• Re-examine culture and philosophy	• Formalize total quality management (TQM) philosophy and means of establishing and maintaining
Step 3	
Identification of a corporate mission, values and ideals	Formalization of critical corporate mission and values
• Clarification of mission	• Codification of more formal structural design
• Acknowledgement of	

Table 5.3: (continued)

Poor Employment Relationships	Good to Excellent Employment Relationships
critical role of employee	rather than vague, verbal generalities
• Develop pattern of management support to establish credibility	• Continuing acts of faith on part of company towards employees
• Share TQM philosophy	• Implementation of TQM programme
	• Considering empowerment for future

Step 4

Design of internal work processes	Refinement of TQM and employee involvement programmes
• Seek to gain support for a TQM effort	• Retaining programmes
• Work with managers to establish participative outlook	• Mentoring
• Work with employees to gain their involvement	• Carry out employee involvement/participative management (EI/PM) culture
• Emphasize teamwork	

Step 5

Movement towards a high-commitment/ high-productivity corporate environment #1	Participation in a high-commitment/ high-productivity proactive organization
• Seek to manage participation and involvement philosophies	• Furtherance of corporate credibility
• Establish credibility and emphasis on co-operation	• Watch and maintain programmes
• Seek to implement a TQM programme	• Be willing to revise or totally revamp
• Promote and support employee empowerment	• Exploit high-commitment/ high-productivity opportunities
• Launch training initiatives	

Table 5.3: (continued)

Poor Employment Relationships	Good to Excellent Employment Relationships
Step 6	
Movement towards a high-commitment/ high-productivity corporate environment #2 • Implementation and refinement of TQM effort • Seek to establish loyalty and commitment • Continue to reinforce new employment relations and philosophy	Maintaining high-commitment/ high-productivity organization and quality philosophy • Emphasis on continuous improvement, refinement of process and activities • Continuing cross-training and empowering process • Facilitate career mobility
Step 7	
Participation in high-commitment/ high-productivity organization • Establishment of a clear and explicit psychological contract • Instil quality, value and service standards as part of total quality efforts • Maintain high-support systems	Maintaining high-commitment/ high-productivity organization and TQM philosophy #2 • Review of designs, programmes and processes • Reorientation meetings

Source. After Durack *et al.,* 'New Paradigm Approaches' (1994) p 154

efficiency. Learning processes concern the achievement of these outcomes, the *how* and the *why*, rather than the *what* questions. Organization learning can occur through:

• Learning with clients; asking how, beyond market research, does the organization achieve a constant symbiosis and exchange with clients?

- Learning from outsiders; asking how does the organization tap the knowledge of consultants, academics, subcontractors, the community?
- Learning from each other; asking how is knowledge passed on within the group, from group to group, from division to division, or even from sector to sector?
- Learning from schemes for systematic knowledge capture and dissemination.[72]

According to McKinsey, managers in innovative firms learn that an appropriate top manager's role is proactive, committed, hands-off the detail, goal-setting and motivating; that dream-driven goals should be the company aspirations; that it demands an ability to 'zoom in' on customer needs, company strengths and the innovations required to ensure their match.[73] Project management will stress cross-functional teams, senior management sponsorship of projects and championing separate from the day-to-day organization politics. The focus will be on integrated innovation that improves existing products and processes, as well as aiming to supersede them, through changes that are pursued in close dialogue with the customers by managers, including senior management.

According to Goldman and Nagel, organizations and their managers must also *un*learn old rhetorics implying that co-operation is less desirable than competition; that labour-management relations have to be adversarial; that information is power and can be shared only to one's detriment; that trusting others makes one vulnerable; that complex problems admit of single technological solutions.[74] Additionally, for some organizations unlearning about innovation means realizing that breakthroughs are not the only targets to aim for; that markets will not create themselves once better mousetraps are invented; that infrastructure requirements do not take care of themselves; and that standards need not be constraining and their formulation need not be dull work. Incremental innovation, in other words, can be more valuable than radical transformations of systems.

Comparing companies that are winning with those that are losing market position, Hayes, Wheelwright and Clark conclude that the key difference is that winners constantly strive to be better, placing great emphasis on experimentation, integration, training and the building of critical organizational capabilities.[75]

Microsoft: A World-Class Organization?

Microsoft is a classic case of a company founded on the initial intelligence of a few people who have systematized that intelligence into an organization that learns through continuous self-critique, feedback and sharing of information. While Microsoft makes extensive use of the virtual technologies that it designs, spatially it is also quite a concentrated company, headquartered in Redmond, Washington State, in the USA. Consequently, as well as the virtual systems of feedback and communication there are many opportunities for face-to-face communication, often of a quite informal kind. Retreats are widely used. 'Postmortem reports' are also used for most post-project launches: these resemble aspects of Maoism, where one reflects rigorously and self-critically on the project process. Postmortem reports may take between three and six months to produce. They address not just what went well, but also what could have gone better or failed, looking at a detailed inventory covering the people involved, the product, its quality, the schedule and the process of production. Cusumano and Selby detail with remarkable frankness the many glitches involved in the development of major Microsoft products such as the various versions of Word and the slowness, and costs, with which the emergence of a learning organization took place in Microsoft.[76]

Microsoft hires smart people who must know the software business really well; only 2 or 3 per cent of those who apply to be software developers are invited to join Microsoft. But the company is not so successful just because it makes good selection decisions: it also nurtures creative people and technical skills through its organization design.[77] Multifunctional teams are the norm, comprised of distinctive functional skills and responsibilities that overlap at the boundaries. As new competencies are required they are hired in and people learn on the job, rather than from formal rules, regulations or training programmes. The organization seeks to ensure that technical skills have career paths associated with them. Of course, if there are to be careers there have to be products and services shifting rapidly in the marketplace. Microsoft's strategy has always been to make its own products the market standard and then to make them obsolescent before their competitors do so: hence, the market grows dynamically.

Managing dynamic technologically discontinuous markets

premised on complex innovation can be the reef of unmanageable creativity on which enterprise founders. Microsoft development is project-based, but project teams must maintain market, not just technical, focus. This focus is sustained by promoting innovation not in the technically feasible but in the commercially marketable under pressure of managerial limits on time, people and other resources. At any time several project teams will be working in parallel but they will also be in frequent communication with each other, and under central co-ordination. Project teams are encouraged to synchronize design and iron out conflicts in parallel process development with other teams. Strict time guidelines achieve this: teams have to report progress by a specified time and date so that any problems of design incompatibility that require debugging are spotted immediately. Similarly, any bugs inadvertently built in to a program must be fixed by its designers – rather like the Toyota 'lean production' line, where operatives fix faults that they spot or create, as Cusumano and Selby note.[78]

Microsoft is an entirely innovation- and marketing-focused company. Frequent incremental innovation is aided by the use of open-plan offices, a single site location, common tools and frequent customer trials (and feedback – there are over 2,000 people receiving customer calls in the USA alone). Moreover, a small range of specific measures monitors progress (such as individual daily reports on project development and brief monthly status reports on project team progress, formatted in terms of set of headings and sub-headings, both of which are e-mailed to supervisors; and three-monthly programme reviews for each project chaired by Bill Gates and other senior executives and attended by one or two key people from each project team). The use of quantitative metrics and benchmarks at Microsoft became a well-established practice over the years. Whatever is at issue, any case that relies on politics or emotion rather than data is unlikely to be received favourably by senior management. Use of such data typically addresses issues of quality, product and process.

Microsoft is based on teams whose members learn from each other, from other teams, from customers and from past mistakes. Teams seek to 'share knowledge in project management and quality control, as well as to build components that more than one project can utilize. Sharing and standardization save engineering and testing costs, make products more coherent to customers, and reduce the need for large customer support staffs'.[79] All of this takes place in a context where teams are continually pushed by senior management to imagine tomorrow today, forcing continuous innovation and improvement in a process that Cusumano and Selby term 'synch-and-stabilize',[80] in an iterative, incremental and concurrent process that 'continually synchronize[s] what people are doing as individuals and as members of different teams, and periodically stabilize(s) the product in increments – in other words, as the project proceeds, rather than once at the end'.[81]

The cultural, structural and personnel context in which this occurs, while it may be 'fervently antibureaucratic', is also simultaneously structured.[82] The structure is based not so much on rules for, and formalization of, operating procedures, as on formal reporting of loosely structured project work. Thus chunks of process development constructed by small teams are rendered manageable and are closely linked to customer feedback from the marketplace. Firmly structured but informal reporting mechanisms on daily progress keep a tight check; sophisticated personnel management practices help to compensate for the overwhelming technical, rather than managerial, skill-biases of most of the managers. The staff are the brightest and technically the best available from the élite universities in the USA, so 'it is not surprising that the company culture emphasizes technical competence and shipping products rather than adhering to rules and regulation, respecting formal titles, or cultivating skills in political infighting'.[83] The downside of this culture is that solutions are continually being reinvented because they have not been abstracted and systematized into the operating practices of the firm. As Microsoft develops its metrics it is attempting to transform the tacit knowledge of its employees into generalizable abstractions through standardizing, commodifying and abstracting that knowledge.

None of the systems that Microsoft uses was the result of a conscious design decision: rather they were emergent from the company's historical development, the problems that it faced and the disasters and solutions that it stumbled into, or shipped in, with the buying-in of key management expertise that brought solutions pioneered elsewhere. One of these was the realization that as Microsoft's product-range grew it resembled a series of distinct business lines that were best managed as organic entities rather than as projects staffed by interchangeable people, without 'ownership' of the projects. Organic entities grew into distinct small business units, where functional specialists worked in small teams with overlapping responsibilities. While Microsoft employees are expected to be flexible they are not expected to be so at the expense of career path and career ladders within the company. As stakeholders in the company, not just employees, they receive generous stock-options as part of their compensation package.

Microsoft developed as a company that wanted to make 'paradigm shifts' that flow from technological discontinuities in the digital world.[84] Talk of 'paradigm shifts' is not regarded as academic at Microsoft but is part of the core business, overseen by a 'brains trust' of a dozen senior people who 'run the key product areas and new initiatives as well as constitute an informal oversight group to critique what everybody else is doing'. Many of its members were previously senior executives elsewhere or research professors before joining Microsoft.

Microsoft has not only learnt from professional expertise hired from elsewhere: it also learns from its customers. Customer support is regarded as a part of the product and as data for improvement. Such a strategy allows Microsoft to make a strength out of a weakness, the weakness being their propensity to ship products that are not totally debugged, despite all the in-house work. Over time they have evolved a complex cycle of customer input as a part of the product cycle.

The customer-cycle input begins by integrating internal data analysis with that derived from customers through phone-in services. These are of two types: 'wish lines' and 'off-line plus'. Wish lines are for customers who tell the company what they would like to see developed; off-line plus analyses data from the thousands of customer calls that come in every month. Information derived from these sources is fed in to the internal product development that takes place in the testing of prototypes in Microsoft's usability labs. While these prototypes are widely tested within Microsoft they are also released to selected customers for further testing. Microsoft's product support services division also tests its 'supportability services' through the usability labs to find to what extent the new features are supportable, as well as experimenting with new ways of diagnosing problems. At product-release time product developers and testers staff the product support services telephone lines so that they can hear, respond to and learn from customer complaints directly. Product support services also run extensive post-launch market research on customer satisfaction, not only with the new products but with the company as a whole. Finally, the product support services division also run focus groups with marketing agencies to discover how customers actually use the products as well as releasing versions of the product that have been manufactured to track every mouse move and keyboard entry used by the customer when working with the product.[85] Customers are key stakeholders in Microsoft.

Despite all the positive things that one can say about Microsoft's achievements, it is hardly a total quality organization: there have been too many infamously bugged or late product launches for anyone to claim that. Indeed, firms like Microsoft, dealing with abstract representations rather than highly tangible machined objects, point to some of the limitations of the quality movement. It can handle issues of probability and efficiency very well; it is far less able to address issues of representation. Managing probability focuses on the management of stochastic events, while the management of continuous events will be focused on efficiency. While managing both these areas is important for Microsoft, the key focus is on the management of representations. Quality is much more difficult to achieve here.

Stochastic events are probabilistic, not deterministic, because they have no clear cause and affect relations between 'what is to be done, how it is done, and when it is to be done'.[86] Most recent management fashions founder on the reef of stochastic events. For instance, if an organization trained its members rigorously and prescriptively in one-best-way processes, it would never learn. This is because organizations require more skills than they know. The repertoire of skills that must be maintained if that organization is to learn, if it is to be intelligent, must be larger than the skill-set in use at any time. This is particularly the case where a new procedure or technology is introduced, and especially where diagnosis is required to make the start-up work smoothly. In these circumstances learning occurs through error and its rectification: if an organization knew already there would be no error, and no learning. A further corollary of this is that diagnosis and monitoring, as much as operation, become crucial skill-sets. Stochastic events form the essence of an organization's exploratory learning about *reliability*, the hallmark of the industrial era.[87] Employees should be able to offer more skills than, vocationally, they need right now, and much of Microsoft's unorthodox selection procedures (such as asking candidates impossible questions and studying the processes they use in trying to answer them) seek to identify people who do.

In the post-industrial era, where continuous events tie together disparate geographical spaces, *efficiency* has become the hallmark of quality. Here, exploratory learning arises not so much from learning how to avoid unanticipated or random events but in learning from the way in which disorder interrupts the order of due process and its management. The emphasis is on rapid responses to emergencies, the ability to keep cool while managing tense environments, on early detection of malfunctions in continuous systems. Much of the 'bug-testing' that occurs in Microsoft is of this order: the processes are in simultaneous development and, as existing bugs are resolved in one application, they may simultaneously introduce errors in another. As Cusumano and Selby detail, in Microsoft this has led to several disastrous or late product launches.[88] In such environments, 'supervisors often pay more attention to processes and products than to people'.[89]

Microsoft is typical: while the technical management skills are excellent the people management skills have not been so well developed. Over-attention to process and under-attention to people produces problems. Process does not encourage causal analysis: when events flow seamlessly it is much more difficult to work out what or who is responsible for what. One consequence is that as supervisors pay more attention to process, people working closely with the processes pay less attention to their conception of the causal linkages at work in sound and unsound operation, thus compounding the stochastic probabilities. Unless they are closely monitored, the cognitive interactive capacities of people working close to continuous processes in intelligent organizations routinely produce slower learning capacities, as Microsoft came to realize. Intelligent organizations, paradoxically, can produce slower people who rely on process rather than intuitive judgement. And if that intuitive judgement cannot be standardized, commodified and abstracted, then the learning that smarter people achieve will not be generalized.

Increasingly, technology in the postmodern era is a source of abstract events; their hallmark is neither reliability nor efficiency, both of which are assumed, but their *representation*. New technologies have an essentially dual character: one aspect is the essentially invisible material processes that unfold in applications, while the other is the equally unavailable mental maps of the imagined processes with which operators work. In this we all try to construct socially a sense of the world in which we live and work: as it becomes ever more remote and inaccessible technologically, the less able we are to learn what to attend to. Operating a lathe through feel, rhythm and visual cues is a very different operation to reading from a computer graphic applied to an automatic process from which the usual sense data are absent: 'The result is inadequate sampling of displayed information, inattention to information on the periphery, and distractions when building problem representations'.[90]

Abstract events require a kind of learning without environmental stimuli in the form of cues: hence, organizations that make use of technologies premised on the abstraction of events require learning capacities that are equally abstract; that 'can intervene at any time, pick up the process and assemble a recovery'.[91] Learning is often sufficiently abstract as to be tacit, ineffable, inimical to programming. Even if the ineffable can subsequently be translated into the do-able, through learning from the captured image, as Microsoft developers have done in trying to transmit tacit learning, this can never capture the initial exploratory breakthroughs that render the ineffable into the knowable. A further corollary of this is that diagnosis and monitoring, as much as operation, become crucial skill-sets.[92] Intelligent organizations are not smart enough to know all of what they need to know: that's why they need to employ people who are smart enough to know that they need to know more than they do (the definition that proved Socrates to be the wisest man in ancient Athens).

Microsoft appears to be a virtual monopoly – an image reinforced by the lawsuits pending in many of its spheres of operation. More organizationally significant than Microsoft, in the long run, may be not virtual monopolies but virtual organizations made possible by innovative software.

Virtual Organizations

Virtual is a term with considerable currency in the natural sciences: in physics, since the mid-nineteenth century the term has indicated 'structure and objects whose ontological status lies in the fuzzy realm between facts and apparition'; thus 'virtual image' refers 'to an image from which light *seems* to emanate but does not in truth do so'.[93]

Most readers will probably be familiar with the computer

concept of 'virtual memory', even if they are unclear what it is exactly. Users of the Internet know that when they 'surf the net' they exist in cyberspace, a 'virtual' space. Virtual organizations share many features with these other uses of 'virtual': members of networked organizations interact with others whom they may rarely, if ever, see face-to-face, and their transactions take place in a virtual space. Computers make virtuality possible.

Intelligent organizations would not exist without computers and information technology. Only a decade ago the nature of the relationship was still a matter for speculation: in 1988 *Fortune* magazine predicted that, in the future, organizations would not just be aided by computers, but that they 'will live by them, shaping strategy and structure to fit new information technology'. Among the early oft-cited prodigies of the relationship are: airline reservation, where strategic advantage attaches to the booking system rather than the flying system (SABRE); automated teller machines in developed economies like Australia, where outlets now exceed conventional bank sites with staff; and computer-aided design/manufacturing (CAD/CAM), which has developed within, albeit not always integrally, many organizations systems.[94] However, the most significant impact of information technology is not in its effect on specific products or services but in the way in which it dematerializes modern organization. Electronic information can be everywhere simultaneously, worked on by everyone simultaneously, from anywhere in the world with electronic access. Organization, as a container or an envelope of activity, ceases to be important.

In the past considerable resources, including IT, were committed to organization design. For many years its adoption mirrored the organizations that produced it (IBM) and used it: they were bureaucracies in which IT enhanced centralization, formalization, standardization and control. More recent developments make virtuality possible. Leaner organizations began to emerge that no longer needed armies of supervisors: supervision became more immediate through technologies; employees were subjected less to an external supervisory gaze and more either to team or self-supervision, in an environment that was measured and monitored electronically.

Organization structure loses its historic role of managing power relations at a distance: for one thing, distance disappears electronically; for another, power relations flatten as teams proliferate, work becomes a series of projects, and the supervisory gaze is both internalized and becomes part of peer pressure.

Davidow and Malone identified *The Virtual Corporation* (1992) as a distinctive model premised on these changes. A simple thesis characterized their book. New technologies make old assumptions irrelevant. Organization design needs to catch up with the technological capacities of personal computers, remote access, networked databases and e-mail. Yet, as should be apparent from the discussion thus far, digitization is just one part of the tendencies towards 'virtuality'. It is the enabling mechanism that allows time and space to be collapsed, superseding the informational controls inscribed in bureaucracy which sought to manage across them.

> In the virtual organization . . . the file cabinets of bureaucratic ritual disappear, replaced by devices that shatter the traditional physical instantiation of information and knowledge . . . When employees in contemporary organizations use electronic mail or build reports from network databases, there is no original physical reality to which this information refers, unless such reference be to a tangle of code and writing that, to most workers, remains opaque or even mystical.[95]

The virtual organization is almost the exact opposite of the modern organizations that Weber first identified (see Table 5.4, in which we contrast Weber's modern organization with its 'virtual' counterpoint).

While the rhetoric of the 'virtual organization' has few concrete referents at present, in its totality, aspects of the ideal type may be glimpsed in many organizations that deal with essentially 'representational data' as the core of their workflow: data in a digitized form can be effortlessly globalized and worked on globally and simultaneously in ways that, for instance, the automobile, however much of a 'world car' it is, cannot. The latter is still very much a complex final assembly that takes place in a congruent space and time, at a given locale, rather than something that is distributed across space and through time but is tied together in a virtual organization.

Table 5.4: Modern and Virtual Organization Compared on Weber's Criteria

Modern Organization	Virtual Organization
Functionality in design structure	Defunctionalized project-based design held together by network capabilities.
Hierarchy governing formal communication flows and managerial imperative the major form and basis of formal communication	Instantaneous remote computer communication for primary interaction; increase in face-to-face informal interaction; decrease in imperative actions and increased governance through accountability in terms of parameters rather than instructions or rules.
The files	Flexible electronic immediacy through IT.
Impersonal roles	Networking of people from different organizations such that their sense of formal organizational roles blurs.
Specialized technical training for specific careers	Global, cross-organizational computer-mediated projects.

Source: Nohria and Berkely, 'The Virtual Organization' (1994)

Network Organizations

The widespread use of the software produced by Microsoft within the company, while it is still in process, leads to a network-based organization. Networks may be characterized in terms of the strength or intensity of their linkages, the symmetricality, reciprocity and multiplexity of their flows. The strength of a network linkage depends on the extent to which it is an 'obligatory passage point' in the network: can information flow elsewhere or must it route that way? The greater the amount of information or resources flowing through the passage point, then the more powerful will be those whose knowledge decodes it.[96] The proportions of different knowledge, embodied in different peoples, around these obligatory passage points may be more or less symmetrical: that is, some will be more or less dependent or independent within the flow of relations. Reciprocity refers to the degree of mutual or non-reciprocal obligation that occurs in the relationship. Multiplexity refers to the degree to which those who relate to one another do so more or less exclusively or are also involved in other networks. Finally, the content of the linkages is important, in terms of its degree of 'classification' and 'framing': how strongly or loosely framed or bounded it is, and how tightly or loosely coded is its classification.

Under these circumstances it should be clear that while intelligent organizations may not have the same kind of hard, zero-sum power that characterized the hierarchical and industrial relations power plays of modern organizations, they are certainly not bereft of power. Power need not be negative, though: it depends on the type of learning – whether it is virtuous or vicious. Learning implies both outcomes and processes. The notion of virtuous learning circles suggests comparative improvement in efficiency, however one chooses to measure it and in whatever stakeholder terms: profits; quality of working; supply of jobs; consumer satisfaction; environmental impact or macro-economic outcomes. Vicious learning, by contrast, implies diminished efficiency.

CONCLUSIONS

There are those who argue that the shift to intelligent organizations is based on such an increasing transparency of power/knowledge that the creativity of all employees is effortlessly incorporated without resistance for use by the organization.[97] Hence, virtuous learning (seen from the point of view of the organization's management) will characterize the future. Employees will be subject to such surveillance, either through technology or through the gaze of their work team as a normative device, picking up on kanban cues displayed prominently in the workplace, that the transparency of their actions allows space only for virtuosity and virtuousness.

Some commentators see these conditions as beneficial, allowing for the exercise of enhanced individual discretion,[98] while others see them as inimical, reflecting a totalitarian nightmare of total control through total surveillance.[99]

Neither view is likely to be correct. While employee desire, understanding and trust may become aligned with employer governance strategies they are highly unlikely to do so seamlessly. Intelligent organizations will still operate in careless ways, on recalcitrant problems, using flawed systems; intelligent people will still strive for selective advantage; intelligent systems of surveillance will still break down, fail and be subverted. But the rhetoric of intelligent organizations does open opportunities for employees to try to make them live up to their slogans.

Future organizations and networks, concrete or virtual, will be paradigmatic systems built from the flows of power and knowledge that people use to create them, fused around technologies that carry both past design and future applications. The trick will be to create the kind of learning in the intelligent organization that is not so locked into past design that it cannot reach for future, unknown applications.

Chapter 6

STAKEHOLDERS

One of the safest and simplest assumptions of orthodox management belief is that the business is basically there to serve the interests of the shareholders. This view derives from the earliest forms of enterprise, which were invariably owner managed. The arrival of the joint stock company presented many dilemmas for investors and company managers. In the minds of classical economists concerned with property rights these agency problems could only be resolved by the application of objective and demanding financial performance indicators to ensure that managers served the interests of the ultimate owners and not their own. As businesses became larger and more complex, this assumption of direct accountability to shareholders alone has become increasingly untenable, though it is often tenaciously defended. In 1932 Berle and Means were the first to record the profound implications of the separation of ownership and control.

In this chapter we examine how in practice managers find they need to develop good relationships with more stakeholders than *introduction* simply investors if their business is to succeed. Relations with customers, suppliers, employees, lenders and the wider community are critical for the viability of most enterprises. Stakeholder values are reinforced by the realization that the intangible assets of a company are often its most precious resource, and these are often embodied in the knowledge and skills of employees. The conception of the company as a set of relationships rather than a series of transactions, in which managers adopt an inclusive concern for the interests of all stakeholders, is much closer to European and Asian business values; in practice, however, most companies are increasingly being run this way. It represents an important step towards a sense of corporate citizenship – in an organization with a mature appreciation of its rights and responsibilities.

Table 6.1: Paradigm Shifts

Shareholders/financial performance indicators	Stakeholders/ non-financial performance indicators
Agency/stewardship theory	Stakeholder theory
Short term	Long term
Shareholder value	Stakeholder values
Tangible assets	Intangible assets
Anglo-Saxon	European/Asian
Property	Knowledge
Transactions	Relationships
Exclusive	Inclusive
Corporate image	Corporate citizenship

GOVERNANCE SYSTEMS

Different economic systems, business strategies and management practices compete, co-exist and sometimes co-operate. As Tricker has noted, corporate governance systems are in a state of transition in every industrial country, the greatest impelling force being the internationalization of financial markets. A likely outcome is increased diversity within an overall impulse towards convergence.[1] A discernible trend is the increasing influence of Anglo-Saxon shareholder value-based approaches to corporate governance, even among European and Asian companies which have formerly sustained stakeholder or collective conceptions of governance (Figure 6.1). Simultaneously there has been a revival of interest in stakeholder approaches in both the United States and the UK, partly influenced by the evident industrial strength of German and Japanese companies, but also drawing upon indigenous inclinations towards the development of a more durable business system.

Business leaders are being called upon to face in two apparently different directions at once, a feat some are happy to attempt to accomplish, but which leaves others looking for an alignment of strategies and values that is more convincingly consistent. The paradox of contemporary management is:

Figure 6.1: Convergence and Divergence of Governance Systems

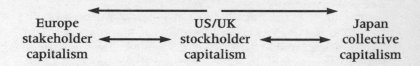

| Europe stakeholder capitalism | US/UK stockholder capitalism | Japan collective capitalism |

- In response to the excesses of the 1980s a renewed emphasis upon business values, the integrity of companies and the responsibility of business executives. Also a sense that the short-term orientation and narrow focus upon financial performance is ultimately self defeating, relative to the longer horizons and deeper commercial relationships of competitors not subjected to these narrow performance indicators. Finally the wider social and environmental responsibilities and the part played in the community by business enterprise is once again on the agenda.
- In the context of global competition, international investment patterns and the aggressive growth of mergers and acquisitions a reinvigorated sense of the significance of releasing shareholder value. (In 1988, at the height of the merger and acquisition activity of this period, in the United States $335 billion of corporate assets were involved; in the first eight months of 1997 a total of $639 billion was in play. Worldwide there was a similar growth in acquisition activity to $600 billion in 1989, with £1,300 billion estimated in 1997).[2]

The New York-based takeover expert Martin Lipton suggests that 'Unlike the financially motivated, highly leveraged bust-up takeovers of the 1980s, most of the current mergers are soundly financed, strategically motivated [and will] result in better products and services at lower real prices'.[3] If this logic is marginally more convincing than it was in the eighties, it is still easier to square with the conception of the company as a bundle of assets than a set of stakeholder interests. Reflecting on an earlier phase in the corporate battleground, Peacock and Bannock suggested: 'Compared with the slow process of internal growth, which requires detailed planning, trial and error, recruitment of personnel, product development, investment in plant perhaps with long lead times, the building of relationships with suppliers, the establishment of marketing strategies and channels of distribution, an acquisition that can be pushed through in a matter of weeks or months is fast indeed'.[4]

Commenting on the intended sale at the end of 1997 of Rolls-Royce Motor Cars by Vickers to a German car-manufacturer, John Harvey-Jones, a former chairman of ICI argued, 'The same people who tell us ownership doesn't matter are those who tell us the sole role of business is to reward shareholders. Despite attempts to broaden board responsibilities to balance the interests of investors, employees, customers, suppliers and community (jobs I believed I was doing) the prevalent view still seems to be that shareholder interests are the sole driver'.[5]

Though ascendant in financial circles, the shareholder view of the firm has only occasionally enjoyed a strong voluntary commitment from industrial managers, who have to wrestle with the more practical concerns of running a business. A more broadly based stakeholder conception of the objectives of companies has a long intellectual lineage beginning with the pioneering work of Berle and Means. Corporate governance is once again at the top of the agenda on business policy throughout the industrial world.

Corporate Governance

Put simply, corporate governance is the operation of the system of government of companies. Bob Tricker, editor of *Corporate Governance – An International Review*, offers the best full definition: 'Corporate governance is concerned with the processes by which corporate entities, particularly limited liability companies, are governed; that is, with the exercise of power over the direction of the enterprise, the supervision of executive actions, the acceptance of a duty to be accountable and the regulation of the corporation within the jurisdiction of the states in which it operates'.[6] This definition stresses the political, supervisory and regulatory aspects of governance, which are paramount, whatever other functions the boards fulfil. For those who prefer a more operational definition, the International Institute for Management Development offers a view of the work of the board of directors as 'the fulcrum where a comprehensive view of corporate activity comes together with the responsibility for understanding social, economic and stakeholder demands for performance accountability'.[7] The OECD offers the most direct definition: 'Corporate governance refers to the discipline and control of firms designed to ensure that they are efficiently managed and that economic welfare of society is maximized'.[8]

Corporate governance has in recent years become a subject of great controversy, with a string of well-publicized scandals occurring in most countries, prompting numerous efforts at regulatory reform. The fact that public fascination with the subject has increased rather than diminished as a result suggests that issues of corporate governance are more complex, deeply rooted and enduring than originally envisaged. Critical issues of governance include:

- Standards of audit and financial control.
- Accountability, disclosure and transparency of company direction.
- The influence of the changing pattern of the distribution of share ownership with the rise of institutional investors upon corporate direction.
- The selection, quality and competence of directors.
- The weakness of self-regulation, and the efficacy of external regulation.

There are some common misconceptions concerning corporate governance, unintentionally fostered by regulatory reports such as that of the Cadbury Committee in the UK:[9] firstly, that corporate governance is essentially about the financial aspects of corporate control and, secondly, that corporate governance is concerned exclusively with boardroom behaviour. Corporate governance is about more than company board structure, representation and behaviour; fundamentally it concerns:

- The organization, direction and operation of companies.
- The institutions, markets and environments in which companies operate.

The efficiency and effectiveness of corporate governance influence not only company performance, but ultimately the overall economic performance of individual countries. These links may be complex and difficult to analyse, but their significance is none the

conclude for corporate governance

less real. In 1995 the OECD launched research into corporate governance and national economic performance, and there seems to be a correlation between different approaches to governance and the competitive qualities and performance results of companies from different parts of the world.

Berle and Means were the first to explore the political ramifications of the separating of ownership and control in the modern corporation, and their 1932 study was very prescient of the kinds of problems companies would face in the future. However, they did not anticipate the impact of the rise of institutional shareholders, the heavyweight players inserted between company directors and the amorphous mass of individual shareholders, which further complicates the task of executive directors, who have to successfully deal with lenders, customers, suppliers and employees. It is around these relationships that the debate on corporate governance has revolved over the last sixty years, with rival explanations of the orientations of company directors.

Agency theory: Which questions company directors' willingness and capacity to represent shareholders' interests without careful safeguards.

Stewardship theory: Which suggests directors are best placed to reconcile the different interests and aspirations of the members of the company.

Stakeholder theory: Which suggests that company directors can and do move beyond an exclusive focus upon shareholder interests to consider the interests of a wider set of stakeholders.

Other theoretical perspectives include that of *resource dependence*, in which directors are there to reduce uncertainty and span boundaries; *managerial hegemony*, in which boards of directors are seen as a legal fiction masking executive domination of companies; and finally, *class hegemony*, in which boards of directors are essentially regarded as protectors of class interests (Table 6.2). The fundamental questions of corporate governance are therefore:

• Who has control of companies?
• For whom is control exercised?

The way in which these questions are resolved has a direct impact upon the performance and sustained success of companies.

Figure 6.2: Revised 'Berle–Means' Model, with Institutional Investors

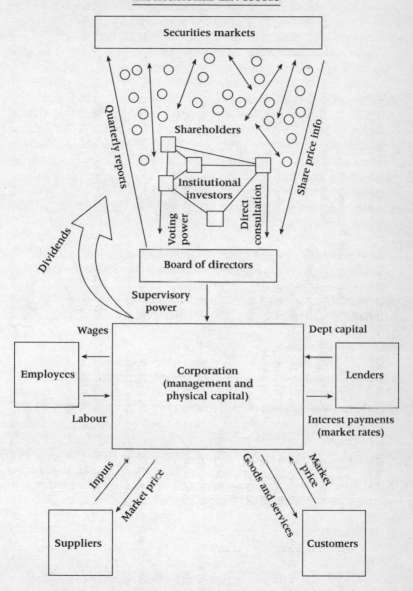

Source: M. Blair, *Ownership and Control* (1995), p. 47

Table 6.2: Theoretical Perspectives on Corporate Governance

Dimension	Theoretical Perspective					
	Agency	Stewardship	Resource Dependence	Stakeholder	Managerial Hegemony	Class Hegemony
Board Role	Ensure match between managers and shareholders	Ensure the stewardship of corporate assets	Reduce uncertainty; boundary spanning	Inclusive pursuit of stakeholder interests	Board 'a legal fiction'	Perpetuate élite and class power
Theoretical Origin	Economics and finance	Organization theory	Sociology	Politics, law and management theory	Organization theory	Sociology
Representative Studies	Fama and Jensen (1985) Jensen and Meckling (1976) Kosnik (1987)	Donaldson and Davis (1991) Donaldson and Davis (1994)	Pfeffer (1972) Pfeffer and Salanick (1978)	RSA (1995) Blair (1995)	Mace (1971) Lorsch and MacIver (1989)	Mills (1971) Useem (1980)

Source: Derived from Philip Stiles, London Business School (1997) T. Clarke, 'Corporate Governance Research' (1998)

Short-termism and Long-termism

In the 1980s there was increasing concern in both the United States and the UK that companies were being driven either in the short-term interests of equity returns to shareholders, or in the even more narrow self-interests of executive directors themselves. The consequences of industry serving these sectional interests appeared to be a failing competitive performance in US and UK manufacturing industry, as Japanese and German companies seized larger shares in cars, electronic goods and other important product markets, most painfully in US and UK domestic markets. The Confederation of British Industry (CBI) recorded the plight of UK industry:

> Despite this record and the combined constraints imposed in many cases by lower sales and tighter margins, companies remain under pressure at least to maintain dividends, 'rewarding' shareholders for loyalty. Hence, of the largest 600 quoted companies reporting in the first half of 1992, 57 per cent had increased dividends while only 10 per cent had reduced them. The gravity of the situation is all the more apparent when compared with other countries. Dividends as a percentage of post tax profits have been persistently higher in the UK throughout the past decade. Furthermore this differential has widened since the beginning of 1991. There is a risk that companies will seriously deplete their capital resources especially as recovery in profits could be slow to come through. A more flexible approach to dividends is essential. Companies should not allow themselves to pay out an excessive level of dividend which weakens their balance sheet or causes them to abandon capital spending required to secure their long term competitive position.[10]

In the United States there is a similar lack of supportive relationships between investors and industry, as Michael Porter has observed in a research project on corporate investment sponsored by the Council on Competitiveness and Harvard Business School. Unlike his work on competitive strategy, Porter's findings, reported in 1992, have never received the attention they deserve, and were in summary:

The US system of allocating investment capital is threatening the competitiveness of American firms and the long term growth of the national economy. Although the US system has many strengths, including efficiency, flexibility, responsiveness and high rates of corporate profit, it does not seem to be effective in directing capital to the firms that can deploy it most productively and to the most productive investment projects. As a result of this system, many American firms invest too little in those assets and capabilities most required for competitiveness (such as employee training), while wasting capital on investments with limited financial or social rewards (such as unrelated acquisitions).[11]

The US research was prompted by evidence that for more than a decade US industrial investment was being made at a lower rate and with a shorter time horizon than those of German or Japanese competitors. A variety of measures of comparative rates, patterns and outcomes of US investments and the behaviour of US investors were noted by Porter:

- The competitive position of important US industries had declined relative to those of other nations, notably Japan and Germany.
- Aggregate investment in property, plant and equipment, and intangible assets, such as civilian R&D and corporate training, is lower in the US than in Japan and Germany.
- Leading American companies in many manufacturing industries such as construction equipment, computers and tires are outinvested by their Japanese counterparts.
- American companies appear to invest at a lower rate than both Japanese and German companies in non-traditional forms such as human resource development, relationships with suppliers, and start-up losses to enter foreign markets.
- R&D portfolios of American companies include a smaller share of long-term projects than those of European or Japanese companies.
- Hurdle rates used by US companies to evaluate investment projects appear to be higher than estimates of the cost of capital.
- US CEOs believe their companies have shorter investment horizons than their international competitors and that market pressures have reduced long-term investment.

- The average holding period of stock has declined from more than seven years in 1960 to about two years.
- Long-term growth has declined as an influence on US stock prices.
- Many recent US policy proposals such as government funding of specific industries, R&D consortia, and joint production ventures implicitly reflect a private investment problem.[12]

Porter's further findings included industry and company variation; a good US performance on funding high-risk start-up companies; higher profitability than Japanese or German industry, yet no better returns for American shareholders; over-investment in some forms such as acquisitions, and under-investment in intangible assets; efficient capital markets but suboptimal investment behaviour. In explaining some of these paradoxes Porter contrasts the fluid capital structure of the United States with the dedicated capital structure of Germany and Japan (see Figure 6.3). Overall, Japan and Germany have a system of dedicated capital in which the funds of principal owners remain invested in companies over long periods of time. *Dedicated capital* is characterized by:

- Continued aggressive investment in existing businesses to boost productivity and upgrade capabilities.
- Internal diversification into closely related fields, building upon and extending corporate capabilities.
- Retention of ownership by principal shareholders over long periods of time.
- Close ties between banks and companies, with bank finance being the most important source of external funds.[13]

In contrast, the *fluid capital* investment system of United States (and to a great extent in the UK):

- The goals of institutional investors are purely financial and are focused on quarterly or annual appreciation of their investment portfolio compared with stock indices.
- Because managers are measured on their short-term performance, their investment goals understandably focus on the near-term appreciation of shares.
- Because of their fragmented stakes in so many companies, short holding periods and lack of access to proprietary information

Figure 6.3: The External Market: Fluid Capital and Dedicated Capital

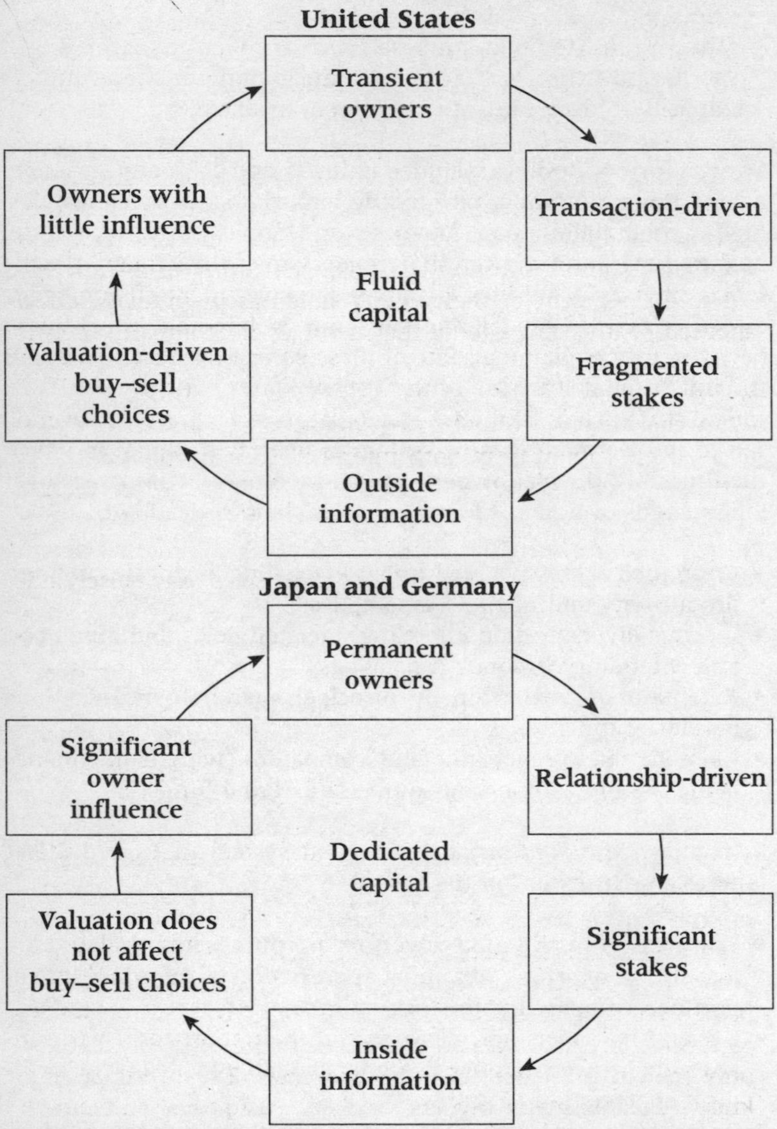

United States

Fluid capital

Transient owners → Transaction-driven → Fragmented stakes → Outside information → Valuation-driven buy–sell choices → Owners with little influence → Transient owners

Japan and Germany

Dedicated capital

Permanent owners → Relationship-driven → Significant stakes → Inside information → Valuation does not affect buy–sell choices → Significant owner influence → Permanent owners

Source: Porter, *Capital Choices* (1992)

through disclosure or board membership, institutional investors tend to base their investment choices on limited information that is oriented towards predicting near-term stock price movements.

- The system drives investors to focus on easily measurable company attributes, such as current earnings or patent approvals, as proxies of a company's value on which to base market timing choices.
- The value proxies used vary among different classes of companies and can lead to under-investment in some industries or forms of investment, while allowing over-investment in others.
- Given the difficulty of outperforming the market with this approach, some institutions have moved to invest as much as 70 to 80 per cent of their equity holdings in index funds, a method of investing capital that involves no company-specific information at all.[14]

The internal capital market, the system by which companies allocate available capital from both internal and external sources to investment projects, mirrors the external capital market (Figure 6.4). The relationship and information flow between capital budget holders and business unit managers will affect the investment decisions of the company, but Porter emphasizes how closely this is geared to the external capital market:

The US internal market is structured to maximize measurable investment returns. It is organized to stress financial returns, to motivate managers to achieve financial targets, to raise accountability for unit finance, and to base decision making and investment allocation heavily on financial criteria. In the US system, corporate goals centre on earning high returns on investment and maximizing current stock prices. Management exercises the dominant influence on corporate goals, interpreting signals about desired behaviour from the external capital market, influenced by compensation based on current accounting profits or unrestricted stock options that heighten price sensitivity. Boards, which have come to be dominated by outside directors with no other links to the company, exert only limited influence on corporate goals. The presence of knowledgeable major owners, bankers, customers, and suppliers on corporate boards has diminished. An estimated 74 per cent of the directors of the largest US corporations are

Figure 6.4: Internal Market Overview

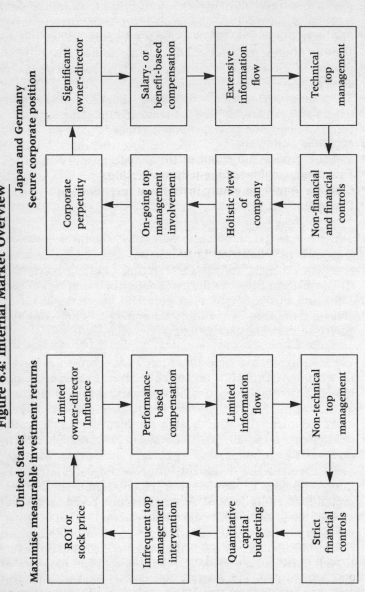

Source: Porter, *Capital Choices* (1992)

now outsiders, and 80 per cent are CEOs of other companies. The move to outside directors arose out of calls for greater board objectivity. But the cost of objectivity has been directors who lack ties to the company and whose own companies are in unrelated businesses.[15]

The outcome of Porter's research was a series of policy recommendations for government, institutional investors and companies. Among them were proposals:

For public policy to:
• Increase private and public sector saving.
• Encourage employee long-term ownership.
• Create a long-term equity investment incentive.
• Encourage board membership by customers, suppliers, financial advisers, employees and community representatives.

For institutional investors to:
• Increase the size of stakes.
• More carefully select companies based on fundamental earning power.
• Encourage changes in agent measurement and evaluation procedures to reflect long-term investment performance.
• Transform interactions with management into productive, advisory discussions.

For companies to:
• Seek long-term owners and give them a direct voice in governance.
• Nominate significant owners, customers, suppliers and employee representatives to the board of directors.
• Move away from unrelated diversification.
• Transform financial control structures into position-based control systems with a broader definition of assets and measurement of asset quality in addition to quantity.[16]

The recovery of the US economy distracted attention from the warnings of the US Council on Competitiveness of which Porter's report formed part. The longest bull market in American history lasted through most of the 1990s, massively inflating the Dow Jones (the index surged 22 per cent to more than 7,900 points in the first nine months of 1997, and quickly recovered from the stock market crash originating in Asia in October 1997, causing Alan Greenspan of the Federal Reserve to caution against 'irrational exuberance'.[17] Following the huge increase in jobs in the service sector and the reduction of unemployment below 5 per cent, its lowest level in decades, it seemed the US economy was fully revived and had escaped the long period of retrenchment and self-doubt of the seventies and eighties.

The US economy undoubtedly possesses vast capabilities, and remains the world leader in important product markets such as computers and software, aerospace, pharmaceuticals and professional services. However, the increase in US corporate profitability in the 1990s was primarily due to lower taxes and interest rates, and it is questionable whether this can be sustained into the next century without a new direction. Despite the Clinton administration's policy on big emerging markets, the Commerce Secretary said, 'Our competitors continue to dedicate more resources to gaining footholds in these emerging markets'.[18]

Meanwhile Toyota announced plans to leapfrog Ford to become the world's second largest car-maker, with a new range of low-emission, safety-conscious vehicles. The structural problems of the US – and particularly those in the investment system – may well return to undermine the economy as the Asian and European economies recover.

International Corporate Governance

The different systems of corporate governance in industrial countries reflect different legal and institutional arrangements, the historical development of the country and the structure of the financial system.[19] The OECD distinguishes two contrasting models of governance: a market-based *outsider* model, and a representation-based *insider* model.

Market-based Governance
In this outsider model boards are closely allied with managers, and discipline is exercised by the capital market. Shares are owned by dispersed investors, and if the company is poorly managed or shareholder value is neglected investors will react by selling shares, depressing the share price, and exposing the company to hostile

takeover. This model assumes good information flows, full disclosure of information, adherence to trading rules and liquid stock markets. It is the Anglo-Saxon model of the United States and UK, but the Netherlands, Sweden and Switzerland appear to be moving in this direction.

Representation-based Governance

This insider model relies on the representation of interests on the board of directors, which is expected to play a strong monitoring role over management. More diverse groups of stakeholders are recognized, including workers, banks, other companies with close ties, local communities and the national government. Stable investments and cross shareholdings mean that discipline of management by the securities market is not strong; similarly the market for corporate control is weak, with hostile takeovers rarely occurring. This is the continental European system, with a supervisory board for oversight of management, banks playing an active role as shareholders, inter-corporate shareholdings, and often close ties to a political/administrative élite. In Japan the largest associations of *keiretsu*, often acting as suppliers and subcontractors to each other, with a main bank and other financial institutions as part of the group, are central to understanding the conduct of corporate governance. In this system managers are relatively free from external monitoring and tend to work on the basis of internal consensus.[20]

Corporate Finance

A major determinant of governance patterns is the structure of corporate finance, and there are sharply contrasting debt/equity ratios among industrial countries. Debt finance is much more important in Japan, Germany and Italy than in France, the UK or the United States. Corporate equity is of much greater importance in the US and UK (and Japan), where there is a much higher proportion of exchange-listed joint-stock companies, than in continental Europe; there is also a much higher ratio of market capitalization to gross domestic product. Table 6.3 illustrates the central importance of listed companies in the United States in terms of the market value of listed domestic shares and the turnover of domestic stocks. In contrast, in Germany the equity market, though now growing, remains comparatively undeveloped.

The distribution of shares among investors also varies markedly among industrial countries over time. In all major industrial countries there has been a pronounced shift from individual shareholding towards shareholding by the financial institutions, including banks, securities firms and institutional investors (collective investment institutions, insurance companies and pension funds). In the United States and UK pension funds and collective investment institutions (mutual funds and unit trusts) have gained; in Germany and Japan the banks and insurance companies have a significant role. Table 6.4 indicates that the United States remains the only major industrial country with a large proportion of individual shareholders; it also emphasizes the burgeoning influence of the pension funds in both the US and UK, and the importance of non-financial enterprise cross-holdings in France and Germany.

The impact of the internationalization of equities markets due to liberalization and electronic trading has become a major feature of global capital markets, and is likely to further influence the institutional structure of governance in every country. Similarly the volume and scale of international mergers and acquisitions have greatly increased over the last decade.

The Growing Influence of Institutional Investors

The phenomenal growth of the institutional investors since the early 1980s is the most important development in the structure of corporate financing in the United States, the UK and Japan, and will influence the funding of companies around the world. Pension funds, insurance companies and collective investment institutions have accumulated massive funds for investment. The largest institutional investors are the pension funds: in the US pension fund assets grew from $400 billion in 1974 to $3.6 trillion by 1994.[21] In the English-speaking world insurance companies and mutual funds have gathered huge amounts of private savings. These have been invested in diversified portfolios and attracted to high historical equity returns.

However, institutional investors have traditionally kept a low profile in corporate governance, their main objective being to secure a high return on their portfolio rather than to become directly involved in particular companies. As the OECD comments:

Table 6.3: The Relative Importance of Listed Companies

	Frankfurt	Total Germany (8 exchanges)	NYSE	United States (NYSE + Amex + NASDAQ)[1]	Tokyo	Paris	United Kingdom/ Ireland	Toronto
Number of listed domestic companies, end-1993	409	664	2203	7313	1667	726	1865	1124
Turnover of domestic stocks[2] DM billion, 1993	688[3]	920[3]	3605	5929[4]	1345	281	721[3]	189
Market value of listed domestic shares, DM billion, end-1993	–	800	7471	9006	5019	791	2056	559
Stock market capitalization, per cent of GDP, average 1991–4	–	29	65	–	125[5]	39[5]	112	54

1. Figures shown are the simple sum of data concerning the three markets and may involve some double counting.
2. Precise comparisons are not possible because of divergent statistical methods, even within countries. Figures are rounded. Some totals are skewed by including various warrants and drawing rights.
3. Since raw data for Germany and United Kingdom/Ireland include both ends of each trade, they have been halved to bring them on a base roughly comparable with those of the other countries.
4. Assuming all turnover on Amex to relate to domestic shares.
5. All domestic stock exchanges.

Source: *Roby Securities Markets Moving Ahead,* (1994); OECD.

Table 6.4: Distribution of Outstanding Corporate Equity among Different Categories of Shareholders

	United States	Japan	Germany	France	United Kingdom	Italy	Sweden
Financial sector	46	45	29	8	62	19	24
of which:							
Banks		22[1]	14	3	1	10	1
Insurance companies	5	17[1]	7	1[2]	17	2	8
Investment funds							8
Pension funds	26	1			34		
Mutual funds	11	3	8	2	7	6	6
Other financial institutions	4	1		2	3	1	
Non-financial enterprises		24	39	59	2	32	34
Public authorities		1	4	4	1		7
Individuals	49	24	17	19	18	28	16
Foreign	5	7	12	11	16	17	9
Other					2	5	10
Total	100	100	100	100	100	100	100

1. Division between banks and insurance companies estimated.
2. Including pension funds.

Note: Due to rounding, the figures may not add up to the total.

Sources: Flow of funds. Board of the Federal Reserve System; Round Table of National Stock Exchanges; Survey of Stock Ownership Distribution, (March 1994); Deutsche Bundesbank, Banque de France, CSO, Consob, Banca d'Italia.Statistika Centralbyran, Sweden

In the 1980s, the ability of portfolio managers to integrate equities into asset portfolios and to use risk management techniques including equity derivatives, improved considerably ... In a fully 'commoditized' equity market strategy, the pension fund will seek to have its portfolio replicate the benchmark index or may use the derivatives market to achieve a desired portfolio exposure. The growing sophistication of investment management has not been accompanied by similar development in the use of equities as ownership stakes in productive enterprises. Indeed, some critics contend that the extremely sophisticated use of equities and equity derivatives has led to a 'commoditization' of equity markets. In the more extreme cases, the institution may be completely disinterested in the performance of the companies of which they are nominal owners.[22]

Recently political pressure has encouraged institutional investors to abandon this passivity towards the governance of the companies they invest in, with frequent calls for more institutional shareholder activity to increase the accountability of company directors. There has been an effort – particularly among the American public pension funds – to improve information about company performance, to define issues of interest for shareholders, to vote proxies more actively, to identify under-performing management and to modify their behaviour. Networks of institutional investors and advisory services have formed, making it easier for institutional investors to fulfil their voting duties, and organize coalitions around particular policies.

The Market for Corporate Control

The share-price mechanism and hostile takeovers are the means of holding management accountable in market-based systems; however, they appear to have mixed effects on company strategy. The hostile takeover boom in the US and the UK during the 1980s, often driven by financial entrepreneurs looking for undervalued assets to take over and sell at a profit, prompted companies to develop elaborate anti-takeover devices. In Europe and Japan hostile takeovers are rare: regulations protecting employees, creditors, suppliers and subcontractors present obstacles to immediate corporate restructuring. In the United States shareholders and managers are protected by bankruptcy codes, while in Europe and Japan employees and creditors are shielded.[23]

There is some evidence that the threat of takeover imposes short-term investment horizons on managers concerned about the possibility that major long-term investments may temporarily depress share prices. In the 1990s it appears that the market for corporate acquisition is driven largely by the desire to establish strategic linkages, and speculative, highly leveraged bids have become the exception. Blue-chip companies, rather than dubious green-mailers, are likely to be making the acquisitions, and institutional pressure means that protracted battles are giving way to quicker conclusions of hostile bids. However, the explosion of mega-deals in the late 1990s is creating considerable instability. In the United States in the first nine months of 1997 the largest bid in history was announced, with WorldCom offering $30 billion for MCI Communications, disturbing a protracted courtship between MCI and British Telecommunications. In addition, fifteen other deals worth more than $5 billion, and 120 deals worth more than $1 billion were announced during this period. Following this frenzy of M & A activity Alan Greenspan, chairman of the Federal Reserve, claimed that the US economy was on an 'unsustainable track': a principal indication of over-heating was the huge increase in stock market activity; moreover, as in the boom of the 1980s, takeovers are being funded without cash:

> WorldCom's all-paper offer for MCI means that the acquisitive company is using its high stock market rating of more than 40 times expected 1998 earnings to buy MCI's profit stream without paying out any cash to MCI shareholders. Analysis by J. P. Morgan shows that WorldCom's offer to MCI shareholders is hardly unusual. It says that 43 per cent of the value of deals done so far in 1997, and 44 per cent in 1996, was funded entirely or partly through stock. That compared with just 7 per cent in 1998, the 1980s M & A market peak.[24]

The Role of Boards

United States

In the US boards of directors are unitary structures often dominated by management. An attempt to restructure boards to achieve greater accountability was made by introducing a majority of non-executive directors. However, according to Lorsch and MacIver, outside directors have limited time, knowledge and expertise in the companies they are in principle responsible for. Non-executives often lack any group cohesion of their own, but fit into the values of the companies they join. The OECD comments: 'It is generally conceded in English-speaking countries boards have great difficulty in fulfilling the oversight function in a meaningful way, because they have traditionally worked on a collegial basis under the dominance of senior management. Until recently one tier boards have, more often than not, tended to ratify strategic decisions of management.'[25]

To improve the oversight functions of boards and limit the domination of chief executives, committees for critical tasks were established in the 1980s in US corporations; these tasks included the remuneration of executive directors, nomination of board members and auditing. CEOs can no longer decide their own pay and choose their own board, but in many companies they still wield considerable power in the boardroom. Lipton and Lorsch have proposed the reform of US boards, with recommendations for:

- A board maximum of ten directors, with two independent directors for every inside director.
- An outside director to be nominated as the 'lead' director where the CEO is also the chairman.
- Boards to meet several times a year with the major shareholders.
- The independent directors to describe remedial action in the annual report if the company under-performs for three out of five years.[26]

United Kingdom

In the UK management has also traditionally dominated the board if institutional shareholders are not inclined to intervene. As in the US, the debate concerning corporate governance was sparked by the weak performance of domestic companies, the lack of accountability of executive management and the fact that management compensation appeared unrelated to performance.[27] The Cadbury recommendations quickly effected the reforms rehearsed in US corporations, and introduced a new sense of the significance of corporate governance, and the need for effective monitoring of boards of directors. The Cadbury Code, which became a model for international standards of governance, recommended the following:

- There should be a clearly accepted division of responsibility at the head of a company, ensuring a balance of power and authority.
- Boards should include non-executive directors of sufficient calibre and number to carry significant weight in the board's decisions.
- Non-executive directors should bring an independent judgement to bear on issues of strategy, performance and resources, including key appointments and standards of conduct.
- Each board should have an audit committee composed entirely of non-executives, and a remuneration committee composed largely of non-executives.
- The directors should report on the effectiveness of the system of internal financial control, showing that the business is a going concern.
- The audit committee should meet the auditors at least once a year, without the executive directors, to ensure that there are no unresolved areas of concern.[28]

Following this reform of corporate governance by Cadbury, and the Greenbury proposals to regulate executive pay, the appetite for further self-regulation waned in the UK, and the ensuing Hampel Report, intended to develop the work of Cadbury, was largely an exercise in complacency, which left both government and institutional shareholders searching for some more robust means to both regulate corporate governance and ensure that companies are directed towards sustained generation of wealth.

Germany
Significant differences are generally perceived between the corporate governance structures of Anglo-American companies and those of European companies, with the German model of governance often portrayed as the most distinctive of the European types.[29]

Among the notable features of the German business sector are: the relatively strong concentration of ownership of individual enterprises; the importance of small- and medium-sized unincorporated companies, with a close correspondence between owners and managers; and the limited role played by the stock market.[30] More broadly, the dominant feature of German commercial enterprises is the insider basis of their governance systems, through which all interested stakeholders – managers, employees, creditors, suppliers and customers – are able to monitor company performance:

> A stylized version of the German model is that it relies on continuous monitoring of managers by other stakeholders, who have a long-term relationship with the firm and engage permanently in the important aspects of decision-making and in the case of dissatisfaction, take action to correct management decisions through internal channels. In the case of incorporated firms (*Kapitalgesellschaften*) stakeholder influence is exerted through a two-tier company board structure. The importance of the banks, in their double role as both lenders and important share owners, has often, perhaps too often, been stressed. In contrast the Anglo-American model is typically taken to imply that individual stakeholders have little direct influence on management and that dissatisfied stakeholders 'vote with their feet', e.g. firms shifting subcontractors or shareholders selling their equity holdings in a firm. Resulting downward pressure on share prices, however, serves as an indirect disciplining device on management. As a result of these differences, the stock market is seen to be much more central to the Anglo-American model than the German model which, in contrast, relies importantly on continuous participation by banks, business partners and employees in the running of companies, creating greater potential for conflict of interest.[31]

The economic debate concerning corporate governance is often posed in terms of a potential dilemma between strong direction and accountability: paradoxically, assets are most efficiently valued when information to shareholders is maximized, while operational efficiency suggests that shareholders should delegate surveillance and decision-making to managers. The German model of governance, being based, unlike the market-oriented Anglo-American model, on a pattern of institutional relations, diminishes such tensions by relying much less on market assessment, and by including a wide range of stakeholders in the governance process:

> The issues in a German context are then how to ensure that this alignment – as an alternative to a market for corporate control – can ensure the effective allocation of capital, especially to new firms and 'innovations', and related to this, whether the trend towards greater international integration and capital and product market liberalization will call for a further evolution in existing arrangements . . . The incentives which led to a particular German model of enterprise control seem set to undergo further rapid change. Among the pressures for change are the on-going processes of technical change and internationalization as well as the financing patterns that are likely to follow from future changes in private saving and its allocation.[32]

The recent apparent weaknesses in the German economy have led people to ask questions about the continued viability of the German mode of corporate governance, including:

- Whether the German system is capable of taking advantage of the internationalization of the capital market.
- Whether German industry can respond to the more rapid processes of technical change that require more frequent restructuring of industry.
- Whether the rigidities of the German labour market, which threaten the competitiveness of industry, can be overcome.

Some major corporate failures emphasized the vulnerabilities of the German system, and following the $500 million rescue of Klockner-Humboldt-Deutz engine-makers, in which the Deutsche Bank was the major shareholder, the chief executive of Deutsche Bank could only suggest plaintively, 'No system of corporate governance is perfect'. More seriously, the overseas investment of German industry expanded massively in the 1990s, partly in response to the problems in the domestic economy of Germany, though also in order to seize new opportunities in emerging international markets.

Japan

The Japanese system of corporate governance relies on trust and implicit contracting and a relationship-oriented approach. As in the German system, there are close ties between banks and industry and a web of cross-shareholdings, making hostile takeovers virtually impossible and allowing companies to focus on the accumulation of assets and long-term research and development strategies.[33] As a result Japanese industry can concentrate on the long-term interests of the company and invest in R&D, capital, employee training and skills development. This system which, like the German one, concentrates on the long-term interests of many stakeholders at the expense of short-term returns for stockholders only, is fundamentally different from the Anglo-Saxon model. However, the increasing activity of international institutional investors demanding greater returns on their investments may well change this.

Mergers are quite common in Japan, and tend to be with businesses in the same industry and often within the same group; they are particularly likely to occur if a member within a group is in financial difficulties. However, more recently Japanese companies have been diversifying into unrelated areas, often resulting in unprecedented conflicts of interest between different stakeholders.[34] At present acquisitions are far more unusual than mergers but Aron Viner suggests that an increasing number of Japanese companies will not be able to survive in Japan's fiercely competitive environment and will be looking abroad for friendly buyers.[35]

One of the major features of Japanese corporate governance is the reliance on cross-shareholdings. In the 1980s, when stock prices rose rapidly, turnover of shares also increased. Growing competition in the capital markets will discourage institutional investors from keeping low yielding equities in their portfolios. This process has begun in Japan and could weaken Japan's preference for capital gains at the expense of dividend yield. If this occurs institutional investors may gradually adopt American strategies, including the practice of selling blocks of shares to potential hostile bidders. This is ever more likely with further breakdowns in trust, a decreasing emphasis on cross-shareholdings and a rising number of buyouts. However, there has been no dramatic shift in the pattern of stable cross-shareholdings in the recent period of recession in the Japanese economy.[36]

In the past Japan's huge institutional investors, including the life insurance companies and banks, have not been keen to exercise their influence on management unless a company was facing financial or other difficulties; even then, any influence tends to be behind the scenes. Toru Ishiguro argues that this passive shareholder approach is changing and that investors are increasingly becoming less friendly towards management.[37] The big institutions are becoming aware of their obligations to maximize shareholder value. Thus long-term institutional shareholdings and cross-shareholding of shares by several or a group of companies, which used to guarantee management a reliable basis of control over the company, may no longer continue in the same way.

The paradox of this system, cruelly exposed since the bursting of the bubble economy in the early 1990s with the onset of a prolonged and dispiriting recession, is the strength of Japanese industrial management, and the weakness of Japanese corporate governance. Companies are inward looking; there is inadequate and inefficient monitoring of top management except through the product market; cross-shareholdings, cross-directorships and long-term business relationships isolate managers from shareholders and takeover threats. Annual general meetings are very short and ritualistic and, in most major companies, are held on the same day to limit the incursion of criminals. Boards are far too large, composed mainly of company executives, entirely ritualistic, highly secretive, totally loyal, and exclusively appointed by the company president. Statutory auditors are ineffective, and have failed to warn of the imminent collapse of large sections of the Japanese banking and finance industry.[38] The collapse of Japanese share prices and the fall in the yen finally punctured the intimations of commercial invulnerability that had occasionally surfaced in the 1980s. However, before the industrial might of Japan is written off completely, it should be realized that the reduced value of the yen is giving Japanese car-manufacturers and consumer electronics firms an opportunity to confirm their pre-eminence in world markets.

Convergence or Divergence of Governance Systems?

Different systems of corporate governance result from different historical development, different cultures and different economies. It is not realistic to assume that all this will simply be overwhelmed by an inevitable process of global convergence. Tricker suggests:

> The one thing that seems certain is that the existing diversity and complexity of forms of corporate enterprise and patterns of corporate governance will continue and, very probably, increase. Alternative paradigms of corporate governance will be needed to improve the effectiveness of governance, to influence the healthy development of corporate regulation, and to understand the reality of the political processes by which companies are governed, rather than the structures and mechanisms through which governance is exercised. In any development it will be important to avoid the polar extremities of governance based on an expensive bureaucracy of regulation and the adversarial clash of vested interests. Governance powers and processes need to provide for the many different constitutional bases of modern enterprise and to reflect the reality of power over that entity, balancing independence and objectivity with executive commitment and motivation.[39]

Each of the regional corporate systems of governance has strengths and weaknesses (Table 6.5). A sage professor of management, Derek Pugh, once suggested that to discover the weaknesses of a company you have to understand its strengths. The *Pugh Paradox* also applies to governance systems. In the Anglo-Saxon model there is a dynamic market orientation in which highly fluid capital will seek out business opportunities internationally, particularly in innovative and new industries where the promise of high returns is greatest: for example, the UK provides almost as much venture capital each year as the rest of Europe put together (in 1996 the UK invested 2.9 billion ecu of a European total of 6.7 billion ecu).[40] This vitality is associated with the success of leading-edge companies like Motorola, Microsoft, Merck and Glaxo. The obverse of this is a volatility of finance which leads to a focus on the short-term, and impatience with the long haul of gradually improving companies in mature industries where returns are modest. This transaction-driven system is characterized by inadequate governance structures that are not dynamic or robust enough to match the demands made of it.

Table 6.5: Strengths and Weaknesses of Governance Systems

Anglo-Saxon Model (US and UK)
Strengths
- Dynamic market orientation
- Fluid capital
- Internationalization extensive

Weaknesses
- Volatile instability
- Short termism
- Inadequate governance structures

European Model (Germany)
Strengths
- Long-term industrial strategy
- Very stable capital
- Robust governance procedures

Weaknesses
- Internationalization more difficult
- Lack of flexibility
- Inadequate investment for new industries

Asian Model (Japan)
Strengths
- Very long-term industrial strategy
- Stable capital
- Major overseas investments

Weaknesses
- Financial speculation
- Secretive, sometimes corrupt governance procedures
- Weak accountability

Source: Clarke and Bostock, 'International Corporate Governance' (1994)

In contrast the European model, as represented by Germany, has as its core rationale a commitment to long-term industrial strategy, with stable capital investment structures and robust, representative governance procedures. This has been the foundation of the great German manufacturing companies such as Siemens, Daimler-Benz and Volkswagen. However, the very stability and security of the relationships in the German system has caused a degree of rigidity and lack of flexibility in the face of new competitive threats. Until quite recently internationalization was more difficult for German companies, who have had to adapt to Anglo-Saxon accounting practices. Finally, the lack of a developed equity market has inhibited the growth of new companies in innovative businesses.

Japan has exposed the greatest paradoxes of all, with industrial companies devoted to very long-term strategies of growth and gradual winning of market share, supported by patient capital investment based on close relationships, a formula that has led to the domination of world product markets by companies such as Toyota, Matsushita, Mitsubishi and Sony. On the other hand, the speculative boom provoked by this industrial wealth revealed the weakness of governance institutions and the inadequacy of secretive and sometimes corrupt procedures. The resulting growth of shareholder activism, together with the influence of international investors and regulatory standards, is likely to lead to significant changes in Japanese governance practices.

It is not surprising that the different governance systems have different outcomes, since the values and objectives of the systems are quite different. Lester Thurow colourfully contrasts the definitions of business success:

America and Britain trumpet individual values: the brilliant entrepreneur, Nobel prize winners, large wage differentials, individual responsibility for skills, ease of firing and quitting, profit maximization and hostile mergers and takeovers. In contrast, Germany and Japan trumpet communitarian values: business groups, social responsibility for skills, teamwork, firm loyalty, industry strategies, and active, growth promoting industrial policies. Anglo-Saxon firms are profit maximizers; Japanese firms play a game that might be better known as 'strategic conquest' – they are more focused on market share than on profit. These different visions of capitalism have profound effects on everything from labour relations to public education.[41]

Corporate governance is in a state of transition in every country in the world, with the strongest force being the internationalization and globalization of financial markets. The outcome is likely to be an increase in diversity within an overall trend towards convergence:

Looking ahead towards the next decade it is possible to foresee a duality in the developing scenarios. On the one hand, we might expect further diversity – new patterns of ownership, new forms of group structure, new types of strategic alliance, leading to yet more alternative approaches to corporate governance. More flexible and adaptive organizational arrangements, entities created for specific projects, business ventures and task forces are likely to compound the diversity. Sharper differentiation of the various corporate types and the different bases for governance power will be necessary to increase the effectiveness of governance and enable the regulatory processes to respond to reality ... But on the other hand, we might expect a convergence of governance processes as large corporations operating globally, their shares traded through global financial markets, are faced with increasing regulatory convergence in company law, disclosure requirements and international accounting standards, insider trading and securities trading rules, and the exchange of information between the major regulatory bodies around the world.[42]

QUESTIONS OF GOVERNANCE

To understand the forces shaping the development of corporate governance it is necessary to return to the basic fundamentals, and in the beginning there was Berle and Means: they were the first to explore the structural and strategic implications of the separation of ownership and control. Berle wrote in the preface of *The Modern Corporation and Private Property* that 'It was apparent to any thoughtful observer that the American corporation had ceased to be a private business device and had become an institution'.[43] The dispersal of equity ownership of companies raises a number of governance issues:

- For firms to operate efficiently managers must have the freedom to take risks, make strategic decisions and take advantage of opportunities as they arise, and though they should remain subject to effective monitoring mechanisms, they cannot submit every decision to a shareholder vote.
- A group of shareholders with a large total share of the equity might be more effective at monitoring management, but their powers must also be restrained to prevent them taking advantage of other shareholders.
- Many investors prefer the advantages of liquidity and diversity in their portfolios to the time and resource commitment involved in monitoring.
- Investors require accurate accounting information, but any performance measures can provide misleading information or distort incentives by encouraging managers to focus attention on inappropriate goals. Further, releasing some kinds of information can weaken a firm's competitive position.[44]

The attenuation of the shareholders' role in managing the business, and the rise of professional management, are associated with a growing recognition of the significance of the role and contribution of other stakeholder groups to the performance of the company. With management assuming responsibility for the supervision of the physical capital of the corporation, each of the primary stakeholder groups – shareholders, lenders, customers, suppliers and employees – have a relationship with the company in which they provide some resource vital for the company's survival and in return receive some value. Berle and Means argue:

> Neither the claims of ownership nor those of control can stand against the paramount interest of the community ... It remains only for the claims of the community to be put forward with clarity and force. Rigid enforcement of property rights as a temporary protection against plundering by control would not stand in the way of the modification of these rights in the interests of other groups. When a convincing system of community obligations is worked out and is generally accepted, in that moment the passive property right of today

must yield before the larger interests of society. Should corporate leaders, for example, set forth a programme comprising
fair wages, security to employees, reasonable service to their
public, and stabilization of business, all of which would divert
a portion of the profits from the owners of passive property,
and would the community generally accept such a scheme as
a logical and human solution of industrial difficulties, the
interests of passive property owners would have to give way.
Courts would almost of necessity be forced to recognize the
result, justifying it by whatever of the many legal theories
they might choose. It is conceivable, indeed it seems almost
essential if the corporate system is to survive, that the 'control'
of the great corporations should develop into a purely neutral
technocracy, balancing a variety of claims by various groups
in the community and assigning to each a portion of the
income stream on the basis of public policy rather than private
cupidity.[45]

In 1932, the same year their book was first published, Berle
insisted, 'You cannot abandon emphasis on the view that business
corporations exist for the sole purpose of making profits for their
shareholders until such time as you are prepared to offer a clear
and reasonably enforceable scheme of responsibilities to someone
else'.[46] He could not have foreseen that, after sixty-five years of
patient and deliberate effort by company managers to balance their
responsibilities and objectives, no 'clear or enforceable scheme' for
them to do this had emerged; or that, though the law has struggled
to keep pace with industrial reality, the changes in the fundamental
principles of company law would have proved so modest.

The Corporate Constituency

In the United States thirty-eight state legislatures attempted to
protect the companies in their local economies from hostile
takeover by passing stakeholder laws that permitted or required
directors to consider the impact of all their activities on constituencies other than shareholders, including employees, customers, suppliers and the community.[47]

Steven M. H. Wallman, an SEC commissioner who helped to
draft the 'corporate constituency' law passed in Pennsylvania,

defines the corporation's interest as 'enhancing its ability to produce wealth indefinitely . . . both profit from today's activities and expected profit from tomorrow's activities'.[48] This could provide the basis of a new interpretation of what it means for directors to act 'in the interests of the corporation'. Defining the interests of the corporation in terms of maximizing the wealth-producing potential of the enterprise, and linking the interests of the various constituencies to the interests of the corporation 'resolves much of the tension that would otherwise exist from competing and conflicting constituent demands'.[49]

Over half of the Standard & Poor's 500 corporations in the United States are listed in the state of Delaware, which does not have a 'corporate constituency' statute; however, in a case involving Paramount Communications the Delaware supreme court was understood to give the same freedom to management to judge the short-term and long-term interests of the company, though in 1993 this ruling was altered in a case involving the same company, leaving it unclear whether directors of companies incorporated in Delaware can consider the effects of takeover decisions on all stakeholders rather than on shareholders alone.[50]

Martin Lipton offers a precise legal interpretation:

> Under Delaware law the objective of the corporation is the *long-term* growth of shareholder value; assuming the board of directors has used due care (followed reasonable procedures) and did not have a conflict of interest, the board may prefer *long-term* goals over *short-term* goals except when the decision is to sell control of the corporation or to liquidate it in which case the board must use reasonable efforts to get the best value obtainable for the shareholders. Under this standard the board has the right to invest for the *long-term* in people, equipment, market share and financial structure even though the financial markets do not recognize (or overtly discount) the future value and even though the board's strategy results in elimination of dividends and reduction in market price of the stock. Also under this standard, the board has the right to 'just say no' to a premium takeover bid. However, the board does remain subject to shareholder control and the shareholders have the right at least once a year to replace at least some of the directors who have followed a strategy or taken a position disliked by the shareholders.[51]

The Shareholder Theory of the Firm

Though the law in the United States has inched towards acknowledging the rights of other stakeholders, at least in the extreme
circumstances of company takeovers, for most of this century a
'property conception' of the company has predominated in the
Anglo-Saxon world. This has received most robust expression in
the 'Chicago School' of law and economics, which treats the company as a nexus of contracts through which the various participants
arrange to transact with each other. Their theory claims that assets
of the company are the property of the shareholders, and managers
and boards of directors are viewed as agents of shareholders, with
all the difficulties of enforcement associated with agency relationships but without legal obligations to any other stakeholder: 'the
rights of creditors, employees, and others are strictly limited to
statutory, contractual, and common law rights'.[52]

Any broadening of the social obligations of the company was
dangerous, according to this school of thought: 'Few trends could
so thoroughly undermine the foundations of our free society as
the acceptance by corporate officials of a social responsibility other
than to make as much money for their stockholders as possible'.[53]
The difficulty is whether, in trying to represent the interests of all
stakeholders, company directors simply slip the leash of the one
truly effective restraint that regulates their behaviour – their
relationship with shareholders. In apparently seeking to become
the arbiter of the general interest, executives become a self-
perpetuating group of princes:

> So long as the management has the one overriding duty of
> administering the resources under its control as trustees for
> the shareholders and for their benefit, its hands are tied; and
> it will have no arbitrary power to benefit from this or that
> particular interest. But once the management of a big enter-
> prise is regarded as not only entitled but even obliged to con-
> sider in its decisions whatever is regarded as of social interest,
> or to support good causes and generally to act for the public
> benefit, it gains indeed an uncontrollable power – a power
> which would not be left in the hands of private managers but
> would inevitably be made the subject of increasing public
> control.[54]

These views were expressed with vigour by liberal economists, and enjoyed the support of some business leaders and senior politicians. More practically, such views reflected how US and UK companies were driven in the seventies and eighties, with an emphasis upon sustaining share price and dividend payments at all costs, and freely using merger and takeover activity to discipline managers who failed in their responsibility to enhance shareholder value. It was the economic instability and insecurity created by this approach that was criticized in the report by Michael Porter.[55]

Monks and Minnow have recently attempted to restate the essential principles of the shareholder theory of the firm, which is more tolerant of the interests of other constituents but insists they are best served by acknowledging the supremacy of the ultimate owner:

> It seems to make most sense to envision a hypothetical long-term shareholder, like the beneficial owner of most institutional investor securities, as the ultimate party at interest. That allows all other interests to be factored in without losing sight of the goal of long term wealth maximization. But without a clear and directly enforceable fiduciary obligation to shareholders, the contract that justifies the corporate structure is irreparably shattered. It is difficult enough to determine the success of a company's strategy based on only one goal – shareholder value. It is impossible when we add in other goals . . . The only way to evaluate the success of a company's performance is to consult those who have the most direct and wide-reaching interest in the results of that performance – the shareholders. The problem is one of effective accountability (agency costs). Only owners have the motive to inform themselves and to enforce standards that arguably are a proxy for the public interest.[56]

It could be contested whether a focus upon shareholder interests really has been the key to good corporate performance and effective accountability in the recent past in the US and UK. In an age of more active participation by consumers, employees and other economic groups, to assume that shareholders alone are capable of effective monitoring is perhaps merely wishful thinking. An irony is that shareholders, particularly the scattered army of individual shareholders, have not been particularly well looked after or informed in the recent past, even by companies espousing share-holder-value views.

The arguments against the stakeholder view have recently been summarized by John Argenti:

- Companies have a relatively homogenous group of shareholders but diverse stakeholders to relate to.
- It is clear what shareholders expect, but unclear what stake-holders expect.
- The pursuit of the profit motive is simple, but if all stakeholder interests are to be balanced, trade-offs will become increasingly complex.
- There is a need for a single bottom line to provide a focus for managers.
- There is difficulty in measuring and verifying values to other stakeholders.[57]

As Andrew Campbell suggests, this straightforward view of management underestimates the existing complexity of the task, and confines the objectives of business to a single purpose, when in fact the 'market economy allows each company to define its own "deal" for each stakeholder group. This in turn encourages creativity'.[58] For example, the latest annual report of Enterprise Oil plc includes among its central corporate objectives 'nurturing an environment in which the best people want to work towards delivering a strong growth in *values*'. (Apparently the plural caused problems for one of the company's non-executives.)

THE STAKEHOLDER THEORY OF THE FIRM

Stakeholding: A Concept with Many Meanings

The Shorter Oxford English Dictionary definition of 'stakeholding' records the first use of the term in 1708 as a bet or deposit; 'to have a stake in (an event, a concern, etc.): to have something to gain or lose by the turn of events, to have an interest in; especially to have a stake in the country (said of those who hold landed property). Hence specifically a shareholding (in a company)'. A stakeholder theory of the firm has existed in various forms, based on different economic principles, since the origins of industrialism.

The philosophical antecedents of stakeholder theory reach back into the nineteenth century, to the ideals of the co-operative movement and mutuality.[59] Periodically such theory has become marginalized and forgotten, only to be reclaimed later in response to changing economic circumstances. Because of its fragmented development and its marginal status, it has never been elaborated or explained as fully and coherently as the shareholder theory of the firm.

One explanation for the recent widespread enthusiasm for the idea of stakeholding is that, like the concepts of *democracy* and *citizenship*, *stakeholding* has many meanings which stretch across the political spectrum and have multiple practical implications. In its broadest meaning Jacobs identifies three fundamental elements:

Philosophical: Stakeholding represents a general sense of social inclusion; an economy or society in which every citizen is a valued member, everyone contributes and everyone benefits in some way.

Participatory: Whether at the level of the economy as a whole, or in relation to individual companies, stakeholding implies an active participation in processes of accountability.

Financial: Participation is reinforced by the acknowledgement of the stakeholders' direct financial or material interest in the well-being of the economy or company; this in turn legitimates their participation.[60]

Edith Penrose in *The Theory of the Growth of the Firm* (1959) laid the intellectual foundations for stakeholder theory in her concept of the company as a bundle of human assets and relationships. The term 'stakeholder theory' was first used in 1963 at the Stanford Research Institute, where stakeholder analysis was used in the corporate planning process by Igor Ansoff and Robert Stewart.[61] However, Igor Ansoff was cautious in his use of the concept: 'While . . . responsibilities and objectives are not synonymous, they have been made one in a "stakeholder theory" of objectives. This theory maintains that the objectives of the company should be derived by balancing the conflicting claims of the various "stakeholders" in the firm, managers, workers, stockholders, suppliers, vendors'.[62]

Freeman provides a history of the US use of the concept.[63] In 1975 Dill argued:

For a long time we have assumed that the views and initiatives of stakeholders could be dealt with as externalities to the strategic planning and management process: as data to help management shape decisions, or as legal and social constraints to limit them. We have been reluctant, though, to admit the idea that some of these outside stakeholders might seek and earn active roles with management to make decisions. The move today is from stakeholder influence to stakeholder participation.[64]

The Wharton School in Pennsylvania began a stakeholder project in 1977 exploring the implications of the stakeholder concept as a management theory; as a process for practitioners to use in strategic management; and as an analytical framework.[65]

The stakeholder theory is deceptively simple. Definitions of who the stakeholders are range from the highly specific and legal to the general and social. The Stanford Research Institute's definition of stakeholders was: 'those groups without whose support the organization would cease to exist'. Max Clarkson organized an academic conference on the subject at the University of Toronto in May 1993: following this, a special edition of the *Academy of Management Review* was issued in January 1995; it offered the following definition of stakeholder theory: 'The firm is a system of stakeholders operating within the larger system of the host society that provides the necessary legal and market infrastructure for the firm's activities. The purpose of the firm is to create wealth or value for its stakeholders by converting their stakes into goods and services'.[66]

Who Are the Stakeholders and What Do They Want?

Whatever approach to stakeholding is adopted by business, the first question must be: 'Who are your stakeholders and what do they want?' The answer to this will be rather different for every company, depending on its ownership, size and structure, product or service market and so forth. Jonathan Charkham suggests a distinction between *contractual* stakeholders, who have some legal relationship with the company, and *community* stakeholders, whose relationship with the business is more diffuse but none the less real (Table 6.6).

In their configuration of the key stakeholders, Wheeler and Sillanpää, from the environmental wing of stakeholding, suggest

Table 6.6: Contractual and Community Stakeholders

Contractual stakeholders	Community stakeholders
Shareholders	Consumers
Employees	Regulators
Customers	Government
Distributors	Pressure groups
Suppliers	The media
Lenders	Local communities

Source: J. Charkham, 'Corporate Governance: Lessons from Abroad' (1992)

a division between primary social stakeholders and primary non-social stakeholders (Figure 6.5).

Ascertaining what stakeholders want is the next critical task. Again, the interests, desires and preferences of stakeholders will vary for every company, but a template for stakeholder expectations and forms of accountability is summarized in Table 6.7.

Creating a Measurement Framework
Once it has been established who key stakeholders are, and what it is they value in their relationship with a business, there remains the tricky job of assessing whether, over time, relationships are improving as planned. This task is made easier if the variables are easily quantified, but many aspects of stakeholder relationships and business processes are complex and qualitative, and in the past this may have excluded them from the careful consideration received by the 'hard' data. Companies are developing and utilizing more effective measurement frameworks, and the RSA report suggested several useful principles for any measurement system:

- To manage complexity to create clarity – encompassing a coherent set of selected key measures.
- To match the success model – for example, General Electric's success model is expressed in terms of customers, employees and cash, and the key measures are customer loyalty, employee morale, and cash flow.
- To include one leading indicator from each relationship.
- To include measures of the strategic health of the business – for example, the rate of introduction of new products, or the progress in staff development.

Figure 6.5: Constellation of Influences on the Stakeholder Corporation

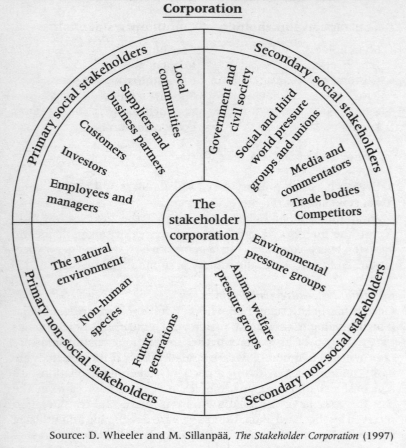

Source: D. Wheeler and M. Sillanpää, *The Stakeholder Corporation* (1997)

- To enable benchmarking against the performance of world-class companies.
- To balance immediate results with future capabilities.
- To include measures which assist the board in risk assessment and management.[67]

Accountability to Whom?
A related and unresolved problem is to work out how or whether stakeholder interests should be more formally represented in a company's aims; which are the appropriate spheres of influence

Table 6.7: What Do Stakeholders Want?

Stakeholder	Expectations of Stakeholder *From* the Company	Nature of Accountability *By* the Company
Employees	Remuneration, employment security, conditions, training	Company reports, employment news, bargaining information
Owners	Dividends and share price appreciation	Annual report and accounts, merger and takeover information
Customers	Quality, service, safety, value for money	Sales literature, advertising, servicing
Bankers	Liquidity and solvency of company, value of security, cash generation	Cover ratios, collateral cash forecasts
Suppliers	Stable and enduring relationship	Payment according to terms
Government	Compliance with law, jobs, competitiveness, accurate data	Reports to official bodies, press releases
General Public	Safety of operations, contribution to the community	Safety reports, press reports
Environment	Benign operations, substitution of non-renewable resources	Environmental reports, compliance reports

Source: Adapted from D. G. Woodward, F. Edwards, and F. Birkin, 'Organizational Legitimacy and Stakeholder Information Provision', *British Journal of Management*, 7, 4 December 1996, p. 340

of the different parties; and whether there is any need to change company law. In his review of the centrality of stakeholder models to the running of enterprises in Germany, France and Japan, Charkham argues:

In one important respect the law does not need to be changed: namely the bodies to which the board is accountable. In the 'other constituencies' debate, it is argued that management has a great many interests to consider other than the shareholders, such as employees, customers, suppliers, bankers, and the community. Of course it does: it cannot hope to succeed unless it takes all these interests properly into account . . . Shareholders may come at the end of the queue for dividends (and for distribution if the company ceases to trade), but they are the anchormen. If the board's accountability to them is lessened it will be altogether weakened: the distinction between 'taking into account' and 'being responsible to' must be maintained.[68]

It was this critical distinction which allowed the Hampel Committee on Corporate Governance in the UK to avoid formally recognizing stakeholder interests among the duties of company directors:

A company must develop relationships relevant to its success. These will depend on the nature of the company's business; but they will include those with employees, customers, suppliers, credit providers, local communities and governments. It is management's responsibility to develop policies which address these matters; in doing so they must have regard to the overriding objective of preserving and enhancing the shareholders' investment over time . . . This recognizes that the directors' relationship with the shareholders is different in kind from their relationship with other stakeholder interests. The shareholders elect the directors. As the CBI put it in their evidence to us, the directors are responsible *for relations with* stakeholders; but they are accountable *to* the shareholders. This is not simply a technical point. From a practical point of view, to redefine the directors' responsibilities in terms of the stakeholders would mean identifying the various stakeholder groups; and deciding the nature and extent of the directors' responsibility to each. The result would be that the directors were not effectively accountable to anyone since there would be no clear yardstick for judging their performance. This is a recipe neither for good governance nor for corporate success.[69]

Identifying and communicating with relevant stakeholder groups, deciding the nature of responsibilities to each, and being judged by a wider range of performance indicators that relate to stakeholder concerns is precisely what enlightened companies are striving to do, as Wheeler and Sillanpää illustrate in their work on *The Stakeholder Corporation* (1997). As John Kay insists, there is an alternative to the shareholder-agency model of the corporation, which recognizes the existence of the corporate personality, and accepts that the large public corporation is a social institution, not the creation of private contracts. Well-established principles of English law govern the behaviour of individuals or groups who control assets they do not beneficially own – which results in the concept of trusteeship:

> The notion that boards of directors are the trustees of the tangible and intangible assets of the corporation, rather than the agents of the shareholders is one which the executives of most German and Japanese companies, and of many British firms, would immediately recognize. The duty of the trustee is to preserve and enhance the value of the assets under his control, and to balance fairly the various claims to the returns which these assets generate . . . The responsibility of the trustees is to sustain the corporation's assets. This differs from the value of the corporation's shares. The difference comes not only because the stock market may value these assets incorrectly. It also arises because the assets of the corporation, for these purposes, include the skills of its employees, the expectations of customers and suppliers, and the company's reputation in the community. The objectives of managers as trustees therefore relate to the broader purposes of the corporation, and not simply the financial interests of shareholders . . . Thus the trusteeship model demands, as the agency model does not, the evolutionary development of the corporation around its core skills and activities because it is these skills and activities, rather than a set of financial claims, which are the essence of the company.[70]

A more fundamental question, which Hampel failed to ask, is: What are the principal assets of the contemporary company?

The Principal Assets of Knowledge-based Companies

The principles of corporate governance to which the Hampel Committee refers were established almost two centuries ago. Charles Handy in an essay on 'The Citizen Corporation' explains why clinging to former certainties is no longer appropriate:

> The old language of property and ownership no longer serves us in the modern world because it no longer describes what a company really is. The old language suggests the wrong priorities, leads to inappropriate policies, and screens out new possibilities. The idea of a corporation as the property of the current holders of shares is confusing because it does not make clear where power lies. As such, the notion is an affront to natural justice because it gives inadequate recognition to the people who work in the corporation, and who are, increasingly, its principal assets.[71]

In a study of intellectual capital and the end of assets as we know them, Thomas A. Stewart, a board member of *Fortune* magazine, insists,

> The knowledge company travels light. When information has replaced stockpiles of inventory and when it has left its material body and taken on a business life of its own, a company ultimately becomes a different kind of *creature*. A traditional company is a collection of physical assets, bought and owned by capitalists who are responsible for maintaining them, and who hire people to operate them. A knowledge company is different in many ways . . . not only are the assets of a knowledge company intangible, it's not clear who owns them or who is responsible for them. Indeed, a knowledge company might not own much in the way of traditional assets at all. Just as information replaces working capital, so intellectual assets replace physical ones. A knowledge company's financial structure can be so different from that of an industrial company that it is incomprehensible in traditional terms.[72]

A report was prepared by Arthur Anderson in response to the concerns of UK industry that they were failing adequately to identify, value and improve intangible assets.[73] The issue came to prominence for the first time in 1988, when Nestlé bid for Rowntree more than twice its pre-bid market capitalization. At the same time a string of leading UK companies announced they were going to capitalize their brands. The valuing of intangible assets has been based on:

- The prospects for the future commercial exploitation of the intangible asset.
- The parameters that should be applied to capitalize the cash flows or earnings attributable to such future operations.[74]

Intangible assets are the result of past efforts and possess the following attributes:

- They are non-physical in nature.
- They are capable of producing future economic net benefits.
- They are protected legally or through a *de facto* right.[75]

Intangible assets must be separable for the purpose of measurement from the business as a whole, and the most common categories of intangible assets are:

- Brands.
- Publishing rights.
- Intellectual property.
- Licences.[76]

A classification of the most frequently encountered intangible assets is provided in Table 6.8. (A study by Interbrand and *Financial World* in 1996 identified the most valuable brands and attributed astonishing value to the brands alone: Marlboro $44 billion; Coca-Cola $43 billion; McDonald's $19 billion; IBM $18 billion; Disney $15 billion. This is put into perspective when it is appreciated that Coca-Cola has a fixed asset base of only $4.4 billion.)[77]

Stewart illustrates the true value of intangibles by comparing the finances of Microsoft and IBM. Firstly, it is important to remember that IBM, as the most powerful computer company of the middle decades of the twentieth century, assured Microsoft's

Table 6.8: Classification of Intangible Assets

Brands	Intellectual property
Consumer goods brand	Patent
Industrial brand	Copyright
Service brand	Trademark
Trademark, including	Know-how
– name	Technology
– logo	Trade secret
– device	
– colour combination	
Corporate name	Product design/style
	Database
	Software
	Drawing/blueprint

Publishing rights	Licences
Magazine	TV/radio franchise/licence
Book title	Airline route/slot
Masthead	Production right
Film library	Import quota
Music library	Operating licence
Photographic library	(e.g. transport)
TV/radio programme listing	Mineral exploitation
Copyright	Franchise operation
Imprint	Distribution right
Subscriber/advertiser list	Licence of right
	(e.g. pharmaceutical)
Trademark	Non-compete agreements
Exhibition right	

Source: Arthur Andersen, *The Valuation of Intangible Assets* (1992)

future when in 1983 it selected the MS-DOS software to run its personal computers. IBM's sales are more than fifteen times greater than Microsoft's, and its software business generates more sales than the whole of Microsoft. IBM's one-word motto, 'THINK', its array of Nobel Prize-winning scientists, and the 3,768 patents granted to its employees between 1993 and 1995 – all testify to the formidable intelligence at its disposal.

Yet Microsoft in 1996 had a market capitalization of $85.5 billion and IBM a total market capitalization of $70.7 billion. The asset-base of the two companies was totally different. IBM owned, net of depreciation, $16.6 billion worth of property, plant and equipment; Microsoft's net fixed assets totalled just $930 million. A $100 investment in IBM buys $23 worth of fixed assets, and a little over $1 worth of fixed assets in Microsoft. Margaret Blair of the Brookings Institute calculated the relationship between tangible assets (property, plant and equipment) and total market value for every US manufacturing and mining company in the Compustat database. In 1982 physical assets accounted for 62.3 per cent of companies' market value; ten years later they made up only 37.8 per cent, and these were industrial companies; the physical assets of high-technology and service companies would be much lower.[78]

This argument has particular resonance with regard to knowledge-based companies, and of course all companies are becoming more knowledge based: 'You would be hard-pressed to find a single industry, a single company, a single organization of any kind, that has not become more "knowledge intensive", dependent on knowledge as a source of what attracts customers and clients and on information technology as a means of running the place'.[79] Drucker argues that in the new economy, knowledge is not just another resource alongside the traditional factors of production of labour, land and capital, but the only meaningful resource.

According to Drucker, the fact that knowledge has become *the* resource, rather than *a* resource, makes the new society unique. In a society based on knowledge, the 'knowledge worker is the single greatest asset'.[80] Robert Reich argues that the only true competitive advantage will be through symbolic analysts who are equipped with the knowledge to identify, solve and broker new problems.[81]

Nonaka and Takeuchi in *The Knowledge Creating Company* suggest that while Western companies focus on information-processing of formal, codified knowledge, Japanese companies succeed because they understand the significance of tacit, subjective knowledge.[82] Robert Grant claims that 'If knowledge is the pre-eminent productive resource, and most knowledge is created by and stored within individuals, then employees are the primary stakeholders. The principal management challenge . . . is establishing mechanisms by which co-operating individuals can co-ordinate their activities in order to integrate their knowledge into productive activities.'[83]

Silicon Valley, which has given the world Intel, Apple, Silicon

Graphics, Netscape and a host of other high-technology companies, fully recognizes this fact. This triumph of technological innovation could only be achieved by attracting the brightest people to start-up companies with the most generous employee stock options in the history of corporate America. As Matt Ward of WestWard Pay Strategies puts it, 'Silicon Valley is the economic engine of the world, and options the fuel.' Before the recent meteoric rise in the value of Microsoft shares, a Wall Street analyst calculated that 2,200 of Microsoft's 11,000 employees each held options worth at least $1 million. By 31 March 1997, $23 billion was outstanding in unexercised employee stock options, equivalent to $1 million per employee, and the company is now facing legal action from employees who felt excluded from this largesse. According to Sanford C. Bernstein & Co., the total value of shares set aside for employee options was $59 billion in 1985; this had reached $600 billion by 1996, when 90 per cent of US public companies had employee stock-option programmes.[84] In 1996, of the 200 largest US companies, fifteen had at least 24 per cent of their shares set aside for employee options and other stock awards (Table 6.9).

Table 6.9: US Companies Employee Options and Stock Awards 1996

Morgan Stanley	91.36%
Merrill Lynch	40.26%
Travelers	39.42%
Warner-Lambert	35.00%
Microsoft	32.95%
J. P. Morgan & Co.	29.62%
Lehman Brothers	28.25%
US Airways	26.71%
Sun Microsystems	25.99%
Marriott	25.81%
Bankers Trust	25.53%
General Mills	25.41%
MCI	24.39%
Allied Signal	24.23%
ITT Industries	24.14%

Source: Pearl Meyer & Partners, *Fortune*, July 1997

Stakeholder Strategies in Practice

In practice, executives leading companies and managers operating them have increasingly utilized elements of the stakeholder approach. The growing emphasis upon customer relations, employee relations, supplier relations and, indeed, investor relations is an indication that managers are having to grapple with the need to satisfy the interests of more complex constituencies than shareholder theory would suggest.

The defence of shareholder rights sits uneasily with the way in which companies are, increasingly, being managed. According to the Tomorrow's Company Inquiry, launched by the RSA in 1992, businesses need to fundamentally examine their objectives, relationships and performance measures if sustainable commercial success is to be achieved. Convincing evidence was cited of the perils of focusing too narrowly on short-term financial indicators.

Kotter and Heskett studied 200 companies over twenty years and clearly correlated superior long-term profitability with corporate cultures that express the company's purpose in terms of all stakeholder relationships.[85] John Kay defines success in terms of value added, and – arguing that outstanding businesses derive their strength from a distinctive structure of relationships with employees, customers and suppliers – explains why continuity and stability in these relationships are essential for a flexible and co-operative response to change (1993).[86] He offers a hard-headed interpretation of how a stakeholder approach is an essential basis for industrial viability:

> Inclusion and shared values promote trust, co-operative behaviour and the ready exchanges of information. These things also yield hard-nosed commercial advantages. Such values encourage closer working together, which is why the Japanese have achieved unmatched levels of component reliability, implemented just-in-time production processes and shortened model cycles. They help explain why the Germans and Swiss have secured exceptional standards of production engineering.[87]

Paradoxically, companies driven by financial indices to satisfy shareholders often appear capable of doing so for limited periods of time, but 'Companies that set profits as their No. 1 goal are actually less profitable in the long run than people-centred companies'.[88] Of the eleven companies named as Britain's most profitable between 1979 and 1989 by *Management Today*, four subsequently collapsed and two were acquired.[89] A BOC/London Business School survey, *Building Global Excellence*, commented on the preoccupation of UK managers with financial performance: 'To be in a position to predict the future and discover you need to change 3-4 years before the crisis comes, today's managers need to switch their attention away from the *financial* health of their companies and start measuring the *strategic* health'.[90]

Schools of Thought
The deep philosophical underpinnings of stakeholder theory have been operationalized in a great variety of practical ways. The multiple interpretations and applications have created a degree of confusion, with different parties claiming allegiance to different understandings, some of which are contradictory. Among the influential proponents of rival stakeholding propositions are:

- A political economy of stakeholding.
- Institutional approaches to a stakeholding economy.
- A stakeholder theory of the firm.
- The inclusive company.
- Integrated stakeholder communications.
- Quality and improvement stakeholding.
- Sustainable enterprise.

A Political Economy of Stakeholding
As countries traditionally associated with essentially stakeholding principles appear to be drifting away from them, the UK, which under Mrs Thatcher launched a free-market property-rights counter revolution upon the world, has travelled in the opposite direction. Will Hutton, presently editor of the *Observer* newspaper in the UK, launched an impassioned defence of new Keynesianism in his bestselling book, *The State We're In*. His robust advocacy of stakeholder capitalism helped to provoke an on-going public discussion.[91] His central thesis is that a market economy needs democratic institutions that generate social capital, particularly trust, and that, contrary to the individualistic neo-classical model, businesses function best on the basis of internal commitment and trust:

In market capitalism there will always be a constant tension between relationships of commitment and relationships of flexibility; between market contracts and non-market contracts. My central argument is that many of the present instabilities within society are the result of the balance being tilted too far in favour of an emphasis on free markets. This creates an environment which is so unstable, and which leads to such exclusion and polarization that it actually destroys the social habitat within which a successful regulated market system needs to be embedded. The pattern is particularly clear in the US where you see atomistic markets throwing up, for example, an excessively large financial services industry as people try desperately to protect themselves against unquantifiable and unmeasurable degrees of risk. Simultaneously 2 per cent of the black population of America are incarcerated for turning to crime due to their exclusion from the labour market.[92]

Hutton's vision involves reframing the relationship between finance and business; reforming workplace relations; transforming the welfare state and the benefit system; reformulating macroeconomic policy; and reconstructing the democratic system. On a tour of the Far East in January 1996 Tony Blair briefly entered the debate with a speech on stakeholder economics, before quickly retreating to the safer ground of the stakeholder society. John Plender of *The Financial Times* has focused on how reform of the pensions system is necessary to give people *A Stake in the Future* (1997). A new journal, the *Stakeholder*, is helping to extend the analysis to public sector management, where stakeholder principles are particularly useful in defining management roles and responsibilities.

Mario Nuti remains sceptical of such an ambitious extension of the stakeholder principle, and suggests, 'Once the set of a country's stakeholders coincides with the set of all citizens, the concept of stakeholders becomes completely redundant'; however, he may be underestimating the appeal of an 'inclusive society' in economies that have felt the consequences of the cold draught of exclusion in poverty, crime and failing economic performance.[93]

Institutional Approaches to a Stakeholding Economy

It is often suggested that the institutional foundations of stakeholding were essential to the post-war economic success of the German and Japanese economies. In Germany this was provided by the high concentration of owner-managers, the limited role of the equity market, and the inside characteristic of their governance systems, with their emphasis on the representation of all interested stakeholders.[94] In Japan collective stakeholder conceptions are deeply embedded in corporate thinking and practice, from the *keiretsu* principle of related companies, to *kaizen*, for continuous improvement, to the *kanban* of just-in-time production and the suppliers it depends upon: the importance of relationships is paramount.[95] Both systems are now under stress.

In Europe and Japan companies have traditionally adhered consciously to a stakeholder model, which is often pointed to as the basis of their industrial success and social stability. However, more recently, following the development of their equity markets and the increasing activity of international investors, particularly from the United States, some major European and Japanese companies have for the first time come under pressure to focus upon shareholder value. Whether this system can survive in major German companies such as Mercedes Benz and Hoechst following their listing on the New York Stock Exchange, and the insistent pressures they will face to yield shareholder returns, is open to question. At the other end of the scale, up to 700,000 of the family-run companies that constitute the Mittelstand, the locally based backbone of German enterprise, could be up for sale within the next ten years, as their post-war founders retire.[96]

Rainer Zimmerman has recorded the sea change sweeping through German industry:

> The late 1980s and early 1990s ushered in a phase of far reaching change for German companies. 'Go global' pressure and both political and private-sector deregulation force market players to adopt new competitive approaches and rethink their self-images. The potential for pure streamlining as a cost-cutting tool had effectively been exhausted. A new era began, one marked by a focus on growth, restructuring, corporate downsizing, portfolio shifts, consolidation, mergers and acquisitions, divestment, production shifts abroad and, more than anything, value management.[97]

Figure 6.6: Commitments of German Companies

Targeted themes (examples)

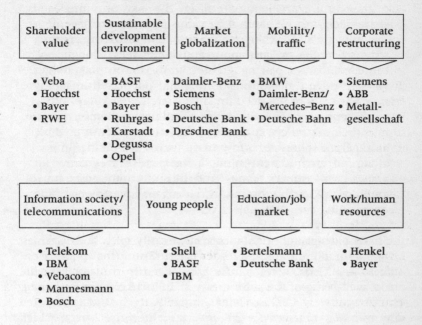

Shareholder value	Sustainable development environment	Market globalization	Mobility/ traffic	Corporate restructuring
• Veba	• BASF	• Daimler-Benz	• BMW	• Siemens
• Hoechst	• Hoechst	• Siemens	• Daimler-Benz/	• ABB
• Bayer	• Bayer	• Bosch	Mercedes–Benz	• Metall-
• RWE	• Ruhrgas	• Deutsche Bank	• Deutsche Bahn	gesellschaft
	• Karstadt	• Dresdner Bank		
	• Degussa			
	• Opel			

Information society/ telecommunications	Young people	Education/job market	Work/human resources
• Telekom	• Shell	• Bertelsmann	• Henkel
• IBM	• BASF	• Deutsche Bank	• Bayer
• Vebacom	• IBM		
• Mannesmann			
• Bosch			

Source: R. Zimmerman, *No Entity Without Identity* (1998)

According to German analysts Trinkhaus and Burkhard, a string of leading German companies, including BASF, Bayer, SAP, Daimler-Benz, Linde, Mannesmann, VEBA, Deutsche Bank, Shering, BMW, Lufthansa and Metro had explicitly chosen to focus on shareholder value.[98] German companies have made commitments to a wide range of social themes which help to identify their image and direction (Figure 6.6). Zimmerman notes that many German corporations are trying to project shareholder values and stakeholder values simultaneously, having approached the shareholder/stakeholder dilemma from the opposite direction to UK and US corporations. German companies that emphasize shareholder value must also take into account the interests of all reference groups:

It goes without saying that none of these companies can afford the luxury of underweighting the reference group of customers, so vital to their survival, or that of employees, so vital to their future development, all for the sake of a one-sided shareholder focus. Shareholder value and value management are only possible when companies first focus on creating strong benefits to customers and employees. Conversely, those companies placing greater emphasis on stakeholder value both in terms of positioning and public self-image by no means ignore the need for high shareholder value. While most companies generally position and depict themselves *vis-à-vis* their customers, their employees and society as a whole as expert, responsible, transparent, forward-thinking, innovative and environment-minded, the picture they draw for analysts, investment banks and business journalists must embrace the ideal of optimum returns on investment as the overarching corporate objective.[99]

Shareholder-value orientations sit uneasily with both German corporate traditions and the legal system. Gruner has pointed out that by law German companies are obliged to contribute to the social well-being of the community.[100] In 1918 Walter Rathenau, chief executive of AEG and later German Foreign Minister, created the term *'das Unternehmen an sich'* (the enterprise itself), which must meet not only the interests of the owner, but those of others. Yet German corporations want to appear more attractive on the national and international capital market, and companies such as Seimens, Henkel and Daimler-Benz have been measuring business performance more and more in terms of market value and equity return. In recent years shareholder returns have consistently risen, while wages have fallen.[101]

In Japan stakeholder principles are deeply embedded in corporate thinking and practice. Yoshimori highlights a company survey in which 97 per cent of companies agreed with the statement that a firm exists for the interest of all stakeholders. Asked whether a CEO should opt to maintain dividends or to lay off employees, a similar percentage of companies felt that job security was more important. When asked which stakeholder was most important as a source of support, 63 per cent of Japanese chief executives said that it was the employees, and only 11.5 per cent suggested it was shareholders.[102] Japanese firms have favoured long-term growth and sustained a policy of low dividend payments, with share-holders more concerned with total returns. However, in 1993 Japanese company law was changed to strengthen the powers of shareholders, and pressure to improve performance is coming from institutional investors, including those from overseas. As institutional investors become more influential in Japan and the influence of banks diminishes, Japanese corporations are likely to be under increasing pressure to alter their stakeholder orientations in favour of shareholder interests.[103]

The Origins of the Stakeholder Approach

In the United States Freeman traced the origins of the stakeholder approach, if not the actual use of the term, to the depression of the 1930s, when GEC identified four major stakeholder groups: shareholders, employees, customers and the general public. In 1947 Johnson and Johnson's president listed the company's 'strictly business' stakeholders as customers, employees, managers and shareholders; these then formed the basis of the Johnson and Johnson credo mission statement. In 1950 the CEO of Sears, which enjoyed rapid post-war growth, listed the 'four parties to any business in the order of importance as customers, employees, community and stockholders'.[104]

With the present proliferation of employee-stock-ownership plans (ESOPs) and other stakeholder forms, there is a growing literature in North America which regards the firm as a *nexus of contracts* between itself and its stakeholders. Thus Hill and Jones develop the principal-agent paradigm of financial economics to create a stakeholder-agency theory – 'a generalized theory of agency' in which managers are seen as agents for all stakeholders, not simply shareholders.[105]

The 'quest for a business and society paradigm' has covered corporate social performance and the social control of business as well as stakeholder models, in an as yet unresolved effort to produce an analysis with descriptive accuracy, instrumental power and normative validity.[106] 'Managers may not make explicit reference to stakeholder theory but the vast majority of them apparently adhere in practice to one of the central tenets of the stakeholder theory, namely, that their role is to satisfy a wider set of relationships, not simply the shareowners.'[107] The law in the United States has responded to this new thinking by encouraging company directors to look to the longer term, and to take into account a wider set of community interests, but this does not seem to have checked the huge escalation in the rate of takeovers and merger activity.

The Inclusive Company

In its search for the sources of sustainable business success (and for something more acceptable to the business community than either the prevailing competitive individualism or the demands of stakeholder theory), the RSA Tomorrow's Company Inquiry (1992–5), sponsored by twenty-five leading companies in the UK, concluded that 'only by giving due weight to the interests of all key stakeholders can shareholders' continuing value be assured'.[108] This *inclusive* approach to business leadership 'has the courage to put across a consistent message which is relevant to all stakeholders – giving the same vision for the company to shareholder and employee, to investor and supplier, to customer and the community at large'. Similar conclusions were reached by the Tomorrow's Corporation conferences, which met in Aspen, Colorado (1992–4), sponsored by the Polaroid Corporation; and by the Karpin Industry Task Force on Leadership and Management Skills, which reported in Australia.[109]

The key message of the RSA Tomorrow's Company Inquiry was that: 'As the business climate changes, so the rules of the competitive race are being re-written. The effect is to make people and relationships more than ever the key to sustainable success. Only through deepened relationships with – and between – employees, customers, suppliers, investors and the community will companies anticipate, innovate and adapt fast enough, while maintaining public confidence'.[110]

Durable competitive success could be achieved by focusing less exclusively on shareholders and financial measures of success, and including all stakeholder relationships within a broader range of measures, and in thinking and talking about business people, performance and actions. A company adopting an *inclusive* approach:

- Clearly defines its own distinctive purpose and values.
- Communicates these consistently to all stakeholders.
- Develops its model of success, indicating how this may be sustained, and the importance of each relationship to the success of the enterprise

Figure 6.7: The Inclusive Approach

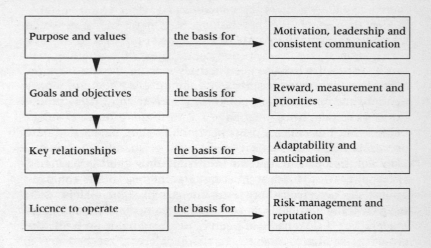

Source: SPL (1997)

- Engages in reciprocal rather than adversarial relationships with all those who contribute to the business.
- Works actively to build a partnership approach with employees, customers, suppliers and other stakeholders.
- Works actively to maintain public confidence in the legitimacy of its operations and business conduct; in other words, to maintain a *licence to operate*.

The Strategic Partnership (SPL) consultancy, which was in part inspired by the Tomorrow's Company Inquiry, seeks to facilitate this pursuit of an *inclusive* approach by examining how clarity of purpose and values can sustain leadership and motivation; how well-defined goals and objectives can be the basis of performance measurement and priorities; how a focus on key relationships can promote adaptability and anticipation; and how a strong licence to operate can support risk management (Figure 6.7).

The Centre for Tomorrow's Company, which also grew out of the RSA Inquiry, acts as a pressure group and research agency, encouraging a network of sympathetic companies and investment institutions to adopt an inclusive approach in their business activity. A task force was established jointly with the Institute of Public Relations to examine how company annual reports could more adequately address the concerns of a wider group of stakeholders than simply the shareholders: statements of values would be made, along with accurate assessments of progress in meeting them, without the necessity for complex external auditing processes. The centre has also been actively seeking to make directors appreciate that under existing UK common law they owe a duty firstly to the *company*, and not to any specific third-party group. Directors as fiduciaries must have regard to the interest of shareholders, but this obligation is not to the holders of shares at one particular time, but to the general body of shareholders over a length of time. That is, the law in the UK, as in the United States, allows directors to balance the long-term interests of the company against the perceived short-term interests of shareholders. (It is not practically possible to be accountable immediately to all shareholders. The AGM, badly in need of overhauling, is presently the great theatre of accountability to shareholders.)

Quality and Improvement Stakeholding

The logical outcome of the total quality management movement of the last twenty years, in part inspired by the industrial success of Japanese enterprise, is a focus on the quality of relationships between every stakeholder who contributes to the production of goods and services with zero defects. Other measures, such as the balanced business scorecard, aim to improve the whole business, and not just immediate financial results.

International quality models are concerned with company performance in all key stakeholder relationships: the criteria used both by the US Baldridge Quality Award and by the European Quality Award (1992) acknowledge this in their stakeholder emphasis. The assessment model of the European award proposes that the *enablers* of leadership, people management, policy and strategy, resources and processes are the means to achieve business *results*, which are achieved through people satisfaction, customer satisfaction and impact on society (Figure 6.8). It is interesting that the values ascribed by the model as a result of consultations with the several hundred corporate members of the European Foundation for Quality Management include:

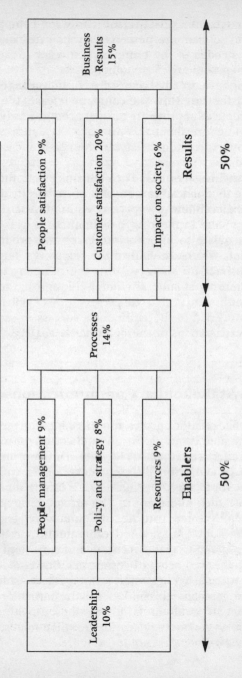

Figure 6.8: The European Quality Award Assessment Model

Leadership 10%

People management 9%
Policy and strategy 8%
Resources 9%

Enablers 50%

Processes 14%

People satisfaction 9%
Customer satisfaction 20%
Impact on society 6%

Results 50%

Business Results 15%

Source: European Foundation for Quality Management, *The European Quality Award* (1993)

20 per cent customer satisfaction: How the company and its products and services are perceived by its external customers. Evidence is needed of the company's success in satisfying the needs and expectations of customers.

18 per cent people, in the form of people management and people satisfaction: How the company releases the full potential of its people to improve its business continuously, and what people's feelings are about the company. Evidence is needed of the company's success in satisfying the needs and expectations of its people.

15 per cent business results: The company's continuing success in achieving its financial targets and objectives in meeting the needs and expectations of everyone with a financial interest in the company; and in meeting non-financial targets and objectives, which relate to internal processes and products/service improvements which are vital to the company's success.

6 per cent impact on society: How the company is perceived by the community at large, including its approach to quality of life, the environment and to the preservation of global resources. Evidence is needed of the company's success in satisfying the needs and expectations of the community at large.

Integrated Stakeholder Communications

Within the public relations profession there is an increasing realization that integrated communications and consistent messages are necessary for effective corporate identity. Different management functions may be addressing different stakeholders with different, and sometimes conflicting, messages, so it is important to structure and co-ordinate such information. The arrival of the professional investor, the sophisticated customer, the empowered employee, the information revolution, a knowledgeable public and government regulation has served to make accurate and consistent communications vital to the well-being of companies. Stakeholders actively communicate with each other when forming relationships with and views about the company; this makes it all the harder for companies to manage what are insubstantial impressions. Employees are pivotal to the whole process: they are the frontline representatives of the company with other stakeholders (Figure 6.9).

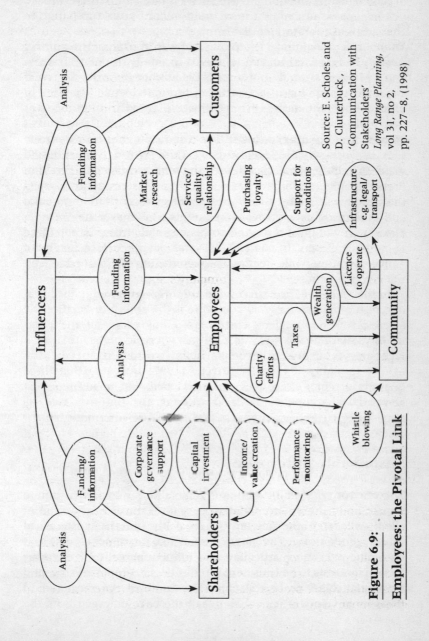

Figure 6.9:

Employees: the Pivotal Link

Source: E. Scholes and
D. Clutterbuck,
'Communication with
Stakeholders'
Long Range Planning,
vol 31, no 2,
pp. 227–8, (1998)

Scholes and Clutterbuck cite some recent corporate casualties of stakeholder retaliation. British Airways faced a cabin-crew strike just as it was launching a new multi-million-pound initiative to change its corporate identity from a company that was seen as 'monolithic' and 'inflexible', to one that was 'warm' and 'genuinely caring'. Some passengers were moved to side with the cabin crew and switched airlines in protest. Dissatisfaction with the chief executive's handling of the incident prompted some investors to offload stock. Similarly, Disney's image of good triumphing over evil took a knock when the World Development Movement accused it of boasting to shareholders about huge profits from the film *Hercules*, while allegedly using Third World sweatshops to make the clothing associated with the merchandising of the film. Premières of the film were picketed by protesters, who usurped the headlines. Finally, Shell, as a result of recent environmental and human rights controversies, saw its position in the *Financial Times* survey of most respected companies slide from the top three to number eleven. In contrast, BP was described as achieving a global operation while steering through the minefield of ethics and the environment.

In the *Financial Times* survey the CEOs interviewed judged that one of the marks of a good company is the ability to balance the interests of shareholders, customers, employees and the community; share analysts placed this characteristic higher than new technology, quality, or even satisfying customers' needs. The MORI Captains of Industry Survey (1997) indicated that three quarters of chief executives questions said that a business best serves its shareholders by also catering for the needs of its employees, customers, suppliers and the wider community.[111]

Sustainable Enterprise

The environment is the ultimate stakeholder, and the corporate impact upon the environment is the most critical relationship of all: it will determine not only the wealth, but the existence of future generations. The environmentalist movement, which is becoming ever more articulate and influential, calls for environmental interests to be considered in business decision-making, and for sustainability to be the objective. Some of the most radical ideas for developing stakeholder dialogue have emerged from the movement for sustainable enterprise. The competitive global economy is increasingly characterized by complexity and uncertainty: according to Wheeler and Sillanpää, 'One way to make sense of chaos is to base decisions on the maximum amount of information. The only way to secure information is to actively request it. In the case of key relationships with stakeholders this means regular conversations, focus groups and opinion surveys. It also means that the firm must organize itself to be receptive to inputs of opinion. In this context there are few more important sources of advice than the company's own employees'.[112]

Wheeler and Sillanopää suggest a generalized cycle of dialogue and inclusion for all stakeholders, aimed at continuous improvement of processes, products performance and relationships (Figure 6.10). The stages involved in the cycle include company commitment to a stakeholder-inclusive ethos and a review of policies which delineate the company's intentions with respect to shareholders – for example, health and safety programmes for employees, customer service programmes and dividend policies for shareholders. For each stakeholder group the scope of the audit feasible within numerical and geographic constraints needs to be determined: a retail company with millions of transactions will require representative samples of customers; a multinational oil company will have to gauge the level of consultation feasible in many local communities in different cultures.

There must be agreement on valid indicators of performance based on quantifiable factors and perceptions. Such surveys are becoming standard practice for leading companies; however, the distinction here is in both consulting stakeholder groups on relevant indicators and questions, and in sharing the results in a verifiable way. As Michael Power notes, 'audits are needed when accountability can no longer be sustained by informal relations of trust alone, but must be formalized, made visible and subject to independent validation.'[113]

Thus whether the subject is financial control, social performance or environmental management, formal processes of information collecting, reporting and auditing are essential if the issue is to be understood and managed effectively. This can lead to agreements on objectives which secure stakeholder commitment, such as improvements in product quality, employee development or environmental management, adding *stakeholder value*.

How exacting these processes of stakeholder dialogue and

Figure 6.10: Generalized Cycle of Inclusion for Stakeholders

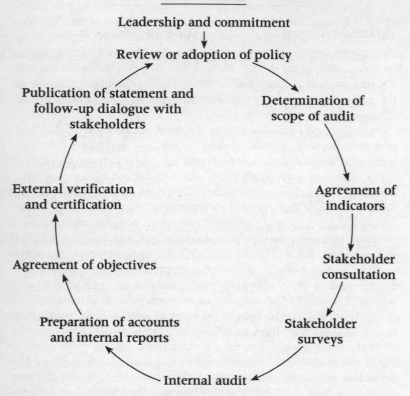

Leadership and commitment

Review or adoption of policy

Publication of statement and follow-up dialogue with stakeholders

Determination of scope of audit

External verification and certification

Agreement of indicators

Agreement of objectives

Stakeholder consultation

Preparation of accounts and internal reports

Stakeholder surveys

Internal audit

Source: D. Wheeler and M. Sillanpää, *The Stakeholder Corporation* (1997), p. 169.

reporting can be, and how far they have become part of official policy with regard to sustainable enterprise is revealed by the UN Environment Programme. The UNEP provided a set of measures which companies could use to benchmark the quality of environmental and social disclosure; this meant that a company could no longer argue that disclosure of social information was not possible or that indicators of sustainability were too diffuse.

The UNEP rating requires systematic and active engagement with stakeholders on the full range of environmental, social and

Table 6.10: UNEP Sustainability Programme –
Ten Transitions for the Future

Established focus on		Emerging focus on:
1 One-way, passive communication	→	Multi-way, active dialogue
2 Verification as option	→	Verification as standard
3 Single company progress reporting	→	Benchmarkability
4 Management systems	→	Life-cycles, business design, strategy
5 Inputs and outputs	→	Impacts and outcomes
6 *Ad hoc* operating standards	→	Global operating standards
7 Public relations	→	Corporate governance
8 Voluntary reporting	→	Mandatory reporting
9 Company determines reporting boundaries	→	Boundaries set through stakeholder dialogue
10 Environmental performance	→	Triple bottom line – economic, environmental and social – performance

Source: SustainAbility and United Nations Environment Programme,
Engaging Stakeholders (1996)

economic questions – *the triple bottom line*. It describes ten transitions in corporate environmental and social reporting for the future, which are benchmarks for corporations wishing to build a reputation for transparency and integrity (Table 6.10).

NON-FINANCIAL PERFORMANCE
INDICATORS

The Firmness of Financial Indicators

Buttressing the traditional financially based approaches to corporate governance and management are accounting systems which track the flow of physical and financial assets. Of course, the modern corporation would not be manageable, or even feasible, without a system of debits and credits that gives a coherent picture of the many different streams of goods and money that flow through an enterprise, combined with a system of financial controls to ensure they flow in the right direction. The first accounting textbook was written by Luca Pacioli, a Venetian monk, in 1494: *Summa de arithmetica, geometrica, proportioni et proportionalita* introduced the world to double-entry bookkeeping. This framework of measurement has survived for 500 years, simply assembling more rules – several thousand of them – over time.[114]

But the rock to which investors cling – firm financial indicators – can often disappear in heavy seas. Terry Smith, who wrote an influential critique of creative company accounting, commented on the failure of companies in the recession of 1990–92: 'I was struck by the extent to which investors, even professional fund managers and analysts, were quite naive in thinking that published company accounts were in some way a protection against losing money in this maelstrom'.[115]

When companies that have published healthy annual reports suddenly fail in a recession it is disturbing, but the veracity and reliability of company accounts are open to question even in more normal times. Commenting on the weaknesses of the Generally Accepted Accounting Principles (GAAP) in the United States, Monks and Minnow argue:

> Existing standards are too often seen as far more objective and meaningful than they are. For example 'earnings' are one of the critical components of value in the market place, yet essentially, earnings are what accountants say they are. Earnings, are subject to manipulation. Much of it is legal and some even appropriate, but some goes far beyond what should be acceptable. In recent years there has been an increasing tendency towards what has been called 'big bath' accounting. This is the practice when a company decides at the end of the year that it must take a one-time only 'restructuring charge'. This charge is not assessed against current earnings, it is levied against the accumulated earnings of the venture.[116]

In this world of corporate bath-taking Monks and Minnow offer some home-truths: 'More important than the *worth* of a company, which measures (imperfectly) today's value, is the *health* of a company, which predicts tomorrow's'.[117] In putting into perspective some of the commonly used financial measures, they refer to

Freidheim's critique of earnings per share, which can be driven up by restructuring and weakening the balance sheet, by acquisitions, and changing conventions, which do not add anything to the real value of the enterprise. Similarly, all 'the Rs – ROI, ROE, ROCE, ROA, ROS, ROT. They all have a place in business . . . but each can pay off without performance if followed as *the* measure'. Scepticism about over-reliance on any single financial measure has not prevented the search for a more all-embracing metric, and the current one is EVA (economic value added). EVA is the after-tax operating profit minus the weighed average cost of capital multiplied by the total capital (ATOP–WACC×TC). Basically, this is the net cash return on capital employed – 'what investors really care about'.[118]

It was Alfred Rappaport in his book on *Creating Shareholder Value: The New Standard for Business Performance* (1986) who launched the enthusiastic drive among leading companies around the world to introduce value-creating business strategies. Though these may be oriented to the longer term than some of the more immediate financial measures, and though they accept that to create value stakeholders have to be on board the corporate enterprise, they focus on financial return for shareholders as the ultimate objective of the company:

> Business strategies should be judged by the economic returns they generate for shareholders, as measured by dividends plus the increase in the company's share price. As management consider the alternative strategies, those expected to develop the greatest sustainable competitive advantage will be those that will also create the greatest value for shareholders. The 'shareholder value' approach estimates the economic value of an investment (e.g. the shares of a company, strategies, mergers and acquisitions, capital expenditures) by discounting forecasted cash flows by the cost of capital. These cash flows, in turn, serve as the foundation for shareholder returns from dividends and share-price appreciation.[119]

In contract, Drucker claims that multiple financial and non-financial performance measures should be used to assess more accurately both the present performance and the future potential of the company:

Neither the quantity of output nor the 'bottom line' is by itself an adequate measurement of management and enterprise. Market standing, innovation, productivity, development of people, quality, financial results – are all crucial to an organization's performance and to its survival. Non-profit institutions too need measurements in a number of areas specific to their mission. Just as a human being needs a diversity of measures to assess its health and performance, an organization needs a diversity of measures to assess its health and performance. Performance has to be built into the enterprise and its management; it has to be measured – or at least judged – and it has to be continuously improved.[120]

The overwhelming of traditional accounting practices by the arrival of intangible assets is detailed by Thomas A. Stewart in *Intellectual Capital: The New Wealth of Organizations*:

At bottom, accounting measures a company's accumulation and concentration of capital, and is based on costs – that is, it assumes that the cost of acquiring an asset fairly states (after some adjustments for items like depreciation) what an asset is worth. The model falls apart when the assets in question are intangible. As knowledge and its wrapper become separated, the relationships between current value and historical costs has broken down. The cost of producing knowledge bears much less relationship to its value or price than the cost of producing, say, a ton of steel. In the Industrial Age an idea couldn't become valuable unless a measurable collection of physical assets was assembled around it to exploit it. Not so now ... Netscape, for example, concentrated an enormous amount of intellectual capital that assumed scarcely any physical or institutional form until, released into the market as an initial public offering in 1995, the capital manifested itself financial – to the tune of £2 billion.[121]

Non-financial Indicators

Recognition that purely financial measures of business performance are inadequate in modern business leads to the consideration of the use of non-financial performance measures, as Elaine Monkhouse has argued:

> Financial measures explicitly ignore a range of resources which, in an age when products and services can be rapidly duplicated, are being recognized as keys to sustainable business success. Resources such as skills, technological and management competency, innovation, information, brand loyalty, and demonstrable concern for the environment and community are rising to the top of the management agenda. Yet ability to systematically monitor management's efforts to improve the effectiveness of such resources through appropriate performance measures is dramatically underdeveloped. Decisions to invest in training or R&D for example, still require a leap of faith. Knowledge of how and why available measures are being used is scarce beyond the domain of quality measures . . . dispelling the popular misconception that the use of non-financial measures is widespread and sophisticated.[122]

A framework for developing non-financial performance measures was drawn up by the London Business School and the University of Warwick for the Chartered Institute of Management Accountants (CIMA). Their structured approach has six dimensions: financial, competitiveness, quality, resource utilization, flexibility and innovation:

Financial: The traditional means of steering a company and evaluating potential investment projects.

Competitiveness: Performance relative to competitors whether in overall company performance, or in defined fields such as technical excellence, retaining staff, etc.

Quality: Quality as defined by the customer, whether internal or external.

Resource utilization: Both the obvious use of tangible resources, such as machinery, and the less obvious use of intangible resources, such as corporate knowledge and communications.

Flexibility: The ability of a company to meet changing customer needs, and to redirect resources in a timely fashion to maintain business efficiency.

Innovation: The ability to encourage and support new ideas, products or processes, and turn them into commercial reality.[123]

Of course, to be of use these measures require careful and appropriate definition, in the context of the industry and company concerned, accurate and verifiable assessment, and some form of rigorous internal and external benchmarking in order to lead to superior performance.[124]

The Balanced Business Scorecard

In the United States, Kaplan and Norton's concept of the balanced business scorecard was developed by a number of leading companies, including DuPont, General Electric and Hewlett Packard, who were looking for a new performance measurement model:

> The collision between the irresistible force to build long range competitive capabilities and the immovable object of the historical cost financial accounting model has created a new synthesis: the balanced scorecard. The balanced scorecard retains traditional financial measures. But financial measures tell the story of past events, an adequate story for industrial age companies for which investment in long term capabilities and customer relationships was not critical for success. These financial measures are inadequate, however, for guiding and evaluating the journey that information age companies must make to create future value through investment in customers, suppliers, employees, processes, technology and innovation.[125]

However, Kaplan and Norton caution against too literal a pursuit of quality objectives:

> With the proliferation of change programmes under way in most organizations today, it is easy to become preoccupied with such goals as quality, customer satisfaction, innovation and employee empowerment for their own sake. While most of these goals can lead to improved business-unit performance, they may not if these goals are taken as ends in themselves. The financial problems of some recent Baldridge Award winners give testimony to the need to link operational improvements to economic results.[126]

Kaplan and Norton propose instead a *balanced scorecard*, which retains traditional financial measures but recognizes that these record *past* events and are not adequate to guide and evaluate the challenge of information age companies to create future value through investment in customers, suppliers, employees, processes, technology and innovation. Hence the balanced scorecard complements financial measures of past performance with measures of the drivers of future performance. Derived from the organization's vision and strategy, the scorecard measures organizational performance from four perspectives: financial, customer, internal business processes and learning and growth.[127]

CONCLUSIONS

In the West we are encouraged to conceive of the company as a bundle of assets, property rights over which are the key to economic performance. As Boisot and Child have suggested, in the East a company is conceived as a set of relationships; this 'system of network capitalism works through the implicit and fluid dynamic of relationships. On the one hand this is a process that consumes much time and energy. On the other hand, it is suited to handling complexity and uncertainty'.[128] As the value attributed to intangible assets grows in the knowledge-based companies of the late twentieth century, conceptions of the company are beginning to change in the West.

To some business people the stakeholder concept remains largely a public relations exercise. However, a stakeholder approach may be not just a moral imperative, but a commercial necessity 'in a world where competitive advantage stemmed more and more from the intangible values embodied in human and social capital'.[129] The importance of developing good stakeholder relationships for successful enterprise in the information age is becoming increasingly apparent. This involves not simply acknowledging the significance of these relationships, but making consistent efforts to measure and manage stakeholder relations, in order to achieve continuous improvement in all company operations and, ultimately, increased stakeholder values. In this context many companies are likely to investigate how stakeholder strategies may usefully be applied in business, and how stakeholding is interpreted in other companies and countries. It is harder for companies driven by narrow self-interest to survive public scrutiny; it is still possible for them to make money, but this form of enterprise is invariably short term. Companies that are durable invariably possess a wider and deeper sense of their responsibilities.

Chapter 7

SUSTAINABILITY

One of the most difficult paradigm shifts to make in business is to realize that the goals of profit and growth are no longer sustainable as the ultimate objectives of enterprise. Sustainability itself has become the central business imperative. A basic element of the traditional belief system of managers is that in competitive markets the only choice is to grow or die. However, this competitive struggle to accumulate profits and grow has disturbed the natural balance of the earth to the point where we are perilously close to losing essential environmental life-support systems. Of course, this does not mean the abandonment of enterprise and consumption, but it does mean that, instead of freely destroying the natural environment, business has to find ways of integrating its activity in balance with nature – replenishing natural resources, not merely ignoring or exploiting them.

In this chapter we investigate how sustainability may be achieved by replacing materials and labour with information and intelligence as the essential inputs of commercial activity. Advancing knowledge enables industry to design production processes and products which are not environmentally hazardous, and which use minimal amounts of raw materials and energy. The eternal search for domination over nature is replaced by the pursuit of harmony with nature. This environmental imperative is respected by a growing number of businesses, but will become a commercial necessity as government and consumers become less forgiving of those who take recklessly and destructively from the environment rather than contributing to it.

Sustainability is now generally accepted to be the core concept when considering mankind's interaction with the physical environment. It is now seen as a desirable and often essential measure

Table 7.1: Paradigm Shifts

Profit/Growth/Control	Sustainable Enterprise
Profitability	Sustainability
Growth	Balance
Control	Integration
Materials	Information
Labour	Intelligence
Design for style	Design for environment
Technical efficiency	Environmental efficiency
Domination over nature	Harmony with nature

of the impact of economic activity upon global survival. However, the question of how to operationalize the concept gives rise to considerable disagreement as there are direct consequences for the way in which people organize their lives and industry is developed.[1] A generally accepted definition of sustainability is that people must 'ensure the development needs of the present without compromising the ability of future generations to meet their own needs'.[2] The strategy and operations of corporations are crucial to the achievement of sustainability as they control much of the world's resources, technology and innovation, and exert considerable influence over the choices available to people.

Most people have certain preconceived ideas about business and the natural world:

- It is often forgotten that what is conventionally defined as success – growth, profits, consumption – derive not just from business activity, but from the physical environment.
- It is often not realized that there is a limit to the extent to which the physical environment can continue to support the activities that have generated what is defined as material success.

Orthodox economic theory assumes that all wealth derives from man and the use of generally unlimited resources; moreover, that continued economic growth is an inalienable right and duty of those responsible for business. This is supported by a belief in the ability of markets and technology to solve problems. Environmental concerns, while they are recognized as legitimate in principle, are regarded as readily solvable within the existing framework of business operations. Another view which is rapidly gaining influence – not simply with governments and the general public but with a growing number of business leaders – is that environmental concerns have become critical, that environmental damage is worsening, and that the way in which economic activity is presently organized and oriented is fundamentally *unsustainable*.

There are significant indications that many companies are shifting their focus: their previous disregard for the damage they do to the environment is giving way to a more willing compliance with environmental regulation, and a commitment to environmental standards. Some companies have taken an important further step, and embraced sustainability as a core philosophy of their business existence. Sustainability represents a new paradigm for strategic thinking and business activity. Sustainability strategies may improve the performance of a firm because they result in lower costs, or give the firm the opportunity to differentiate itself, and its products, from those of other companies (Table 7.2). Traditionally environmental management has been seen as a cost to the economy – perhaps necessary, but to be minimized. Now it is accepted that environmental concerns can help to improve corporate profitability, competitiveness and employment:

Sustainability should be a core value as it supports a strategic vision of firms surviving over the long term by integrating their need to earn an economic profit with their responsibility to protect the environment. Such a vision demonstrates the interconnectedness of economic success and the health of the ecosystem: the organization would see itself as part of the greater society and natural environment, to whom its survival is tied . . . It is important to note that sustainability strategies are not compromise strategies: they are not designed merely to earn a profit while doing as little damage as possible to the ecosystem. Rather, they are seen as integrative strategies: they provide competitive advantages to organizations by simultaneously enhancing the quality of the ecosystem and the long-term survivability of the firm.[3]

Table 7.2: Assessing and Achieving a Sustainable Business

Achieving Sustainability

'Never Thought about It.' Carry on with existing technology and products	Focus: Paradigm shift Business strategy New products and markets Cultural change

Uninvolved   **Involved**

'Environment Does Not Affect Us.' Wait for public recognition of environmental damage	Focus: Compliance Cost-saving Reputation Health and safety

Reducing Environmental Impact

Source: Adapted from Hutchinson, 'Corporate Strategy' (1996), p. 96

EARTH SUMMIT

The present activities of the exploding world population are threatening and, in many cases, already destroying the planet's ecosystem: recognizing the gravity of the situation, the United Nations held the first Conference on Environment and Development in Rio de Janeiro in 1992. This was the first meeting between representatives of all of the people of the world to discuss 'our common future'. It coincided with the 500th anniversary year of Columbus's voyage to America, which saw the beginning of the economic domination of the world by Europe and, later, America. These representatives were prompted to attend the summit by the weight of evidence that increasing ecological damage will present a danger, not simply to economic well-being, but to human existence. Most environmental pressures are increasing exponentially, and mankind is faced with an accelerating:

- Rate of ozone depletion.
- Rate of species extinction.
- Rate of habitat depletion.
- Rate of increase in technological and scientific disaster.
- Desertification.
- Deforestation.
- Incidence of acid rain.
- Depletion of fishing stocks.
- Decline of the planet's waste-sink-absorption capacity.
- Erosion of soil.
- Pressure on water resources.
- Rates of poverty and starvation.
- Rate of usage of non-renewable resources.[4]

Table 7.3: Spheres of the Earth

Stratosphere:	30 miles, −225°F at top
Ecosphere:	Directly maintains its structure using the energy flow from sun. Contains the biosphere, atmosphere (including protective ozone layer), hydrosphere and pedosphere
Ozone:	50°F. Ultraviolet rays from the sun are absorbed in the ozone layer. The ozone makes up only .005% of total stratosphere, so even minor depletions can have profound effects
Troposphere:	10 miles, −75°F at top. Weather as experienced on earth occurs in the troposphere
Biosphere:	Where plant and animal life exist: approximately 5 miles above and 5 miles below earth's surface
Lithosphere:	Comprised of the crust and upper mantle extending 60 miles below the earth's surface. Contains minerals, fossil fuels and soil chemicals (nutrients) needed to support plant life

Source: Interface Inc., *Sustainability Report* (1997)

Suddenly the planet seemed very vulnerable, and mankind was reaching the limits of the earth's capacity in every sphere (Table 7.3). It was hoped that a robust set of conventions and treaties would emerge from the Rio Earth Summit:

- The rich countries would commit themselves to concentrating on improving the quality of life, while reducing the per capita ecological impact to a sustainable level.
- The developing countries and Eastern Europe would accept they could never attain the level of per capita material throughput, pollution and waste of the rich world today, and would commit themselves to a new path of sustainable development, including population policies and an enhanced development role for women.
- In their own self-interest the rich countries would commit themselves to technical and financial support for sustainable development elsewhere in the world, recognizing that ecological damage there affects the global ecosystem on which they depend.
- The rich countries would also accept the huge 'development debt' to the less developed countries, arising from damage done historically by the rich countries to the global environment, and as part of this would agree to write off the outstanding debt of the third world as part of a global agreement on sustainable development.
- Finally, agreement would be reached on how to restructure the UN to enable effective monitoring of policies for equitable and sustainable development.[5]

Rather than reaching clear and binding agreements on these critical issues the Rio Conference reinforced doubts about the willingness or capacity of the West to provide world leadership when its own immediate vested interests were perceived to be at stake.

At the following 1997 summit in Kyoto, Japan, only modest progress was made in securing environmental commitments, highlighted by the reluctance of the United States to do any more than stabilize carbon dioxide emissions at 1990 levels by 2010; the European Union was prepared to aim for a 15 per cent reduction from 1990 levels by the year 2010. Meanwhile the major developing countries of China, India and Brazil are standing aside from the process until they see more evidence of a willingness in the developed world to shoulder a proper share of the burden for which it is primarily responsible after 100 years of industrialization.

Global Interdependencies

The global economy is really three different interdependent, and overlapping economies:[6]

The Market Economy

The market economy is the familiar world of international production and trade, comprised of both the developed nations and the emerging economies. Around 1 billion people – one quarter of the world's population – live in the developed market economies. These account for 75 per cent of the world's energy and resource consumption, and create the bulk of the industrial, toxic and consumer waste. Pollution levels are now being reduced in the developed economies by stringent environmental regulations, the voluntary greening of industry and the relocation of the most polluting activities (such as commodity processing and heavy manufacturing) to the emerging economies: 'Thus to some extent the greening of the developed world has been at the expense of the environments in emerging economies'.[7]

The emerging economies of Latin America and Asia, together with Eastern Europe and the former Soviet Union, have added nearly 2 billion people to the market economy over the past forty years. As they acquire the production and consumption patterns of the developed market economies the environmental impact will be severe. Acid rain is a growing problem, and the World Bank estimates that by 2010 there will be more than 1 billion motor vehicles in the world. Concentrated in the cities, these vehicles will double the current levels of energy use, smog and emissions of greenhouse gas.

The Survival Economy

The survival economy is the traditional, village way of life found in the rural parts of developing countries. Three billion people in this economy, mainly in Africa, India and China, are subsistence oriented and meet their basic needs directly from nature. Because of the rapid development of the market economy, existence in the survival economy is becoming increasingly precarious. Extractive industries and infrastructure development have degraded the ecosystems upon which these people depend. As they compete for scarce resources, rural populations are driven into poverty. The

Figure 7.1: Global Income Distribution

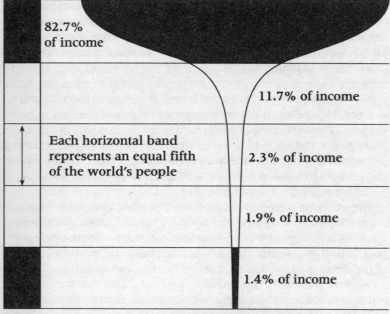

World
population
arranged
by income

Distribution of income

82.7%
of income

11.7% of income

Each horizontal band
represents an equal fifth
of the world's people

2.3% of income

1.9% of income

1.4% of income

The poorest fifth receives
1.4% of total world income

Source: UNDP, *Human Development Report 1992* (New York:
Oxford University Press, 1992)

absolute poverty of three fifths of the world's population is a source
not only of widespread misery, but of political instability and
environmental degradation from which the developed world can
no longer be insulated (Figure 7.1).

Nature's Economy

Nature's economy consists of the natural systems that support the
market and survival economies. There are finite, non-renewable

resources, such as oil, metals and other minerals, and renewable resources, such as soils and forests, which will replenish themselves as long as they are not used beyond critical thresholds. Forests, soil, water and fisheries are all being pushed beyond their limits by human population growth and rapid industrial development. For example, as agricultural, commercial and residential use of water increases, water tables are being drawn down at an alarming rate, particularly in heavily populated China and India. Ten per cent of the world's topsoil is seriously eroded, and many animal species are near to extinction. All eighteen of the world's major fisheries have now reached or exceeded the maximum yields compatible with sustainability.

> By some estimates, humankind now uses more than 40 per cent of the planet's net primary productivity. If, as projected, the population doubles over the next forty years, we may outcompete most other animal species for food, driving many to extinction. In short, human activity now exceeds sustainability on a global scale ... As we approach the twenty-first century, the interdependence of the three economic spheres is increasingly evident. In fact, the three economies have become worlds in collision, creating the major social and environmental challenges facing the planet: climate change, pollution, resource depletion, poverty, and inequality.[8]

In the survival economy major infrastructural development, including dams, highways and power plants, often aided by international agencies and banks, provides new access to raw materials and industry, but tend to benefit élites rather than those in the survival economy. Infrastructural developments help to contribute to the global glut of raw materials, and the long-term fall in the price of commodities relative to manufactured goods. The terms of trade of the developing countries have become weaker, and as their purchasing power declines, their substantial debt burden increases. This intensifies the vicious circle of resource exploitation and pollution in the developing world to service mounting debts. The developing world today has a combined debt of more than $1.2 trillion, which is equivalent to nearly half their total gross national product.[9]

According to Hart, there are three stark choices facing humanity if the environmental burden is to be reduced:

Table 7.4: Major Challenges to Sustainability

	Developed economies	Emerging economies	Survival economies
Pollution	• Greenhouse gases	• Industrial emissions	• Dung and wood burning
	• Use of toxic materials	• Contaminated water	• Lack of sanitation
	• Contaminated sites		• Ecosystem destruction due to development
		• Lack of sewage treatment	
Depletion	• Scarcity of materials	• Over exploitation of renewable resources	• Deforestation
			• Overgrazing
	• Insufficient reuse and recycling	• Overuse of water for irrigation	• Soil loss
Poverty	• Urban and minority unemployment	• Migration to cities	• Population growth
		• Lack of skilled workers	• Low status of women
		• Income inequality	• Dislocation

Source: Hart, *Strategies for a Sustainable World* (1997), p. 70

• Decreasing the human population.
• Lowering the level of consumption.
• Changing fundamentally the technology used to create wealth.[10]

Decreasing the human population is not likely, and lowering consumption would be counter-productive in the survival economy as population and poverty go hand in hand: the birth rate is inversely correlated with the standard of living. The emphasis must therefore be upon transforming the technology used to create the goods and services that constitute the material wealth of the world. 'Although population and consumption may be societal issues, technology is the business of business.'[11]

Alternative Environmental Paradigms

Three environmental paradigms are identified by Gladwin, Kennelly and Kranse: technocentrism, sustaincentrism and ecocentrism (Table 7.5). Technocentrism is the existing dominant paradigm which neglects the environment and ignores calls for sustainability. Why does the dominant paradigm ignore sustainability? In large part because environmental pollution and waste are considered as 'externalities', off-balance-sheet items that, lacking a cost or a price, have not figured. The core of the problem is the distinction between prices and costs – market prices do not always reflect the total costs of products. If a corporation receives more monetary value for a product than the cost of producing and delivering it, theoretically it manages those economic conditions conducive to survival. However, other factors, although they constitute empirical examples of environmental costs, such as noise, emissions, industrial accidents and the post-consumption costs of collecting, recycling and depositing waste-products in landfills, are usually not part of most companies' accounting systems, except where changes to the regulatory environment make them salient.[12] The dominant paradigm finds no place for them: they remain, simply, externalities. Thus, most of today's physical pollution consists of corporate costs that have been *externalized* from the organization on to other citizens and their organizations, in the states in which they operate and the societies in which they are embedded.

Externalized costs are the core issues of the 'risk society' that Beck (1986) identifies in the post-Chernobyl world. It is a world in which the notion of unanticipated consequences of social action takes on an added, and dangerous, dimension. In the face of the risks posed to life on earth by manufacturing products and processes, sustainability should not be seen simply as a lifestyle option but an option *for* life, against death, destruction and despoliation. The dominant social paradigm hardly considers such issues at all.

The natural 'wealth of nations' exists only to be exploited. The effects of this resource-exploitation (and despoliation) are just a necessary, if unfortunate, side-effect of progress.

The dominant social paradigm sees unlimited human progress resulting from the exploitation of infinite natural resources. In other words, humanity stands apart from nature, at the centre of all life. People's relationships with nature are based on exploitation and control: the natural environment must serve human needs, and organizations are central to the achievement of this end. Management theorists and practitioners must work to improve the efficiency of these organizations. The question is always how to make organizations more efficient, not what they are or what their purpose is. The way to the future, to progress, to growth lies through the domination of nature. The idea of growth is central for organizations in all spheres of society, and manufacturing companies in particular reproduce this logic in the form of economies of scale. The assumptions of the dominant paradigm in both the social and the natural worlds open a gap: between society and nature; between organizations and environments; and between humankind at the centre stage of the human drama and nature at its margins.

The dominant social paradigm barely considers issues of sustainability. Gladwin et al. regarded the dominant paradigm as 'technocentric', characterized by a mechanical ontology focused on anthropocentric humankind, acting fearlessly on nature to enhance economic well-being.[13] The reform environmentalist paradigm (termed the 'sustaincentric' paradigm by Gladwin et al.) is a modified, indeed a reformed version of the dominant paradigm. Adherents of this paradigm seek to retain the efficiencies achieved under the dominant social paradigm, in terms of the availability of the products and services associated with an industrial society, but wish to do so in such a way that the ecological impact of industrialism is minimized. Adherents of the radical environmentalist paradigm (which Gladwin et al. term 'ecocentric', as do Purser et al.)[14] will, if they believe it is in the interests of the preservation of the ecology to do so, forswear the benefits of industrialism in favour of the affinity and attachment that they feel for an unpolluted nature, a nature that they will fight to protect and preserve against the depredations of any exploitation, even when it is 'green' in intent. They believe that biospecies egalitarianism is a prerequisite for economic advancement in harmony with nature.

Table 7.5: Alternative Environmental Paradigms

Key Assumptions	Technocentrism	Sustaincentrism	Ecocentrism
A. Ontological & Ethical			
1. Metaphor of earth	Vast machine	Life support system	Mother/web of life
2. Perception of earth	Dead/passive	Home/managed	Alive/sensitive
3. System composition	Atomistic/parts	Parts and wholes	Organic/wholes
4. System structure	Hierarchical	Holarchical	Heterarchical
5. Humans and nature	Disassociation	Interdependence	Indisassociation
6. Human role	Domination	Stewardship	Plain member
7. Value of nature	Anthropocentrism	Inherentism	Intrisicalism
8. Ethical grounding	Narrow homocentric	Broad homocentric	Whole earth
9. Time/space scales	Short/near	Multiscale	Indefinite
10. Logic/ reason	Egoist-rational	Vision/network	Holism/ spiritualism
B. Scientific & Technological			
1. Resilience of nature	Tough/robust	Varied/fragile	Highly vulnerable
2. Carrying capacity limits	No limits	Approaching	Already exceed
3. Population size	No problem	Stabilize soon	Freeze/reduce
4. Growth pattern	Exponential	Logistic	Hyperbolic
5. Severity of problems	Trivial	Consequential	Catastrophic
6. Urgency of solutions	Little/wait	Great/decades	Extraordinary/ now
7. Risk orientation	Risk taking	Precaution	Risk aversion

Table 7.5: (continued)

Key Assumptions	Technocentrism	Sustaincentrism	Ecocentrism
B. Scientific & Technological			
8. Faith in technology	Optimism	Scepticism	Pessimism
9. Technological pathways	Big/centralized	Benign/ decoupled	Small/ decentralized
10. Human vs. Natural capital	Full substitutes	Partial substitutes	Complements
C. Economic & Psychological			
1. Primary objective	Efficient allocation	Quality of life	Ecological integrity
2. The good life	Materialism	Postmaterialism	Antimaterialism
3. Human nature	Homo economicus	Homo sapient	Homo animalist
4. Economic structure	Free market	Green economy	Steady state
5. Role of growth	Good/necessary	Mixed/modify	Bad/eliminate
6. Poverty alleviation	Growth trickle	Equal opportunity	Redistribution
7. Natural capital	Exploit/convert	Conserve/ maintain	Enhance/ expand
8. Discount rate	High/normal	Low/ complement	Zero/ inappropriate
9. Trade orientation	Global	National	Bioregional
10. Political structure	Centralized	Devolved	Decentralized

Source: Gladwin, Kennelly and Krause, 'Shifting Paradigms . . .' (1995)

Approaches such as 'deep ecology', 'spiritual ecology', 'social ecology' and 'ecofeminism' characterize the radical environmentalist paradigm.

The radical and the dominant paradigms are mirror-images: each is virtually the opposite of the other, so that their adherents seek to achieve what the other does not. Reform environmentalism is more mediated: it is within these parameters that the paradigm strategies that seem to be viable alternatives for twenty-first-century business may be found. While the dominant social paradigm is scarcely sustainable, the radical environmentalist paradigm, however attractive it may be to many people as an ethical position, is hardly viable as a business posture.

Having analysed a wide and diverse literature, Gladwin et al. suggest that sustainability implies the achievement of human development that expands rather than narrows people's choices.[15] Thus they provide the framework for a definition of sustainability that environmental reformist paradigms might adopt. Sustainability should be:

Inclusive: In a systems framework that emphasizes the interconnectedness of the 'natural' and the 'social'.

Connective: The environmental should be interconnected with social and economic goals.

Equitable: Both across contemporary space and time and also across the generations; solutions for today should not be foreseeable problems for tomorrow.

Prudent: Characterized by safeguards, reversible actions, safety margins; being prepared to be perpetually surprised.

Secure: Characterized by care *vis-à-vis* the 'health' of both eco- and social systems; stocks of irreplaceable natural assets; self-organization, carrying capacities of both eco and social systems, and human freedom enshrined in universalized rights and democracy.

According to Gladwin et al., 'the global eco-system is finite, non-growing, materially closed, vulnerable to human interference, and limited in its regenerative and assimilative capacities.'[16] They accept the limitations of crude and difficult-to-operationalize axioms like: waste emissions must not exceed natural assimilative capacity; harvest rates for renewable resources should not exceed regeneration rates; and human activities should not result in a net loss of genetic, species or ecosystem diversity. However, they offer a tentative set of operational principles and associated techniques of biophysically sustainable behaviour (Table 7.6).

Table 7.6: Operational Principles and Techniques of Biophysically Sustainable Behaviour

Sustainability Principles	Operational Principles	Sample Techniques
Assimilation	Waste emissions $\leq$ Natural assimilative capacity	Pollution prevention Natural products Detoxification Biodegradability Low input agriculture Synthetic reduction
Regeneration	Renewable harvest rate $\leq$ Natural regeneration rate	Sustained yield management Safe minimum standards Harvest certification Access restriction Exclusive harvest zones Resource right systems
Diversification	Biodiversity loss $\leq$ Biodiversity preservation	Biosphere reserves Extractive reserves Buffer zones Polyculture farming Ecotourism Debt for nature swaps
Restoration	Ecosystem damage $\leq$ Ecosystem rehabilitation	Reforestation Mine reclamation Site decontamination Bioremediation Species reintroduction Habitat restoration
Conservation	Energy-matter throughput per unit of output (time 2) $\leq$ Energy-matter throughput per unit output (time 1)	Fuel efficiency Mass transit Cogeneration Computer controls Demand side management Smart buildings
Dissipation	Energy-matter throughput (time 2) $\leq$ Energy-matter throughput (time 1)	Depackaging Durable design Repair/reconditioning Telecommuting Bioregional sourcing Dematerialization

Table 7.6: (continued)

Sustainability Principles	Operational Principles	Sample Techniques
Perpetuation	Nonrenewable resource depletion $\leqslant$ Renewable resource substitution	Solar energy Wind power Hydrogen fuel Bioenergy Hydropower Geothermal energy
Circulation	Virgin ÷ recycled material use Close-loop manufacturing (time 2) $\leqslant$ Virgin ÷ recycled material use (time 1)	Industrial ecosystems Internal recycling Waste recovery Design for disassembly Water recirculation

Source: Gladwin, Kennelly and Krause, 'Shifting Paradigms...' (1995), p. 892

THE SEARCH FOR ENVIRONMENTAL SOLUTIONS

A conventional view, still frequently expressed in many industries, is that environmental regulation inevitably leads to increased costs to business and often serves to lower international competitiveness. The US Vice-President, Al Gore, takes a more optimistic view, in the Foreword to his book *The Earth in Balance: Forging a New Common Purpose*: 'We can prosper by leading the environmental revolution and producing for the world market place the new products and technologies that foster economic progress without environmental destruction'. Similarly Michael Porter emphasizes the potential gains of environmental awareness and regulations:

The conflict between environmental protection and economic competitiveness is a false dichotomy. It stems from a narrow view of the sources of prosperity and a static view of competition. Strict environmental regulations do not inevitably hinder competitive advantage against foreign rivals; indeed, they often enhance it. Properly constructed regulatory standards which aim at outcomes and not methods will encourage companies to re-engineer their technology. The result in many cases is a process that not only pollutes less but lowers costs or improves quality.[17]

In the United States, in the sectors where environmental standards have lagged behind other countries, the patenting and exporting of associated anti-pollution equipment technologies has also slipped. In contrast, the US leads the world in industries where regulations have been strictest, such as pesticides.[18]

Regulation

In this field more than any other, regulation is necessary as a spur to innovation, an encouragement of high standards and a guard against the irresponsible. Table 7.7 highlights the progress of regulation in OECD countries in the 1990s in protecting water, air, waste and nature. Hence regulation serves:

- To create pressure that motivates companies to innovate. Outside pressure overcomes organizational inertia and fosters creative thinking.
- To improve environmental quality in cases where innovation and the resulting improvements in resource productivity do not completely offset the cost of compliance, or when it takes time for the learning curve to reduce the overall cost of innovative solutions.
- To alert and educate companies about likely resource inefficiencies and potential areas for technological improvement.
- To encourage environmentally friendly product and process innovations.
- To create demand for environmental improvement until companies and customers are better able to perceive and measure the resource inefficiencies of pollution.
- To level the playing-field during the transitions period to innovation-based environmental solutions, ensuring that one company cannot gain temporary advantage by avoiding environmental investments.[19]

Thus regulation provides a buffer for innovative companies until new technologies are proven and the learning process can begin to reduce technological costs.

Table 7.7: Managing Water, Air, Waste and Nature

Water: major policy directions and challenges
- Implement appropriate charges, in line with the user-and-polluter-pays principles, in order to:
  - finance the necessary investment in water supply and waste water treatment infrastructure
  - reduce sources of point and diffuse water pollution
  - promote water conservation.
- Design and introduce lower-cost innovative waste water treatment techniques.
- Introduce cleaner production methods, e.g. through integrated permitting that stresses pollution prevention, and greater use of voluntary agreements with specific industry branches to meet specified reductions in pollutant discharges.
- Adopt and implement whole-basin approaches to water quantity and quality management, ensuring that these are integrated with land-use policies.

Air: major policy directions and challenges
- Improve energy efficiency and develop the use of cleaner fuels, through a mix of instruments, including extended recourse to economic instruments.
- Continue efforts in support of implementation and enforcement of regulations, while improving the efficiency of the regulatory framework and devoting more attention to prevention.
- Develop cost-effective strategies to reduce emissions of conventional pollutants by using various policy instruments.
- Address human health issues by: i) strengthening measures on local air pollution problems in urban areas, and ii) developing cost-effective programmes to reduce hazardous air pollution.
- Strengthen measures on vehicle emissions by: i) more stringent emission standards, especially for heavy-duty diesel vehicles, and better inspection and maintenance programmes; and ii) development of policies to contain private vehicle traffic volumes and to promote public transport in urban areas.

- Give greater attention to regulations and voluntary programmes aimed at stabilizing emissions of greenhouse gases, and promote full application of measures with no net costs (win/win strategies).

Waste: major policy directions and challenges

- Fully implement and enforce regulations on hazardous waste management, including controls on imports and exports.
- Strengthen measures for waste minimization, especially for prevention of waste generation through co-ordination with relevant programmes concerning cleaner technology, life-cycle management of products and extended producer responsibility.
- Increase the use of economic instruments to promote prevention and recycling, including waste disposal fees, product charges and deposit-refund systems; and of other instruments, such as voluntary agreements, information and education.
- Ensure the availability of necessary waste treatment and disposal capacity for hazardous and other waste, with better planning and full public involvement.

Nature: major policy directions and challenges

- Implement national nature conservation and biodiversity strategies to better co-ordinate the actions of responsible authorities at all levels.
- Strengthen the integration between nature conservation, pollution control and sectional policies (e.g. agriculture and forestry, fisheries, tourism).
- Set aside a significant share of the national territory as protected, including ecological corridors and all major ecosystem types, terrestrial as well as marine.
- Strengthen nature conservation efforts outside protected areas and implement landscape protection policies.
- Establish and implement effective management regimes for coastal and marine fisheries.
- Improve funding schemes for nature protection.

Source: *Environmental Performance in OECD Countries; Progress in the 1990s*
(OECD, 1996)

Well-conceived regulation need not drive up costs, and Michael Porter and Claas van der Linde suggest principles of regulatory design which, they claim, will promote innovation, resource productivity and competitiveness:

Focus on outcomes, not technologies: The regulations in the past prescribed remedial technologies, such as catalysts. Phrases such as 'best available technology' are deeply rooted and imply that one replacement technology is best, discouraging innovation.

Enact strict rather than lax regulation: Regulation should promote real innovation, not end-of-pipe or secondary treatment solutions.

Regulate as close to an end-user as practical while encouraging upstream solutions: Normally this may allow more innovation or flexibility in the end product, and in all the production and distribution stages. Avoiding pollution entirely or mitigating it early in the value chain is almost always less costly than late-stage remediation or cleaning up.

Employ phase-in periods: Well-defined phase-in periods tied to industry capital-investment cycles will allow companies to develop innovative resource-saving technologies rather than force them to implement expensive solutions too hastily, often merely patching over problems.

Use market incentives: Market incentives such as pollution charges and deposit-refund schemes draw attention to resource inefficiencies.

Harmonize or converge regulations in associated fields: Inconsistent regulation on alternative technologies deters beneficial innovation.

Develop regulations in sync with other countries or slightly ahead of them: When standards in a country's industry lead world developments, companies get early-mover advantage in international markets.

Make the regulatory process more stable and meaningful: If governments commit to stability in standards then companies can tackle root-cause problems instead of waiting for the next change in government policy.

Require industry participation in setting standards from the beginning: Industry should assist in developing phase-in periods, the content of regulation and the most effective regulatory process.

Develop strong technical capabilities among regulators: Regulators must understand an industry's technology, economies and what drives its competitiveness.

Minimize the time and resources used by the regulatory process itself: Self-regulation with periodic inspection is more efficient than seeking formal approval. Litigation creates uncertainty over long periods of time; arbitration procedures can lower costs and encourage innovations.[20]

Voyt compares the old approaches to environmental regulation with newer models (Table 7.8). The problem is seen as regional and global, not just local, and viable strategies are developed through public participation, not just through governmental remedies. Anticipation and prevention are preferred, with an emphasis on performance standards to encourage innovation.

Table 7.8: A Comparison of the Old and New Models of Environmental Regulations

Old	New
Environmental protection and economic growth seen as opposed	Sustainable development links environmental and economic decision-making
Focus is on local problems	Focus is on regional, global problems
Agenda driven by domestic consideration	Agenda responsive to international trade and climate for investment
Public looks to government to prioritize problems, find solutions	Public participation in identifying problems and developing solutions
Jurisdictional fragmentation leads to duplication and overlap	Jurisdictional co-operation strives to eliminate duplication and overlap

Table 7.8: (continued)

Old	New
Mindset is to react and cure	Mindset is to anticipate and prevent
Command-and-control is instrument of choice	Broad array of instruments, including voluntary action and economic instruments, are utilized
Regulations prescribe technical solutions, inhibit innovation	Performance standards give industry flexibility, encourage innovation
Address, large, easy-to-identify and manage point sources of pollution	Address diffused and difficult to manage non-point sources of pollution

Source: Voyt (1995)

Some companies seek to take the driving seat in environmental performance improvement, insisting that they know best where the most significant gains can be made at the least cost. Companies are in a position to address environmental degradation because they can obtain efficiency gains and cost savings; find new commercial opportunities in the emerging environmental pressures; and ultimately, demonstrate leadership in responding to environmental issues. Bernard Teissier of the European Chemical Industry Council believes that 'industry . . . can probably achieve the most effective progress through voluntary actions, moving towards specific targets. These targets cannot be decided by industry alone; they must be decided by political authorities who represent the broader interests of society.'[21]

A Multi-Stakeholder Approach

Determining what is good for the environment is highly complex in scientific terms; it is even more difficult to figure out how to link this to business practice, taking into account the preferences of customers and the wider community. When trying to develop an environmental policy companies are continually asking themselves the following questions:

- What do consumers value?
- What are the regulators demanding?
- What does science suggest?
- What does the local community value?
- What do environmentalists want?

Miller and Szekely identified twenty environmental stakeholders who make judgements about the environmental performance of companies, and discovered that there were considerable variations in their definitions and understanding of environmental criteria, metrics and assessment systems. As Kuhn recognized, new paradigms tend to emerge from entirely new fundamentals without a full set of concrete rules or standards. Rather than condemn this embryonic state of affairs, it is important to work with the unfolding process of debate: science and understanding advance as a result of alternative interpretations being considered and discounted. Miller and Szekely identify four clusters of environmental stakeholders:

The international community: Including United Nations bodies, the European Commission and other international agencies.
Financial agents: Including institutional investors, banks, investment companies and not-for-profit groups who provide investment information.
Environmental pressure groups: Such as campaign organizations, conservation groups and consumer organizations.
Industry: Working through industry associations, consultants and companies to develop systems for managing and reporting environmental performance.

Miller and Szekely conclude that there is some agreement on what is green and what companies need to do across the four stakeholder groups; however, there is a reluctance to set specific criteria: with insufficient knowledge about environmental impact, people are unsure what their priorities should be.[22] There is a general desire to see the integration of environmental considerations and a reduction of environmental impact across the entire ecosystem, but there is little guidance on what this means specifically. All groups believe that good companies should adopt an environmental policy with targets that can be measured over time. Greener companies are identified by traditional principles of conservation: *reduce, reuse, recover, recycle*, with the emphasis on source reduction of emissions and materials. As yet there are no adequate systems to check whether criteria are applied consistently, and the measures being employed are embryonic. All the interested groups seek to develop quantitative metrics and facilitate comparison among industry peers on a per unit output basis. Assessment systems currently rely upon readily observable information that is publicly available.

Financial agents are interested in risk assessment and quantified performance data. Environmental groups are willing to accept less tangible performance data, and are willing to work with companies to develop environmental policies. The international community is interested in bringing together multiple stakeholders to assemble a range of criteria and methods for improving corporate environmental performance. Industry tends to focus on what is achievable in terms of existing methods, processes and materials. However, Gray, Owen and Adams note the emergence of green business networks, and a few consortia with more proactive aspirations (Figure 7.2).

The dilemmas involved in environmental policies are highlighted by Miller and Szekely:[23] everyone is demanding quantitative metrics while accepting that it is too early to measure environmental impact accurately. The current reference points in existing measurement systems are average environmental performance within a sector, or best performance among peers. However, it is not known if this performance, replicated across an entire industry, might exceed the limits of the planet's capacity. Finally, there is a division between companies which are prepared to do only the minimum in terms of compliance; others which would like to work voluntarily on a programme of continuous improvement; and those which will make radical changes to improve their corporate environmental performance.

Figure 7.2: The Changing Role of Industry Associations

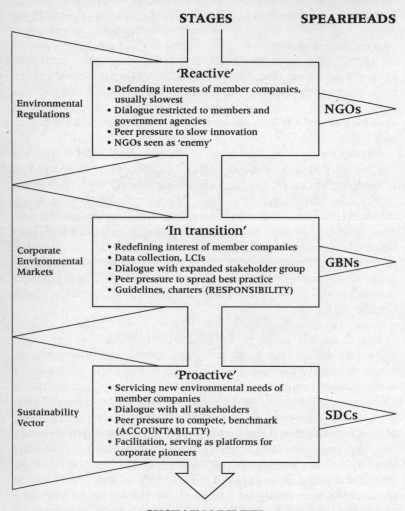

STAGES   **SPEARHEADS**

'Reactive'
- Defending interests of member companies, usually slowest
- Dialogue restricted to members and government agencies
- Peer pressure to slow innovation
- NGOs seen as 'enemy'

Environmental Regulations

NGOs

'In transition'
- Redefining interest of member companies
- Data collection, LCIs
- Dialogue with expanded stakeholder group
- Peer pressure to spread best practice
- Guidelines, charters (RESPONSIBILITY)

Corporate Environmental Markets

GBNs

'Proactive'
- Servicing new environmental needs of member companies
- Dialogue with all stakeholders
- Peer pressure to compete, benchmark (ACCOUNTABILITY)
- Facilitation, serving as platforms for corporate pioneers

Sustainability Vector

SDCs

SUSTAINABILITY

NGOs = Non-governmental organizations
GBNs = 'Green business networks' (e.g. ACBE, BAUM, BiE, BCSD, WICE)
SDCs = Sustainable development consortia

Source: From UNEPIE (1994); Gray, Owen and Adams, *'Accounting and Accountability'* (1996) p. 132

Figure 7.3: Environmental System Analysis

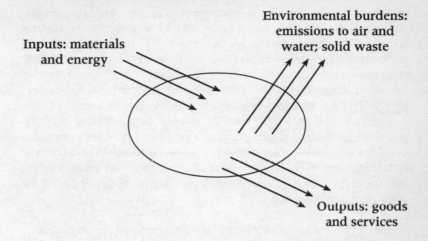

Source: After Azapagic and Clift; Clift and Longley, 'Introduction to Clean
Technology' (1996), p. 112

Clean Technology

There is an important distinction between *remediation* or repairing
environmental damage caused by industrial activity; *clean-up technology*, which reduces environmental damage by modifying or adding 'end-of-pipe' pollution abatement measures to existing plants
or processes; and *clean technology*, which avoids environmental
damage at source. 'In the process industries, a clean-up technology
may capture a potential emission from a process and transform it
to another state, such as by "scrubbing" or filtering a gas stream
to collect an atmospheric pollutant as liquid or sludge or solid for
disposal by other means. A clean technology will avoid producing
the pollutant in the first place or will recycle it within the process.'[24]

Environmental life-cycle assessment defines and evaluates the
total environmental load associated with providing a service, following material and energy flows from their 'cradle' to their
'grave', from primary resources to ultimate resting place as solid
waste or dispersed emissions. This is a form of environmental
system analysis in which the productive system is identified, the

inputs of materials and energy assessed, and the outputs of goods and services, together with the undesirable outputs of emissions to the air and solid waste, measured (Figure 7.3). Site-specific environmental impact assessment (EIA) draws the boundary around the manufacturing plant. However, environmental life-cycle analysis attempts to account for upstream and downstream environmental effects, as well as those directly involved in the manufacturing process. A boundary is drawn around the entire life-cycle of the materials and energy flows (Figure 7.4).

The goal of clean technology is to provide goods and services with the minimum consumption of energy and primary materials: the *dematerialization of the economy.*[25] Clean technology demands a systematic approach to the reuse of materials and components, and this approach requires changes not only in technology but in commercial relationships:

> The term 'industrial ecology' has been coined to denote a relationship in which systems providing different services and products 'metabolize' successive uses of materials and energy. The 'once through' use of resources which characterizes the profligate behaviour of much human activity is represented by the 'open loop' system. An ideal 'dematerialized' system would be represented by the 'closed loop' system. However, this popular view of recycling is obviously a simplistic misconception. Very rarely does reuse or recycling entail no resource consumption or environmental load.[26]

What happens in a real closed-loop recycling system is illustrated in Figure 7.6; so can the resources and environmental load involved offset the benefit of material recycling? Assessment of the practicalities of reuse and recycling leads to the concept of a general industrial ecology for material use (Figure 7.7). As a material passes through the economy it will have several uses, each with a lower performance specification. If a material passes through a cascade of uses a further element of clean technology is introduced: materials should not be contaminated with unnecessary additives that will increase the environmental loads associated with subsequent uses. Rather than optimizing a single use of a material, the whole use cascade should be considered in the initial product design.

A framework for the product life-cycle assessment is offered by Hutchinson, in which for each product at every stage of pro-

Figure 7.4: Environmental Life-cycle Analysis

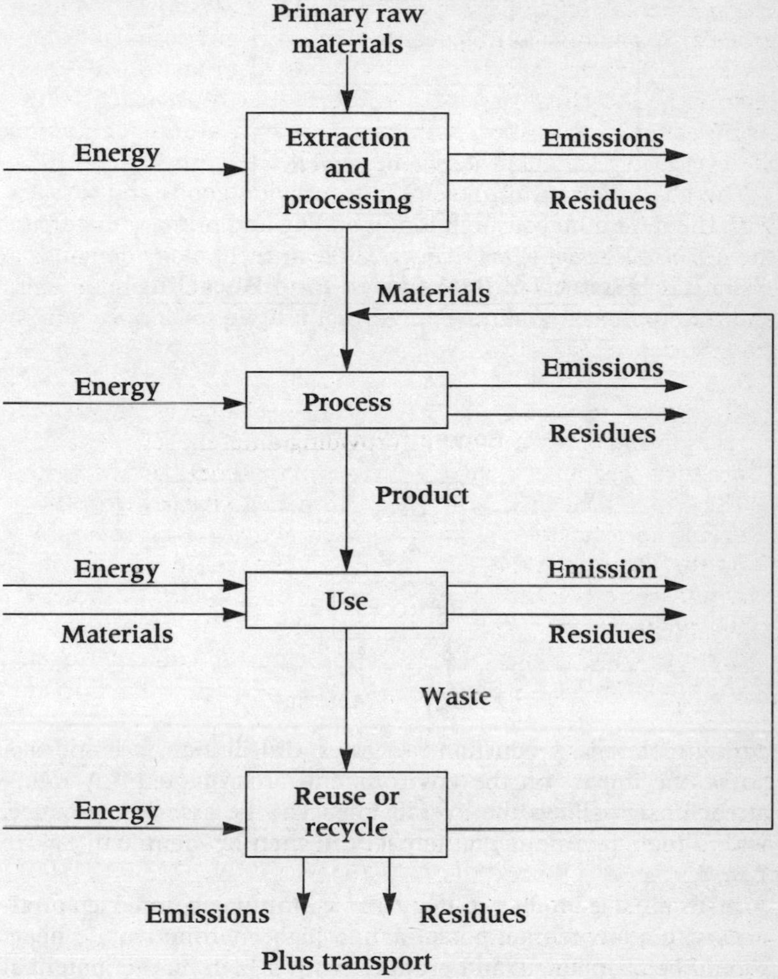

Primary raw
materials

Energy → **Extraction and processing** → Emissions
→ Residues

Materials

Energy → **Process** → Emissions
→ Residues

Product

Energy → **Use** → Emission
Materials → → Residues

Waste

Energy → **Reuse or recycle**

Emissions ↓ ↓ Residues

Plus transport

Source: Clift and Longley, 'Introduction to Clean Technology' (1996), p. 113

Figure 7.5: Idealized View of Recycling: Closed-loop

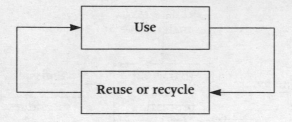

Figure 7.6: Real Closed-loop Recycling

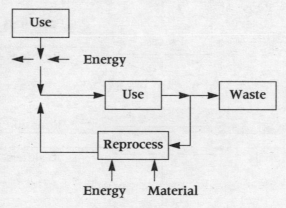

curing materials, production processes, distribution, use and disposal, the impact on the environment is considered.[27] A rating at each stage allows the overall impact to be assessed; products with a high environmental impact can then be identified (Figure 7.8).

A sustainable product strategy mix is formulated, in which products with a low market potential and high environmental impact should be abandoned, and products with a high market potential and high environmental impact need to be modified to minimize their environmental impact. The priorities for development are clearly those products which happily combine high market potential and high sustainability (Figure 7.9).

Industrial ecosystems view organizations through the total cycle of the materials they use. These may be optimized in terms of

Figure 7.7: General Industrial Ecology for Material

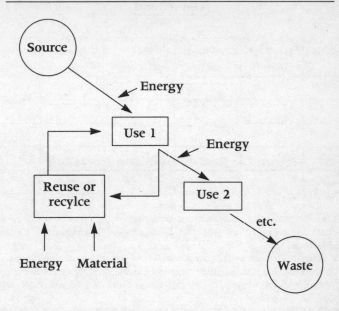

Source: Clift and Longley, 'Introduction to Clean Technology' (1996), pp. 120–1

resources, energy, environmental impact and capital.[28] The application of industrial ecosystems requires an interdependent system of materials, processes and energy. Wastes and by-products of one company become raw material for another. In the absence of any regulatory process, organizations establish an efficient flow of materials and energy. At the same time as they reduce their environmental impact, they reduce costs through the optimal use of resources.

In principle it is possible to design industrial ecosystems that emulate the self-sufficient, dynamically balanced ecosystem. These consist of a network of organizations seeking to minimize environmental degradation by using each other's by-products and waste, and sharing the use of natural resources. An illustration of such a co-operative strategy is a network of companies in Kalundborg, Denmark, which includes a power plant, enzyme plant, refinery, chemical plant, cement plant, wallboard plant and

Figure 7.8: A Framework for Product Life-cycle Assessment

Products	Procuring materials	Production processes	Product distribution	Products in use	Disposal after use
A					
B					
C					
D					
E					

Consider: Resource depletion, wastes, pollution of air, water and soil recovery procedures, impact on community and damage to the environment at each stage of the life-cycle.

Quick rating: Give scores ranging from 1 (low impact) to 5 (high impact) for each product and each stage of the process. Develop strategies for dealing with any scores of 3 and above for any individual rating and all products which achieve a score of 12 or more.

In-depth analysis: Develop descriptive information for each stage of one product. Review the method and the criteria being used. Redefine as necessary to suit your business and then complete the analysis.

Source: Hutchinson, 'Corporate Strategy' . . .' (1996), p. 98

some farms.[29] In this industrial ecosystem water is saved, the amount of waste to landfills is minimized, pollution is reduced, energy conserved, and there is an ongoing exchange of ideas on how to further improve environmental performance (Figure 7.10).

In traditional management the priorities are goals such as growth, and shareholder returns; there is a 'rational' conception of how to achieve these through the values, products, systems, organization designs, relationship to the environment and to the appropriate role of business functions. These contrast with the views embedded within ecocentric management, according to Shrivastava:

Figure 7.9: Sustainable Product Strategy Mix

	High		
		Modify	Priorities for development
Market Potential			
		Abandon	Strengthen market acceptance
	Low		*High*

Potential for Sustainability

Source: Hutchinson, 'Corporate Strategy . . .' (1996), p. 97

The action consequences of ecocentric management proliferate all aspects of organizations: their mission, inputs, throughputs and outputs. Ecocentric management seeks eco-friendly products through ecological designs, packaging and material use. It encourages the use of low energy, smaller amounts of resources, and environmentally efficient and appropriate technologies of production. Organizations in the ecocentric paradigm are appropriately scaled, provide meaningful work, have decentralized participative decision making, have low earning differentials among employees, and have nonhierarchical structures. They establish harmonious relationships between their natural and social environments. They seek to systematically renew natural resources and to minimize waste and pollution. All business functions assume more ecologically centred roles. Marketing seeks to educate consumers about responsible consumption, instead of promoting unrestricted consumption. Finance aims for long-term sustainable growth, instead of short-term profits. Accounting seeks to incorporate social and environmental costs of production, instead of externalizing them. Management seeks to provide meaningful work and safe working conditions, instead of single-mindedly pursuing labour productivity.[30]

Figure 7.10: An Industrial Ecosystem

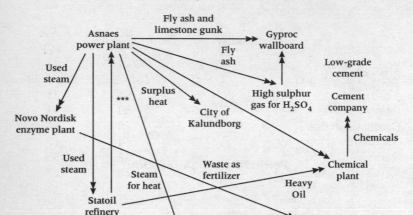

*** Treated waste water for cooling and desulphurized gas for fuel
Result:
Minimization of water use
Ecology cooperation
Maximization of energy use
Image/public relations
Resource reuse/recycling

Source: Shrivastava, 'Ecocentric Management . . ' (1995), p. 129

BUSINESS STRATEGY

Although it is not yet contemplating industrial ecosystems, mainstream business was grappling with sustainability issues long before there was a term for the concept. Well-formulated strategies can lead to better quality, reduced costs, improved environmental image and the opening of new markets. The business opportunities offered by environmental action now represent one of the largest sectors of new business for many industries (Table 7.9).

Most large companies already have refined environment policies, and over 80 per cent of the Fortune 500 companies have

Table 7.9: Business Opportunities in the Environment

Estimated expenditure (£bn 1991–2000)

Issues	UK	EC	USA
Greenhouse effect	48	237	443
Water quality	25	75–100	71
Waste management	19	180–200	120–170
Acid rain	11	51	25
Heavy metals	9	80	52
Ozone depletion	7	70	76
Air quality	7	34	17
Noise	6	32	33
VOCs and smells	3	26	27
Persistent organics	2	23	15
Contaminated land	2	25	150
Major spills	1	7	7
Total	140	860	1060

Source: Centre for Exploitation of Science and Technology, Industry and the Environment: *A Strategic Overview*, 1990

written environmental charters; however, 'at some point strategy has to degenerate into work'. The real challenge is to move from value statements to implementation.

Those who believe that ecological disaster will somehow be averted must also appreciate the commercial implications of such a belief: over the next decade or so, sustainable development will constitute one of the biggest opportunities in the history of commerce. Nevertheless, as of today few companies have incorporated sustainability into their strategic thinking. Instead, environmental strategy consists largely of piecemeal projects aimed at controlling or preventing pollution. Focusing on sustainability requires putting business strategies to a new text. Taking the entire planet as the context in which they do business, companies must ask whether they are part of the solution to social and environmental problems or part of the problem.[31]

Implementing Environmental Strategies

Three stages of environmental strategy are identified by Hart: pollution prevention, product stewardship and clean technology:

Pollution Prevention

The first step for companies is the shift from pollution control to pollution prevention. Pollution control involves cleaning up waste after it has been created; pollution prevention minimizes or eliminates waste before it is created. As with total quality management, pollution prevention strategies depend on continuous improvement efforts to reduce waste and energy use. An incentive for pollution prevention is cost-saving, combined with adherence to emerging global standards for environmental management systems, such as ISO 14000. The emerging economies cannot afford the reckless waste of Western development, and must learn from these mistakes. The imperative of sustainability encouraged BASF, the German chemical giant, in designing and building giant chemical plants in China, Indonesia, India and Malaysia, to *collocate* facilities that in the West are geographically dispersed. In this way BASF was able to create industrial ecosystems in which the waste from one process becomes the raw material for another. Collocation solves the problem found in the West, where the difficulty and cost of transporting waste from one site to another makes recycling unfeasible.

Product Stewardship

Product stewardship focuses on minimizing not only the pollution from manufacturing, but the environmental impact associated with the full life-cycle of the product. As companies move closer to zero emissions, reducing the use of materials and waste production involves fundamental changes in product design. *Design for the environment* (DFE) – a tool for creating products that are easier to recover, reuse or recycle – is becoming increasingly popular. All the effects that a product will have upon the environment are examined when designing for the environment. This includes a full assessment of all of the inputs to the product, and an examination of how customers use and dispose of it.

In reducing materials and energy consumption DFE can contribute to profitability. Xerox corporation's Asset Recycle Management

(ARM) uses leased Xerox machines as a source of quality components for new machines: in 1995 it saved between $300 and $400 million in raw materials and labour and waste disposal. To do this, 'Xerox has reconceptualized its business. By redefining the product-in-use as part of the company's asset base, Xerox has discovered a way to add value and lower costs. It can continually provide its lease customers with the latest product upgrades, giving them state-of-the-art functionality with minimal environmental impact'.[32]

Clean Technology

Having realized that the existing technology in many industries is environmentally unsustainable, some companies are planning for the future by researching tomorrow's technologies – for example, how to replace the bulk chemicals used in modern agriculture with biotechnology that does the same job without the accompanying pollution. Bioengineering, rather than chemical pesticides and fertilizers, could produce sustainable agricultural yields.

However the wider ecological impact of this technology is as yet unknown, and there are worrying indications of bio-engineering development being driven by the profit motive rather than scientific discovery, and of a disturbing desire on the part of multi-national bio-engineering companies to capture intellectual property of important crop species which presently peasant farmers, who developed the original species over thousands of years, rightly have free access to.

Similarly Asia is presently experiencing the most rapid industrialization in the world, and is therefore facing unprecedented environmental threats; however, since new technologies are being adopted there, in principle traditional technologies could be replaced with clean technology, but there are few indications that this opportunity is being taken, and widespread evidence of an unthinking acceptance of the most despoiling technologies as long as they are considered modern. The governments and people of the developing world are continually confronting a tragic dilemma the consequences of which threaten to impact seriously upon the developed world. They feel compelled to pursue the most rapid economic growth possible to lift their country out of poverty, and too often the most immediately available technologies are the most polluting. Trading economic growth for environmental damage is a reckless gamble. Increasingly this is recognised in the developing world, though often only when poisoned rivers and polluted skies begin to exact a deadly toll.

Figure 7.11:

	Clean technology	Sustainability vision
Tomorrow	Is the environmental performance of our products limited by our existing competency base? Is there potential to realize major improvements through new technology?	Does our corporate vision direct us towards the solution of social and environmental problems? Does our vision guide the development of new technologies, markets, products and processes?

	Pollution prevention	Product stewardship
Today	Where are the most significant waste and emission streams from our current operations? Can we lower costs and risks by eliminating waste at the source or by using it as useful input?	What are the implications for product design and development if we assume responsibility for a product's entire life-cycle? Can we add value or lower costs while simultaneously reducing the impact of our products?

Internal   **External**

Source: Hart, 'Strategies . . .' (1997), p. 74

Proactive Environmental Strategies

Companies around the world are progressing through the three stages of pollution prevention, product stewardship and clean technology with varying levels of enthusiasm (Figure 7.11). In Germany the 'take-back' law of 1990 requires manufacturers to take responsibility for their vehicles until the end of their useful lives. BMW have influenced new car design with their *design for disassembly*. However, the auto industry has not begun to face the real challenge of mass transportation in the developing world. There are currently only 1 million cars on the roads in China, but with a population of 1.2 billion, a 30 per cent market penetration would raise this number to 12 to 15 million units per year – the size of the US car market. Rather than supplying this enormous increase in demand with products that will further compound environmental damage, the industry should reassess vehicle production: with new technology *hypercars*, manufactured from composites with hybrid engines, metal stamping and the internal combustion engine could be abandoned.[33]

A struggle between information technology and biotechnology on the one hand and environmental degradation on the other is anticipated by Shapiro: 'Information technology is going to be our most powerful tool. It will let us miniaturize things, avoid waste, and produce more value without producing and processing more stuff. The substitution of information for stuff is essential to sustainability'.[36]

Three companies attempting a proactive environmental strategy are examined by Maxwell, Rothenberg, Briscoe and Marcus.[37] Volvo, Polaroid and Procter and Gamble have each adopted programmatic alternatives to environmental management (Table 7.10).

Volvo

In 1989 the Volvo chairman Pehr Gyllenhammar formed an environmental task force of the senior managers of each Volvo company and adopted a strategy whereby, within financial constraints, they would adopt manufacturing processes which had the least possible impact on the environment. Volvo initiated one of the most extensive environmental training programmes in corporate history: all 70,000 employees, including suppliers and dealers, were

Table 7.10: Programmatic Alternatives in Environmental Management

Structures for environmental goal setting	A structure for environmental management to internalize and meet regulatory and more proactive environment goals, through allocating environmental responsibility, specifying the flow of internal and external information, and offering guidelines on how to carry out its environmental goals
Mechanisms to monitor and review environmental performance	Monitoring of environmental achievement through direct reporting of environmental activity and environmental auditing
Incentives and controls to encourage environmental achievement	Establishment of incentives and controls to emphasize the company's commitment to environmental performance, and to encourage employees to perform in a manner that is consistent with this commitment
Guidelines and tools for environmental investments	Creation of financial guidelines and management tools to suggest how managers can consider such benefits as long-term financial savings and avoided costs when making environmental investments
Methodologies and tools to assist in environmental decision-making	Development of tools to help evaluate the environmental impacts of product and process decisions, systems to record company activities and their associated risks, and/or standard operating procedures to guide employees when performing environment-related tasks
Guidelines for communication and negotiation with stakeholders	Communication and negotiation with company stakeholders, including participation in environmental debates and financial support of environmental activities

Source: Maxwell, Rothenberg, Briscoe and Marcus, 'Green Schemes' (1997), p. 120

trained in environmental awareness. Whether they worked in Gothenburg, Sweden, or in Curaciba, Brazil, Volvo employees knew that being sensitive to environmental impact was at the top of the company agenda. Corporate-wide working groups were formed in recycling, environmental information, production and EMAS (the European Eco-management and Auditing System). Environmental goals were set throughout the product life-cycle, and the 850 model incorporated design changes that enhanced fuel efficiency and recyclability. The Torslanda plant had the lowest emissions of volatile organic compounds of any auto plant in the world. Volvo announced the likely introduction by the year 2000 of the first complete life-cycle declaration, which will cover 80 per cent of the car's life-cycle. However, at the same time Volvo was implementing a design and marketing change: it sought to broaden the appeal of its cars – the 'boring but safe' image was replaced by one of power and speed. In contrast, Mercedes Benz has responded to environmental pressures by revising their product strategy and offering a small, fuel-efficient 'city car'. Volvo, like its competitors, is locked into a paradigm of twentieth-century car-production that seems destined to survive into the first decades of the twenty-first century. In a flash of insight Gyllenhammar once startled a British radio audience by suggesting that 'the car was an inappropriate means of urban transport' – an apparently surprising view which is explained by the fact that Volvo's bus division has a substantially larger share of the world market than its car division.

Polaroid

Polaroid Corporation has designed and manufactured cameras, lenses, filters and chemical optical and industrial products since 1937. In the past Polaroid's commitment to pollution control took the form of 'end-of-pipe' controls; it incinerated waste. The Polaroid director of health and safety, Harry Fatkin, began to find compliance an 'elusive goal which required running hard to stay in place'.[38] Compliance seemed to be a losing strategy, and at an annual stockholders' meeting Fatkin announced the Toxic Use and Waste Reduction (TUWR) programme, which aimed to eliminate nearly all toxic emissions to the environment. The use of toxins was measured by a tracking system called Environmental Accounting and Reporting (EARS), which grouped chemicals into toxicity categories, targeting the most toxic. Although engineers felt that control was being taken from them as the ranking was decided by toxicity not the manufacturing system, the tracking was continued, though results were harder to achieve after the first years. For example, it took some years to move to aqueous-based film-coating, a process finally initiated in 1997. Polaroid's strategy kept it ahead of the frequently changing environmental regulations, but then a decision to introduce disposable cameras upset the environmentalists.

Procter and Gamble

P & G consumer products company was also established in 1937, and by 1995 had net sales in excess of $30 billion. As a company whose products kept it close to consumer thinking, it appreciated that environmental questions were becoming more pressing. For John Smale, the chief executive, making products that were more environmentally compatible was not only socially responsible but a valuable opportunity in the market place. P & G's strategy focused on reducing the environmental impact of product and packaging design, manufacture, distribution, use and disposal: 'Equally important to this technical strategy was to sell these environmental improvements just as they would any other product improvement demanded by the public, and to communicate extensively about its environmental activities with company stakeholders'.[39] The benefits of this policy exceeded expectations within the company: for example, the sale of a super-concentrated fabric softener reduced package size by 75 per cent, costing consumers less and increasing market share. Other consumer products companies, such as Colgate and Unilever, followed P & G's lead by developing super-concentrated detergents and powders, using more recycled plastic and advertising these attributes to customers. In general this policy improved P & G's relations with stakeholders, regulators and environmentalists. However, it made the mistake of advertising the recyclability and environmental friendliness of its disposable nappies, and was subsequently sued by attorney-generals in ten states in the US.

According to Maxwell, Rothenberg, Briscoe and Marcus (Table 7.11), the processes of environmental change are facilitated by the following characteristics:

Table 7.11: Environmental Management Programme
Compared

Programmatic Choices	Volvo	Polaroid	P & G
Structure for environmental goal-setting			
• Management structure	Groups at division level and managers at lower levels to set goals	Committee at corporate level	Broad goals set by corporate level team; specific goals set by each division, guided by teams
• Focus of goals	All areas – product, production, training, management	Use and disposal of hazardous material in production	Product waste management and consumer research
• Flexibility	Very flexible	Less flexible	Some flexibility
Mechanisms to monitor and review environmental performance			
• Reporting structure	Reviewed at each level of organization	Reviewed by top management	Reviewed by top management
• Auditing	Plant audits	Chemicals monitors through database	Plant audits
Incentives and controls to encourage environmental achievement	Environmental training used as informal incentive	Division performance reviews; training to encourage employees	Brand performance reviews

Table 7.11: (continued)

Programmatic Choices	Volvo	Polaroid	P & G
Guidelines and tools for environmental investment	Pick best technology with regard to environment or send decision to higher level	No formal criteria	Resources available for customer demanded changes
Methodologies and tools to assist environmental decision-making	Life-cycle tool; chemical database	Chemical database for risk identification	Life-cycle analysis
Guidelines for communication and negotiation with stakeholders	At group and company level; environmental standards and suppliers and dealers	Mainly at corporate staff level	At corporate and brand level; work with suppliers customers and community groups

Source: Maxwell, Rothenberg, Briscoe and Marcus, 'Green Schemes' (1997),
p. 129

→ Visible commitment of senior management to environmental policy, with active encouragement for initiatives that come from other levels

→ Creation of a management structure that removes buffers, and encourages integration between environmental issues and all other business operations

→ Formulation of an environmental strategy and supporting management system that blends with the attributes of the existing corporate culture

→ Recognition of and adaptation to the initiatives of domestic and international environmental and consumer groups.[40]

Environmental Standards and Management

The search for a better use of organizational resources can prompt companies to adopt environmental strategies. In the everyday life of an organization decisions aiming at optimal performance are made by the classical administrative functions, such as marketing, production, finance and human resources. In these spheres it is imperative to work towards better performance in relation to what competitors are doing or the demands emanating from the main stakeholders. Consider the well-known example of programmes of total quality management (TQM): although in their early stages these were considered a source of competitive advantage, today they have become a prerequisite for companies wishing to compete and to maintain their market position. TQM became an organizational imperative for global competitiveness in the eighties just as total quality environmental management (TQEM) may possibly become in the coming years. In this respect, the inclusion of environmental goals into quality programmes follows the same logic of a continuous search for productivity – in this case, resource productivity. As with TQM, pioneering companies that incorporate environmental standards in their strategies will gain a competitive advantage, but only until the competition process transforms it into another generalized organizational imperative.

The developed countries are adopting standards of environmental management that will strongly influence the competitiveness of national and overseas corporations. The British Standards Institution's BS-7750 requires companies doing business in the UK to conform to the UK Environmental Protection Act of 1990, and to develop environmental management systems that take corporate practice beyond compliance. European standards, along with those of Japan, the United States and Canada, are reflected in the European Union's Eco-Management and Audit Scheme (EMAS), and in the ISO 14000 standards drafted by the International Organization for Standardization.[41]

Most national and international environmental management standards focus on how corporations implement their environmental policies. ISO 14000 states that an environmental policy 'establishes an overall sense of direction and sets parameters of action for an organization. It sets the overarching goal as to the level of environmental performance required of the organization,

Figure 7.12:
ISO 14000 Environmental Management Systems Standard

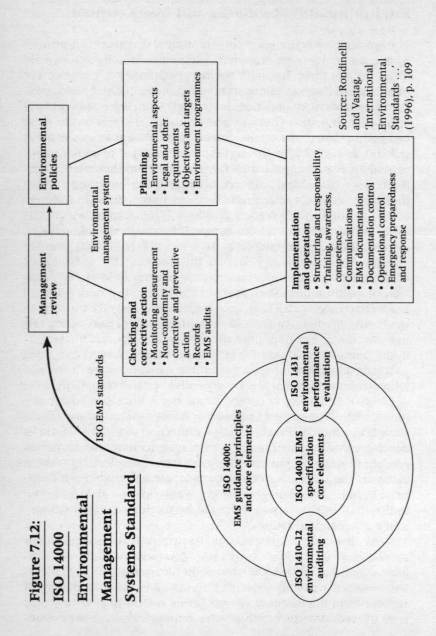

Source: Rondinelli and Vastag. 'International Environmental Standards ...'. (1996), p. 109

against which all subsequent actions shall be judged.'[42] Corporations are responsible for the scope and content of environmental policies (Figure 7.12).

Corporate environmental policies must reflect the environmental impacts of the organization's activities; they must also express a commitment to continual improvements and the prevention of pollution, give assurances that the company will comply with relevant laws and regulations, and provide a framework for regularly reviewing environmental objectives and targets. This policy must be documented and available to the public.[43] In many companies the enthusiasm dedicated in the 1980s to total quality management systems is now being used in the pursuit of environmental standards. Sayre provides a helpful flowchart of the necessary stages in the development of an environmental policy, through adoption of ISO 14000 to implementation, monitoring and review. The critical final stage is public communication with all stakeholders, which is of unique importance since it is also their environment which is being managed (Figure 7.13).

Rondinelli and Vastag offer a classification of corporate environmental policies based on endogenous and exogenous risks, of reactive, proactive, strategic and crisis prevention.[44] According to the classification, companies with reactive policies have low levels of emissions and their pollutants are not environmentally dangerous; the number of people affected is likely to be small. Such companies use non-exhaustible raw resources as raw materials, their production is not energy intensive, and their activities are not environmentally hazardous. Examples of such companies would be precision-technology companies, food producers or other companies employing clean technology. Reactive companies avoid legal violations, and establish programmes for regulatory compliance and periodic review. Proactive companies are those whose technologies and processes involve potentially high levels of pollution that can be environmentally dangerous; however, location, climate or environmental infrastructure can minimize adverse ecological or health consequences of their pollutants. This involves a more significant environmental function, concerned not only with compliance, but with continuous risk-assessment and effective management of those parts of the operations which have negative environmental impacts. Examples of companies in this category are distilleries or food-processing plants in rural areas. Managers also have to anticipate changes to environ-

Figure 7.13: System Flowchart for Environmental Management

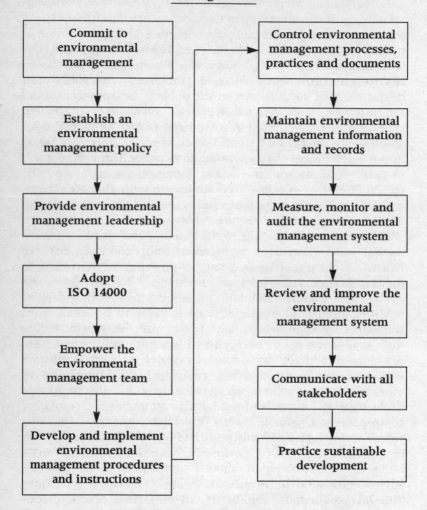

Source: Sayre, *Inside ISO 14000* (1996), p. 201

mental legislation, technology and public concern (Figure 7.14). In the crisis prevention group, companies are not heavy pol-

Figure 7.14: Classification of Environmental Policies

	Small	**Large**
Endogenous environmental risks	Group B **Proactive**	Group C **Strategic**
	Group A **Reactive**	Group D **Crisis preventive**

Exogenous environmental risks

Source: Rondinelli and Vastag, 'International Environmental Standards . . .'
(1996), p. 114

luters, either because they do not use large volumes of dangerous materials, or because pollution happens indirectly. Companies adopt a crisis prevention policy because their levels of pollution from production are usually low; however, when pollution does occur through ineffective waste disposal or degradation of natural resources, it may be highly visible, and the public perception of environmental damage may exceed actual negative impacts. Fast-food or tourist companies, for example, must rely on 'fail-safe' technologies and processes to prevent crisis situations, and on strong communication programmes concerning safety. Adherence to international standards and effective emergency response plans are essential.

Finally, the strategic environmental group of companies are in industries that are highly polluting, and operate in a social or physical context in which risks are further increased by external conditions and by hostile public attitudes towards environmental hazards. Large chemical and heavy manufacturing plants located in cities are examples of critical environmental risks. These companies require aggressive safeguards to prevent environmental damage, with well-defined, highly visible policies (Table 7.12).

Table 7.12: Comparison of Environmental Policies

Activity	Reactive	Proactive	Crisis Prevention	Strategic
Management level for environmental reporting and decision-making	Middle-level managment external consultants	Senior engineering or manufacturing managers at the plant level	Senior management leadership; corpora- tion-wide reporting and monitoring	Top management (CEO or board chairman level); senior management corporation- wide
Operational control of environmental management	Plant/site level guidelines and control	Plant-level controls; headquarters supervision	Corporate guidelines; plant/site-level control	Corporate-level guidelines and control
Environmental managagement actions	Required corrective action as regulations and norms change	Immediate corrective action as potential risks appear	Because of public exposure, continuous emergency monitoring procedures and immediate intervention if emergency occurs	Continuing improvements in all aspects of business activity towards pollution prevention and waste elimination
Training and education	Special training for plant environmental managers and/ or middle-level management	Corporation- wide environ- mental management training for senior and middle management	Corporation- wide specific training for senior and middle management	Corporation- wide general training for top management and board of directors; specific training for senior and middle management and awareness training for all employees and suppliers

Corporate Environmental Reports

As Gray suggests, there is little evidence that corporations will make public data which may have an adverse effect upon them.[45] But there is some indication that companies are beginning to

Table 7.12 (continued)

Activity	Reactive	Proactive	Crisis Prevention	Strategic
Driving force for environmental improvements	Current regulations and norms	Anticipated (future) regulations and norms; appearance of potential risks	Favourable public perception of company operations; avoidance of legal liabilities; protection of company reputation	Competitive positioning in global market; clean corporate image; current and anticipated regulations; favourable public perceptions
Nature of environmental improvements	Monitoring equipment 'end-of-pipe' filters	Technology improvements to reduce pollution and waste	Adoption of emergency prevention and response procedures; public communication campaigns; 'green' marketing	Seek innovative technology for pollution prevention; more effective public communication programmes; green labelling; frequent auditing and reporting; frequent management reviews and policy improvements
Environmental management technologies	Use of conventional technologies that meet compliance standards	Adoption of state-of-the-art technologies for pollution reduction	Use of proven, reliable technology for risk minimization; adoption of 'fail-safe' systems	Adoption of state-of-the-art 'clean' technology for pollution prevention and waste elimination

Source: Rondinelli and Vastag, 'International Ennvironmental Standards' (1996), p. 115

respond to the proposals for environmental reporting made by UNEPIE and other international agencies (Figure 7.15). This involves more than the green glossies of corporate PR campaigns:

Figure 7.15: Stages in Corporate Environmental Reporting

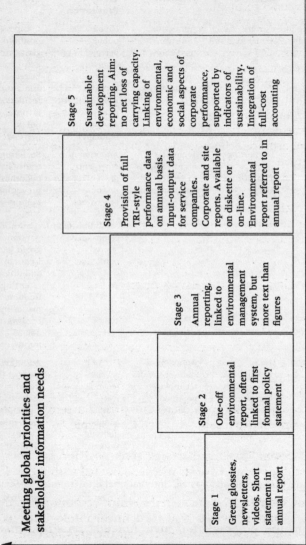

Meeting global priorities and stakeholder information needs

Time, effort

Stage 1

Green glossies, newsletters, videos. Short statement in annual report

Stage 2

One-off environmental report, often linked to first formal policy statement

Stage 3

Annual reporting, linked to environmental management system, but more text than figures

Stage 4

Provision of full TRI-style performance data on annual basis. Input-output data for service companies. Corporate and site reports. Available on diskette or on-line. Environmental report referred to in annual report

Stage 5

Sustainable development reporting. Aim: no net loss of carrying capacity. Linking of environmental, economic and social aspects of corporate performance, supported by indicators of sustainability. Integration of full-cost accounting

Source: UNEPIE *'Company Environmental Reporting'* (1994)

input/output data and full site reports should be made available. The final stage is sustainable development reporting in which the environmental, economic and social aspects of corporate performance are linked.

International companies such as BT now make regular environmental performance reports, giving a detailed public account of the policies and practices of the company, together with an assessment of how BT operations impact upon the environment. This is an important first step towards a comprehensive analysis of how a vast company with wide-ranging activities can calculate its full effect upon the environment, diminish that effect wherever it occurs, and closely monitor its success (Figure 7.16).

For some companies this has become an environmental crusade whose importance eclipses all other aspects of their business. Ray C. Anderson, the chief executive of Interface Inc. of Atlanta, Georgia, the world's largest manufacturer of carpet tiles, read Paul Hawken's *The Ecology of Commerce*, and felt 'a spear in my chest which remains to this day'. This led to the enthusiastic implementation of some of the most sophisticated environmental policies and commitments ever voluntarily engaged in (Figure 7.17).

Accounting for the Environment

Implementing effective business strategies for sustainability requires robust and meaningful measurement and reporting systems. Rob Gray has pioneered corporate and social environmental reporting and has encouraged accountants, in the most conservative profession, to take a more critical look at their methods and at the potential for more substantial measures of the true contribution to wealth creation of enterprise. Currently accounting and reporting activity depends upon four simple factors:

Organizations: The organizations accounted for are defined in times and space, and events which do not fall within the defined organization are ignored.

Economic events: The only events which accounting recognizes are the 'economic events' that are defined tautologically as those events which have *financial* effects on the organization.

Financial description: The events that accounting recognizes are further limited to events which can be described in financial

Figure 7.16: BT and the Environment

BT's Environmental Policy

BT is committed to minimizing the impact of its operations on the environment by means of a programme of continuous improvement. In particular BT will:

- Meet and, where appropriate, exceed the requirements of all relevant legislation – where no regulations exist BT shall set its own exacting standards
- Seek to reduce consumption of materials in all operations, reuse rather than dispose whenever possible, and promote recycling and the use of recycled materials
- Design energy efficiency into new services, buildings and products and manage energy wisely in all operations
- Reduce wherever practicable the level of harmful emissions
- Market products that are safe to use, make efficient use of resources, and which can be reused, recycled or disposed of safely
- Work with its supplier to minimize the impact of their operations on the environment through a quality purchasing policy
- Site its buildings, structures and operational plant to minimize visual, noise and other impacts on the local environment
- Support through its community programme the promotion of environmental protection by relevant external groups and organizations
- Include environmental issues in discussions with BT unions, the BT training programmes and encourage the implementation by all BT people of sound environmental practices
- Monitor progress and publish an environmental performance report on an annual basis.

How BT Affects the Environment

Fuel and energy

The combustion of fossil fuels generates emissions of carbon dioxide, sulphur oxides and nitrogen oxides. Increased atmosphere carbon dioxide is an important factor in global warming, while the latter two gases contribute to regional environmental problems such as acid rain.

Wastes

Significant BT wastes, in proportion to the UK totals, include telephones, exchanges, cable, batteries and PCB/PCN capacitors. BT acknowledges its responsibility to carefully manage its wastes in order to minimize any environmental impacts caused by their disposal.

Procurement

BT is the UK's largest civilian purchaser, and spends around £4 billion a year on goods and services. BT acknowledges its duty to practise environmentally responsible purchasing, a responsibility shared with its suppliers.

Emissions to air

BT's fleet of vehicles is responsible for an estimated 0.2 per cent of the UK's total road vehicle-related VOC (volatile organic compound) emissions. These compounds affect local air quality. BT uses refrigerants, fire extinguishers and other materials whose emissions damage the ozone layer.

Product stewardship

BT is the UK's principal supplier of telecommunications services and a major supplier of telecommunication equipment. BT acknowledges its responsibility to make them energy and resource efficient, safe in disposal, and to support their recycling or reuse.

Local impacts

BT operates from more than 9,000 properties. In additions, BT's network include 122,000 payphones, 4 million poles, 3.7 million covered manholes, 86,000 roadside cabinets and 210 radio stations. Careful planning is required to minimize impacts on local communities.

Environmental risk management

BT is formalizing the procedures for the assessment and management of the environmental risks posed by underground storage tanks, holdings of potentially damaging chemicals and contaminated land.

Source: BT, *Environmental Performance Report* (1994)

Figure 7.17: Interface Inc. Sustainability Report

Front	Problem	Solution
Eliminate waste	Industrial processes generate enormous amounts of waste which cannot be assimilated by nature or reused by industry. The volume of waste reflects inefficiencies which degrade the environment, harm the environment, harm the economy and reduce customer value	Our goal is to create zero waste. To accomplish this, we are re-examining our current sources of waste and creating progammes to first reduce and then eliminate them. We are redesigning products and process to reduce and simplify the amount of resources used in production. Waste can then be remanunfactured into new resources, becoming technical 'nutrients' for the next cycle of production
Benign emissions	Though less visible, industry creates more molecular garbage than solid waste. Small concentrations of poisons, persistent man-made chemicals, greenhouse gases and localized heating are affecting all living systems, accumulating in animal tissue, fouling water and air systems, affecting reproductive cycles and changing our climate	Interface will proceed toward eliminating all harmful releases into the ecosphere, striving to create factories with no smokestacks, effluent pipes or hazardous waste. Because it is difficult to safeguard against such releases, toxic emissions will be eliminated at the source. Ultimately, the only substances emitted from our plants should be valuable products, such as carpet and fabric, and clean air and water

Figure 7.17: (continued)

Front	Problem	Solution
Renewable energy	Modern industry has become dependent on the availability of seemingly inexpensive energy from fossil fuels: oil, coal and natural gas. Their combustion destroys a valuable source of feedstock and is the main cause of global climate change	We are focusing on improving production methods and equipment to consume less energy, thereby reducing demand. At the same time we are pursuing renewable energy supplies. This includes installing alternative technologies at our facilities, as well as contracting with power companies to provide us with energy from renewable sources
Closing the loop	Industrial systems are linear, take-make-waste systems. Natural, cyclical, living systems are destroyed when resources are depleted and waste accumulates in the biosphere	Interface is redesigning its processes and products into cyclical material flows where 'waste equals food'. We are reducing use of raw materials and working to get most value out of the materials that we employ. This includes careful recycling of synthetic materials so that waste materials in society become valuable raw materials in industry. It also means keeping organic materials uncontaminated so they can return to their natural cycles

Figure 7.17: (continued)

Front	Problem	Solution
Resource-efficient transportation	Dependence on readily available fossil fuels worldwide has led to centralized manufacturing facilities and long supply lines. This is not a viable model for sustainable transportation if the goal is resource efficiency	Transportation includes moving people, products, information and resources. Interface is working to make its transportation more ecologically efficient: changing packaging so products weigh less, manufacturing closer to the customer, and moving information instead of matter
Sensitivity hook-up	Most of society does not understand the basic principles of natural systems of how individual and collective human actions affect them	To progress towards sustainability we will help all of our associates and business partners gain a better understanding of the environment and the challenge that lies ahead. We hope to demonstrate to our customers, suppliers and friends – even our competitors – that it is not only the right thing to do, it is the smart thing to do

Figure 7.17: (continued)

Front	Problem	Solution
Redesign commerce	Existing business practices are focused on producing and distributing goods and services. A multitude of economic distortions make it difficult, if not impossible, for markets to recognize the true cost of what they produce	Interface is creating new methods of delivering value to customers, changing its purchasing practices, and supporting initiatives to bring about market-based incentives for sustainable commerce. It is focusing on the services, delivered by multiple life-cycles of its products. It is working to shift taxation away from economic and social benefits – such as labour, income and investment – to detriments including pollution, waste and the loss of primary resources

Source: Interface Inc, Sustainability Report (1997)

terms: that is, those which in the past have generated cash receipts or cash payments, or will do so in the future.

The users of information: The way in which events are recognized and then processed is determined largely by assumptions about the eventual users of this information. Users are assumed to be predominantly management, investors and lenders; their interests are taken to be predominantly financial in nature.[46]

Social and environmental accounting questions each of these characteristics of reporting:

• How do we define organizations? To what extent can we include externalities?
• Why account for only economic events? How might we account and report on social and environmental events as well?
• What are the consequences of restricting our accounting and reporting to only financial description? How can we account in other ways?
• Why do we restrict our reporting to a selected set of participants?

How might we set about accounting and reporting to society, employees, communities, other countries or future generations?

The ultimate objective of environmental reporting is to ensure there is *'constancy of natural capital stock'*.[47] The capital available to humanity can be conceived of as falling into three categories:

Critical natural capital: Those elements of the biosphere that are essential for life and which, for sustainability, must remain inviolate (for example, the ozone layer, a critical mass of trees, etc.)

Other sustainable natural capital: Those elements of the biosphere which are renewable (for example, non-extinct species, woodlands), or for which a reasonable substitute can be found (for example, energy from fossil fuels versus energy from renewable sources).

Man-made capital: Those elements created from the biosphere which are no longer part of the harmony of the natural ecology (machines, buildings, roads, products, wastes, intangible assets).

The point is that man-made capital, which is covered by economics and accounting, is created and expanded at the expense of the natural capitals. Man-made capitals are measured by GNP and by profit, but as man-made capital expands *it is almost inevitable that natural capital declines* – unless some way of managing sustainability is found. If sustainability is to be achieved the critical capital must not be touched, and all diminutions in other natural capital must be replaced, renewed or substituted.[48]

Gray concludes with a notion of sustainable cost, derived directly from accounting concepts of capital maintenance and the need, within all definitions of sustainability, to maintain the natural capital for future generations: 'Translating the most basic concept of sustainability to the level of the organization we would say that a *sustainable organization is one which leaves the biosphere at the end of the accounting period no worse off than it was at the beginning of the accounting period.* It must be the case then that the vast majority of, if not all, organizations do not comply with this'.[49]

CONCLUSIONS

There are many forces driving paradigmatic changes in business and management, but there is none more important than the need to discover and develop sustainable enterprise for ecological survival. New paradigm organizations are capable of rapid learning, from a wide range of stakeholders, and the most compelling lesson must be the vulnerability of the physical environment to the impact of human industry. Sustainability is the key strategic imperative of the future. As we have seen, this does not necessarily involve the abandonment of industry and consumption. It does involve the application of intelligence to ensure that neither production processes nor end products cause irreparable harm to the natural environment. By using knowledge as the key resource, rather than destructive exploitation of limited natural resources, sustainability may be achieved.

Chapter 8

CONCLUSIONS

MANAGEMENT FOR THE NEW MILLENNIUM

With one century ending and a new century beginning, it is a natural time to take stock. What have we achieved? What are we doing right? What could we do better? What new challenges will we face? How will we meet them? The answers to these questions may be different for every individual and every business, but there are some issues we will all face. Posing such questions can have a sobering effect at any time. Doing so at the end of a troubled but immensely inventive millennium of human civilization, and at the beginning of a millennium that promises even more dramatic changes in how we live our lives, and in our economics and societies, provokes some fairly profound thoughts and emotions.

In business terms the first and most obvious thought is that we cannot carry on as we are. The dominant global paradigm of Western industrialism may have provided previously unimaginable material wealth and opportunities to the people of the advanced industrial countries. However, this has resulted in widespread environmental degradation, man-made climactic change, accumulating toxic wastes, receding forests, diminishing topsoil, expanding deserts and a depleting ozone layer. The numbers of plants and animal species are shrinking at the same time as the human population continues to grow, and the gap between rich and poor countries continues to widen.

These environmental problems are different facets of a fundamental crisis of perception. In the industrial world most people and organizations are clinging to an outdated world view that is no longer able to deal with an under-resourced, overpopulated and globally interconnected planet.[1] Unlimited material progress through economic growth is unsustainable. The poorer countries of the South have long been confronted by this bitter reality, but even in the industrial countries more people now accept that we cannot sustain this rate of resource depletion and interference with life-supporting ecological systems.

Schumpeter characterized the industrial market system as one of *creative destruction*.[2] The search for industrial paradigms for the new millennium needs to concentrate on finding ways in which the creativity of industry and technology can be harnessed without the reckless and despoiling destruction that was formerly taken as an inevitable, if regrettable, result of business activity. A dematerialization of the economy is required whereby goods and services will be provided with the minimum consumption of energy and primary materials, closing the loop of manufacturing systems, sustaining and restoring rather than exhausting natural resources.

Creative Paradigms

The imperative of environmental responsibility is unlikely to be observed unless business also respects the increasing demand for social responsibility. Its traditional response to the call for environmental and social responsibility is often a reluctant acceptance that while this may be necessary, there will be additional costs which businesses must bear and, ultimately, a potential brake upon the drive for efficiency and profitability. However, recent evidence shows that companies are adopting more creative business paradigms, in which they regard a deep respect for the environment and a genuine concern for their stakeholders as a fundamental strength, not just of their value system, but in their business practice.

Studies like that undertaken by Collins and Porras of companies that have achieved sustainable business success reveal the fundamental importance of strong values to their existence and continued vitality and, in particular, the high value placed upon relationships.[3] Good relationships with, and between, employees, customers, suppliers, investors and the community not only allow companies to anticipate, learn and adapt; they also provide them with the public support that allows them to maintain and develop their operations. When based on reciprocity and partnership these relationships can form invaluable corporate resources of extensive knowledge, new ideas, growing sales, stable investment and a sense of purpose and long-term security. Again, it is a question of how we regard the business world: are companies simply a bundle of short-term assets, or are they essentially a set of long-term relationships and commitments?

Businesses that may have only recently recovered from restructuring, down-sizing, business-process re-engineering and other shock therapy, are faced with the fact that creativity, innovation and the accumulation of intellectual capital are the positive routes to business success. Commitment to the generation and sharing of knowledge can only be inspired in employees, suppliers, customers and others who feel a sense of connection with the company and who share its values and objectives.

Knowledge-based Business

All business is becoming knowledge based – that is, the utilization of state-of-the-art knowledge is now the critical ingredient for commercial viability. Developing better information systems is only part of this challenge. It is necessary to create collaborative cultures, group technologies, supportive infrastructures and sensitive measurement systems to facilitate the effective acquisition and deployment of new knowledge.

In knowledge-based business, learning and innovation are the critical drivers of business development. Redefining the workplace as a central mechanism for knowledge-exchange encourages the discovery and utilization of knowledge at every level, making the organization more alert, informed and responsive. For some companies this has involved transforming training programmes into virtual universities; for others, the development of the company Intranet has facilitated knowledge-sharing among employees across the globe; in some cases vast knowledge databases have been created – knowledge centres enabling a company to offer world-class best practice to customers.

Virtual Organization

Companies that capture the technological capacity of networked databases, remote access and the Intranet begin a process of dematerialization whereby the physical structures which previously bound organizational life become less important. What is important is the accumulation of collective state-of-the-art knowledge and the speed of its transmission and use throughout the company. The old methods of structure and control – hierarchy, systems and budgets – become less significant when staff are more mobile, informed and autonomous. What holds people together in virtual organizations is not so much authority structures and detailed instructions, but parameters of accountability, clear objectives and guiding values.

Understandably, in virtual organizations people feel an over-powering need to belong to *something* they can identify with and feel proud of. In this relationship it is even more important that their company can offer a sense of purpose that gives meaning to work. The paradox inherent in virtual forms of organization is that, while people are physically released from traditional organizational structures, other forms of connection – including inspiring ideas, binding values and shared objectives – become considerably more important to them.

The New Paradigm Business

The assumptions that underpinned the business structures of the past are as antiquated as the structures themselves. But this does not mean that one worn-out set of business goals and solutions should be exchanged for another universally applicable business paradigm. The new business paradigm is not simply a fixed template of criteria that a company must try to fulfil; it is not a checklist or a ten-step programme. Increasingly, new business paradigms will be about images of *forming*, not images of *form*; processes of development and achievement, values and vision. More than ever before management will be based on intelligence, creativity and the capacity to question and to learn. Sustaining energy and direction without the support of the material structures that earlier defined the organization of enterprise will be the key management challenge of the new millennium.

APPENDIX

Top 25 Companies by Market Capitalization, 1997

Rank	Company Name	Country	Market Cap. $ million	Turnover $ million	Profit $ million	Employees
1	General Electric	US	222748.3	78541.0	7280.0	239000
2	Royal Dutch/Shell	Nuk	191002.3	131557.9	17417.9	101000
3	Microsoft Corp.	US	159659.6	11358.0	3454.0	22232
4	Exxon Corp.	US	157970.4	116728.0	7510.0	79000
5	Coca-Cola	US	151287.6	18546.0	3492.9	26000
6	Intel Corp	US	150837.8	20847.0	5157.0	48500
7	Nippon Tel. & Telephone	Jap	146138.7	65436.4	4573.4	231000
8	Merck	US	120757.0	19828.7	3881.3	49100
9	Toyota Motor Corp.	Jap	116585.4	101305.9	5860.5	150736
10	Novartis	Swi	104467.6	24639.9	1766.1	116178
11	Int Business Machines Corp.	US	104119.6	75947.0	5429.0	240615
12	Phillip Morris	US	100666.4	54553.0	6303.0	154000
13	Proctor & Gamble	US	93291.9	35764.0	3415.0	106000
14	HSBC Holdings	UK	91339.4	N/R	7251.2	109298
15	Bank of Tokyo-Mitsubishi	Jap	88818.9	N/R	721.2	
16	British Petroleum	UK	85905.0	71695.8	5877.5	53700
17	Roche Holdings	Swi	85852.8	10857.5	3202.3	48972
18	Wal-Mart Stores	US	82533.0	104859.0	3056.0	728000
19	Bristol Myers Squibb	US	82482.2	15065.0	2850.0	51200
20	Glaxo	UK	79715.9	13369.1	4750.8	53808
21	Johnson & Johnson	US	76898.1	21620.0	2887.0	89300
22	Pfizer Inc	US	75468.9	11306.0	1929.0	47000
23	American Int Group	US	72359.4		2897.3	36600
24	Hewlett-Packard Co.	US	72267.8	38420.0	2586.0	112000
25	Lloyds TSB Group	UK	72094.9	N/R	4015.1	90383

Source: FT500, Financial Times, Thursday 22 January, 1998

Top 25 Companies by Turnover, 1997

Rank	Company Name	Country	Turnover $ million	Market Cap. $ million	Profit $ million	Employees
1	General Motors	US	160121.0	48293.8	4953.0	647000
2	Mitsubishi Corp.	Jap	147235.9	15171.2	748.4	13100
3	Ford Motor	US	146991.0	54150.0	4446.0	371702
4	Mitsui & Co.	Jap	144962.6	12434.6	656.6	11378
5	ITOCHU Corp.	Jap	135096.5	4929.6	436.9	
6	Sumitomo Corp.	Jap	133791.7	7926.6	426.2	
7	Royal Dutch/Shell	Nuk	131557.9	91002.3	17417.9	101000
8	Marubeni Corp.	Jap	121291.3	4944.6	120.2	6702#
9	Exxon Corp.	US	116728.0	157970.4	7510.0	79000
10	Wal-Mart Stores	US	104859.0	82533.0	3056.0	728000
11	Toyota Motor Corp.	Jap	101305.9	116585.4	5860.5	150736
12	General Electric Co.	US	78541.0	222748.3	7280.0	239000
13	Nissho Iwai Corp.	Jap	78173.1	3009.8	−139.4	
14	Int Business Machines Corp.	US	75947.0	104119.6	5429.0	240615
15	British Petroleum	UK	71695.8	85905.0	5877.5	53700
16	Mobil Corp.	US	71129.0	58248.1	2964.0	43000
17	Hitachi	Jap	70520.4	28998.8	2178.8	330152
18	Nippon Tel. & Telephone	Jap	65436.4	146138.7	4573.4	231000
19	Daimler-Benz	Ger	59513.7	42709.9	1097.5	291268
20	Chrysler Corp.	US	59333.0	24387.9	3720.0	126000
21	Matsushita Elec. Ind Co.	Jap	56220.9	38099.2	634.0	265538
22	Volkswagen	Ger	56034.2	19055.3	1103.6	242770
23	Phillip Morris	US	54553.0	100666.4	6303.0	154000
24	Tomen Corp.	Jap	54110.5	1069.4	97.0	
25	AT&T	US	52184.0	71918.8	5608.0	130400

Source: FT500, Financial Times, Thursday 22 January, 1998

Top 25 Companies by Employees, 1997

Rank	Company Name	Country	Employees	Market Cap. $ million	Turnover $ million	Profit $ million
1	Wal-Mart Stores	US	728000	82533.0	104859.0	3056.0
2	General Motors	US	647000	48293.8	160121.0	4953.0
3	Pepsico	US	486000	61532.5	31654.0	1149.0
4	Siemens	Ger	378800	37357.7	52708.8	1823.4
5	Gazprom	Rus	375000	31947.1	22508.5	6470.9
6	Ford Motor Co.	US	371702	54150.0	146691.0	4446.0
7	Sears Roebuck	US	335000	22319.4	38236.0	1271.0
8	Tricon Global Restaurants	US	335000	4913.7	10232.0	−53.0
9	Hitachi	Jap	330152	28998.8	70520.4	2178.8
10	Unilever plc/NV	Nuk	306000	57484.2	53729.8	4258.7
11	Daimler-Benz	Ger	291268	42709.9	59513.7	1097.5
12	Columbia/HCA Healthcare	US	285000	18792.9	19909.0	1505.0
13	Philips	Net	272270	29015.5	34391.2	454.3
14	Matsushita Elec. Ind. Co.	Jap	265538	38099.2	56220.9	634.0
15	K Mart Corp.	US	265000	6828.4	31437.0	231.0
16	Penny (JC) Co.	US	252000	14498.2	24290.0	565.0
17	Volkswagen	Ger	242770	19055.3	56034.2	1103.6
18	Fiat	Ita	240888	14801.0	44431.3	2182.6
19	Int Business Machines Corp.	US	240615	104119.6	75947.0	5429.0
20	General Electric Co.	US	239000	222748.3	78541.0	7280.0
21	McDonald's Corp.	US	237000	32766.0	10686.5	1572.6
22	Deutsche Telekom	Ger	236812	52515.4	35300.5	1850.2
23	Nippon Tel. & Telephone	Jap	231000	146138.7	65436.4	4573.4
24	Nestlé	US	221144	54315.6	41135.7	3358.0
25	Dayton Hudson Corp.	US	218000	13140.5	25371.0	474.0

Source: FT500, Financial Times, Thursday 22 January, 1998

Top 25 US Companies by Market Capitalization, 1997

Rank	Company Name	Market Cap. $ million	Turnover $ million	Profit $ million	Employees
1	General Electric	222748.3	78541.0	7280.0	239000
2	Microsoft Corp.	159659.6	11358.0	3454.0	22232
3	Exxon Corp.	157970.4	116728.0	7510.0	79000
4	Coca-Cola	151287.6	18546.0	3492.0	26000
5	Intel Corp.	150837.8	20847.0	5157.0	48500
6	Merck	120757.0	19828.7	3881.3	49100
7	Int. Business Machines Corp.	104119.6	75947.0	5429.0	240615
8	Philip Morris	100666.4	54553.0	6303.0	154000
9	Proctor & gamble	93291.9	35764.0	3415.0	106000
10	Wal-Mart Stores	82533.0	104859.0	3056.0	728000
11	Bristol Myers Squibb	82482.2	15065.0	2850.0	51200
12	Johnson & Johnson	76898.1	21620.0	2887.0	89300
13	Pfizer & Co.	75468.9	11306.0	1929.0	47000
14	American International Group	72359.4		2897.3	36600
15	Hewlett-Packard Co.	72267.8	38420.0	2586.0	112000
16	AT&T Corp.	71918.8	52184.0	5608.0	130400
17	Du Pont (EI) De Nemours	69654.9	38504.0	3636.0	97000
18	Lilly (Eli)	67305.5	7346.6	1523.5	29200
19	Bell Atlantic Corp.	62470.5	13081.4	1739.4	62600
20	Pepsico	61532.5	31645.0	1149.0	486000
21	Citicorp	61355.4		3788.0	89000
22	Mobil Corp.	58248.1	71129.0	2964.0	43000
23	Compaq Computer Corp.	56585.8	18109.0	1313.0	18863
24	SBC Communications	56150.1	13898.0	2101.0	61540
25	Berkshire Hathaway	55193.6	10500.3	2488.6	34500

Source: FT500, Financial Times, Thursday 22 January, 1998

Top 25 European Companies by Market Capitalization, 1997

Rank	Company Name	Country	Market Cap. $ million	Turnover $ million	Profit $ million	Employees
1	Royal Dutch/Shell	Nuk	191002.3	131557.9	17417.9	101000
2	Novartis	Swi	104467.6	24639.9	1766.1	116178
3	HSBC Holdings	UK	91339.4	N/R	7251.2	109298
4	British Petroleum	UK	85905.0	71695.8	5877.5	53700
5	Roche Holdings	Swi	85852.8	10857.5	3202.3	48972
6	Glaxo Wellcome	UK	79715.9	13369.1	4750.8	53808
7	Lloyds TSB Group	UK	72094.9	N/R	4015.1	90383
8	Unilever plc/NV	Nuk	57484.2	53729.8	4258.7	306000
9	Allianz Holding	Ger	56013.3	N/R	2215.1	65836
10	Nestlé	Swi	54315.6	41135.7	3358.0	221144
11	Smithkline Beecham	UK	53304.1	12702.4	2476.4	52900
12	Deutsche Telekom	Ger	52515.4	35300.5	1850.2	236812
13	ENI	Ita	49876.9	49934.0	4727.2	86422
14	Ericsson LM	Swe	46174.0	16156.9	1452.3	89391
15	Daimler-Benz	Ger	42709.9	59513.7	1097.5	291268
16	BT	UK	42017.5	23938.1	5133.8	129600
17	Barclays	UK	40636.1	N/R	3776.2	87400
18	Siemens	Ger	37357.7	52708.8	1823.4	378800
19	ING Group	Net	37345.8	N/R	2265.9	58106
20	Deutsche Bank	Ger	36991.1	N/R	2736.7	66833
21	Elf Aquitaine	Fra	35997.4	38747.7	3290.0	85400
22	Telecom Italia	Ita	34666.1	23244.2	3946.5	133211
23	Gazprom	Rus	31947.1	22508.5	6470.9	375000
24	Zeneca	UK	30735.3	8595.9	1562.8	31100
25	Astra	Swe	29673.2	5069.2	17719.5	19851

Source: FT500, Financial Times, Thursday 22 January, 1998

Top 25 Japanese Companies by Market
Capitalization, 1997

Rank	Company Name	Market Cap. $ million	Turnover $ million	Profit $ million	Employees
1	Nipon Tel. & Telephone	146138.7	65436.4	4573.4	231000
2	Toyota Motor Corp.	116585.4	101305.9	5860.5	150736
3	Bank of Tokyo-Mitsubishi	88818.9	N/R	721.2	
4	Sumitomo Bank	47300.5	N/R	507.7	17418
5	Matsushita Elec. Industrial Co.	38099.2	56220.9	634.0	265538
6	Sony Corp.	37171.3	46857.0	2585.0	163000
7	Sanwa Bank	35532.0	N/R	458.0	19737
8	Dai-Ichi Kangyo Bank	35374.5	N/R	−2620.3	19292
9	Honda Motor	33939.6	43797.0	3232.8	101100
10	Fuji Bank	31886.7	N/R	820.0	17756
11	Industrial Bank of Japan	31518.9	N/R	368.0	5000
12	Seven-Eleven Japan	31217.9	2106.7	956.2	2718#
13	Hitachi	28998.8	70520.4	2178.8	330152
14	Takeda Chemical Industries	26291.0	6630.3	1040.8	10676
15	Tokyo Electrical Power	25969.3	41816.4	1400.3	43448
16	Nomura Securities	25499.5	N/R	1249.7	
17	Canon Inc.	25294.5	21166.9	1512.2	75628
18	Fujitsu	23234.6	37261.9	1183.8	167000
19	Ito-Yokado	22481.5	24978.2	1755.8	38149
20	Denso	21436.2	11770.7	843.7	56385
21	Fuji Phote Film	21205.0	8977.0	1085.1	29903
22	Mitsubishi Trust & Banking Corp.	20257.6	9304.3	573.2	6092
23	Bridgestone Corporation	19695.1	16200.8	1078.7	92458
24	NEC Corporation	19423.0	36382.5	1252.0	152719
25	Mitsubishi Estate	18919.1	N/R	−659.0	

Source: FT500, Financial Times, Thursday 22 January, 1998

Top 25 Asia-Pacific Companies by Market Capitalization, 1997

Rank	Company Name	Country	Market Cap. $ million
1	HSBC Holdings	Hong Kong	60147.8
2	Hutchinson Whampoa	Hong Kong	38141.1
3	Sun Hung Kai Properties	Hong Kong	28079.6
4	Hong Kong Telecommunications	Hong Kong	2686.7
5	Singapore Telecom	Singapore	26058.2
6	Cheung Kong Holdings	Hong Kong	25811.9
7	Hang Seng Bank	Hong Kong	23757.2
8	Broken Hill Proprietary	Australia	23490.8
9	National Australia Bank	Australia	21755.2
10	Taiwan Semiconductor	Taiwan	19063.1
11	Cathay Life Insurance	Taiwan	15839.3
12	Henderson Land Development	Hong Kong	14875.3
13	Korea Electric Power	S Korea	14016.5
14	China Light & Power	Hong Kong	13688.3
15	ANZ Bank	Australia	12313.6
16	CITIC Pacific	Hong Kong	12092.8
17	Swire Pacific	Hong Kong	11878.8
18	New World Development	Hong Kong	11541.5
19	Commonwealth Bank of Australia	Australia	11470.2
20	Telekonumikasi Indonesia	Indonesia	11264.4
21	Westpac Banking Corp.	Australia	11206.4
22	United Micro Electronics	Taiwan	10692.8
23	Hua Nan Commercial Bank	Taiwan	10022.8
24	News Corporation	Australia	9991.7
25	First Commercial Bank	Taiwan	9851.8
#	*Parent Company Accounts*		

Source: FT500, Financial Times, Thursday 22 January 1998

NOTES

For full publishing details of works referred to in the Notes, please see the Bibliography (p. 460),

Introduction

1. T. A. Stewart, *Intellectual Capital: The New Wealth of Organizations* (1997), p. 33.
2. C. Handy, *The Age of Unreason* (1991).
3. G. Hamel and C. K. Prahalad, *Competing for the Future* (1994).
4. N. Negroponte, *Being Digital* (1995).

1: Paradigms

1. S. Covey, *The Seven Habits of Highly Effective People* (1989), p. 23.
2. G. Burrell, 'Organization Paradigms', 1997 p. 34.
3. G. Morgan, *Images of Organizations* (1985); L. G. Bolman and T. E. Deal, *Reframing Organizations: Artistry, Choice and Leadership* (1991).
4. J. A. Barker, *Paradigms: Understand the Future in Business and Life* (1992), p. 164.
5. Ibid., pp. 51–2.
6. T. S. Kuhn, *The Structure of Scientific Revolutions* (1970).
7. G. Burrell and G. Morgan, *Sociological Paradigms and Organizational Analysis* (1979).
8. N. D. Kondratiev, 'The Longwaves in Economic Life' (1935).
9. J. A. Schumpeter, *Business Cycles* (1934).
10. P. G. Keen and E. M. Knapp, *Every Manager's Guide to Business Processes* (1996), p. 89.
11. Keen and Knapp, *Every Manager's Guide to Information Technology* (1995), p. 88.

12. R. G. Eccles and N. Nohria, *Beyond the Hype: Rediscovering the Essence of Management* (1992), p. 7.
13. R. Pascale, *Managing on the Edge* (1990), p. 19.
14. Ibid., p. 20.
15. J. Micklethwaite and A. Wooldridge, *The Witch Doctors* (1997), p. 147.
16. M. Porter, *The Competitive Advantage of Nations* (1990), p. 20.
17. C. Handy, *The Age of Unreason* (1989).
18. Ibid.
19. B. H. Schmitt and A. Simonson, *Marketing Aesthetics* (1997).
20. R. M. Kanter, *World Class* (1995), p. 331.
21. P. M. Senge, *The Fifth Discipline* (1992), p. 3.
22. Pascale, op. cit.
23. W. Bennis, J. Parikh and R. Lessem, *Beyond Leadership: Balancing Economics, Ethics and Ecology* (1994), pp. 4–8.
24. R. H. Hall, *The Soul of the Enterprise* (1993), p. 24.
25. C. A. Bartlett and S. Ghoshal, *Transnational Management* (1995).
26. T. Cannon, *Welcome to the Revolution* (1996), p. 44.
27. Ibid., p. 137.
28. R. D. Hames, *The Management Myth* (1994).
29. J. Fulk and G. DeSanctis, 'Electronic Communication and Changing Organizational Forms' (1995).
30. Hames, op. cit.
31. D. Tapscott and A. Caston, *Paradigm Shift: The New Promise of Information Technology* (1993), p. 9.
32. Ibid., p. 18.
33. W. H. Davidon and M. A. Malone, *The Virtual Corporation* (1992).
34. C. K. Prahalad and G. Hamel, 'Strategy As a Field of Study: Why Search for a New Paradigm?' (1990).
35. G. Hamel and C. K. Prahalad, *Competing for the Future* (1994), p. 23.
36. Karpin Industry Task Force on Leadership and Management Skills, 'International Models of Management Development' (1995).
37. Ibid., p. 4.
38. Ibid., pp. 15–49.
39. Rand (1995).
40. Karpin Industry Task Force, p. 16.
41. Ibid., p. 17.
42. *Business Week*, 12 December 1994.
43. Boston Consulting Group, 'The Australian Manager of the Twenty-first Century' (1995).
44. L. A. Hill, *Becoming a Manager* (1992).
45. Gouldner, *Patterns of Industrial Bureaucracy*.
46. Boston Consulting Group, op. cit.
47. Ibid., p. 1234.

48. G. Stalk, P. Evans and L. Schulman, 'Competing on Capabilities: The New Rules of Corporate Strategy' (1992).

49. I. Hawryszkiewycz, *Designing the Networked Enterprise* (1997).

50. Stalk et. al., op. cit.

51. Boston Consulting Group, op. cit., pp. 1255–6.

52. Handy, op. cit.; P. Drucker, *The New Realities* (1989).

53. K. Ohmae, *The Borderless World* (1990).

54. Boston Consulting Group, op. cit.

55. Ibid., p. 1229.

56. D. Limerick and B. Cunnington, *Managing the New Organization* (1993).

57. S. Lash and J. Urry, *The End of Organized Capitalism* (1987).

58. See also R. Rothwell, 'Successful Industrial Innovation: Critical Factors for the 1990s'.

59. Bryman, *Charisma and Leadership of Organizations* (1992).

60. Bennis, Parikh and Lessem, op. cit; W. Bennis, 'Creative Leadership' (1993).

61. J. C. Collins and J. I. Porras, *Successful Habits of Visionary Companies* (1996), pp. 43–4.

62. A. de Geus, *The Living Company* (1997), p. 22.

63. See, for example, P. Anderson, *The Transition from Feudalism to Capitalism* (1979).

64. De Geus, op. cit., pp. 12–14.

65. Ibid., p. 14.

66. Collins and Porras, op. cit.

67. De Geus, op. cit., p. 21.

68. H. M. Maynard and S. E. Mehrtens, *The Fourth Wave, Business in the 21ˢᵗ Century* (1996), p. 6.

69. R. D. Hames, *Burying the 20th Century: New Paths for New Futures* (1997), pp. 35, 41.

70. Ibid., p. xiv.

71. Ibid., pp. 39–40.

72. Ibid., p. 141.

2: Globalization

1. R. Petrella, 'Globalization and Internationalization: The Dynamics of the Emerging World Order' (1996).

2. L. Thurow, *The Future of Capitalism* (1996), p. 115.

3. OECD, *Globalization of Industry* (1996), p. 9.

4. Hirst and Thompson (1996), pp. 74, 2–3.

5. OECD (1996a), p. 15.

6. Kenneth Ohmae, *Managing in a Borderless World*, in Bartlett and Ghoshal (1995), pp. 102–4.

7. Petrella, op. cit., p. 71.
8. *The Economist, World Economy Survey* (28 September 1996), p. 4.
9. R. Buckley, *Fairer Global Trade? The Challenge for the WTO, Understanding Global Issues* (1996).
10. Thurow, op. cit., pp. 21–4.
11. R. Reich, *The Work of Nations* (1991).
12. *Economist*, op. cit., p. 4.
13. R. Wade, 'Globalization and Its Limits: Reports of the Death of the National Economy Are Greatly Exaggerated' (1996), p. 66.
14. L. Weiss, 'Globalization and the Myth of the Powerless State' (1997), p. 7.
15. Wade, op. cit.
16. Petrella, op. cit., p. 77.
17. C. A. Bartlett and S. Ghoshal, *Transnational Management* (1995), pp. 3, 5.
18. OECD (1996a), p. 16.
19. Ibid., p. 17.
20. J. Kay, *Foundations of Corporate Success: How Business Strategies Add Value* (1993).
21. E. Bowman and B. Kogut, *Redesigning the Firm* (1995), pp. 5–7.
22. R. Boyer and D. Drache, *States Against Markets: The Limits of Globalization* (1996), p. 13.
23. OECD (1996a), p. 20.
24. P. J. Lloyd, 'Regionalization and World Trade' (1992).
25. OECD (1996a).
26. Ibid., p. 26.
27. Congress of the United States, *Multinationals and the US Technology Base* (1994).
28. D. Drache, 'From Keynes to K-Mart: Competitiveness in a Corporate Age' (1996), p. 52.
29. W. Ruigrok, *Paradigm Crisis in International Trade Theory* (1991).
30. Buckley, op. cit.
31. Ibid., pp. 2–5.
32. *Far Eastern Economic Review*, 20 March 1997.
33. OECD, 'Recent Trends in Foreign Direct Investment' (1996e), p. 37.
34. Ibid., pp. 39–40.
35. Ibid., p. 41.
36. Glynn (1995), pp. 48–9; Weiss, op. cit., p. 9.
37. OECD, 'Recent Trends . . .', p. 42.
38. Ibid., p. 43.
39. Ibid., p. 45.
40. Ibid., p. 46.
41. Ibid.
42. United Nations, *World Investment Report: Transnational Corporations and Integrated Production* (1993).
43. OECD, 'Recent Trends . . .', p. 47.

44. Weiss, op. cit., p. 10.
45. OECD, 'Recent Trends . . .', p. 56.
46. OECD, *Globalization of Industry* (1996a), p. 41.
47. N. Kumar, *Intellectual Property Protection and Location of Overseas R&D Activities by Multinational Enterprises* (1995).
48. OECD, *Globalization of Industry* (1996a), p. 42.
49. Weiss, op. cit., p. 8.
50. OECD, *Globalization of Industry* (1996a), p. 20.
51. Ibid., p. 21.
52. T. Levitt, 'The Globalization of Markets' (1983).
53. Bartlett and Ghoshal, op. cit., pp. 11–14.
54. Ibid., p. 16.
55. OECD, *Globalization of Industry* (1996a), pp. 16–17.
56. J. H. Dunning, *International Production and the Multinational Enterprise* (1981).
57. Bartlett and Ghoshal, op. cit., p. 144.
58. M. Porter, *The Competitive Advantage of Nations* (1990), p. 21.
59. M. Porter, *The Competitive Advantage of Nations* (1990).
60. Porter, *The Competitive Advantage*.
61. Bartlett and Ghoshal, op. cit., p. 127.
62. J. Stopford and L. T. Wells, *Managing the Multinational Enterprise: Organization of the Firm and Ownership of the Subsidiaries* (1972); T. W. Malknight, 'Globalization of an Ethnocentric Firm: An Evolutionary Perspective' (1995).
63. H. Mintzberg, *The Structure of Organizations* (1979).
64. B. Kogut, 'Designing Global Strategies: Profiting from Operational Flexibility' (1985).
65. C. A. Bartlett and S. Ghoshal, *Managing Across Borders: The Transnational Solution* (1990).
66. C. K. Pralahad and Y. L. Doz, *The Multinational Mission: Balancing Local Demands and Global Vision* (1987).
67. G. Hedlund, 'The Hypermodern MNG: A Hierarchy?' (1986).
68. M. Hanna, 'The Varieties of Multinational Firm Structures' (1995), pp. 209–15.
69. Ibid., p. 215.
70. J. Farley and S. Kobrin, 'Organizing the Global Multinational Firm' (1995), pp. 197–9.
71. Ibid.
72. Ibid., p. 208.
73. Petrella, op. cit., p. 76.
74. J. Bleeke and D. Ernst, *Collaborating to Compete: Using Strategic Alliances and Acquisitions in the Global Marketplace* (1993), pp. 1–2.
75. Bartlett and Ghoshal, *Transnational Management*, p. 368.
76. Ibid., pp. 368–9.

77. M. Y. Yoshino and U. S. Rangan, *Strategic Alliances: An Entrepreneurial Approach to Globalization* (1995), p. 17.
78. Ibid., pp. 19–21.
79. OECD, *The Globalization of Industry* (1996a), p. 44.
80. Ibid., p. 46.
81. Bartlett and Ghoshal, *Transnational Management*, pp. 376–8.
82. Ibid., pp. 379–82.
83. W. Vanhonacker, 'Entering China: An Unconventional Approach' (1997).
84. Bleeke and Ernst, op. cit., p. 9.
85. Bartlett and Ghoshal, *Transnational Management*, p. 116.
86. Levitt, op. cit.
87. *Guardian*, 8 February 1997.
88. Farley and Kobrin, op. cit., pp. 198–9.
89. Drache, op. cit., p. 57.
90. Bartlett and Ghoshal, *Transnational Management*, p. 117.
91. Ibid., p. 119.
92. OECD, *The Globalization of Industry* (1996a); J. de Vet, 'Globalization and Local and Regional Competitiveness' (1993); M. Storper and A. J. Scott, *The Wealth of Nations: Market Forces and Policy Imperatives in Local and Global Context* (1993).
93. OECD, *The Globalization of Industry* (1996a), p. 52.
94. De Vet, op. cit.
95. OECD, *The Globalization of Industry* (1996a), pp. 54–5.
96. Ibid., p. 55.
97. Ibid., p. 63.
98. Ibid., p. 59.
99. Lyon Group of Seven Meeting, 'Making a Success of Globalization for the Benefit of All' (June 1996).
100. Boyer and Drache, *States Against Markets* (1996).
101. *The Economist, World Economy Survey* (28 September 1996), p. 24.
102. A. Wood, *North–South Trade, Employment and Inequality* (1994).
103. *Economist*, op. cit., p. 33.
104. Ibid., p. 34.
105. Ibid.
106. Ibid.
107. M. Porter, 'Capital Disadvantage: America's Failing Capital Investment System' (1992).
108. *Economist*, op. cit., pp. 34, 37.
109. B. Arthur, 'Increasing Returns and the Two Worlds of Business' (1996).
110. Ibid.
111. Petrella, op. cit., pp. 78–9.
112. Ibid., pp. 80–81.
113. Kenneth Ohmae, 'The Rise of the Regional State' (1993), p. 78.
114. Drache, op. cit., p. 32.

115. J. Bhagwati, *Protectionism* (1998), p. 33.
116. L. Tyson, *Who's Bashing Whom? Trade Conflict in High Technology Industries* (1992).
117. Drache, op. cit., p. 44.
118. Ibid., p. 54.
119. T. Clarke, 'Rethinking Management in Government' (1994).
120. Weiss, op. cit., p. 10, citing Y.-S. Hu, 'Global or Stateless Corporations Are National Firms with International Operations' (1992).
121. Petrella, op. cit.; Weiss, op. cit.
122. Dicken, *Global Shift* (1992), p. 358.
123. O. Bertrand and T. Noyelle, *Human Resources and Corporate Strategy: Technological Change in Banks and Insurance Companies* (1988).
124. N. J. Thrift, 'The Geography of International Economic Disorder' (1989), p. 38.
125. Dicken, op. cit., p. 364.
126. D. Harvey, *The Condition of Postmodernity* (1992), p. 161.
127. B. Cohen, *The Edge of Chaos* (1997), pp. 27–9.
128. Harvey, op. cit.; V. Niederhoffer, *The Education of a Speculator* (1997).
129. Harvey, op. cit., p. 194.
130. Ibid., pp. 331–5.
131. Cohen, op. cit.
132. Harvey, op. cit., pp. 168–70.
133. Ibid., p. 166.
134. CBI, *Making It in Britain* (1992), p. 22.
135. Harvey, op. cit., pp. 162–3.

3: Digitalization

1. N. Negroponte, *Being Digital* (1995).
2. M. Estabrooks, *Electronic Technology, Corporate Strategy and World Transformation* (1995), p. ix.
3. *The Economist*, 28 September 1996.
4. D. Tapscott, *The Digital Economy: Promise and Peril in the Age of Networked Intelligence* (1996), p. 11.
5. Spectrum Strategy Consultants, *Development of the Information Society: An International Analysis* (1996), p. 4.
6. OECD, *Information Technology and New Growth Opportunities* (1989), p. 137.
7. Estabrooks, op. cit., p. 5.
8. *Economist*, 28 September 1996.
9. Kuhn; G. Dosi, *Technical Change and Industrial Transformation* (1983).
10. R. E. Freeman, 'The Challenges of New Technologies' in OECD (1987).
11. Ibid., p. 130.
12. J. A. Schumpeter, *Business Cycles* (1939); Freeman, op. cit.

13. Estabrooks, op. cit., p. 7.
14. D. B. Yoffie (ed.), *Competing in the Age of Digital Convergence* (1997), p. 4.
15. Estabrooks, op. cit., p. 3.
16. Ibid., p. 10.
17. Ibid., p. 8.
18. P. G. Keen, *Every Manager's Guide to Information Technology* (1995), p. 9.
19. Tapscott, op. cit., p. 75.
20. Keen, op. cit., pp. 8–30.
21. Estabrooks, op. cit., p. x.
22. *Economist*, 28 September 1996.
23. Ibid.
24. Estabrooks, op. cit., p. 2.
25. Ibid., p. 59.
26. Ibid., p. 63.
27. *New Statesman*, 18 January 1997.
28. D. Tapscott and A. Caston, *Paradigm Shift: The New Promise of Information Technology* (1993).
29. C. Y. Baldwin and K. B. Clarke, 'Competition Within a Modular Cluster 1985–1900' (1997), p. 127.
30. Estabrooks, op. cit., pp. 134–6.
31. Yoffie, op. cit. p. 18.
32. A. Rappaport and S. Halevi, 'The Computerless Computer Company' (1991).
33. Spectrum, op. cit., p. 100.
34. Tapscott, op. cit., p. 114.
35. Estabrooks, op. cit., p. 199.
36. J. K. Galbraith, *The New Industrial State* (1985), pp. 73–4.
37. *Economist*, 28 September 1996.
38. C. Goldfinger, 'The Intangible Economy and Its Implications for Statistics and Statisticians' (1996); D. Quah, 'The Invisible Hand and the Weightless Economy' (1996).
39. *Economist*, 28 September 1996.
40. A. Wyckoff, 'The Growing Strength of Services' (1996).
41. Estabrooks, op. cit., p. 200.
42. Ibid., p. 161.
43. Ibid.
44. Ibid., pp. 205–7.
45. S. Lash and J. Urry, *The End of Organized Capitalism* (1987), p. 117.
46. L. Thurow, *The Future of Capitalism* (1996).
47. Negroponte, op. cit., p. 23.
48. Estabrooks, op. cit., p. 130.
49. Tapscott, op. cit., p. xiv.
50. Spectrum, op. cit., pp. 86–7.

51. Tapscott, op. cit., p. 16.
52. Spectrum, op. cit., p. 87.
53. Ibid., p. 93.
54. Tapscott, op. cit., p. 18.
55. Spectrum, op. cit., p. 96.
56. Estabrooks, op. cit., p. 212.
57. *Economist*, 28 September 1996.
58. *Financial Times*, 4 December 1997.
59. Estabrooks, op. cit., p. 243.
60. L. Groth, *Building Organization With Information Technology* (1997).

4: Strategy

1. C. K. Prahalad and G. Hamel, 'Strategy as a Field of Study' (1994b), p. 5.
2. G. Hamel and C. K. Prahalad, *Competing for the Future* (1994).
3. Ibid., p. 9.
4. H. Mintzberg, *The Rise and Fall of Strategic Planning* (1994a).
5. G. Hamel and A. Heene, *Competence Based Competition* (1994), p. 1.
6. R. Whipp, 'Creative Deconstruction: Strategy and Organizations' (1996), p. 266.
7. J. Kay, *Foundations of Corporate Success: How Business Strategies Add Value* (1993), p. 337.
8. Prahalad and Hamel, op. cit., pp. 7–9.
9. M. de Kare-Silver, *Strategy in Crisis* (1997), p. 22.
10. P. Joyce and A. Woods, *Essential Strategic Management: From Modernism to Pragmatism* (1996), p. 25.
11. Hamel and Heene, op. cit., pp. 2–3.
12. Joyce and Woods, op. cit.
13. Ibid., p. 34.
14. Mintzberg, op. cit.; R. Stacey, *The Chaos Frontier* (1991).
15. J. B. Quinn, 'Strategic Change: Logical Incrementalism' (1991).
16. I. Ansoff and E. McDonnell, *Implanting Strategic Management* (1990)
17. Quinn, op. cit.
18. Mintzberg, op. cit.
19. Joyce and Woods, op. cit., pp. 34-44.
20. Kalchas Group, *Growth Through Revenues vs. Cost Cutting* (1995).
21. De Kare-Silver, op. cit.
22. Prahalad and Hamel, 'The Core Competence of the Corporation' (1991), p. 281.
23. De Kare-Silver, op. cit., pp. 37–52.
24. S. Makridakis, 'Metastrategy: Learning and Avoiding Past Mistakes' (1997), p. 132.
25. Hamel and Prahalad, op. cit., pp. 6–8.

26. Ibid., p. 9.
27. Mitchell and Co., 'Amputating Assets: Companies That Slash Jobs End Up with More Problems than Profits' (1992).
28. Hamel and Prahalad, op. cit., p. 21.
29. B. Burnes, *Managing Change* (1992); K. Lewin, 'Group Decisions and Social Change'; R. M. Kanter, *When Giants Learn to Dance*; E. H. Schein, *Organizational Culture and Leadership* (1992).
30. G. Morgan, *Imagination* (1991), p. 286.
31. B. G. Dale and C. L. Cooper, *TQM and Human Resources: An Executive Guide* (1992).
32. P. B. Crosby, *Quality Is Free* (1979); W. E. Deming, *Quality, Productivity and Competitive Advantage* (1982); J. M. Juran, *Quality Control Handbook* (1988); G. Taguchi, *Introduction to Quality Engineering* (1986).
33. Burnes, op. cit.
34. G. Rommel, F. Bruck, R. Diederichs, R. Kempis, H. Kaas, G. Fuhry and V. Kurfess, *Quality Pays* (1996).
35. H. Hammer and J. Champy, *Re-engineering the Corporation: A Manifesto for Business Revolution* (1993), p. 32.
36. Ibid., p. 35.
37. R. K. Talwar, 'Re-engineering – A Wonder Drug for the 90s?' (1994), pp. 43–5.
38. Ibid., pp. 50–52.
39. Kalchas Group, op. cit.
40. American Management Association, 'Downsizing' (1994).
41. C. Baden-Fuller and J. Stopford, *Rejuvenating the Mature Business* (1992).
42. Prahalad and Hamel, 'The Core Competence . . .', p. 280.
43. Baden-Fuller and Stopford, op. cit.
44. B. P. Burgers, C. W. L. Hill and W. C. Kim, 'A Theory of Global Strategic Alliances: The Case of the Global Auto Industry' (1993), p. 432.
45. P. Dussauge, S. Hart and B. Ramanantsoa, *Strategic Technology Management: Integrating Product Technology into Global Business Strategies for the 1990s* (1992), pp. 167–90.
46. R. Reich, *The Work of Nations* (1991), pp. 68–9.
47. Bogaert, Martens and van Cauwenbergh, 'Strategy as a Situational Puzzle' (1994).
48. J. Barney, 'Firm Resources and Sustained Competitive Advantage' (1991).
49. R. Hall, 'The Strategic Analysis of Intangible Resources' (1992).
50. R. Amit and P. J. H. Schoemaker, 'Strategic Assets and Organizational Rent' (1993).
51. R. M. Grant, 'The Resource Based Theory of Competitive Advantage' (1991).
52. I. Dierickx and K. Cool, 'Competitive Advantage' (1988).

53. H. Itami, *Mobilizing Invisible Assets* (1987).
54. R. Hall, 'The Contribution of Intangible Resources to Business Success' (1991).
55. Barney, op. cit.
56. G. Stalk, P. Evans and L. Schulman, 'Competing on Capabilities: The New Rules of Corporate Strategy' (1992).
57. B. Wernerfelt, 'A Resource Based View of the Firm' (1984).
58. D. Aaker, 'Managing Assets and Skills' (1989).
59. Itami, op. cit., p. 125.
60. Bogaert, Martens and van Cauwenbergh, op. cit., pp. 57–60.
61. R. P. Rumelt, 'Foreword' in Hamel and Heene, op. cit., p. xv.
62. Prahalad and Hamel, 'The Core Competence of the Corporation' (1990), p. 82.
63. Ibid., p. 83.
64. Rumelt, op. cit., p. xvii.
65. Hamel and Prahalad, *Competing for the Future* (1994), p. 19.
66. D. Band and G. Scanlon, 'Strategic Control Through Core Competencies' (1995), p. 110.
67. Hamel and Prahalad, *Competing for the Future*, p. 23.
68. Ibid., p. 293.
69. J. C. Collins and J. I. Porras, *Successful Habits of Visionary Companies* (1996), p. 43.
70. Ibid., p. 112.
71. P. Wack, 'Scenarios: Shooting the Rapids' (1985); van der Heijden, *Scenarios: The Art of Strategic Conversation* (1996).
72. P. O. Gaddis, 'Strategy Under Attack' (1997), p. 39.

5: Organization

1. See S. R. Clegg, *Modern Organizations: Organization Studies in the Postmodern World* (1990).
2. M. Weber, *The Protestant Ethic and the Spirit of Capitalism* (1936).
3. N. Albertsen, 'Postmodernism, Post-Fordism, and Critical Social Theory' (1988), p. 347.
4. M. Cusumano, *The Japanese Automobile Industry: Technology and Management at Nissan and Toyota* (1985).
5. K. Koike, 'Human Resource Development and Labor Management Relations' (1987).
6. M. Kenney and R. Florida, 'Beyond Mass Production: Production and the Labor Process in Japan' (1988), p. 132.
7. Ishikawa, *What is Total Quality Control* (1985), p. 45.
8. Imae, *Kaizen: The Key to Japan's Competitive Success* (1986), p. xxiii.
9. Sewell and Wilkinson, 'Someone to Watch Over Me' (1992).

10. C. F. Sabel, *Work and Politics* (1982), p. 220.
11. M. J. Piore and C. F. Sabel, *The Second Industrial Divide: Possibilities for Prosperity* (1984).
12. H. C. Katz and C. F. Sabel, 'Industrial Relations and Industrial Adjustments in the Car Industry' (1985); M. J. Piore, 'Perspectives on Labor Market Flexibility' (1986); see also C. Smith, 'Flexible Specialization, Automation and Mass Production' (1989), pp. 210–11.
13. E. H. Schein, *Organizational Culture and Leadership* (1992); K. E. Weick, 'The Social Psychology of Organizing' (1979).
14. Sewell and Wilkinson, op. cit.
15. W. Lewchuck and D. Robertson, 'Working Conditions under Lean Production: A Worker-Based Benchmarking Study?' (1996), p. 79.
16. Ibid., p. 61.
17. J. P. Womack, D. T. Jones and D. Roos, *The Machine That Changed the World* (1990).
18. Ibid., p. 102.
19. N. Oliver and B. Wilkinson, *The Japanization of British Industry* (1988); J. Morris and B. Wilkinson, 'The Transfer of Japanese Management to Alien Institutional Environments' (1995).
20. B. Sandkull, 'Lean Production: The Myth Which Changes the World?' (1996), p. 71.
21. K. Williams, C. Haslam, S. Johal and J. Williams, *Cars: Analysis, History, Cases* (1994).
22. C. Haslam and K. Williams, with S. Johal and J. Williams, 'A Fallen Idol? Japanese Management in the 1990s' (1996), p. 36.
23. W. E. Deming, *Japanese Methods for Productivity and Quality* (1981); *Quality, Productivity and Competitive Position* (1982); J. M. Juran, *Quality Control Handbook* (1988).
24. P. Dawson and G. Palmer, *Quality Management: The Theory and Practice of Implementing Change* (1995), pp. 3–4.
25. Ibid., Appendix III; Deming, *Quality, Productivity* . . . ; Juran, op. cit.; P. B. Crosby, *Quality Without Tears* (1984).
26. T. Kono and S. R. Clegg, *The Transformation of Japanese Corporate Cultures* (1998).
27. R. M. Hodgetts, F. Luthans and S. M. Lee, 'New Paradigm Organizations: From Total Quality to Learning to World-Class' (1994).
28. Kono and Clegg, op. cit.
29. Crosby, op. cit; *The Externally Successful Organization* (1984).
30. Dawson and Palmer, op. cit., pp. 29–37.
31. Ibid., pp. 29–30.
32. Ibid., p. 163.
33. Kono and Clegg, op. cit.
34. P. Dawson, *Organizational Change: A Processual Approach* (1994); Dawson and Palmer, op. cit.

35. Dawson and Palmer, op. cit., p. 181.

36. Ibid., p. 182.

37. A. Wilkinson, T. Redman and E. Snape, *Quality and the Manager* (1993); Dawson and Palmer, op. cit.

38. E. R. Burack, M. D. Burack, D. M. Miller and K. Morgan, 'New Paradigm Approaches in Strategic Human Resource Management' (1994), p. 142.

39. Ibid., p. 145.

40. M. Parker and J. Slaughter, *Choosing Sides: Unions and the Team Concept* (1988).

41. Dawson and Palmer, op. cit.

42. Ibid., pp. 183–4.

43. E. Mayo, *The Social Problems of an Industrial Civilization* (1947).

44. G. Zeitz and V. Mittal, 'Total Quality Management (The Deming Method As New Management Ideology: Institutionalization Patterns in the United States' (1993).

45. S. Gherardi, 'Organizational Learning' (1997), pp. 542–3.

46. C. Argyris and D. Schon, *Organizational Learning* (1978).

47. Gherardi, op. cit., p. 543.

48. Argyris and Schon, op. cit.

49. Gherardi, op. cit., p. 543.

50. R. Rothwell, 'Successful Industrial Innovation: Critical Factors for the 1990s' (1992).

51. Womack et al., op. cit.

52. Clegg, op. cit.; S. R. Clegg, W. Higgins and T. Spybey, '"Post-Confucianism", Social Democracy and Economic Culture' (1990); J. Marceau (ed.), *Reworking the World: Organizations, Technologies and Cultures in Comparative Perspective* (1992).

53. Rothwell, op. cit.

54. R. H. Hayes, S. C. Wheelwright and K. B. Clark, *Dynamic Manufacturing: Creating the Learning Organization* (1988), pp. 252–3.

55. P. S. Adler, 'The Learning Bureaucracy: New United Motor Manufacturing, Inc.' (1993); P. S. Adler and R. E. Cole, 'Designed for Learning: A Tale of Two Plants' (1993).

56. Especially J. G. March, 'Exploration and Exploitation in Organizational Learning' (1991); see also J. G. March, 'The Future, Disposable Organizations, and the Rigidities of Imagination' (1995); D. A. Levinthal and J. G. March, 'The Myopia of Learning' (1993).

57. W. B. Brown and N. Karagozoglu, 'Leading the Way to Faster New Product Development' (1993).

58. S. R. Clegg, *Frameworks of Power*; L. G. Bolman and T. E. Deal, *Deframing Organizations: Artistry, Choice and Leadership* (1991).

59. R. L. Daft and K. E. Weick, 'Towards a Model of Organizations As Interpretation Systems' (1982).

60. K. E. Weick, 'Drop Your Tools: An Allegory for Organization Studies' (1996); M. Janowitz, 'Changing Patterns of Organizational Authority: The Military Establishment' (1959).
61. K. E. Weick and F. Westley, 'Organizational Learning: Affirming an Oxymoron' (1996), p. 450.
62. Adler and Cole, op. cit.
63. K. Ellegård, 'Volvo – A Force for Fordist Retrenchment or Innovation in the Automobile Industry' (1996), p. 118.
64. Weick and Westley, op. cit., p. 450.
65. Ellegård, op. cit., p. 120.
66. T. Clarke, 'Imaginative Flexibility in Production Engineering at the Volvo Uddevalla Plant' (1991).
67. Levinthal and March, op. cit., p. 105.
68. M. Rawlinson and P. Wells, 'Taylorism, Lean Production and the Automotive Industry' (1996), p. 203.
69. Ibid.
70. Hodgetts, Luthans and Lee, op. cit., p. 14.
71. Burack et al., op. cit., pp. 153–4.
72. T. Peters, *Liberation Management* (1992).
73. McKinsey & Co. Inc., *Emerging Exporters: Australia's High Value-Added Manufacturing Exporters* (1993), p. 57.
74. S. L. Goldman and R. N. Nagel, 'Management, Technology and Agility: The Emergence of a New Era in Manufacturing' (1993).
75. R. H. Hayes, S. C. Wheelwright and K. B. Clark, *Dynamic Manufacturing: Creating the Learning Organization* (1988).
76. M. A. Cusumano and R. W. Selby, *Microsoft Secrets – How the World's Most Powerful Software Company Creates Technology, Shapes Markets, and Manages People* (1996).
77. Ibid., p. 9; what follows is taken from this account.
78. Ibid., p. 12.
79. Ibid., pp. 12–13.
80. Ibid., pp. 13–19.
81. Ibid., p. 14.
82. Ibid., p. 15.
83. Ibid., pp. 70–71.
84. Ibid., p. 56.
85. Ibid., Figure 6.1, p. 361.
86. K. H. Roberts and M. Grabowski, 'Organizations, Technology and Structuring' (1996), p. 411.
87. Ibid., p. 412.
88. Cusumano and Selby, op. cit.
89. Roberts and Grabowski, op. cit., p. 412.
90. Ibid.
91. Ibid., after Weick (1990).

92. Weick, 'Technology as Equivoque: Sense-making in New Technologies' (1990)

93. N. Nohria and J. D. Berkely, 'The Virtual Organization: Bureaucracy, Technology, and the Implosion of Control' (1994), p. 113.

94. D. G. Copeland and J. L. Mckenney, 'Airline Reservation Systems: Lessons from History' (1988).

95. Nohria and Berkely, op. cit., p. 119.

96. Roberts and Gradowski, op. cit., p. 416; Clegg, *Frameworks or Power*.

97. For instance, J. Rule and P. Brantley, 'Computerized Surveillance in the Workplace: Forms and Distribution' (1992).

98. S. Zuboff, *In the Age of the Smart Machine* (1992).

99. K. Robins and F. Webster, '"Revolution of the Fixed Wheel"': Information, Technology and Social Taylorism' (1993).

6: Stakeholders

1. R. Tricker, *Corporate Governance – An International Review* (1994), p. 520; T. Clarke and R. Bostock, 'International Corporate Governance: Convergence and Diversity' (1994).

2. *Financial Times*, 10 October 1997.

3. Ibid.

4. Peacock and Bannock, *Corporate Takeovers and the Public Interests* (1991), p. 10.

5. *Observer*, 2 November 1997.

6. Tricker, op. cit., pp. 482–3.

7. Demb and Neubauer, *Adding Value With the Corporate Board* (1989).

8. OECD, *OECD Economic Surveys: Japan* (1996), p. 143.

9. Committee on Corporate Governance, *The Financial Aspects of Corporate Governance* (The Cadbury Report) (1992).

10. CBI, *Making It in Britain* (1992), p. 23.

11. M. Porter, *Capital Choices: Changing the Way America Invests in Industry* (1992).

12. Ibid., p. 67.

13. D. Brewster, 'Short-termism, Stock Market Efficiency and the Takeover Process – An Overview' (1993).

14. M. Porter, 'Capital Disadvantage: America's Failing Capital Investment System' (1992), p. 70.

15. Ibid., p. 71.

16. Porter, *Capital Choices*, pp. 16–17.

17. *Observer*, 19 October 1997.

18. *Financial Times*, 29 October 1997.

19. OECD, *Financial Market Trends* (1995), p. 13.

20. Ibid., pp. 13–14.

21. Ibid., p. 23.
22. Ibid., p. 24.
23. Ibid., pp. 27–8.
24. *Financial Times*, 29 October 1998.
25. OECD, *Financial Market Trends* (1995), p. 22.
26. M. Lipton and J. Lorsch, 'A New Compact for Owners and Directors' (1991).
27. OECD, *Financial Market Trends*, p. 28.
28. Committee on Corporate Governance, op. cit.
29. Tricker, op. cit.; R. A. G. Monks and N. Minnow, *Corporate Governance* (1995); T. Clarke and R. Bostock, 'Governance in Germany: The Foundations of Corporate Structure' (1997).
30. OECD, *OECD Economic Surveys: Germany* (1995).
31. Ibid., pp. 85–6.
32. Ibid., pp. 84–5.
33. A. Viner, 'The Coming Revolution in Japan's Board Rooms' (1993).
34. C. Kester, *Japanese Takeovers: The Global Contest for Corporate Control* (1992).
35. Viner, op. cit.
36. OECD, *OECD Economic Surveys: Japan* (1996), p. 155.
37. T. Ishiguro, 'Japan' (1990).
38. K. Yoshimori, 'The Concept of the Corporation in Japan and the West' (1995).
39. Tricker, op. cit., p. 520.
40. *Financial Times*, 5 June 1997.
41. L. Thurow, 'Who Owns the 21st Century?' (1992), p. 6.
42. Tricker, op. cit., p. 520.
43. A. A. Berle and G. C. Means, *The Modern Corporation and Private Property* (1932), p. v.
44. M. M. Blair, *Ownership and Control: Rethinking Corporate Governance for the 21st Century* (1995), pp. 32–3.
45. Berle and Means, op. cit., p. 312.
46. A. A. Berle, 'For Whom Are Corporate Managers Trustees?' (1932).
47. J. J. Hanks, 'From the Hustings: The Role of States with Takeover Control Laws' (1994); Orts 'Beyond Shareholders' (1992); Hanks goes on to describe stakeholder theory as 'an idea whose time should never have come'.
48. S. M. H. Wallman, 'The Proper Interpretation of Corporate Constituency Statutes' (1991), p. 170.
49. Ibid., p. 170; Blair, op. cit.
50. Blair, op. cit., pp. 220–22.
51. Ibid., p. 222.
52. W. T. Allen, 'Our Schizophrenic Conception of the Business Corporation' (1992), p. 10.
53. M. Friedman, *Capitalism and Freedom* (1962), p. 113.

54. F. A. Hayek, *Law, Legislation, Liberty*, Vol. 3: *The Political Order of a Free People* (1979), p. 82.
55. Porter, *Capital Choices*.
56. Monks and Minnow, op. cit., p. 41.
57. J. Argenti 'Stakeholders: The Case Against' (1997).
58. A. Campbell, 'Stakeholders: The Case in Favour' (1997), p. 448.
59. T. Clarke 'Alternative Modes of Cooperable Production' (1984); 'In Defence of Mutuality' (1998).
60. Jacobs, 'The Environment as Stakeholder' (1997).
61. R. E. Freeman and D. L. Reed, 'Stockholders and Stakeholders: A New Perspective on Corporate Governance' (1983), p. 89.
62. I. Ansoff, *Corporate Strategy* (1965), p. 33.
63. R. E. Freeman, *Strategic Management: A Stakeholder Approach* (1983).
64. W. R. Dill, 'Public Participation in Corporate Planning' (1975), p. 60.
65. Freeman and Reed, op. cit., p. 91.
66. M. Clarkson, 'A Stakeholder Framework for Analysing and Evaluating Corporate Social Performance' (1995), p. 21.
67. RSA, *Tomorrow's Company: Final Report* (1995), p. 13.
68. J. Charkham, *Keeping Good Company: A Study of Corporate Governance in Five Countries* (1994), p. 336.
69. Hampel Committee on Corporate Governance (1997), pp. 1.16–1.17.
70. J. Kay, 'The Stakeholder Corporation' (1997), p. 135.
71. C. Handy, 'The Citizen Corporation' (1997).
72. T. A. Stewart, *Intellectual Capital: The New Wealth of Organizations* (1997), p. 32.
73. A. Anderson, *The Valuation of Intangible Assets* (1992).
74. Ibid., p. 8.
75. Ibid., p. 21.
76. Ibid., p. 22.
77. De Kare-Silver, *Strategy in Crisis* (1997), p. 204.
78. Stewart, op. cit., p. 33.
79. Ibid., p. 18.
80. P. Drucker, *Post-Capitalist Society* (1993).
81. R. Reich, *The Work of Nations* (1991).
82. I. Nonaka and H. Takeuchi, *The Knowledge Creating Company* (1995), p. 8.
83. R. M. Grant, 'The Knowledge-Based View of the Firm', *Long Range Planning*, Vol. 30, No. 3, 1997, p. 452.
84. *Fortune* magazine, July 1997, pp. 52–62.
85. J. P. Kotter and J. L. Heskett, *Corporate Culture and Performance* (1992).
86. J. Kay, *Foundations of Corporate Success: How Business Strategies Add Value* (1993).
87. *Financial Times*, 17 January 1996.
88. R. Waterman, *The Frontiers of Excellence – Learning from Companies That Put People First* (1994), p. 26.

89. P. Doyle, 'Setting Business Objectives and Measuring Performance' (1994).

90. BOC, *Building Global Excellence* (1994), p. 16.

91. W. Hutton, *The State We're In* (1995); *The State to Come* (1997).

92. Hutton, 'An Overview of Stakeholding' (1997); *The State to Come*.

93. M. Nuti, 'Democracy and Economy: What Role for Stakeholders?' (1997), p. 19.

94. OECD, *OECD Economic Surveys*: Germany, 1995; *OECD Economic Surveys*: Japan, 1996.

95. K. Yoshimori, 'The Concept of the Corporation in Japan and the West' (1995); T. W. Zimmerer and R. F. Green, 'Pressure from Stakeholders Hits Japanese Corporations' (1996); OECD (1996).

96. *Financial Times*, 10 October 1997.

97. R. Zimmerman, 'No Entity Without Identity – Communication Strategies of Corporate Germany in the Early 1990s' (1998), pp. 251–257.

98. *Manager* magazine, July 1997, p. 133.

99. Zimmerman, op. cit.

100. H. Gruner, 'The Current Situation of the Conception of Stakeholder in German Industry' (1998).

101. Ibid.

102. Yoshimori, op. cit.

103. OECD, *Economic Surveys: Japan* (1996).

104. Preston, 'Stakeholder Management and Corporate Performance' (1990), p. 362; Clarkson, op. cit.

105. C. W. Hill and T. M. Jones, 'Stakeholder Agency Theory' (1994), pp. 132–4.

106. T. Jones, 'Instrumental Stakeholder Theory: A Synthesis of Ethics and Economics' (1995).

107. T. Donaldson and L. E. Preston, 'The Stakeholder Theory of the Corporation: Concepts, Evidence, and Implications' (1995), p. 75.

108. RSA, op. cit., p. iii.

109. Karpin Industry Task Force on Leadership and Management Skills, *Enterprising Nation: Renewing Australia's Managers to Meet the Challenge of the Asia-Pacific Century* (1995).

110. RSA, op. cit., p. 1.

111. E. Scholes and D. Clutterbuck, 'Planning Stakeholder Communication' (1998).

112. D. Wheeler and M. Sillanpaa, *The Stakeholder Corporation* (1997).

113. M. Power, *The Audit Explosion* (1994).

114. Stewart, op. cit.

115. T. Smith, *Accounting for Growth* (1996), p. 10.

116. Monks and Minnow, op. cit., p. 49.

117. Ibid., p. 56.

118. Ibid.

119. A. Rappaport, *Creating Shareholder Value: The New Standard for Business Performance* (1986), p. 12.

120. P. Drucker, *The New Realities* (1990), p. 222.

121. Stewart, op. cit., p. 59.

122. E. Monkhouse, *Benchmarking SMEs: Innovation, Quality and Performance* (1995), p. i.

123. Ibid., p. 28.

124. R. C. Camp, *Benchmarking* (1989).

125. R. S. Kaplan and D. P. Norton, *The Balanced Scorecard* (1996), p. 7.

126. Ibid., p. 150.

127. Ibid.

128. M. Boiset and J. Child, 'From Fiefs to Clans: Explaining China's Economic Order' (1996).

129. J. Plender, *A Stake in the Future: The Stakeholding Solution* (1997), p. 2.

7: Sustainability

1. R. Gray, 'Corporate Reporting for Sustainable Development' (1996), p. 173.

2. World Commission on Environment and Development, 'Our Common Future' (1987), p. 80.

3. W. E. Stead and J. G. Stead, 'Strategic Management for a Small Planet' (1996), pp. 79, 82.

4. Gray, op. cit., p. 182.

5. J. Robertson, 'Shaping the Post-Modern Economy' (1996), p. 20.

6. V. Shiva, *Ecology and the Politics of Survival* (1991).

7. S. L. Hart, *Strategies for a Sustainable World* (1997), p. 68.

8. Ibid., p 69

9. Ibid., p. 70.

10. Ibid., p. 71.

11. Ibid.

12. R. Gray, D. Walters, J. Bebbington and I. Thompson, 'The Greening of Enterprise: An Exploration of the (Non) Role of Environmental Accounting and Environmental Accountants in Organizational Change (1995).

13. T. N. Gladwin, J. J. Kennelly and T.-S. Krause, 'Shifting Paradigms for Sustainable Development: Implications for Management Theory and Research' (1995).

14. R. E. Purser, C. Park and A. Montuori, 'Limits to Anthropocentrism: Towards an Ecocentric Organization Paradigm?' (1995).

15. Gladwin et al., op. cit., p. 878.

16. Ibid., p. 891.

17. M. Porter, 'America's Green Strategy' (1996), p. 31.

18. Ibid., p. 33.

19. M. Porter and C. van der Linde, 'Green and Competitive: Ending the Stalemate' (1996), p. 69.

20. Ibid., pp. 71-2.

21. I. Miller and F. Szekely, 'What is Green?' (1995), p. 331.

22. Ibid.

23. Ibid., p. 332.

24. R. Clift and A. Longley, 'Introduction to Clean Technology' (1996), p. 111.

25. Glarinin and Stahel, *The Limits to Certainty* (1989); Jackson, *Clean Production Strategies* (1993).

26. Clift and Longley, op. cit., p. 119.

27. C. Hutchinson, 'Corporate Strategy for the Environment' (1996).

28. P. Shrivastava, 'Ecocentric Management for a Risk Society' (1995).

29. Ibid., p. 128.

30. P. Shrivastava, *Greening Business: Profiting the Corporation and the Environment* (1996), pp. 33–4.

31. Hart, op. cit., p. 71.

32. Ibid., p. 72.

33. Ibid., p. 75.

34. J. Magretta, 'Growth Through Global Sustainability' (1997), p. 79.

35. Ibid., p. 82.

36. Ibid.

37. J. Maxwell, S. Rothenberg, F. Briscoe and A. Marcus, 'Green Schemes: Corporate Environmental Strategies and Their Implementation' (1997).

38. Ibid., p. 123.

39. Ibid., p. 126.

40. Ibid., p. 131.

41. D. A. Rondinelli and G. Vastag, 'International Environmental Standards and Corporate Policies' (1996), p. 107.

42. ISO, *Environmental Management Systems: General Guidelines on Principles, Systems, and Supporting Techniques* (1995), p. 16.

43. Rondinelli and Vastag, op. cit., p. 109.

44. Ibid.

45. Gray, op. cit., p. 185.

46. Ibid., pp. 174–5.

47. Pearce et. al. (1989).

48. Gray, op. cit., p. 184; Blueprint for a Green Economy.

49. Gray, op. cit., p. 189.

8: Conclusions

1. F. Capra, *A Systems Approach to the Emerging Paradigm* (1993).

2. J. A. Schumpeter, *Capitalism, Socialism and Democracy* (1942).

3. J. C. Collins and J. I. Porras, *Successful Habits of Visionary Companies* (1996).

BIBLIOGRAPHY

Aaker, D. A., 'Managing Assets and Skills', *California Management Review*, 31, 2 (1989), pp. 91–106

Abrahamson, E., 'The Emergence and Prevalence of Employee Management Rhetorics: The Effects of Long Waves, Labour Unions, and Turnovers, 1875 to 1992', *Academy of Management Journal*, 40, 3 (1997), pp. 491–533

Ackoff, R. L., *The Democratic Organization* (New York: Oxford University Press, 1994)

Adler, P. S., 'The Learning Bureaucracy: New United Motor Manufacturing, Inc.', *Research in Organization Behaviour* (1993), pp. 111–94

Adler, P. S., and R. E. Cole, 'Designed for learning: a tale of two plants', *Sloan Management Review*, 34, 3 (1993), pp. 85–94

Akerberg, A., *The Process of Transforming Individual Competence into Organizational Competence in Professional Organizations* (Helsinki: Swedish School of Economics and Business Administration, 1989)

Albertsen, N., 'Postmodernism, Post-Fordism, and Critical Social Theory', *Environment and Planning D: Society and Space*, 6 (1988), pp. 339–66

Alchian, A. A., and H. Demsetz, 'Production, Information Costs, and Economic Organization', *American Economic Review*, 62 (1972), pp. 777–95

Allen, W. T., 'Our Schizophrenic Conception of the Business Corporation', *Cardozo Law Review*, 14, 2 (1992), pp. 261–81

American Management Association, 'Downsizing', *AMA Survey* (July 1994)

Amit, R., and P. J. H. Schoemaker, 'Strategic Assets and Organizational Rent', *Strategic Management Journal*, 14, 1 (1993), pp. 33–46

Anderson, A., *The Valuation of Intangible Assets* (London: Arthur Anderson, 1992)

Anderson, P., *The Transition from Feudalism to Capitalism* (London: New Left Books, 1979)

Ansoff, I., *Corporate Strategy* (New York: McGraw-Hill, 1965/London: Penguin, 1968)

Ansoff, I., and E. McDonnell, *Implanting Strategic Management* (London: Prentice Hall, 1990)

Aoki, M., B. Gustafsson and O. Williamson, *The Firm as a Nexus of Treaties* (London: 1990)

J. Argenti, 'Stakeholders the Case Against', *Long Range Planning*, Vol. 30, No. 3 (1997) pp. 442–45

Argyris, C., and D. Schon (eds.), *Organizational Learning* (Cambridge: Addison-Wesley, 1978)

Arthur Anderson, *The Valuation of Intangible Assets*, Report for the Hundred Group of Financial Directors (London: Arthur Anderson, 1992)

Arthur, B., 'Increasing Returns and the Two Worlds of Business', *Harvard Business Review* (July 1996)

Baden-Fuller, C., and J. Stopford, *Rejuvenating the Mature Business* (London: Routledge, 1992)

Baldwin, C. Y., and K. B. Clarke, 'Competition Within a Modular Cluster 1985–1900', in Yoffie (ed.), *Competing in the Age of Digital Convergence*

Band, D., and G. Scanlon, 'Strategic Control Through Core Competencies', *Long Range Planning*, 28, 2 (1995), pp. 102–14

Barker, J. A., *Paradigms: Understand the Future in Business and Life* (Melbourne: Business Library, 1992)

Barley, S. R., and G. Kunda, 'Design and Devotion: Surges of Rational and Normative Ideologies of Control in Managerial Discourse', *Administrative Science Quarterly*, 37 (1992), pp. 363–99

Barney, J., 'Firm Resources and Sustained Competitive Advantage', *Journal of General Management*, 17, 1 (1991), pp. 99–120

Bartlett, C. A., and S. Ghoshal, *Managing Across Borders: The Transnational Solution* (Boston: Harvard Business School Press, 1990)

— 'Changing the Role of Top Management: Beyond Systems to People', *Harvard Business Review* (May–June 1995)

— *Transnational Management* (Chicago: Irwin, 1995)

Beck, U., *Risikogesellschaft* (Frankfurt-am-Main: Suhrkamp, 1986)

Beniger, J. R., The Control Revolution; Technological and Economic Origins of the Information Society (1986)

Bennis, W., 'Creative Leadership', *Management*, 10 (November 1993), pp. 10–15

Bennis, W., J. Parikh and R. Lessem, *Beyond Leadership: Balancing Economics, Ethics and Ecology* (Oxford: Blackwell, 1994)

Berle, A. A., 'For Whom Are Corporate Managers Trustees?' *Harvard Law Review*, 45 (1932), pp. 1365, 1367

Berle, A. A., and G. C. Means, *The Modern Corporation and Private Property* (New York: Commerce Clearing House, 1932; rep. New York: Harcourt, Brace and World, 1962)

Bertrand, O., and T. Noyelle, *Human Resources and Corporate Strategy: Technological Change in Banks and Insurance Companies* (Paris: OECD, 1988)

Bhagwati, J., *Protectionism* (Boston: MIT Press, 1998)

Bidault, F., and T. Cummings, 'Innovating Through Alliances', *R&D Management*, 24, 1 (1994), pp. 33–45

Blair, M. M., *Ownership and Control: Rethinking Corporate Governance for the 21st Century* (Washington, DC: Brookings Institute, 1995)

Bleeke, J., and D. Ernst, *Collaborating to Compete: Using Strategic Alliances and Acquisitions in the Global Marketplace* (New York: Wiley, 1993)

BOC/London Business School, *Building Global Excellence* (BOC/London Business School, 1994)

Bogeart, I., R. Martens, A. Ven Carwenbergh, 'Strategy as a Situational Puzzle: The Fit of Components', in G. Hamel and A. Heene, *Competence-Based Competition* (Chichester: John Wiley & Sons, 1994), pp. 57–76

Boisot, M., and J. Child, 'From Fiefs to Clans: Explaining China's Economic Order', *Administrative Science Quarterly*, 41 (1996), pp. 614–25

Bolman, L. G., and T. E. Deal, *Reframing Organizations: Artistry, Choice and Leadership* (San Francisco: Jossey-Bass, 1991)

Boston Consulting Group, 'The Australian Manager of the Twenty-First Century', in Karpin Industry Task Force on Leadership and Management Skills (eds.), *Enterprising Nation* (1995), pp. 1223–88

Bowman, E., and B. Kogut (eds.), *Redesigning the Firm* (New York: Oxford University Press, 1995)

Boyer, R., and D. Drache, *States Against Markets: The Limits of Globalization* (London: Routledge, 1996)

Bradley, S., *Globalization, Technology and Competition: The Fusion of Computers and Telecommunications in the 1990s* (Boston: Harvard Business School Press, 1993)

Brewster, D., 'Short-termism, Stock Market Efficiency and the Takeover Process – An Overview', *British Review of Economic Issues*, 15, 35 (1993), pp. 1–21

Brown, W. B., and N. Karagozoglu, 'Leading the Way to Faster New Product Development', *Academy of Management Executive*, 7, 1 (1993), pp. 36–47

Bryman, A. *Charisma and Leadership of Organisations* (London: Sage, 1992).

Brynjolfsson, E., T. Malone, V. Gurbaxani and A. Kambi, 'Does Information Technology Lead to Smaller Firms?', *Management Science*, 40 (12 December 1994)

Buckley, R., *Fairer Global Trade? The Challenge for the WTO, Understanding Global Issues* (Cheltenham: Understanding Global Issues Limited, 1996)

Burack, E. R., M. D. Burack, D. M. Miller and K. Morgan, 'New Paradigm Approaches in Strategic Human Resource Management', *Group and Organization Management*, 19, 2 (1994), pp. 141–59.

Burgers, W. P., C. W. L. Hill and W. C. Kim, 'A Theory of Global Strategic Alliances: The Case of the Global Auto Industry', *Strategic Management Journal*, 14 (1993), pp. 419–32

Burnes, B., *Managing Change* (London: Pitman, 1992)

Burns, T., G. and M. Stalker, *The Management of Innovation* (Oxford: Oxford University Press, 1994)

Burrell, G., 'Organization Paradigms', in A. Sorge and M. Warner (eds.), *International Encyclopedia of Business and Management: The Handbook of Organizational Behaviour* (London: International Thomson Business Press, 1997), pp. 33–47

Burrell, G., and G. Morgan, *Sociological Paradigms and Organizational Analysis* (London: Heinemann, 1979)

Callan, V., 'Career Transitions: The Transition from Specialist to Manager', in Karpin Industry Task Force on Leadership and Management Skills (eds.), *Enterprising Nation* (1995), vol. 2, pp. 117–54

Camp, R. C., *Benchmarking* (White Plains, NY: Quality Resources, 1989)

Campbell, A. 'Stakeholders: The Case in Favour', *Long Range Planning*, Vol. 30, No. 3 (1997), pp. 446–49

Capra, F. 'A Systems Approach to the Emerging Paradigm,' in M. Ray and A. Rinzler, *The New Paradigm Business* (New York: G. P. Putnam's and Sons)

Centre for Exploitation of Science and Technology (CEST), *Industry and the Environment: A Strategic Overview* (London: CEST, 1990)

CBI, *Making It in Britain* (London: Confederation of British Industry, 1992)

Chamberlain, N. W., *The Limits of Corporate Social Responsibility* (New York: Basic Books, 1973)

Champy, J., *Re-engineering Management: The Mandate for New Leadership* (London: HarperCollins, 1995)

Chandler, A. D., 'The Evolution of the Modern Global Corporation', in Porter (ed.), *Competition in Global Industries*, pp. 405–48

— *Scale and Scope* (Cambridge, Mass.: Harvard University Press, 1990)

Chappell, T., *The Soul of a Business: Managing for Profit* (New York: Bantam, 1993)

Charkham, J., 'Corporate Governance: Lessons from Abroad', *European Business Journal*, 4, 2 (1992), pp. 8–16

— *Keeping Good Company: A Study of Corporate Governance in Five Countries* (Oxford: Clarendon Press, 1994)

Ciborra, C., 'The Limits of Strategic Information Systems', *International Journal of Information Resource Management*, 2, 3 (1991), pp. 11–17

CIMA, *Performance Measurement in Business Services/The Manufacturing Sector* (Cambridge: Chartered Institute of Management Accountants, 1993)

Clarke, T., 'Rethinking Management in Government', in Clarke and Monkhouse (eds.), *Rethinking the Company*

— 'Corporate Governance Research', *Corporate Governance: an International Review*, 6, 1 (1998), pp. 57–66

— 'The Stakeholder Corporation', *Long Range Planning*, 31, 2 (1998)

— 'Imaginative Flexibility in Production Engineering: the Volvo Uddevalla Plant', in P. Blyton and J. Morris, *A Flexible Future: Prospects for Employment and Organization* (Berlin: Walter de Gruyter, 1991)

— 'Alternative Modes of Co-operative Production', *Economic and Industrial Democracy*, Vol. 5 (1984), pp. 97–129

— 'In Defence of Mutuality', *Business Ethics – A European Review*, Vol. 7, no. 2 (1998), pp. 97–102

Clarke, T., and R. Bostock, 'International Corporate Governance: Convergence and Diversity', in Clarke and Monkhouse (eds.), *Rethinking the Company*

— 'Governance in Germany: The Foundations of Corporate Structure', in Kesey et. al., *Corporate Governance – Economic Management and Financial Issues*

Clarke, T., and E. Monkhouse (eds.), *Rethinking the Company* (London: Financial Times/Pitman Press, 1994)

Clarkson, M., 'A Stakeholder Framework for Analysing and Evaluating Corporate Social Performance', *Academy of Management Review*, 20, 1 (1995), pp. 92–117

Clegg, S. R., *The Theory of Power and Organization* (London: Routledge and Kegan Paul, 1979)

— *Frameworks of Power* (London: Sage, 1989)

— *Modern Organizations: Organization Studies in the Postmodern World* (London: Sage, 1990)

Clegg, S. R., and D. Dunkerley, *Organization, Class and Control* (London: Routledge and Kegan Paul, 1980)

Clegg, S. R., C. Hardy and W. R. Nord (eds.), *Handbook of Organization Studies* (London: Sage, 1996)

Clegg, S. R., W. Higgins and T. Spybey, ' "Post-Confucianism", Social Democracy and Economic Culture', in S. R. Clegg, S. G. Redding and M. Cartner (eds.), *Capitalism in Contrasting Cultures* (Berlin: de Gruyter, 1990)

Clift, R. and A. Longley, 'Introduction to Clean Technology', in R. Welford and R. Starkey (eds.), *Business and the Environment* (London: Earthscan, 1996)

Coase, R., 'The Nature of the Firm', *Economica*, NS 4 (1937), pp. 386–405

Cohen, B., *The Edge of Chaos* (Chichester: Wiley, 1997)

Collins, J. C., and J. I. Porras, *Successful Habits of Visionary Companies* (London: Century, 1996)

Collis, D. J., P. W. Bane and S. P. Bradley, 'Industry Structure in the Converging World of Telecommunications, Computers and Entertainment', in Yoffie (ed.), *Competing in the Age of Digital Convergence*

Committee on Corporate Governance, *The Financial Aspects of Corporate Governance* (The Cadbury Report) (London: Stock Exchange, Gee & Co., 1992)

The Committee on Corporate Governance (Hampel Committee), *Final Report* (London: Gee and Company, 1997)

Common, M., 'What is Ecological Economics?' Proceedings of the Inaugural Conference of the Australia and New Zealand Society of Ecological Economics (Coffs Harbour, NSW: 19 November 1995), pp. 1–16

Conference Board Europe, *Change Management: An Overview of Current Initiatives* (Brussels: Conference Board, 1994)

Congress of the United States, *Multinationals and the US Technology Base* (Washington DC: Office of Technology Assessment, 1994)

Copeland, D. G., and J. L. Mckenney, 'Airline Reservation Systems: Lessons from History', *MIS Quarterly*, 12, 3 (1988), pp. 353–69

Coulson-Thomas, C. *Transforming the Company: Bridging the Gap Between Management Myth and Corporate reality* (London: Kogan Page, 1992)

— (ed.), *Business Process Re-engineering: Myth and Reality* (London: Kogan Page, 1994)

Covey, S., *The Seven Habits of Highly Effective People* (New York: Simon and Schuster, 1989)

Crandell, R. W., and K. Flamm (eds.), *Changing the Rules: Technological Change, International Competition, and Regulation in Communications* (Washington, DC: Brookings Institute, 1989)

Crosby, P. B., *Quality Is Free* (New York: McGraw-Hill, 1979)

— *Quality Without Tears* (New York: McGraw-Hill, 1984)

— *The Externally Successful Organization* (New York: McGraw-Hill, 1984)

Cross, K., J. J. Feather and R. L. Lynch, *Corporate Renaissance: The Art of Re-engineering* (Oxford: Blackwell Business, 1994)

Cusumano, M., *The Japanese Automobile Industry: Technology and Management at Nissan and Toyota* (Cambridge, Mass.: Harvard University Press, 1985)

Cusumano, M. A., and R. W. Selby, *Microsoft Secrets – How the World's Most Powerful Software Company Creates Technology, Shapes Markets, and Manages People* (New York: HarperCollins Business, 1996)

Cusumano, M. A., and S. A. Smith, 'Beyond the Waterfall: Software Development at Microsoft', in Yoffie (ed.), *Competing in the Age of Digital Convergence*, pp. 371–411

Cyert, R. M., and J. G. March, *A Behavioral Theory of the Firm* (Englewood Cliffs, NJ: Prentice Hall, 1963)

Daft, R. L., and K. E. Weick, 'Towards a Model of Organizations as Interpretation Systems', *Academy of Management Review*, 9, 2 (1982), pp. 284–95

Dale, B. G., and C. L. Cooper, *TQM and Human Resources: An Executive Guide* (Oxford: Blackwell, 1992)

Davenport, T. H., and J. E. Short, 'The New Industrial Engineering: Information Technology and Business Process Redesign', *Sloan Management Review*, 11 (Summer, 1990)

Davidow, W. H., and M. A. Malone, *The Virtual Corporation: Structuring and Revitalizing the Corporation for the 21st Century* (New York: HarperCollins, 1992)

Dawson, P., *Organizational Change: A Processual Approach* (London: Chapman, 1994)

Dawson, P., and G. Palmer, *Quality Management: The Theory and Practice of Implementing Change* (Melbourne: Longman, 1995)

DeCieri, H., D. Samson, and A. Sohal, (1991), 'Implementation of TQM in an Australian Manufacturing Company', *International Journal of Quality and Reliability Management*, Vol. 8, No. 5, pp. 55-65

de Geus, A., *The Living Company* (London: Nicholas Brealey, 1997)

de Kare-Silver, M., *Strategy in Crisis* (London: Macmillan, 1997)

de Vet, J., 'Globalization and Local and Regional Competitiveness', *STI Review*, 13 (Paris: OECD, 1993)

de Wit, B., and R. Meyer, *Strategy: Process, Content, Context* (Minneapolis-St Paul: West Publishing, 1994)

DeGreene, K. B., 'Long Wave Cycles of Sociotechnical Change and Innovation: A Macro-psychological Perspective', *Journal of Occupational Psychology*, 61 (1988), pp. 7–23

Demb, A. and F. Friedrich Neubauer, *Adding Value with the Corporate Board* (Lausanne: International Institute for Management Development, 1989)

Deming, W. E., *Japanese Methods for Productivity and Quality* (Washington, DC: George Washington University, 1981)

—*Quality, Productivity and Competitive Position* (Cambridge, Mass.: MIT Press, 1982)

Dicken, P. *Global Shift: The Internationalisation of Economic Activity* (London: Paul Chapman, 1992)

Dicrickx, I. and K. Cool, 'Competitive Advantage', INSEAD Working Paper 88/07 (January 1988)

Dill, W. R., 'Public Participation in Corporate Planning', *Long Range Planning* (1975), pp. 57–63

DiMaggio, P., and W. Powell, 'The Iron Cage Revisited: Institutional Isomorphism and Collective Rationality in Organizational Fields', *American Sociological Review*, 48, 2 (1983), pp. 147–60

Dodgson, M., and R. Rothwell, *The Handbook of Industrial Innovation* (London: Edward Elegar, 1994)

Donaldson, L., *American Anti-Management Theories of Organization: A Critique of Paradigm Proliferation* (Cambridge: Cambridge University Press, 1995)

Donaldson, L., and J. H. Davis, 'Stewardship Theory or Agency Theory: CEO Governance and Shareholder Returns', *Australian Journal of Management*, 16 (1991), pp. 49–64

—'Boards and Company Performance', *Corporate Governance – An International Review*, 2 (1994), pp. 141–50

Donaldson, T., and T. W. Dunfee, 'Toward a Unified Conception of Business Ethics: Integrative Social Contract Theory', *Academy of Management Review*, 19 (1994), pp. 252–84

Donaldson, T., and L. E. Preston, 'The Stakeholder Theory of the Corporation: Concepts, Evidence, and Implications', *Academy of Management Review*, 20, 1 (1995), pp. 65–91

Dosi, G., *Technical Change and Industrial Transformation* (London: Macmillan, 1983)

Doyle, P., 'Setting Business Objectives and Measuring Performance', *Journal of General Management*, 20, 2 (Winter 1994)

Doz, Y. L., and C. K. Prahalad, 'Managing DMNCs: A Search for a New Paradigm', in H. Vernon-Wertzel and L. Wertzel (eds.), *Strategic Management in a Global Economy* (London: Wiley, 1997)

Doz, Y. L., C. A. Bartlett and C. K. Prahalad, 'Global Competitive Pressures and Host Country Demands', *California Management Review*, 223, 3 (1981)

Drache, D., 'From Keynes to K-Mart: Competitiveness in a Corporate Age', in Boyer and Drache, *States Against Markets*

Drucker, P., 'The Coming of the New Organization', *Harvard Business Review* (January–February 1988), pp. 45–53

— *The New Realities* (London: Heinemann, 1989/Mandarin, 1990)

— 'The New Productivity Challenge', *Harvard Business Review* (November–December 1991)

— *Post-Capitalist Society* (Oxford: Butterworth Heinemann, 1993/New York: HarperCollins, 1993)

Dunning, J. H., *International Production and the Multinational Enterprise* (Winchester, Mass.: Allen & Unwin, 1981)

— *Multinational Enterprises and the Global Economy* (Wokingham: Addison Wesley, 1993)

Dussauge, P., S. Hart and B. Ramanantsoa, *Strategic Technology Management: Integrating Product Technology into Global Business Strategies for the 1990s* (Wiley, 1992)

Earl, M. J., *Management Strategies for Information Technology* (London: Prentice Hall, 1989)

Earl, M. J., 'The New and the Old of Business Process Design', *Journal of Strategic Information Systems*, Vol. 3, No. 1 (1994), pp. 5–22

Eccles, R. G., 'The Performance Measurement Manifesto', *Harvard Business Review* (January–February 1991), pp. 131–7

Eccles, R. G., and N. Nohria (with James D. Berkely), *Beyond the Hype: Rediscovering the Essence of Management* (Boston: Harvard Business School Press, 1992)

Economist, *World Economic Survey* (London: Economist Publications, 28 September 1996)

Egan, B. L., *Information Superhighways: The Economics of Advanced Public Communications Networks* (Boston: Artech House, 1991)

Egri, C. P., and L. Pinfield, 'Organizations and the Biosphere: Ecologies and Environment', in Clegg et. al., *Handbook of Organization Studies*, pp. 449–83.

Elkington, J., with T. Burke, *The Green Capitalists: Industry's Search for Environmental Excellence* (London: Victor Gollancz, 1987)

Ellegård, K., 'Volvo – A Force for Fordist Retrenchment or Innovation in the Automobile Industry?', *Asia Pacific Business Review*, 2, 4 (1996), pp. 117–35

Estabrooks, M., *Programmed Capitalism: A Computer Mediated Global Society* (New York: M. E. Sharpe Inc., 1988)

—*Electronic Technology, Corporate Strategy and World Transformation* (Westport, Conn.: Quorum Books, 1995)

European Commission, *Growth, Competitiveness and Employment: The Challenges and Way Forward for the 21st Century* (White Paper) (Brussels: Commission of the European Communities, 1994)

European Foundation for Quality Management, *The European Quality Award* (Eindhoven: EFQM, 1992)

Ezzamel, M., and H. Willmott, 'New Management Thinking', *European Management Journal*, 12 (1993), pp. 454–61

Fama, E., and M. Jensen, 'Agency Problems and Residual Claims', *Journal of Law and Economics*, 26 (1983), pp. 327–49

—'Separation of Ownership and Control', *Journal of Law and Economics*, 26 (1985), pp. 301–26

Farley, J., and S. Kobrin, 'Organizing the Global Multinational Firm', in Bowman and Kogut (eds.), *Redesigning the Firm*

Fayol, H., *General and Industrial Management* (London: Pitman, 1949)

Ferguson, C., 'Computers and the Coming of the US Keiretsu', *Harvard Business Review* (July–August 1990), pp. 55–70

Florida, R., 'Lean and Green: The Move to Environmentally Conscious Manufacturing', *California Management Review*, 39, 1 (1996), pp. 80–105

Forester, T., *High Tech Society: The Story of the Information Technology Revolution* (Cambridge, Mass.: MIT Press, 1987)

Foucault, M., *Discipline and Punish* (Harmondsworth: Penguin, 1976)

Freeman, C., 'The Challenge of New Technologies', in OECD, *Interdependence and Co-operation in Tomorrow's World* (Paris: OECD, 1987)

Freeman, C., J. Clark and L. Soete, *Unemployment and Technical Innovation* (London: Frances Pinter, 1982)

Freeman, R. E., *Strategic Management: A Stakeholder Approach* (Marshfield, Mass.: Pitman, 1983)

Freeman, R. E., and D. L. Reed, 'Stockholders and Stakeholders: A New Perspective on Corporate Governance', *California Management Review*, 25, 3 (1983), pp. 88–106

Friedman, M., *Capitalism and Freedom* (Chicago: University of Chicago Press, 1962)

Fulk, J., and G. DeSanctis, 'Electronic Communication and Changing Organizational Forms', *Organization Science*, 6, 4 (1995), pp. 337–49

Gaddis, P. O., 'Strategy Under Attack', *Long Range Planning*, 30, 1 (1997), pp. 38–45

Galbraith, J. K., *The New Industrial State* (Boston: Houghton Mifflin, 1985)

Garratt, B., *Developing Strategic Thought: Rediscovering the Art of Direction-Giving* (London: McGraw-Hill, 1995)

Garvin, D. A., 'How the Baldrige Award Really Works', *Harvard Business Review* (November–December 1991), pp. 80–93

Gherardi, S., 'Organizational Learning', in A. Sorge and M. Warner (eds.), *International Encyclopedia of Business and Management: The Handbook of Organizational Behaviour* (London: International Thomson Business Press, 1997), pp. 542–5

Ghoshal, S., and C. A. Bartlett, *The Individualized Corporation* (London: Heinemann, 1998)

Gill, J., and S. Whittle, 'Management by Panacea: Accounting for Transience', *Journal of Management Studies*, 30 (1993), pp. 281–95

Gladwin, T. N., 'Environmental Policy Trends Facing Multinationals', *California Management Review*, 20, 2 (Winter 1997), pp. 81–93

Gladwin, T. N., J. J. Kennelly and T.-S. Krause, 'Shifting Paradigms for Sustainable Development: Implications for Management Theory and Research', *Academy of Management Review*, 20, 4 (1995), pp. 874–907

Glarini, O. and W. R. Stahel, *The Limits to Certainty* (Kluwer Academic Publishers, Dordrecht, 1989)

Glyn, A. 'Social Democracy and Full Employment', *New Left Review*, No. 211 (1995, May–June), pp. 33–55

Godet, M., *Prospective et Planification Stratégique* (Paris: Economica, 1985)

Goldfinger, C., 'The Intangible Economy and Its Implications for Statistics and Statisticians', Eurostat–ISTAT seminar (Bologna, February 1996)

Goldman, S. L., and R. N. Nagel, 'Management, Technology and Agility: The Emergence of a New Era in Manufacturing', *International Journal of Technology Management*, 8, 1 (1993), pp. 18–38

Golub, S., *Comparative Absolute Advantage in the Asia-pacific Region*, working paper (Federal Reserve Bank of San Francisco, 1995)

Goodman, P. S., and L. Sproull (eds.), *Technology and Organisation* (San Francisco: Jossey Bass, 1990)

Gouldner, A., *Patterns of Industrial Bureaucracy* (London: Routledge, 1954)

Granovetter, M., 'Economic Action and Social Structure', *American Journal of Sociology*, 91 (1985), pp. 481–510

Grant, R. M., 'The Resource Based Theory of Competitive Advantage', *California Management Review*, 33, 3 (1991), pp. 114–35

— 'The Knowledge-Based View of the Firm: Implications for Management Practice, *Long Range Planning*, Vol. 30, No. 3 (1997), pp. 450–54

Gray, R., 'Corporate Reporting for Sustainable Development', in Welford and Starkey (eds.), *Business and the Environment*

Gray, R., D. Walters, J. Bebbington and I. Thompson, 'The Greening of Enterprise: An Exploration of the (Non) Role of Environmental Accounting and Environmental Accountants in Organizational Change', *Critical Perspectives on Accounting*, 6 (1995), pp. 211–39

Groth, L., *Building Organizations With Information Technology*, Doctoral Dissertation, Norwegian School of Economics and Business Administration, Oslo (1997)

Gruner, H., 'The Current Situation of the Conception of Stakeholder in German Industry', *Journal of Communication Management*, 3, 2 (March 1998)

Habermas, J., *Reason and the Rationalization of Society* (London: Heinemann Educational Books, 1984)

Hagedoorn, J., and J. Schakenraad, 'The Role of Inter-firm Cooperation Agreements in the Globalization of the Economy and Technology', FAST Dossier (Paris: OECD, November 1991)

Hall, R., 'The Contribution of Intangible Resources to Business Success', *Journal of General Management*, 16, 4 (1991), pp. 41–52

— 'The Strategic Analysis of Intangible Resources', *Strategic Management Journal*, 13 (1992), pp. 135–44

— *The Soul of the Enterprise: Creating a Dynamic Vision for American Manufacturing* (New York: HarperCollins, 1993)

Hamel, G., 'Strategy As Revolution', *Harvard Business Review* (July–August 1996), pp. 69–82

Hamel, G., and A. Heene, *Competence Based Competition* (London: Wiley, 1994)

Hamel, G., and C. K. Prahalad, *Competing for the Future* (Boston: Harvard Business School Press, 1994)

Hames, R. D., *The Management Myth: Explaining the Essence of Future Organization* (Sydney: Business Performance, 1992)

— *The Management Myth* (Sydney: Business and Professional Publishing, 1994)

Hames, R. D. (with G. Callanan), *Burying the 20th Century: New Paths for New Futures* (Sydney: Business and Professional Publishing, 1997)

Hamilton, L. and S. Cockerill, 'The Globalisation of Industry', in T. Clarke and E. Monkhouse, *Rethinking the Company* (London: Pitman: Financial Times, 1994)

Hammer, M., 'Re-engineering Work – Don't Automate, Obliterate', *Harvard Business Review* (July–August 1990), pp. 104–12

Hammer, M., and J. Champy, *Re-engineering the Corporation: A Manifesto for the Business Revolution* (London: Nicholas Brealey, 1993)

Hampden-Turner, C., *Charting the Corporate Mind* (Oxford: Blackwell, 1994)

Hampden-Turner, C., and F. Trompenaars, *The Seven Cultures of Capitalism* (London: Piatkus, 1994)

Handy, C., *The Age of Unreason* (London: Business Books, 1989)

— *The Age of Paradox (The Empty Raincoat)* (London: Hutchinson, 1994)

Handy, C. 'The Citizen Corporation', *Harvard Business Review*, Vol. 75, No. 5 (September–October, 1997), pp. 26–28

Hanks, J. J., 'From the Hustings: The Role of States with Takeover Control Laws', *Mergers and Acquisitions*, 29, 2 (September–October 1994)

Hanna, M., 'The Varieties of Multinational Firm Structures', in Bowman and Kogut (eds.), *Redesigning the Firm*

Hart, O., and J. Moore, 'Property Rights and the Nature of the Firm', *Journal of Political Economy*, 98 (1990), pp. 1119–58

Hart, S. L., 'Strategies for a Sustainable World', *Harvard Business Review* (January–February 1997)

Harvey, D., *The Condition of Postmodernity* (Oxford: Blackwell, 1992)

Haslam, C., and K. William, with S. Johal and J. Williams, 'A Fallen Idol? Japanese Management in the 1990s', *Asia Pacific Business Review*, 2, 4 (1996), pp. 21–43

Hawken, P., *The Ecology of Commerce* (London: HarperCollins, 1993)

— 'A teasing Irony', in Welford and Starkey, *Business and the Environment*

Hawryszkiewycz, I., *Designing the Networked Enterprise* (Boston: Artech House, 1997)

Hayek, F. A., *Law, Legislation, Liberty*, Vol. 3: *The Political Order of a Free People* (Chicago: University of Chicago Press, 1979)

Hayes, R. H., S. C. Wheelwright and K. B. Clark, *Dynamic Manufacturing: Creating the Learning Organization* (New York: Free Press, 1988)

Hedlund, G. 'The Hypermodern MMC: A Hierarchy?', *Human Resource Management* (Spring 1986), pp. 9–35

Henry, J. (ed.), *Creative Management* (London: Sage, 1991)

Henry, J., and D. Walker (eds.), *Managing Innovation* (London: Sage, 1991)

Hill, C. W., and T. M. Jones, 'Stakeholder Agency Theory', *Journal of Management Studies*, 29, 31 (1994), pp. 131–54

Hill, L. A., *Becoming a Manager* (Bostom: Harvard Business School Press, 1992)

Hilmer, F. G., *Strictly Boardroom: Improving Governance to Enhance Company Performance*, Report of the Independent Working Party into Corporate Governance (Sydney: Business Library, 1993)

Hilmer, F. G., and L. Donaldson, *Management Redeemed: Debunking the Critics*, (Sydney: Australian Graduate School of Management, 1996)

Hirsch, F. R., *The Social Limits to Growth* (London: Routledge and Kegan Paul, 1978)

Hirst, P., and G. Thompson, *Globalisation in Question* (London: Polity Press, 1996)

HMSO, *Competitiveness: Helping Business to Win*, Cmmd 2563 (London: HMSO, 1994)

Hodgetts, R. M., F. Luthans and S. M. Lee, 'New Paradigm Organizations: From Total Quality to Learning to World-Class', *Organization Dynamics*, Vol 22, Issue 3, Winter (1994), pp. 5–19

Hoffman, R. C., and W. H. Hegarty, 'Top Management Influence on Innovations', *Journal of Management*, 19, 3 (1993), pp. 549–74

Hu, Y.-S., 'Global or Stateless Corporations Are National Firms with International Operations', *California Management Review* (Winter 1992)

Hutchinson, C., 'Corporate Strategy for the Environment', in Welford and Starkey, *Business and the Environment*

Hutton, W., *The State We're In* (London: Jonathan Cape, 1995)

— *The State to Come* (London: Vintage, 1997)

— 'An Overview of Stakeholding', in Kelley, Kelly and Gamble, *Stakeholder Capitalism*

Iansiti, M., 'Managing Chaos: System Focused Product Development in the Computer and Multimedia Environment', in Yoffie (ed.), *Competing in the Age of Digital Convergence*, pp. 413–44

Imae, M. *Kaizen: The Key to Japan's Competitive Success* (New York: McGraw Hill, 1988)

IMF, *Globalization – Opportunities and Threats* (Washington, DC: International Monetary Fund, 1997)

Interface Inc., *Sustainability Report* (Atlanta: Interface Inc., 1997)

Ishiguro, T., 'Japan', in J. Lufkin and D. Gallagher (eds.), *International Corporate Governance* (Euromoney Publications, 1990)

Ishikawa, K. *What Is Total Quality Control? The Japanese Way* (Englewood Cliffs, Prentice Hall, 1985)

ISO, *Environmental Management Systems: General Guidelines on Principles, Systems, and Supporting Techniques*, ISO/TC/SC1 N47, Committee Draft ISO/CD 14001.2 (Geneva, 1995)

Itami, H., *Mobilizing Invisible Assets* (Cambridge, Mass.: Harvard University Press, 1987)

Jackson, T., *Clean Production Strategies* (Boca Raton, Florida: Lewis Publishers, 1993)

Jacobs, M., 'The Environment As Stakeholder', *Business Strategy Review*, Vol. 8, No. 2 (1997), pp. 25-28

Janowitz, M., 'Changing Patterns of Organizational Authority: The Military Establishment', *Administrative Science Quarterly*, 3, 4 (1959), pp. 473–93

Jennings, P. D., and P. A. Zanberger, 'Ecologically Sustainable Organizations: An Institutional Approach', *Academy of Management Review*, 20, 4 (1995), pp. 1015–52

Jensen, M. C., and W. H. Meckling, 'Theory of the Firm: Managerial

Behaviour, Agency Costs and Ownership Structure', *Journal of Financial Economics* (October 1976), pp. 305–60

Johnston, R. J., and P. J. Taylor (eds.), *A World in Crisis? Geographical Perspectives* (Oxford: Blackwell, 1989)

Jones, T., 'Instrumental Stakeholder Theory: A Synthesis of Ethics and Economics', *Academy of Management Review*, 20, 2 (1995), pp. 404–37

Joyce, P., and A. Woods, *Essential Strategic Management: From Modernism to Pragmatism* (Oxford: Butterworth-Heinemann, 1996)

Juran, J. M., *Quality Control Handbook* (New York: McGraw-Hill, 1988)

Kalchas Group, *Growth Through Revenues vs. Cost Cutting* (London: Kalchas Group, September 1995)

Kanter, R. M., *The Change Masters* (London: Routledge, 1983)

— *When Giants Learn to Dance* (London: Routledge, 1989)

— *World Class* (New York: Simon and Schuster, 1995)

Kaplan, R. S., and D. P. Norton, 'The Balanced Scorecard – Measures that Drive Performance', *Harvard Business Review*, 70 (January–February 1992), pp. 71–9

— *The Balanced Scorecard* (Boston: Harvard Business School Press, 1996)

Karpin Industry Task Force on Leadership and Management Skills (eds.), *Enterprising Nation: Renewing Australia's Managers to Meet the Challenge of the Asia-Pacific Century* (Canberra: Australian Government Publishing Service, 1995)

Katz, H. C., and C. F. Sabel, 'Industrial Relations and Industrial Adjustments in the Car Industry', *Industrial Relations*, 24, 2 (1985), pp. 295–315

Kay, J., *Foundations of Corporate Success: How Business Strategies Add Value* (Oxford: Oxford University Press, 1993)

— *The Business of Economics* (Oxford: Oxford University Press, 1996)

— 'The Stakeholder Corporation', in Kelley, Kelly and Gamble, *Stakeholder Capitalism*

Keen, P. G., *Shaping the Future: Business Design Through Information Technology* (Boston: Harvard Business School Press, 1991)

— *Every Manager's Guide to Information Technology* (Boston: Harvard Business School Press, 1995)

Keen, P. G., and E. M. Knapp, *Every Manager's Guide to Business Processes* (Boston: Harvard Business School Press, 1996)

Kelley, G., D. Kelly and A. Gamble, *Stakeholder Capitalism* (Basingstoke: Macmillan, 1997)

Kenney, M., and R. Florida, 'Beyond Mass Production: Production and the Labor Process in Japan', *Politics and Society*, 16, 1 (1988), pp. 121–58

Koehane, R., and E. Ostram (eds.), *Local Commons and Global Interdependence: Heteogeneity and Cooperation in Two Domains* (London: Sage, 1995)

Kesey, K., S. Thompson and M. Wright, *Corporate Governance – Economic,*

Management and Financial Issues (Oxford: Oxford University Press, 1997)

Kester, C., *Japanese Takeovers: The Global Contest for Corporate Control* (Boston: Harvard Business School Press, 1992)

—'Industrial Groups as Systems of Contractual Governance', *Oxford Review of Economic Policy*, 8, 3 (Oxford University Press, Autumn 1992), pp. 24–44

Kieser, A., 'Rhetoric and Myth in Management Fashion', *Organization*, 4, 1 (1997), pp. 49–74

Klein, J. A., and T. Kass, *The World Beyond Markets and Products: Skills and Metaskills* (Cambridge: Generics Limited, 1990)

Klein, J. A., G. M. Edge and T. Kass, 'Skill-Based Competition', *Journal of General Management*, 16, 4 (1991), pp. 1–15

Kogut, B., 'Designing Global Strategies: Profiting from Operational Flexibility', *Sloan Management Review*, 27 (1985), pp. 27–38

Koike, K., 'Human Resource Development and Labor Management Relations', in K. Yamamura and Y. Yasuba (eds.), *The Political Economy of Japan*, Vol. 1: *The Domestic Transformation* (Stanford: Stanford University Press, 1987), pp. 289–330

Kondratiev, N. D., 'The Longwaves in Economic Life', *Review of Economics and Statistics*, 17 (1935), pp. 105–15

Kono, T., and S. R. Clegg, *The Transformation of Japanese Corporate Cultures* (Berlin: de Gruyter, 1998)

Kosnik, R. D., 'Greenmail: A Study of Board Performance in Corporate Governance', *Administrative Science Quarterly*, 32 (1987), pp. 163–85

Kotter, J., *The General Manager* (New York: Free Press, 1982)

Kotter, J. P., and J. L. Heskett, *Corporate Culture and Performance* (New York: Free Press/Macmillan Inc., 1992)

Krubasik, E., and H. Lautenschlager, 'Forming Successful Strategic Alliances in High-Tech Businesses', in Bleeke and Ernst, *Collaborating to Compete*, pp. 55–66

Kuhn, T. S., *The Structure of Scientific Revolutions* (Chicago: University of Chicago Press, 1970)

Kumar, N., *Intellectual Property Protection, Market Orientation and Location of Overseas R&D Activities by Multinational Enterprises*, UNU/INTECH Discussion Papers (March 1995)

Kurtzman, J., *The Death of Money* (New York: Simon and Schuster, 1993)

Landau, M., 'On the Concept of the Self-Correcting Organization', *Public Administration Review* (November–December 1973), pp. 535–7

Lash, S., and J. Urry, *The End of Organized Capitalism* (London: Sage, 1987)

Levinthal, D. A., and J. G. March, 'The Myopia of Learning', *Strategic Management Journal*, 14 (1993), pp. 95–112

Levitt, T., 'The Globalization of Markets', *Harvard Business Review* (May–June 1983), pp. 92–102

Lewchuck, W., and D. Robertson, 'Working Conditions under Lean

Production: A Worker-Based Benchmarking Study?', *Asia Pacific Business Review*, 2, 4 (1996), pp. 60–81

Lewin, K., 'Group Decisions and Social Change', in Swanson et. al. (eds.), *Readings in Social Psychology*

Limerick, D., and B. Cunnington, *Managing the New Organization* (Chatswood, New South Wales: Business and Professional Publishing, 1993)

Lipton, M., and J. Lorsch, 'A New Compact for Owners and Directors', *Harvard Business Review* (July–August 1991), pp. 141–3

Lloyd, P. J., 'Regionalization and World Trade', *OECD Economic Studies*, 18 (Spring 1992)

Lorsch, J., and E. MacIver, *Pawns or Potentates: The Reality of America's Corporate Boards* (Cambridge, Mass.: Harvard University Press, 1989)

Lutahans, F., M. Hodgetts and S. A. Rosencratz, *Real Managers* (Cambridge, Mass.: Ballinger, 1988)

Mace, M., *Directors: Myth and Reality* (Boston: Harvard Business School Press, 1971)

Magretta, J., 'Growth Through Global Sustainability', *Harvard Business Review*, 1997)

Makridakis, S., 'Metastrategy: Learning and Avoiding Past Mistakes', *Long Range Planning*, 30, 1 (1997), pp. 129–35

Malnight, T. W., 'Globalization of an Ethnocentric Firm: An Evolutionary Perspective', *Strategic Management Journal*, 16, 2 (1995), pp. 119–41

Mansell, R., *The New Telecommunications: A Political Economy of Network Evolution* (London: Sage, 1993)

Marceau, J. (ed.), *Reworking the World: Organizations, Technologies and Cultures in Comparative Perspective* (Berlin: de Gruyter, 1992)

March, J. G., 'Footnotes to Organizational Change', *Administrative Science Quarterly*, 26 (1987), pp. 563–77

— 'Exploration and Exploitation in Organizational Learning', *Organization Science*, 2, 1 (1991), pp. 71–87

— 'The Future, Disposable Organizations, and the Rigidities of Imagination', *Organization*, 2, 3/4 (1995), pp. 427–40

Mason, E. S., *The Corporation in Modern Society* (Cambridge, Mass.: Harvard University Press, 1959)

Matheson, D., and J. Matheson, *The Smart Organization* (Boston: Harvard Business School Press, 1998)

Maxwell, J., S. Rothenberg, F. Briscoe and A. Marcus, 'Green Schemes: Corporate Environmental Strategies and Their Implementation', *California Management Review*, 39, 3 (Spring 1997), pp. 118–34

Maynard, H. M., and S. E. Mehrtens, *The Fourth Wave: Business in the 21st Century* (San Francisco: Berrett-Koehler, 1996)

Mayo, E., *The Social Problems of an Industrial Civilization* (London: Routledge and Kegan Paul, 1947)

McGrath, M. E., and R. Hoole, 'Manufacturing's New Economies of Scale', *Harvard Business Review* (May–June 1992), pp. 102–5

McKinsey & Co. Inc., *Emerging Exporters: Australia's High Value-Added Manufacturing Exporters*, Final Report of the Study by McKinsey & Co. for the Australian Manufacturing Council, Melbourne (1993)

Micklethwaite, J., and A. Wooldridge, *The Witch Doctors* (London: Mandarin, 1997)

Miller, J. and F. Szekely, 'What Is Green?', *European Management Journal*, 13, 3 (1995), pp. 332–3

Mills, C. W., *The Power Elite* (Oxford: Oxford University Press, 1956)

Mills, D. Q., *Rebirth of the Corporation* (New York: Wiley, 1991)

Mintzberg, H., *The Nature of Managerial Work* (New York: Harper and Row, 1975)

— *The Structure of Organizations* (Englewood Cliffs, NJ: Prentice Hall, 1979)

— 'Who Should Control the Corporation?' *California Management Review*, 27, 1 (Fall 1984), pp. 90–115

— 'Crafting Strategy', *Harvard Business Review* (July–August 1987), pp. 65–75

— 'The Fall and Rise of Strategic Planning', *Harvard Business Review*, 72, 1 (January–February 1994), pp. 107–14

— *The Rise and Fall of Strategic Planning* (Englewood Cliffs, NJ: Prentice Hall, 1994)

— 'Round Three: Learning 1, Planning 0', reply to Igor Ansoff, in de Wit and Meyer, *Strategy*

Mintzberg, H., and J. B. Quinn (eds.), *The Strategy Process* (Englewood Cliffs, NJ: Prentice Hall, 1991)

Mitchell and Co., 'Amputating Assets: Companies That Slash Jobs End Up with More Problems than Profits', *US News and World Report* (4 May 1992)

Monkhouse, E., *Benchmarking SMEs. Innovation, Quality and Performance*, doctoral thesis (Leeds: Leeds Business School, 1995)

— *The Use of Non-Financial Performance Measures in Small and Medium Sized Enterprises*, unpublished doctoral thesis (Leeds: Leeds Business School, 1995)

Monks, R. A. G., and N. Minnow, *Corporate Governance* (Leeds: Oxford: Blackwell, 1995)

Montgomery, C. A., and M. E. Porter (eds.), *Strategy: Seeking and Securing Competitive Advantage* (Boston: Harvard Business School Press, 1991)

Morgan, G., *Images of Organizations* (Thousand Oaks, Cal.: Sage, 1985)

— 'Emerging Waves and Challenges: The Need for New Competencies and Mindsets', in Henry (ed.), *Creative Management*

— *Imaginization* (Thousand Oaks, Cal.: Sage, 1991)

Morris, D., and J. Brandon, *Re-engineering Your Business* (New York: McGraw-Hill, 1993)

Morris, J., and B. Wilkinson, 'The Transfer of Japanese Management to Alien Institutional Environments', *Journal of Management Studies*, 32, 6 (1995), pp. 719–30

Morrison, N., *The Second Curve: Managing the Velocity of Change* (London: Nicholas Brealey, 1996)

Morton, M. S. S., *The Corporation in the Nineties: Information Technology and Organizational Transformation* (New York: Oxford University Press, 1991)

Naisbitt, J., *Megatrends* (New York: Warner Books, 1982)

— *Asian Megatrends* (London: Nicholas Brealey Publishing, 1997)

Negroponte, N., *Being Digital* (London: Hodder and Stoughton, 1995)

Niederhoffer, V., *The Education of a Speculator* (New York: Wiley, 1997)

Nohria, N., and J. D. Berkely, 'The Virtual Organization: Bureaucracy, Technology, and the Implosion of Control', in C. Heckscher and A. Donneellon (eds.), *The Post-Bureaucratic Organization: New Perspectives on Organizational Change* (Thousand Oaks, Cal.: Sage, 1994), pp. 108–28

Nonaka, I., and H. Takeuchi, *The Knowledge-Creating Company* (Oxford: Oxford University Press, 1995)

Nuti, D. M., 'Democracy and Economy: What Role for Stakeholders?', *Business Strategy Review*, Vol. 8, No. 2 (1997), pp. 14–20

OECD, *Information Technology and New Growth Opportunities, Information, Computer and Communications Policy Committee* (Paris: OECD, 1989)

— *Technology and the Economy: the Key Relationships* (Paris: OECD, 1992)

— *Financial Market Trends*, 62 (Paris: OECD, November 1995)

— *OECD Economic Surveys: Germany* (Paris: OECD, 1995)

— *Environmental Performance in OECD Countries: Progress in the 1990s* (Paris: OECD, 1996)

— *Globalization of Industry – Overview and Sector Reports* (Paris: OECD, 1996)

— *The Knowledge Based Economy* (Paris: OECD, 1996)

— *OECD Economic Surveys: Japan* (Paris: OECD, 1996)

— 'Recent Trends in Foreign Direct Investment', *Financial Market Trends*, 64 (Paris: OECD, 1996)

— *Technology, Productivity and Job Creation* (Paris: OECD, 1996)

Ohara, M., '"CAD/CAM" at Toyota Motor Company', in T. Kitawaga (ed.), *Computer Science and Technologies* (New York: North Holland, 1988)

Ohmae, K., *Triad Power* (New York: Free Press, 1985)

— 'Managing in a Borderless World', *Harvard Business Review* (1989)

— *The Borderless World* (London: Collins, 1990)

— 'The Rise of the Regional State', *Foreign Affairs*, Vol. 72, No. 2 (1993)

Oliver, N., and B. Wilkinson, *The Japanization of British Industry* (Oxford: Blackwell, 1988)

Orts, E. W., 'Beyond Shareholders: Interpreting Corporate Constituency Statutes, *The George Washington Law Review*, Vol. 61, No. 1 (1992), pp. 14–135

Parker, M., and J. Slaughter, *Choosing Sides: Unions and the Team Concept* (Boston: South End Press, 1988)

Pascale, R., *Managing on the Edge* (London: Penguin, 1990)

Peacock, A., and G. Bannock, *Corporate Takeovers and the Public Interest* (Aberdeen University Press, 1991)

Pearce, D., A. Markandya and E. B. Barbier, *Blueprint for A Green Economy* (London: Earthscan, 1989)

Peffer, J., and G. R. Salancik, *The External Control of Organizations: A Resource Dependence Perspective* (New York: Harper and Row, 1978)

Penrose, E., *The Theory of the Growth of the Firm* (Oxford: Oxford University Press, 1959)

Perez, C., 'Microelectronics, Long Waves and World Structural Change: New Perspectives for Developing Countries', *World Development*, 13, 3 (1986), pp. 441–63

Perrow, C., *Complex Organizations: A Critical Essay* (New York: McGraw-Hill, 1986)

Peters, T., *Liberation Management* (New York: Macmillan, 1992)

— *The Pursuit of Wow!* (London: Macmillan, 1994)

— *The Circle of Innovation* (London: Macmillan, 1997)

Peters, T. J., and R. H. Waterman, *In Search of Excellence* (London: Harper-Collins, 1982)

Petrella, R., 'Globalization and Internationalization: The Dynamics of the Emerging World Order', in Boyer and Drache, *States Against Markets*

Pettigrew, A., 'Longitudinal Field Research on Change', *Organization Science*, 1, 3 (1990)

Pfeffer, J., 'Size and Composition of Corporate Boards of Directors: The Organization and Environment', *Administrative Science Quarterly*, 17 (1972), pp. 218–27

Pine, B. J., *Mass Customization* (Boston: Harvard Business School Press, 1993)

Piore, M. J., 'Perspectives on Labor Market Flexibility', *Industrial Relations*, 25, 2 (1986), pp. 156–66

Piore, M. J., and C. F. Sabel, *The Second Industrial Divide: Possibilities for Prosperity* (New York: Basic Books, 1984)

Pitelis, C. N., *Market and Non-Market Hierarchies* (Oxford: Blackwell, 1991)

Plender, J., *A Stake in the Future: The Stakeholding Solution* (London: Nicholas Brealey, 1997)

Porter, M., *Competition in Global Industries* (Boston: Harvard Business School Press, 1986)

— 'The Competitive Advantage of Nations', *Harvard Business Review* (March–April 1990)

— *The Competitive Advantage of Nations* (Basingstoke: Macmillan, 1990)

— *Capital Choices: Changing the Way America Invests in Industry* (US Council on Competitiveness/Harvard Business School, 1992)

—'Capital Disadvantage: America's Failing Capital Investment System', *Harvard Business Review* (September–October 1992), pp. 65–82

—'America's Green Strategy', in Welford and Starkey, *Business and the Environment*

Porter, M., and C. van der Linde, 'Green and Competitive: Ending the Stalemate', in Welford and Starkey, *Business and the Environment*

Powell and Dent-Micallef (1997)

Power, M., *The Audit Explosion*, paper 7 (London: Demos, 1994)

Prahalad, C. K., and G. Hamel, 'Strategy As a Field of Study: Why Search for a New Paradigm?', *Strategic Management Journal*, 15 (1994b), pp. 5–16

—'The Core Competence of the Corporation', in Montgomery and Porter (eds.), *Strategy*, 68, 3 (1990), pp. 79–91.

—'The Core Competence of the Corporation', *Harvard Business Review*, 3 (May–June 1994), pp. 79–91

—'Strategy: Search for New Paradigms', *Strategic Management Journal*, Special Issue, Vol. 15 (Summer 1994)

Prahalad, C. K. and Y. L. Doz, *The Multinational Mission: Balancing Local Demands and Global Vision* (New York: Free Press, 1987)

Preston, L. E., 'Stakeholder Management and Corporate Performance', *Journal of Behavioural Economics*, Vol. 19, No. 4 (1990), pp. 361–375.

Prowse, S., 'The Structure of Corporate Ownership in Japan', *Journal of Finance*, 47 (1992), pp. 1121–40

Purser, R. E., C. Park and A. Montuori, 'Limits to Anthropocentrism: Towards an Ecocentric Organization Paradigm?', *Academy of Management Review*, 20, 4 (1995), pp. 1053–89

Quah, D., 'The Invisible Hand and the Weightless Economy', LSE Centre for Economic Performance, occasional paper 12 (April 1996)

Quinn, J. B., 'Strategic Change: Logical Incrementalism', in Mintzberg and Quinn (eds.), *The Strategy Process*

—*The Intelligent Enterprise* (New York: Free Press, 1992)

Ramsay, H., 'Cycles of Control: Workers' Participation in Sociological and Historical Perspective', *Sociology*, 11, 3 (1977), pp. 481–506

—'Managing Sceptically', in S. R. Clegg and G. Palmer (eds.), *The Politics of Management Knowledge* (London: Sage, 1996)

Rand Corporation, 'International Models of Management Development', *Enterprising Nation: Renewing Australia's Managers to Meet the Challenges of the Asia-Pacific Century*, Research Report Volume 1, Chapter 23, Australian Government Publishing Service (April 1995)

Rappaport, A., *Creating Shareholder Value: The New Standard for Business Performance* (New York: Free Press, 1986)

Rappaport, A., and S. Halevi, 'The Computerless Computer Company', *Harvard Business Review* (July–August 1991), pp. 69–78

Rawlinson, M., and P. Wells, 'Taylorism, Lean Production and the Automotive Industry', *Asia-Pacific Business Review*, 2, 4 (1996), pp. 189–204

Reich, R., 'Entrepreneurship Reconsidered: The Team As Hero', in Henry and Walker (eds.), *Managing Innovation*

— *The Work of Nations* (New York: Alfred A. Knopf, 1991)

Roberts, K. H., and M. Grabowski, 'Organizations, Technology and Structuring', in Clegg et. al. (eds.), *Handbook of Organization Studies*

Robertson, J., 'Shaping the Post-Modern Economy', in Welford and Starkey, *Business and the Environment*

Robins, K., and F. Webster, '"Revolution of the Fixed Wheel": Information, Technology and Social Taylorism', in P. Drummond and R. Paterson (eds.), *Television in Transition: Papers from the First International Television Studies Conference* (London: BFI Publications, 1993)

Roby, E. F., 'Securities Markets Moving Ahead', in Finanzplatz Frankfurt, Landesbank Hessen-Thuringen (1996)

Roddick, A., *Body and Soul: Profits with Principles* (New York: Crown, 1991)

Rogers, E. M., and J. K. Larsen, *Silicon Valley Fever: Growth of High-Technology Culture* (New York: Basic Books, 1984)

Rommel, G., F. Bruck, R. Diederichs, R. Kempis, H. Kaas, G. Fuhry and V. Kurfess, *Quality Pays* (London: Macmillan, 1996)

Roudinelli, D. A., and G. Vastag, 'International Environmental Standards and Corporate Policies', *California Management Review*, 39, 1 (1996), pp. 106–22

Rothenberg, S., J. Maxwell and A. Marcus, 'Issues in the Implementation of Proactive Environmental Strategies', *Business Strategy and the Environment*, 1, 4 (Winter 1993), pp. 1–12

Rothwell, R., 'Successful Industrial Innovation: Critical Factors for the 1990s', *R&D Management*, 22, 3 (1992), pp. 221–39

RSA, *Tomorrow's Company, Final Report* (London: Royal Society of Arts, 1995)

Ruigrok, W., *Paradigm Crisis in International Trade Theory*, Forum on Applied Science and Technology (FAST) (Brussels: Commission of European Community, 1991)

Rule, J., and P. Brantley, 'Computerized Surveillance in the Workplace: Forms and Distribution', *Sociological Forum*, 7 (1992), pp. 405–23

Rumelt, R. P., 'Foreword', in Hamel and Heene, *Competence Based Competition*

Sabel, C. F., *Work and Politics* (Cambridge: Cambridge University Press, 1982)

Sandkull, B., 'Lean Production: The Myth Which Changes the World?', in S. R. Clegg and G. Palmer (eds.), *The Politics of Management Knowledge* (London: Sage, 1996), pp. 69–79

Sayre, D., *Inside ISO 14000: The Competitive Advantage of Environmental Management* (Delray Beach, Fl: St Lucie Press, 1996)

Schein, E. H., *Organizational Culture and Leadership* (San Francisco: Jossey Bass, 1992)

Schmitt, B. H., and A. Simonson, *Marketing Aesthetics* (New York: Free Press, 1997)

Scholes, E., and D. Clutterbuck, 'Planning Stakeholder Communication', *Long Range Planning*, 31, 2 (April 1998)

Schumpeter, J. A., *Business Cycles* (2 vols.) (New York: McGraw-Hill, 1939)
— *Capitalism, Socialism & Democracy* (New York: Harper and Row, 1942)

Scott, W. R., 'The Adolescence of Institutional Theory', *Administrative Science Quarterly*, 32 (1987), pp. 493–511

Senge, P. M., *The Fifth Discipline* (New York: Doubleday, 1990/London: Century Business, 1992)

Sewell, G., and B. Wilkinson, 'Someone to Watch Over Me: Surveillance, Discipline and the Just-In-Time Labour Process, *Sociology*, Vol. 26, pp. 271–289 (1992)

Shapiro, E., *Fad Surfing in the Boardroom* (Oxford: Capstone, 1996)

Shiva, V., *Ecology and the Politics of Survival* (New Delhi: United Nations University Press, 1991)

Shrivastava, P., 'Castrated Environment: Greening Organization Studies', *Organization Studies*, 15, 5 (1994), pp. 705–26
— 'Ecocentric Management for a Risk Society', *Academy of Management Review*, 20, 1 (1995), pp. 118–37
— *Greening Business: Profiting the Corporation and the Environment* (Cincinnati, Ohio: Thomas Executive Press, 1996)

Sibbet, D., '75 Years of Management Ideas and Practice 1922–1977', *Harvard Business Review*, reprint 975000 (Boston: Harvard Business Review Press, 1997)

Simons, R., *Levers of Control: How Managers Use Innovative Control Systems to Drive Strategic Renewal* (Boston: Harvard Business School Press, 1995)

Slater, R., *Portraits in Silicon* (Cambridge, Mass.: MIT Press, 1987)

Smith, C., 'Flexible Specialization, Automation and Mass Production', *Work, Employment and Society*, 3, 2 (1989), pp. 203–30

Smith, T., *Accounting for Growth* (London: Century Business Books, 1996)

Spectrum Strategy Consultants, *Development of the Information Society: An International Analysis* (London: DTI/HMSO, 1996)

Spence, W. R., *Innovation: The Communication of Change in Ideas, Practices and Products* (London: Chapman Hall, 1994)

Staw, B., 'The Experimenting Organization', *Organizational Dynamics* (Summer 1977), pp. 2–18

Stacey, R., *The Chaos Frontier* (London: Butterworth-Heinemann, 1991)

Stalk, G., P. Evans and L. Schulman, 'Competing on Capabilities: The New Rules of Corporate Strategy', *Harvard Business Review* (March April 1992), pp. 57–69

Stalk, G., and T. Hout, *Competing in Time: How Time Based Competition Is Reshaping Global Markets* (New York: Free Press, 1990)

Stead, W. E., and J. G. Stead, 'Strategic Management for a Small Planet', in Welford and Starkey (eds.), *Business and the Environment*

Sternberg, E., 'The Defects of Stakeholder Theory', *Corporate Governance: An International Review*, 5, 1 (1997), pp. 3–10

Stewart, P., and P. Garrahan, 'Globalization, the Company and the Workplace', in A. Scott (ed.), *The Limits of Globalization: Cases and Arguments* (London: Routledge, 1995)

Stewart, T. A., *Intellectual Capital: The New Wealth of Organizations* (London: Nicholas Brealey, 1997)

Stopford, J., and L. T. Wells, *Managing the Multinational Enterprise: Organization of the Firm and Ownership of the Subsidiaries* (New York: Basic Books, 1972)

Storper, M., and A. J. Scott, *The Wealth of Regions: Market Forces and Policy Imperatives in Local and Global Context*, working paper 7 (Lewis Centre for Regional Policy Studies, UCLA, 1993)

SustainAbility and United Nations Environmental Programme, *Engaging Stakeholders 1: The Benchmark Survey* (Paris: United Nations Environment Programme, 1996).

Swanson, G. E., T. M. Newcomb and E. L. Hartley (eds.), *Readings in Social Psychology* (New York: Holt, Rinehart and Winston, 1958)

Taguchi, G., *Introduction to Quality Engineering* (Dearborn, Mich.: Asian Production Organization, 1986)

Talwar, R. K., 'Re-engineering – A Wonder Drug for the 90s?', in Coulson-Thomas (ed.), *Business Process Re-engineering*

Tapscott, D., *The Digital Economy: Promise and Peril in the Age of Networked Intelligence* (New York: McGraw-Hill, 1996)

Tapscott, D., and A. Caston, *Paradigm Shift: The New Promise of Information Technology* (New York: McGraw-Hill, 1993)

Taylor, F. W., *Principles of Scientific Management* (New York: Harper and Row, 1911)

Thrift, N. J., 'The Geography of International Economic Disorder', in Johnston and Taylor (eds.), *A World in Crisis?*

Thurow, L., 'Who Owns the 21st Century?', *Sloan Management Review* (Spring 1992), pp. 5–17

— *The Future of Capitalism* (London: Nicholas Brealey, 1996)

Tricker, R. (ed.), *Corporate Governance – An International Review* (Oxford: Blackwell, 1994)

Tricker, R. I., *International Corporate Governance* (Singapore: Prentice Hall, 1994)

Turnbull, S., 'Stakeholder Governance: A Cybernetic and Property Rights Analysis', *Corporate Governance: An International Review*, 5, 1 (1997), pp. 11–23

Tyson, L., *Who's Bashing Whom? Trade Conflict in High Technology Industries* (Washington, DC: Institute for International Economics, 1992)

UNCTAD, *World Investment Report* (Geneva: UNCTAD, 1995)

UNDP, Human Development Report 1992 (New York: Oxford University Press, 1992)

UNEP IE, *Company Environmental Reporting: A Measure of Progress of Business and Industry Towards Sustainable Development*, Technical Report No. 24, Paris: United Nations Environment Programme Industry and Environment (1994)

United Nations, *World Investment Report: Transnational Corporations and Integrated International Production* (New York: United Nations, 1993)

United Nations, *World Investment Report: Transnational Corporations, Employment and the Workplace* (New York: United Nations, 1994)

University of Western Sydney, 'Embryonic Industries: Leadership and Management Needs', in Karpin Industry Task Force on Leadership and Management Skills (eds.), *Enterprising Nation*, vol. 2, pp. 1289–1349

Useem, M., 'Corporations and the Corporate Elite', *Annual Review of Sociology*, 6 (1980), pp. 41–77

van der Heijden, K., *Scenarios: The Art of Strategic Conversation* (London: Wiley, 1996)

Vandermerwe, S., and M. D. Oliff, 'Customers Drive Corporations Green' *Long Range Planning*, 23, 6, 1990, pp. 10–16

Vanhonacker, W., 'Entering China: An Unconventional Approach' *Harvard Business Review*, March 1997, pp. 108–12 (1997)

Viner, A., 'The Coming Revolution in Japan's Board Rooms', *Corporate Governance – An International Review*, 1, 3 (1993), pp. 112–19

Vogel, D., *Trading Up: Consumer and Environmental Regulation in a Global Economy* (Cambridge, Mass.: Harvard University Press, 1995)

Wack, P., 'Scenarios: Unchartered Waters Ahead', *Harvard Business Review* (September–October 1985), pp. 73–90

— 'Scenarios: Shooting the Rapids', *Harvard Business Review* (November–December 1985), pp. 131–42

Wade, R., 'Globalization and Its Limits: reports of the Death of the National Economy Are Greatly Exaggerated', in S. Berger and R. Dore (eds.), *National Diversity and Global Capitalism* (Ithaca: Cornell University Press, 1996)

Walley, N., and B. Whitehead, 'It's Not Easy Being Green', in Welford and Starkey (eds.), *Business and the Environment*

Wallman, S. M. H., 'The Proper Interpretation of Corporate Constituency Statutes and Formulation of Director Duties', *Stetson Law Review*, 21, pp. 163–92

Waterman, R., *The Frontiers of Excellence – Learning from Companies That Put People First* (London: Nicholas Brealey, 1994)

Learning Resources
Centre